European Integration and Postcolonial Sovereignty Games

This book examines how sovereignty works in the context of European integration and postcolonialism. Focusing on a group of micro-polities associated with the European Union, it offers a new understanding of international relations in the context of modern sovereignty.

This book offers a systematic and comparative analysis of the Overseas Countries and Territories (OCTs), the EU and the four affected Member States: the UK, France, the Netherlands and Denmark. Contributors explore how states and state-like entities play 'sovereignty games' to understand how a group of postcolonial entities may strategically use their ambiguous status in relation to sovereignty. The book examines why former colonies are seeking greater room to manoeuvre on their own, whilst simultaneously developing a close relationship to the supranational EU. Methodologically sophisticated, this interdisciplinary volume combines interviews, participant observation, textual, legal and institutional analysis for a new theoretical approach to understanding the strategic possibilities and subjectivity of non-sovereign entities in international politics.

Bringing together research on European integration and postcolonial theory, *European Integration and Postcolonial Sovereignty Games* will be of interest to students and scholars of International Relations, EU Studies, Postcolonial Studies, International Law and Political Theory.

Rebecca Adler-Nissen is Assistant Professor at the Department of Political Science, University of Copenhagen, Denmark.

Ulrik Pram Gad is a Post-Doctoral Researcher at the Center for Advanced Security Theory, University of Copenhagen, Denmark.

The New International Relations
Edited by Richard Little, *University of Bristol*, Iver B. Neumann,
London School of Economics and Political Science,
and Jutta Weldes, *University of Bristol.*

The field of international relations has changed dramatically in recent years. This new series will cover the major issues that have emerged and reflect the latest academic thinking in this particular dynamic area.

International Law, Rights and Politics
Developments in Eastern Europe and the CIS
Rein Mullerson

The Logic of Internationalism
Coercion and accommodation
Kjell Goldmann

Russia and the Idea of Europe
A study in identity and international relations
Iver B. Neumann

The Future of International Relations
Masters in the making?
Edited by Iver B. Neumann and Ole Wæver

Constructing the World Polity
Essays on international institutionalization
John Gerard Ruggie

Realism in International Relations and International Political Economy
The continuing story of a death foretold
Stefano Guzzini

International Relations, Political Theory and the Problem of Order
Beyond international relations theory?
N.J. Rengger

War, Peace and World Orders in European History
Edited by Anja V. Hartmann and Beatrice Heuser

European Integration and National Identity
The challenge of the Nordic states
Edited by Lene Hansen and Ole Wæver

Shadow Globalization, Ethnic Conflicts and New Wars
A political economy of intra-state war
Dietrich Jung

Contemporary Security Analysis and Copenhagen Peace Research
Edited by Stefano Guzzini and Dietrich Jung

Observing International Relations
Niklas Luhmann and world politics
Edited by Mathias Albert and Lena Hilkermeier

Does China Matter? A Reassessment
Essays in memory of Gerald Segal
Edited by Barry Buzan and Rosemary Foot

European Approaches to International Relations Theory
A house with many mansions
Jörg Friedrichs

The Post-Cold War International System
Strategies, institutions and reflexivity
Ewan Harrison

States of Political Discourse
Words, regimes, seditions
Costas M. Constantinou

The Politics of Regional Identity
Meddling with the Mediterranean
Michelle Pace

The Power of International Theory
Reforging the link to foreign policy-making through scientific enquiry
Fred Chernoff

Africa and the North
Between globalization and marginalization
Edited by Ulf Engel and Gorm Rye Olsen

Communitarian International Relations
The epistemic foundations of international relations
Emanuel Adler

Human Rights and World Trade
Hunger in international society
Ana Gonzalez-Pelaez

Liberalism and War
The victors and the vanquished
Andrew Williams

Constructivism and International Relations
Alexander Wendt and his critics
Edited by Stefano Guzzini and Anna Leander

Security as Practice
Discourse analysis and the Bosnian War
Lene Hansen

The Politics of Insecurity
Fear, migration and asylum in the EU
Jef Huysmans

State Sovereignty and Intervention
A discourse analysis of interventionary and non-interventionary
practices in Kosovo and Algeria
Helle Malmvig

Culture and Security
Symbolic power and the politics of international security
Michael Williams

Hegemony and History
Adam Watson

Territorial Conflicts in World Society
Modern systems theory, international relations and conflict studies
Edited by Stephan Stetter

Ontological Security in International Relations
Self-identity and the IR state
Brent J. Steele

The International Politics of Judicial Intervention
Creating a more *just* order
Andrea Birdsall

Pragmatism in International Relations
Edited by Harry Bauer and Elisabetta Brighi

Civilization and Empire
China and Japan's encounter with European international society
Shogo Suzuki

Transforming World Politics
From empire to multiple worlds
Anna M. Agathangelou and L.H.M. Ling

The Politics of Becoming European
A study of Polish and Baltic post-cold war security imaginaries
Maria Mälksoo

Social Power in International Politics
Peter Van Ham

International Relations and Identity
A dialogical approach
Xavier Guillaume

The Puzzle of Politics
Inquiries into the genesis and transformation of international relations
Friedrich Kratochwil

The Conduct of Inquiry in International Relations
Philosophy of science and its implications for the study of world politics
Patrick Thaddeus Jackson

Arguing Global Governance
Agency, lifeworld and shared reasoning
Edited by Corneliu Bjola and Markus Kornprobst

Constructing Global Enemies
Hegemony and identity in international discourses on terrorism and
drug prohibition
Eva Herschinger

Alker and IR
Global studies in an interconnected world
Edited by Renée Marlin-Bennett

Sovereignty between Politics and Law
Tanja Aalberts

International Relations and the First Great Debate
Edited by Brian Schmidt

China in the UN Security Council Decision-making on Iraq
Conflicting understandings, competing preferences 1990-2002
Suzanne Xiao Yang

NATO's Security Discourse after the Cold War
Representing the West
Andreas Behnke

The Scandinavian International Society
From Norden to the northern dimension?
Laust Schouenborg

Bourdieu in International Relations
Rethinking key concepts in IR
Edited by Rebecca Adler-Nissen

Making Sense, Making Worlds
Constructivism in social theory and international relations
Nicholas Greenwood Onuf

World of Our Making
Rules and rule in social theory and international relations
Nicholas Greenwood Onuf

Maritime Piracy and the Construction of Global Governance
Edited by Michael J. Struett, Jon D. Carlson and Mark T. Nance

European Integration and Postcolonial Sovereignty Games
The EU Overseas Countries and Territories
Edited by Rebecca Adler-Nissen and Ulrik Pram Gad

European Integration and Postcolonial Sovereignty Games

The EU Overseas Countries and Territories

Edited by
Rebecca Adler-Nissen
and Ulrik Pram Gad

Routledge
Taylor & Francis Group

LONDON AND NEW YORK

First published 2013 by Routledge
2 Park Square Milton Park Abingdon Oxon OX14 4RN

Simultaneously published in the USA and Canada
by Routledge
711 Third Avenue, New York, NY 10017

Routledge is an imprint of the Taylor & Francis Group, an informa business.

British Library Cataloguing in Publication Data
A catalogue record for this book is available from the British Library

Library of Congress Cataloging in Publication Data
European integration and postcolonial sovereignty games : the EU overseas countries
and territories / edited by Rebecca Adler-Nissen and Ulrik Pram Gad.
p. cm. — (The new international relations)
Includes bibliographical references and index.
1. European federation. 2. Postcolonialism—European Union countries.
3. European Union countries—Foreign relations. I. Adler-Nissen, Rebecca, 1979-
II. Gad, Ulrik Pram.
JN15.E862 2013
341.242'2—dc23
2012025680

ISBN 13: 978–0–415–65727–3 (hbk)
ISBN 13: 978–0–203–07684–2 (ebk)

Typeset in Times New Roman
by Swales & Willis Ltd, Exeter, Devon

MIX
Paper from
responsible sources
FSC
www.fsc.org   FSC® C004839

Printed and bound by CPI Group (UK) Ltd, Croydon, CR0 4YY

Contents

Notes on contributors

Rebecca Adler-Nissen is Assistant Professor in the Department of Political Science, University of Copenhagen, Denmark. Her main research areas are sovereignty, European integration, diplomacy and international political sociology. Publications include *Opting Out of the European Union: Diplomacy, Sovereignty and European Integration* (2013); *Bourdieu in International Relations: Rethinking Key Concepts in IR* (2012, ed.) and *Sovereignty Games* (2008, co-edited with T. Gammeltoft-Hansen).

Godfrey Baldacchino is Professor in the Department of Sociology and Anthropology, University of Prince Edward Island, Canada, and Visiting Professor at University of Malta. He has published extensively on the subject of microstates and subnational island jurisdictions. His publications include *Island Enclaves: Offshoring Strategies, Creative Governance and Subnational Island Jurisdictions* (2009); and *The Case for Non-Sovereignty: Lessons from Subnational Island Jurisdictions* (2008, co-edited with D. Milne).

Peter Brown is Associate Professor in the School of Language Studies and Associate of the Europe Centre at the Australian National University, Canberra. In 2011 he was a Visiting Fellow at the Collegium Budapest Institute for Advanced Study. He has written widely on New Caledonian literature, culture and politics. Recent publications include 'La société mise en scène (Nouvelle-Calédonie)', in *La Littérature des îles du Pacifique*, eds. J. Bessière and S. André (forthcoming).

Ulrik Pram Gad is a Postdoctoral Researcher at the Centre for Advanced Security Studies, University of Copenhagen, Denmark. From 1998 to 2002, he worked for the Greenland Home Rule Government. Current research focuses on the identity politics and conflicts of Danish 'Muslim relations' and on the postcolonial relation between Greenland and Denmark. Publications include 'Postcolonial identity in Greenland?', *Journal of Language and Politics* (2009).

Siba Grovogui is Professor in the Department of Political Science, Johns Hopkins University, Baltimore, Maryland. Publications include *Sovereigns, Quasi-Sovereigns, and Africans: Race and Self-Determination in International Law* (1996); 'Regimes of sovereignty: rethinking international morality and the

African condition', *European Journal of International Relations* (2002); and 'A revolution nonetheless: the Global South in International Relations', *The Global South* (2011).

Ida Hannibal is Adviser in the Danish Prime Minister's Office. She has co-authored an MSc thesis on *Europe's Permanent Paradox? Sovereignty Games in Brussels by the EU's Overseas Countries and Territories* (2010, with K. Holst); and 'EUs oversøiske lande og territorier', *Politik* (2011, with U.P. Gad *et al.*).

Ulf Hedetoft is Professor and Dean, Faculty of Humanities, University of Copenhagen, Denmark. He has published extensively on European nationalism and national mentality; cultural encounters, migration and ethnic relations; and transatlantic relations. Recent work deals with the impact of globalization and Europeanization on the sovereignty and autonomy of small states. Publications include contributions to the *Globalization and Autonomy* series, UBC Press (2008–2010).

Ulla Holm is Senior Research Fellow in the Danish Institute for International Studies (DIIS). Her expertise includes French domestic and foreign/EU policy; the EU's Neighbourhood policy toward the southern Mediterranean; Algeria and North Africa with regard to internal development and the question about terrorism; Islam and immigration.

Kristine Holst is a Consultant at Devoteam, Copenhagen, Denmark. She was a student assistant on the research project 'Micropolities in the margin of Europe – postcolonial sovereignty games'. She has co-authored an MSc thesis on *Europe's Permanent Paradox? Sovereignty Games in Brussels by the EU's Overseas Countries and Territories* (2010, with I. Hannibal), and 'EUs oversøiske lande og territorier', *Politik* (2011, with U.P. Gad *et al.*).

Cormac Mac Amhlaigh is Lecturer in Public Law, University of Edinburgh, Scotland. Research focuses on the conceptual dimensions of law and politics and the impact of globalization and transgovernmentalism on these concepts including sovereignty and constitutionalism. Recent publications include a contribution to *Europe's Constitutional Mosaic*, eds. N. Walker *et al.* (2011); and *After Public Law* (2013, ed.).

Bill Maurer is Professor in the Department of Anthropology, University of California, Irvine. He conducts research on law, property, money and finance; currently on the shifting regulatory landscape in the offshore Caribbean. Books include *Recharting the Caribbean: Land, Law and Citizenship in the British Virgin Islands* (1997); and *Mutual Life, Limited: Islamic Banking, Alternative Currencies, Lateral Reason* (2005).

Karis Muller is Associate of the Europe Centre at the Australian National University, Canberra. Main research area is French history of ideas and Europe–Africa relations. Publications include 'The Euro in Africa', *Humanitas Journal* *of European Studies* (2008); and 'Europe as a Pacific power', in *EU Law of the Overseas*, ed. D. Kochenov (2011).

Gert Oostindie is Director of the Royal Netherlands Institute of Southeast Asian and Caribbean Studies, and Professor of Caribbean History, Leiden University, The Netherlands. His main research area is Caribbean and Dutch (post)colonial history. Publications include *Postcolonial Netherlands: Sixty-five Years of Forgetting, Commemorating, Silencing* (2012), and *Decolonising the Caribbean: Dutch Policies in a Comparative Perspective* (2004, with I. Klinkers).

Ronen Palan is Professor in the Department of International Politics, City University, London. His work lies at the intersection between international relations, political economy, political theory, sociology and human geography. He has written a number of books and numerous articles, book chapters and encyclopaedia entries on the subject of offshore and tax havens, state theory and international political economic theory.

Bernard Poirine is Professor in the Department of Economics, University of French Polynesia. He has published extensively on the political economy of small island economies. Publications include 'A theory of aid as trade with special reference to small islands', *Economic Development and Cultural Change* (1999); and *Tahiti, une économie sous serre* (2011).

William Vlcek is a Lecturer at the School of International Relations, University of St Andrews, Scotland. His publications on offshore finance and small states include a contribution on the Cayman Islands to *The Non-independent Territories of the Caribbean and Pacific: Continuity or Change?*, ed. P. Clegg and D. Killingray (2012); and 'Behind an offshore mask: sovereignty games in the global political economy', *Third World Quarterly* (2009).

Foreword

This book reflects our common interest in bringing together European integration and postcolonial theory in a discussion of sovereignty. The book also stems from our shared conviction that collective research projects are worthwhile and fun. We are very happy that the highly qualified contributors from various disciplinary backgrounds, including economics, law, anthropology, linguistics, and political science, jumped on board. Writing and editing the book has been nothing less than an adventure.

The book has benefitted from generous input from Tanja Aalberts, Eiríkur Bergmann, Heidi Bojsen, Thomas Gammeltoft-Hansen, Stefano Guzzini, Lene Hansen, Uffe Jacobsen, Pertti Joenniemi, Stephen Krasner, Niels Tannerup Kristensen, Ian Manners, Martin Marcussen, Peter Nedergaard, Iver B. Neumann, Sara Olsvig, Noel Parker, Hanne Petersen, Olivier Rubin, Paul Sutton, Georg Sørensen, Stuart Ward, Wouter Werner, Ole Wæver, and three anonymous reviewers.

The Center for European Politics at the Department of Political Science, University of Copenhagen, funded the opening workshop in Copenhagen in May–June 2009. Further grants from the Carlsberg, Augustinus, and Stjerngren foundations allowed us to proceed with the project and reconvene the contributors in Nuuk, Greenland, in April 2011, where Ilisimatusarfik (the University of Greenland) provided a beautiful and intellectually stimulating setting. A supplementary grant from the Letterstedska Foundation secured the participation of the contributors to the 'twin project' focusing on the EU relations to the Nordic micropolities. Last, but not least, a grant from the Danish Council for Independent Research (Social Sciences) enabled us to complete the editorial work.

We could not have completed this book without the support and help from a number of people. We would like to thank the three editors of Routledge's New International Relations series, in particular Iver B. Neumann, for their support. Moreveover, we owe great thanks to Heidi Bagtazo and Alex Quayle from Routledge's editorial team. In Copenhagen, Ulrik Kirk did more for the project website than we could ever have wished for. In the final round, Sune Petersen patiently assisted us in packaging the manuscript, and Jon Jay Neufeld helped smooth out the language across the chapters. But most importantly: From the very beginning, Kristine Holst has been the backbone of the project first when she wrote an excellent MA thesis with Ida Hannibal (that functioned as our pilot project) and later when she was our invaluable research assistant. We are infinitely grateful for her patience while we both took various breaks from the project to complete a PhD project, work in the Danish Ministry of Foreign Affairs, and enjoy parental leave. We dedicate this book to Kristine's daughter Freja and Ulrik's son Ville.

Rebecca Adler-Nissen and Ulrik Pram Gad
Copenhagen, November 2012

Series editor's preface

Empirically, this is the book about the European Union's Overseas Countries and Territories (OCTs), a variegated group of territories that did not end up as sovereign states during the Cold War thrust for decolonization. It focuses on the British, French, Dutch and Danish territories, leaving the Portuguese and Spanish islands and enclaves to one side. The basic idea is to scrutinize how all these polities are implicated in what the authors refer to as three-way sovereignty games between the overseas territory, the (former) imperial metropole, and the (various institutions of) the EU, whose responsibility for these territories is enshrined in the Treaties. The closest we come to an empirical consensus is that this is a problem complex made up of People, Resource Management, Overseas Engagement, Finance and Transportation (PROFIT).

The OCTs share more than a postcolonial predicament and a strategic positioning in a triangle, however. They are all phenomena of the boundary, in at least two ways. First, their overseas status makes them geographically liminal. The themes of island life are in evidence here; long-distance travel, local tensions between those who leave, those who stay behind and those who come back, tension between island diasporas and metropole natives. Second, and growing out of these tensions, there is the social liminality. And then there is the political liminality that comes with being small and far away. One of the key themes of the book is how this is a disadvantage to start with, but one that may be turned to the advantage of any one OCT. The most direct reminder of this we have in the refusal of the six Dutch Caribbean islands to leave the Kingdom of the Netherlands, despite sustained efforts by den Haag to push them in that direction. The contributors are, not surprisingly, divided on how to weigh the advantages and disadvantages, with Baldacchino and Oostindie stressing how OCTs stand to gain and are therefore not wont to quit, and Grovogui stressing how the OCTs exhibit a particular kind of postcolonial consciousness.

Good studies of liminals always tell us something about the main categories. This book is, therefore, ostensibly about the OCTs, but it is also a book about European states and about the European Union. Forty years ago, Johan Galtung tried to initiate a debate about how European integration could be understood as a process whereby six old empires became a new one. That proved to be a barren exercise. Here we have a new twist that will probably prove more productive, however. In terms of the debate about empires, understood as a category of polities, what is under debate here is a special case of heterogeneous contracting. What this means is simply that empires depend on middle men and women to run their provinces. These middle men each have a unique deal with the metropole, making for a set of heterogeneous contracts between that metropole and its sundry subentities. This book is, to my knowledge, the first one to make a sustained effort at documenting and discussing exactly which these contracts are, how they work, and with which effects. It has, therefore, a lot to offer the student of the European Union and of empires.

In the concluding chapter, the two authors focus on a second job undertaken here, which is to bring together the study of European integration and postcolonialism. This is a theme that will, no doubt, receive more attention in the years to come. Graduate student, pay attention: a number of issues outlined here are worthy of further and sustained scholarly attention. It is my hope that this book will prove to be as seminal as I think it should be.

Iver B. Neumann

List of abbreviations

ACP	African, Caribbean and Pacific states
BES	Bonaire, St. Eustatius, and Saba
BOT	British Overseas Territory
BVI	British Virgin Islands
CoE	Council of Europe
DFID	Department for International Development (UK)
DG	Directorate General (in the European Commission)
DOM	*Départements d'outre-mer* (France)
DROM	Overseas Region and Department (France)
EC	European Community
ECJ	European Court of Justice
ECCC	Eastern Caribbean Commercial Court
ECSC	Eastern Caribbean Supreme Court
EDF	European Development Fund
FDI	foreign direct investment
FLNKS	*Front de Libération National Kanak et Socialiste*
GFCC	German Federal Constitutional Court
GDP	gross domestic product
IR	International Relations
MIRAB	MIgration, Remittances, Aid and Bureaucracy
MLA	Member of the Legislative Assembly
MP	Member of Parliament
MSG	Melanesian Spearhead Group
MFA	Ministry of Foreign Affairs
NDP	National Democratic Party
OCT	Overseas Countries and Territories
OCTA	Overseas Countries and Territories Association
OECD	Organisation for Economic Cooperation and Development
OFC	Offshore Financial Centre
OR	Outermost Region (EU) or Overseas Region (France)
OT	Overseas Territory
PIF	Pacific Islands Forum

PROFIT	People, Resource management, Overseas engagement, FInance, and Transportation
RPCR	*Rassemblement pour la Calédonie dans la République*
SIDS	Small Island Developing States
SITE	Small Island Tourism Economy
SNIJ	Sub-National Island Jurisdiction
TIEA	Tax Information Exchange Agreement
TFEU	Treaty on the Functioning of the European Union
UNCTAD	UN Conference on Trade and Development

EU Overseas Countries and Territories (OCT) and Outermost Regions (OMR)

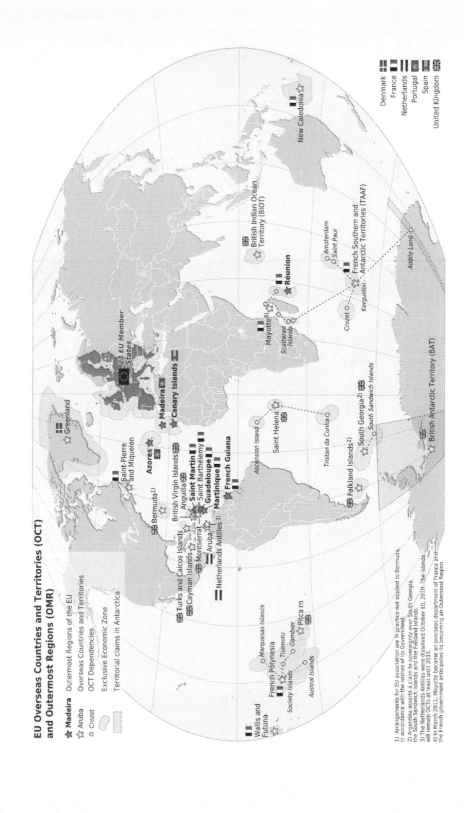

★ Madeira Outermost Regions of the EU
☆ Aruba Overseas Countries and Territories
○ Crozet OCT Dependencies
    Exclusive Economic Zone
    Territorial claims in Antarctica

Denmark
France
Netherlands
Portugal
Spain
United Kingdom

27 EU Member States

Greenland ☆

Saint-Pierre and Miquelon ☆
Azores ★
Bermuda[1] ☆
British Virgin Islands ▓
Anguilla ▓
Turks and Caicos Islands ☆
Cayman Islands ▓
Montserrat ▓
Aruba ☆
Netherlands Antilles[3] ▓

Madeira ★
Canary Islands ★

Saint Martin ▓
Saint Barthélemy ☆
Guadeloupe ★
Martinique ★
French Guiana ★

Ascension Island ○
Saint Helena ☆
Tristan da Cunha ○

Falkland Islands[2] ☆
South Georgia[2] ▓
South Sandwich Islands

British Indian Ocean Territory (BIOT) ☆

Mayotte[4] ◦
Réunion ★
Scattered Islands ☆
Crozet ○
Kerguelen ○
Amsterdam ○
Saint Paul ○
French Southern and Antarctic Territories (TAAF)

New Caledonia ▓

Adélie Land ☆

British Antarctic Territory (BAT) ☆

French Polynesia
Marquesas Islands ○
Tuamotu ○
Society Islands ☆
Gambier ○
Pitcairn ▓
Austral Islands ○

Wallis and Futuna ▓

1) Arrangements for EU association are in practice not applied to Bermuda, in accordance with the wishes of its Government.
2) Argentina asserts a claim to sovereignty over South Georgia, the South Sandwich Islands and the Falkland Islands.
3) The Netherlands Antilles were dissolved October 10, 2010. The islands will remain OCTs at least until 2015.
4) In March 2011, Mayotte became an overseas department of France and the French government anticipates its becoming an Outermost Region.

1 Introduction

Postcolonial sovereignty games

Ulrik Pram Gad and Rebecca Adler-Nissen

How do Greenland, Aruba, Mayotte, and other micropolities use the EU in their efforts to transcend their colonial status? How do the EU and its member states deal with these partially independent polities? While these territories are seeking greater room for manoeuvre on their own, they are at the same time developing a close relationship to the supranational EU in (dis)concert with their former colonizers. This book seeks to address these apparently contradictory processes of fragmentation and integration. Theoretically, we argue that sovereignty cannot be understood as a 'thing' that is either present or absent. On the contrary, sovereignty unfolds in the legal and political games that must be studied as both discourses and practices. By focusing on these arguably odd political entities, we tell an alternative story about how sovereignty works in international relations.

From its very beginnings in the 1950s, the EU has been part of a story of decolonization. We address the interplay of European integration and decolonization through the framework of 'intersecting sovereignty games'. Studying these games allows us to understand how a group of political entities with an ambiguous status in relation to sovereignty can play important roles *precisely* due to their ambiguous status.

Our reconceptualization of sovereignty draws on insights from both EU studies and postcolonialism. The two academic fields – EU studies and postcolonialism – have developed separately despite their obvious theoretical and empirical overlaps (Wæver and Tickner 2009: 3; see also Constantinou 2007; Hansen 2002: 486). In 1994, Darby and Paolini called for the bridging of International Relations (IR) and Postcolonialism. They saw the study of European integration as one of the possible places where state-centrism could be relaxed and where IR theories could become more open to concerns central to postcolonialism (1994: 390). A central aim of this book is to facilitate the cross-fertilization of the two academic sub-fields in order to better theorize international politics in a world of interdependence in which the term 'international' seems to lose its meaning.[1]

This introductory chapter is organized in six sections. The following section introduces the empirical focus of the book – the Overseas Countries and Territories (OCTs) and their relations to the EU and each of their respective metropoles. The second section addresses the IR debates on how best to conceptualize the units and relations of international politics. It briefly presents the various takes on sovereignty in European integration literature and postcolonialism and discusses possible characterizations of the relations between the EU, its member states, and their OCTs. The third section introduces the conceptual framework of the volume, providing a theoretical account of how the triangular relation may be understood as intersecting sovereignty games. The fourth section argues that this triangular relation offers a unique laboratory for studying sovereignty games by comparing these entities and their relations with 'neighbouring' categories of entities which also do not fit the traditional concept of sovereignty. Section five presents the analytical strategies employed in the case studies, and the final section presents an outline of the rest of the book.

Europe's last colonies

Europe's last colonies hold a prominent position on the European political agenda. On 9 June 2009, a majority of the people of Greenland voted in favour of increased independence from Denmark, and this interest in increased independence is combined with widespread interest in closer relations to the EU as a means of diversifying dependency. The EU, Denmark and Greenland alike are preparing for a future with climate change, intensive raw material extraction, new transportation corridors, and new claims to Arctic sovereignty. On the opposite side of the globe, in the Pacific Ocean, French Polynesian separatists advocate switching from a French connection tarnished by its colonial past to a closer relation to the EU, which they see as being free of these connotations. Another French possession, Mayotte in the Indian Ocean, recently voted to integrate further into France, becoming a French Overseas Department and hence fully integrated into the EU. In the Caribbean, a rather different and paradoxical process is taking place as a colony refuses to be decolonized: what is now referred to as the 'Caribbean Netherlands' have successfully resisted Dutch suggestions that the islands should become formally sovereign, opting instead for a process of internal devolution. Turning to the remnants of the British Empire, the situation of the British Overseas Territories is equally diverse: Bermuda resists any association with the EU, the Turks and Caicos has had its self-government arrangement temporarily suspended, while the British Virgin Islands and Cayman Islands are struggling with EU and international authorities seeking to somehow influence, if not control, their offshore financial activities. This book outlines the structural patterns in these seemingly contradictory developments. Seeking to outgrow their colonial status, the polities use the EU to acquire subjectivity without becoming fully independent from their metropoles.

At the same time, the EU is developing a common foreign policy using a range of foreign, environmental, security, development, and trade instruments. In this process, the overseas territories are seen as 'strategically important outposts, spread all over the world, as proponents of the EU's values' (European Commission 2009: 2). Establishing itself as a global 'normative power' (Manners 2002; Whitman 2011), the EU is the world's greatest aid donor and heavily engaged in developing international institutions. Although rarely stated explicitly, much of this involvement is closely linked to Europe's lengthy colonial history. This past has led to an abundance of special relations to former European colonies and dependents around the world. One peculiar type is the so-called 'OCT arrangement'; that is, the unique legal status of the EU's 'Overseas Countries and Territories'. The 21 OCTs arc constitutionally tied to a member state without being part of the EU.[2] Their situation is deeply puzzling. Spread around the world seas, these territories are engaged in constructing their own identities – separate and distinct from their former colonizers – in more or less close cooperation with a supranational EU. The complex relations between these micropolities, metropoles, and the EU have a single characteristic in common: they all dredge up legacies from the colonial period while at the same time demonstrating the significance of the EU for the future of these territories. One symptom of the complexity of these relationships is the language used to describe them: in EU jargon, the official term is 'overseas countries and territories constitutionally related to a member state'. In everyday language, practitioners translate this into 'OCTs and their mother countries'.[3] For reasons argued below, however, we prefer to place the OCTs within the generic category 'micropolity'. Although the Greek word 'metropole' literally means 'mother state', it seems to carry less pronounced maternalistic connotations.

In 2008, the European Commission proposed a comprehensive reform of the OCT arrangement. The objective is to reform the arrangement from a traditional form of development cooperation to a new framework that takes circumstances such as the liberalization of international trade into account. On the one hand, this reform appears to be an attempt at closing the book on Europe's colonial legacy; on the other, it can be seen as a form of neo-imperialism, a way for Europe to govern distant parts of the world.

A more pragmatic motivation for changing the OCT arrangement is financial. A number of the OCTs are now more affluent (per capita) than the average EU member state. Some OCTs have done extremely well in recent decades, possibly due to their peculiar status as 'almost sovereign but not quite' and their positioning on the margins of the EU.[4] Economic reasoning, however, cannot explain the EU's talk of the OCTs as strategic outposts. Indeed, as this book will demonstrate, the debates on the future of the OCTs stem from contrasting ways of imagining and organizing political life. Sovereignty is the dominant way of conceptualizing and ordering the world, but sovereignty is not an exclusive organizational template and may not even appear desirable, as the OCTs amply demonstrate.

Focusing on what appear to be marginal sites of international relations, we are able to see much more heterogeneity than IR theory usually allows a glimpse of. In this volume, we look at a particular site where a special meeting takes place: a meeting between the late sovereign EU, the postcolonial Third World, and autonomous-but-less-than-sovereign entities. The way sovereignty plays out in this site points towards a future which is very different from the (imagined) Westphalian notion of neatly pigeon-holed sovereign states.

This book provides the first comparative analysis of how sovereignty is practised in the triangular relationship between the EU, the micropolities, which have OCT status in relation to the EU, and the member states linking the two.[5] When it comes to natural resources, economic sustainability, collective identity, human rights, and security, the triangular relationship gives rise to what we call 'sovereignty games'. These games involve the interplay of the strategies whereby governments and international organizations attempt to increase their room for manoeuvre and legitimacy by playing on the various meanings of the concept of sovereignty.

Sovereignty in European and Postcolonial Studies

The sovereign state dominates our conception of political order, which prevents us from grasping the dynamics that avoid a strictly sovereign form of life. When reading realist international theory, the state appears to be a given. According to Kenneth Waltz, sovereignty means that a state 'decides for itself how it will cope with its internal and external problems' (Waltz 1979: 97; cf. Morgenthau 1956). This image of political life is strikingly parallel to international legal theory. International law traditionally sees sovereignty as an either/or question: either the state is sovereign or not. From this perspective, sovereignty is the exclusive right to exercise, within a specifiable territory, the functions of a nation-state and be answerable to no higher authority (Espersen, Harhoff and Spiermann 2003:142). This explains why non-sovereign entities such as the OCTs remain objects if viewed from an IR realist or traditional international law perspective. OCTs have no separate identity, no agency, and no subjectivity (Browning and Joenniemi 2004: 700f; 2008: 144; Palan 2003: 74; Anghie 2005: 38–9).

Historians and sociologists, however, paint a different picture of sovereignty. To begin with, the concept of sovereignty has a diverse and uneven past (Bartelson 1995; Grovogui, this volume). Moreover, the conditions for sovereignty have altered over the last few decades (Barkin 1998). Indeed, state sovereignty should not be seen as a permanent situation. Other ways of organizing world politics have been prevalent and continue to exist. This is why Ferguson and Mansbach suggest the label 'polity' to describe 'those entities with a measure of identity, a degree of organisation and hierarchy, and a capacity to mobilize persons and their resources for political purposes.' Moreover, almost all epochs 'have been characterized by layered, overlapping, and interacting polities – coexisting, cooperating and/or conflicting' (Ferguson and Mansbach 2008: 140). The traditional conceptualization of sovereignty is challenged when confronted with self-government arrangements (Petersen 2006; cf. Loukacheva 2007: 6, 145; Baldacchino 2010); and likewise when confronted with the EU (Ruggie 1993; Walker 2003; 2008).

Europe beyond sovereignty?

Jacques Delors once famously described the EU as an 'unidentified political object' (Drake 2000: 24). As Mac Amhlaigh shows in Chapter 3, sovereignty is central to the debate on how to characterize the nature of the EU. Three major positions have emerged that in different ways avoid a traditional understanding of sovereignty to analyse the EU.[6]

One position holds that, in the context of increased integration, the traditional understanding of sovereignty as territorial and inseparable should be replaced with a notion of 'late sovereignty'. This concept refers to functionally differentiated but overlapping claims to authority (Walker 2003; 2008). Within the EU, the late sovereign perspective contends, sovereignty undergoes a particularly radical transformation in which the member states surrender competencies related to everything from financial and trade policy to environmental and legal policy.

A second position holds that the notion of sovereignty is not the best way to conceptualize the present European political configuration. Europe is instead a neo-medieval construction. Ruggie argues that the conduct of politics among EU members resembles the medieval form of rule with its 'overlapping forms of authority' and 'non-exclusive forms of territoriality' (Ruggie 1993: 148–74).[7]

A third position finds that the EU is best conceived of as a kind of empire. While the notion of empire retains some notion of a centre, the absolute territorial limits of the sovereign state are relieved by a notion of gradual fading 'from a central Cosmos to a peripheral Chaos' (Wæver 1997: 65, 86; cf. Motyl 2001). The result is a polity that is internally hierarchically structured in concentric circles of authority and influence (Tunander 1997: 32).

Doyle claims that '[e]mpires are relationships of political control imposed by some political societies over the effective sovereignty of other political societies' (Doyle 1986: 19; cf. 45). Zielonka agrees that 'empire . . . is about a distinct way of organizing political space that is not based on the principle of territoriality and absolute sovereignty' (Zielonka 2006: 192). Doyle goes on to sketch a rather crude relation between metropole and periphery in empire: 'Certain states have centralized government, differentiated economies, and a shared political loyalty . . . Other societies . . . [i.e.] "imperializable peripheries" have no or at best highly divided governments, undifferentiated economies, and absent or highly divided political loyalties' (Doyle 1986: 19). Even historically, however, Zielonka notes that 'the degree of coercion applied by empires has seldom been uniform in terms of territory and policy field' (Zielonka 2006: 192). This relaxation of the definition of empire allows the concept to be applied to the EU.

The European empire is surrounded by other empires, such as the powerful yet fading Soviet and American empires (Zielonka 2006: 13; cf. Ikenberry 2004) and prospective empires such as the Russian, Turkish (Wæver 1997: 77) or Chinese (Wæver 1997: 65; Emmott 2008). A European empire – metaphorically or literally – always appears as an alternative to other imperial projects.[8] Whether the EU appears as a 'benign empire' (Zielonka 2006: 57) – and whether the European imperial project offers an attractive alternative to other imperial projects and to good old Westphalian sovereignty – depends on the perspective from which it is observed.

While Brussels seems to be the obvious political centre of the EU,[9] the periphery of the European empire is more uncertain. In the literature on EU-as-empire, the periphery generally begins with the member states which have opted out of significant areas of cooperation, includes new and prospective member states, and ends with the neighbouring states which have no realistic prospects of becoming part of the EU. Currently, Turkey is the quintessential periphery of the European empire. From this perspective, the OCTs belong to the outermost concentric circles of an emerging European empire, and their situation should be understood as such.

Considering the massive scholarly interest in how the EU has transformed the sovereignty of its member states, one would expect to find a body of literature on how the EU affects the acquisition of sovereignty by Europe's former colonies. Yet this is not the case. Instead, we have a range of studies of how the EU impacts on regional autonomy movements within Europe, in countries such as France and Spain (e.g. Börzel and Hosli 2003). The general argument here is that the EU both promotes and helps contain movements of regional autonomy (Hooghe and Marks 2003) by promoting regional cooperation and self-determination through, for instance, structural funds to disfavoured regions and the protection of sub-state language minorities within the member states (see Keating 1998; 2001). It has been suggested that the EU – partly due to its transformations of sovereignty – is particularly conducive to opening up diplomacy to non-sovereign entities (Mac Amhlaigh, this volume; cf. Cornago 2010: 100–1). But there are no studies of how the transformations of sovereignty inside the EU affect sovereignty in the postcolonial context.

This postcolonial gap in the EU literature is surprising given the important links between the former colonies and the EU. Moreover, the OCTs should be of relevance to integration scholars focusing on the relationship between European integration and autonomy movements on the European continent. To develop our framework which we will later use to analyse the OCTs' use of the integration process to acquire subjectivity, we seek inspiration in a different academic field: postcolonialism.

Postcolonialism, sovereignty, and subjectivity

The most important experience that the world has had with European imperialism is not related to its neighbouring territories – whether in the euro-sceptic North or the (im)patient Balkans. Instead, it has involved Africa, the Americas, Asia, and the Pacific as the 'imperializable periphery' in an asymmetrical relation. When observed from these parts of the world, imperialism meant colonialism. And colonialism implied no or a limited political subjectivity for the colonized. The struggle for decolonization generally meant a fight to make the colonizers leave. The colonized usually 'had a different view of the "benevolence" of their rulers and the desirability of European civilization' (Kohn and McBride 2011: 5). The aim was to replace European empires with independent sovereign states – preferably nation-states.

This is at least how the standard story goes in IR and political geography. Indeed, the postcolonial ambition has generally been taken at face value. The focus on the postcolonial situation has then led to a critique of the traditional perceptions of sovereignty and conceptualized the weak states left by decolonization as an expression of a 'pathological form' of sovereignty (Spruyt 2005; Turner 2002;

Jackson 1990). So the irony seems to be that the European empire left behind the ambition of European-style nation-states. The double irony is that those who judge this ambition to have failed in large parts of the world are European academics (cf. Briggs 1996). As Grovogui details in Chapter 2, this account of colonialism and decolonization grossly glosses over the biases built into the hegemonic discourses of sovereignty to the benefit of white, Western states.

The legal and political decolonization process of Europe's former colonies did not take place in an intellectual vacuum. First of all, as Grovogui recalls in Chapter 2, the independence movements built on European philosophy when they argued for the right to self-determination. Later, the most openly oppressive constructions of European racial superiority were largely delegitimized by the Second World War. Out of the struggles against the European empire grew a distinct strand of thought: postcolonialism. Postcolonial theory developed from 'tricontinentalism', that is, the surprisingly coordinated political efforts of Latin American, African, and Asian leaders from the 1950s onwards to position themselves independently of Western domination (Young 2003; Kohn and McBride 2011: 4). In academia, postcolonialism assumed many forms. What unites the various strands is a sustained concern with the *foundational* question (Kohn and McBride 2011): How is independent subjectivity achieved?

Saïd's (1978) seminal study detailed how Orientalism as a Western discourse immunizes itself from any input from 'the Orientals' – and, hence, serves as an integral aspect of imperialism and colonialism. In relation to various Orientals, the Western subject and particular Western powers thus retained sovereignty. In politics as in academia, this type of analysis often combines with a ferocious critique of Western discourse and policies (cf. Gregory 2004). This critique is usually as timely as the analysis but seldom constructive in the sense of having an impact or presenting viable courses of action.

Especially when combined with an ambition to recover pre-colonial roots to ground a position independent of Western hegemony, the result is often unsustainable both in terms of analytical conclusions (Paolini 1999: 53) and the strategic projects to articulate subjectivity (Mbembe 2002; Darby and Paolini 1994: 376). Concerning Africa, Mbembe shows how influential political and academic postcolonialism implies essentialisms belying a history that is much more complex: either African identity is constructed as victimhood and hence a derivative of the Western 'Other' or it is constructed as a self-sufficient, native alternative (Mbembe 2002: 241). Instead, Mbembe advocates an analysis which acknowledges both diffraction among Africans (2002: 262) and a sustained entanglement among African and non-African agents and cultures (2001; cf. Grovogui, this volume). Such a perspective allows agency on the part of the colonized – in the past, present, and future.[10]

A number of postcolonial scholars have pursued the subjectivity problematique in ways similar to Mbembe's. Spivak (1988) explains how the subaltern is structurally barred from speaking *as subaltern* in relation to Western modernity: subjectivity is only achieved by subjecting to modernity. Bhabha (1994) is more optimistic when he identifies particular ways in which the colonized may utilize cracks in the hegemonic discourse. The very ambiguity of the colonized's *mimicry* of the practices of the colonizer opens room for subjectivity. By appearing 'white, but not quite', the 'white' norm is put into question. A different route to the same aim is followed by Grovogui (2004), as he casts light on the central and active role of the so-called '*evolués*' – well-educated colonial subjects, elevated to French citizenship status – in the repeated re-structuring of the French Empire aiming to slow down African independence. In our study, the way our micropolities *mime* certain aspects of sovereignty – appearing 'sovereign, but not quite' – produces a hybridization which questions sovereignty as an either/or concept.

But what opens up for postcolonial subjectivity and agency is, according to Paolini, not hybridity or ambivalence as such but rather the paradoxical accept of hybridity as part of one's identity and the everyday, practical handling of ambivalent power structures (1999: 107–19).[11] Mbembe describes how the postcolonial subject in its everyday interactions with state power assumes multiple identities 'confirming in passing, the existence of an undoubtable institution . . . precisely in order to better "play" with it and modify it whenever possible' (Mbembe 1992: 23; cf. Paolini 1999: 118). The micropolities in focus in our study – in certain situations, and in varying degrees – assume a state-like identity which allows them to play with and, we contend, possibly modify the institution of sovereignty.

Thus, this book contributes to the study of political subjectivity. It does so in relation to the international system of states as it broadens the study of ways in which formerly colonized entities are acquiring subjectivity from focusing exclusively on full formal sovereignty. To do so, we adopt the perspective of Hall (1996), who describes the postcolonial identity formation process as an oscillation between more or less strategic essentialism (Spivak 1988) and the interplay of differences. At times, he argues, the anti-colonial struggle must coalesce around an identity posing certain fixity to obtain momentum. At other times the de-naturalization of the fixed, modernist categories takes precedence to allow for the emancipations of other identities than the postcolonial nationalist. In this sense, postcolonialism may both advocate modernist categories such as 'identity', 'nation', and 'sovereignty' (Mongia 1996; Appiah 1996; Hall 1996) and challenge the very same categories by promoting hybridization and creolization (Bhabha 1994; Gad 2005). In this vein, we focus on the various ways of acquiring subjectivity as a former colony. These ways to subjectivity each build on acceptance of certain elements of the imperial legacies (Darby and Paolini 1994: 377–8), of Western modernity, and of the state system – including, particularly, a concept of sovereignty. In other words, we reject the understanding that Postcolonial Studies should focus on an 'either/or' choice between submission and resistance. Total resistance to all the categories of Western modernity is a lost cause in any case. Instead, subjectivity may be achieved by selectively accepting some (but not other) categories. 'The state' and 'sovereignty' are both categories that are difficult to escape altogether but can be articulated in very different ways.

Consequently, a rejection of the 'either/or' argument prevalent in certain strands of Postcolonial Studies opens up new avenues for action, which leads away from coloniality proper. In some cases, these new avenues may be more attractive than acquiring formal sovereignty. Indeed, the postcolonial entities that we examine in the book feature a combination of the resistance and instrumentalization of ideas and practices of sovereignty. Today, certain forms of imperial representation have shown themselves to be counterproductive (Darby and Paolini 1994: 388). One of them is the traditional hierarchy between a sovereign, colonizing subject and a subordinate, colonized object: even where both international legal analysis and a realist power analysis would see a traditional, colonial relation, this volume demonstrates that the practical distribution of subjectivity is much more complex. The postcolonial future is never a question of either/or but invariably a choice between different versions of 'both–and'.

Conceptualizing sovereignty games

As indicated above, subjectivity and sovereignty are not interchangeable. One can play strategically with the concept of sovereignty. In the ongoing attempts at manoeuvring between dependency and self-determination, 'sovereignty' is a unique card that can be played – or played on – in a number of different ways. The OCTs and their relations to their metropoles and the EU clearly cannot be accounted for in terms of either sovereignty or empire alone. Rather, sovereign formalities, realities, and prospects as well as the dismantling of old empires and the construction of new ones must all be taken into consideration.

Building on both postcolonial insights and insights from European studies, we approach sovereignty from the perspective of discursive and practical moves. Thus, our concept of sovereignty games does not imply a classical rational choice approach. Of course, with the notion of game we include players with strategies. Some of the players certainly have goals which they seek to achieve. But games also involve moves which are not rationally directed towards any aim that may meaningfully be conceived as included in the game.

Our conceptualization of sovereignty games is inspired by Wittgenstein's idea of a language game. This conceptualization builds on both conventional constructivists (Sørensen 2002) and radical constructivists (Fierke and Nicholson 2001; Aalberts 2004; 2010) who have used Wittgenstein to grasp the strategic aspects of the use of language, that is, language games in relation to sovereignty.

Wittgenstein distinguishes between the constitutive and regulative rules in language. For our purpose, the constitutive rule in sovereignty games is constituted by the 'either/or' distinction of independence.[12] On the background of this constitutive rule, a series of regulative rules may change, most significantly the criteria of admission to the system, but also the distribution of roles between different kinds of players admitted. In Sørensen's analysis, three interrelated sovereignty games currently exist: a modern game (Russia and China are archetypical players); a postmodern game (quintessentially the EU, but the rest of 'the West' plays along); and a postcolonial game (weak states in Africa are ideal type players).[13]

Our perspective differs from Sørensen's approach in three ways. First, and most importantly, Sørensen finds the intrinsic qualities of the individual entity to be decisive for the kind of sovereignty game played out. Accordingly, material capabilities and capacities are decisive for whether a game is postmodern or post-colonial. Conversely, our perspective seeks to explore situations where neither the choice of game nor the rules of each of the games are fixed. Strategic action – and coincidental bi-effects – may lead to a change of game. Second, this also means that more than three games can be played with the concept of sovereignty. Third, some games compromise the very 'either/or' distinction which constituted the game in the first place.

Perhaps the most fitting metaphor for the kind of games we have in mind is that of a group of pre-teens in a playground, making up the rules as they go along. All players participate in an overall game, but most of the time they fan out in pairs or small groups to play their own, smaller games. There is no a priori grammar describing all of the possible moves, so there is room for evolution. Yet each move must have sufficient credibility for the other players to accept it – and there is an elaborate but distinct hierarchy among the players. Some moves require general acceptance – including that of certain central players. Other moves need only to be accepted by one specific player. Some players might have firm ideas of how the partial or overall game should develop – other players may have no long-term goal but a firm will in relation to a short-term goal – yet other players just play along. We thus follow Wittgenstein when he reminds us that 'is there not . . . the case where we play and make up the rules as we go along? And there is even one where we alter them as we go along' (Wittgenstein 1968: §83). At the same time, however, there is a shared understanding of the game being played. So even if the rules can be challenged and changed, there must be some element of the shared purpose of the game for it to make sense to the players.

In line with this conceptualization of a game, we may formally define a sovereignty game like this: a sovereignty game involves two or more players who, in their interaction, make strategic claims about authority and responsibility with reference to a traditional, 'either/or' concept of sovereignty. Contemporary sovereign states *and* polities which qualify as *potential* states manoeuvre between dependence and self-determination; and in these manoeuvrings, sovereignty is a card that can be played – or played on – in different ways. The articulation of the 'either/or' concept of sovereignty need, notably, be neither explicit nor affirmative in order for it to be vital for the game.

With this concept of sovereignty game in mind, we can specify our take on the debates on sovereignty in contemporary Europe and in postcolonial settings recapitulated in the section above.

Within the EU, sovereignty undergoes a particularly radical form of change in which the member states surrender competencies related to everything from financial and trade policy to environmental and judicial policy. As Mac Amhlaigh explains in Chapter 3, the EU has become a 'late sovereign complex' of overlapping claims to sovereignty (cf. Walker 2008). This obviously has consequences for the room for manoeuvre available to the OCTs. The co-existence of two ways of distributing and claiming sovereignty – territory and function – makes for games. They possibly lead to confrontational games over who should be the ultimate arbiter in specific cases (e.g. the constitutional battle between the German

Federal Constitutional Court (GFCC) and the European Court of Justice (ECJ)). They may also give rise to hide-and-seek games in which nobody wants to assume responsibility (Gammeltoft-Hansen and Adler-Nissen 2010). On the one hand, these games build on a traditional either/or concept of sovereignty, while on the other they end up compromising exactly the either/or character of this concept.

Another special category of sovereignty games includes the *postcolonial*. Compared to the variety of sovereignty in the EU, the standard postcolonial situation is rather different. Postcolonial sovereignty games are not merely concerned with the relational distribution of subjectivity (which is a general characteristic of all sovereignty games). At stake is whether one party to the game should be considered a party at all. Should the former colony be awarded *any* subjectivity or none? Postcolonial sovereignty games pertain not (only) to some particular instance of distribution of authority or responsibility, but to the distribution of the very *possibility* of articulating authority and responsibility. Postcolonial sovereignty games, in our definition, involve the constitution of the one of the parties *as a party* to the game.

The standard version of postcolonial sovereignty games involves the acquisition of sovereignty. During the last half of the twentieth century, in what could be seen as the first round of postcolonial sovereignty games, European states saw their empires collapse. A second round of postcolonial games, then, takes place between the former colonizers and the now decolonized but still dependent new states. In this game, the decolonized states play on the outside of both the EU and their former colonizer.

A residual case of entities – the OCTs – are involved in a different postcolonial sovereignty game, however, a game which does not involve the achievement of sovereignty. Instead, it involves the acquisition of whatever you, as a state-like entity, may be able to acquire by distinctively *not* claiming sovereignty. In terms of disturbing the traditional vocabulary, this game is more extreme than the one played in the standard process of decolonization. This is because it necessarily compromises the traditional, binary concept of sovereignty. It involves paradoxically making independent claims to renounce independence. Of course, sovereignty claims may sometimes be a bluff, but they can still induce metropolitan powers to allow micropolities independent subjectivity.

The tiny group of OCTs, hence, also play postcolonial sovereignty games – but they never left the 'first round' by completing the formal process of decolonization. These entities play games on the outside of the EU, but on the inside of their metropoles. To realists, the mere size of these countries would leave their agency inconsequential; sovereign or not, the relations between greater powers will decide their fate.[14] Even approaches in radical opposition to IR realism deem the agency of microentities negligible. Arguably, they are marginalized and discriminated against if we are to believe notions of 'hegemony' (Hout 1996) or 'empire' (Anghie 2005).

In practice, however, non-sovereign polities do have agency. In Chapter 4, Baldacchino explains how sovereignty for a number of micropolities appears not as a precondition for subjectivity, but rather as one tool among others in the toolbox when adapting to the political, social, and economic environment.[15] Moreover, Baldacchino highlights how the 'micro' prefix may be used in different ways, both to detract reality from a formal sovereignty acquired but also to 'dodge the radar' of the responsibilities regularly flowing from sovereignty – whether formal sovereignty resides in the micropolity or in a metropole.[16]

Sutton (2008: 16) stresses that a status as autonomous without formal sovereignty will probably never allow a 'happy', uncontroversial relationship with the metropole. We suggest, however, that the 'unhappiness' and controversies are part of more complex games in which the parties play on two alternatives, integration into the metropole and independent sovereignty, in the ongoing negotiation of the (formally) hierarchical relation. Subjectivity for former colonies may be acquired through a variety of postcolonial sovereignty games with a more or less strategic use of the sovereign state system.

A laboratory of sovereignty games

It appears from most IR literature that sovereign statehood is the most desirable status for any group or large community: 'Today, in contrast to the nineteenth century, it would be almost inconceivable for a country readily to vote to become a colony' (Jepperson, Wendt, and Katzenstein 1996: 36). Yet many former colonies have voted exactly to remain non-sovereign within an empire. As Constantinou notes, 'Certain states of exception are more comfortable than others. Even while they appear problematic or absurd to those experiencing them they can still be judged preferable – less bad, less risky – than available alternatives' (Constantinou 2008: 145). The case studies presented in this volume suggest that this is partly a symptom of a choice which – even on its own premises – is much more complex than simply a choice between sovereign subjectivity and imperial objectification. When this peculiar version of postcolonial sovereignty games is framed by the sovereignty games played in late sovereign Europe, the OCTs clearly offer a unique laboratory for study how polities may play on sovereignty without being formally sovereign.

The OCTs are uniquely *postcolonial, micro-, potentially-sovereign polities.* Each of the four constitutive elements in this label – post, colonial, micro, and potentially-sovereign polity – carries specific meaning. When characterized in this manner, it becomes evident that the OCTs are part of larger groups of entities which do not fit the traditional definition of sovereignty. The unique character of the OCT arrangement as a sovereignty laboratory will be more evident as we discuss each of the elements.

OCTs clearly have a *colonial* history: their present status can only be understood against the background of European colonialism. On this abstract level, they share a fate with many parts of the world. Contrary to most of their neighbours, however, they do not have full sovereignty – they were never formally decolonized. Yet this does not imply that their present status can be adequately characterized as colonial. Rather, the OCTs represent a different kind of *postcoloniality* than their neighbours, which are formally sovereign states.

First, the relation to their metropole is not one of an unconditional colonial submission – the OCTs all have some sort of self-government arrangement.[17] Self-government arrangements may even include the transfer of jurisdiction in some areas of foreign affairs (Loukacheva 2007: 109) – an area traditionally so closely related to sovereignty that it is often considered the prerogative of the sovereign.

Second, and related, full formal sovereignty is for all of them a more or less credible possibility – they are *potentially* sovereign.[18] A few centuries ago, the polities covered in this book would not have sovereignty as a meaningful prospect because decolonization was only 'invented' in Latin America in the early nineteenth century. In the early rounds of decolonization of Africa and Asia in the 1950s and 1960s, size seemed a hindrance to independence. The *micro*polities covered in this book all have less than 300,000 inhabitants.[19] Today, however, a population of only 20,000–300,000 – combined with a distinct identity (politically and, preferably, also culturally delimited)[20] and a 'deep blue ocean' between the OCT and the metropole – makes sovereignty an option. Indeed, to most of these islands, this is a very plausible option: they merely have to look to the neighbouring island, which has its own flag in front of the United Nations (UN) headquarters. The only difference between these islands and the OCTs is the relation to the metropole: the OCT's relation to a current postcolonizer – compared to the relation of the integrated neighbour to the metropole it is formally an equal part of – compared to the relation of a decolonialized neighbour to the former colonizer.

Formally sovereign or not, interdependence is a basic condition of current political life. And sovereign or not, this dependence and exchange with the outside kicks in earlier for micropolities. The absolute limitations regarding educational resources and competencies found in micropolities mean that exchange with, and assistance from, the outside world is necessary (Nielsen 2000: 23) in a way even more acute than for larger entities. The colonial material and social infrastructure has – even with the possibility of increased formal self-government – created a specific dependence upon the former colonizer. In this situation, an interest in the diversification of the relations to the outside world serves as indication that the colonial relationship is in the process of tipping over to a postcolonial situation with greater self-determination (Gad 2009). Also when considering material dependency, the group of entities in focus appears to be postcolonial, even if some of them *are* able to pay for what they need from outside.

In many ways, the OCTs are nation-state-like polities: internally, the 'state' governs its territory and population and the population identifies with the 'state'. Externally, the 'state' represents its population – even if formally only vis-à-vis the metropole. These entities are not sovereign states, however, as they formally only qualify as bureaucratic extensions of the sovereignty of the former colonizer. But as soon as we leave behind the perspective of international law and how this perspective tends to produce binary pictures of sovereignty/non-sovereignty, things become less black and white. While legal texts and practices do not constitute the OCTs as strictly sovereign, when approached from a social science perspective, it becomes evident that the OCTs *do* articulate and refer to the legal and absolute concept of sovereignty.[21] Only the OCTs and sovereignty are articulated in a non-binary manner. Where the international legal scholar may see either state or non-state, the social scientist may see the partial stateness of an entity. Not because sovereignty stops being an either/or concept – but because many stories may be told in which this concept has a role; including stories of evolution or creativity rather than of a single, pre-defined choice. Such stories may – without involving the choice of sovereignty – make the entities more state-like than the 'not-sovereign' label suggests. This is so because, in the ongoing attempts at manoeuvring between dependency and self-determination, 'sovereignty' is an entirely unique card that can be played – or played upon – in a number of different ways by the OCT in relation to the metropole, as well as by the metropole and the outside world in relation to the OCT.

In sum, in the European 'laboratory' for new ways of playing out sovereignty, the OCT arrangement constitutes yet another layer leading to unique sovereignty games. As objects of investigation, the self-governing micropolities included in the OCT arrangement offer the optimal opportunity to study *a multilayered configuration of intersecting sovereignty games*.

Methodology: sovereignty as discourse and practice

The core of this volume consists of nine multi-sited case studies. This section presents the analytical framework applied to the individual case studies, thereby suggesting how we may know a sovereignty game when we see one. The methodological starting point for the case studies has been that sovereignty games – apart from their *codified formalization* in legal texts – can be studied by comparing the *negotiation of meaning* in public debate and specific forms of *diplomatic praxis* (e.g. meetings, negotiations, documents).[22] In all three situations, the concept of sovereignty is often played on in strategic ways. When the EU, the metropole member state or the micropolity relate – in the same strategic move – to both of the two other parties in the triangular relation, the two layers of sovereignty games (the European and postcolonial) intersect. To study these moves, the case studies employ these analytical strategies to study three types of data material, as re-collected in Table 1.1.

First, strategies may be observed indirectly as they have been 'frozen' in *formalized sovereignty arrangements* institutionalized in the form of *legal text*. Agreements such as international treaties or national constitutions are the results of a meeting between (possibly partially conflicting) strategies for how a relation ought to be. From a legal perspective, the relation is constituted by such a founding text – and thereby the sovereignty relation *is* as the law claims. From a social science perspective, however, the legal text is only the point of departure for further sovereignty games.

Second, strategies may be explicated or implicated in *identity discourse* manifested in for instance *public and parliamentary debates* on the triangular relation. Identity discourses delimit who 'we' may credibly become without ceasing to be 'us' – and such delimitations take place by explaining how we relate to 'others' (Wæver 2002; Hansen 2006; Gad 2010). *Discourse analysis* focuses on

Table 1.1 Analytical foci and methods

Method	Institutional analysis	Discourse analysis	Praxis analysis
Site	Formalized sovereignty	Negotiations of identity discourse	Diplomatic praxis
Type of material	Treaties, constitutions, delegation laws, etc.	Parliamentary records, media debate, official statements, and policy papers	Qualitative interviews with representatives of the micropolities, metropole member states, and the EU
Analytical strategy	Understanding the institutionalization of the triangular relation as both result of 'frozen' strategies and the basis for strategies and games	Mapping competing visions of collective identity and strategies for the triangular relations, i.e. the public meanings ascribed to the position of the micropolity vis-à-vis the EU and the metropole member state	Mapping the self-understanding, negotiations, and strategies of the officials involved in the management of the triangular relations – focusing on diplomatic procedures, practices, correspondence, tacit understandings

the role ascribed to the EU in relation to the capacity to act, to be self-supporting, and to an increased (or contracted) room for manoeuvre (formally and in practice) for the OCT. Indeed, it focuses on how agency and structural constraints are articulated; that is, how the sovereignty game frames itself.

Finally, strategies are necessarily implicated in *diplomatic practices* handling the relation between the identity discourses and legal texts. Diplomatic practice can rarely be observed directly. A series of in-depth, qualitative interviews focused on a similar problematique have, however, proven to facilitate the analysis of sovereignty game strategies as they are played out in diplomatic practice (Adler-Nissen 2009). Thus, the interviews serve, first, to establish an overview of how the relations are maintained in *concrete everyday moves* (negotiations, correspondences, tones, frequency of contact). Second, the interviews identify specific experiences casting light on the strategies employed by the respective parties in the triangular relationship – and their degree of success. Third, the interviews reveal how formal sovereignty (as identified in the institutional analysis) and identity discourses (as identified in the discourse analysis) are articulated on a daily basis.

In exploring the configuration of sovereignty games, we argue that the strategic moves can only be fully grasped in their unique settings and regional contexts. The settings involve both the local assemblies on the island, the metropolitan administration, and the Brussels scene in which the local meanings ascribed to the triangular relations can be unpacked. In principle, each corner of the triangular relation – OCT, metropole member state, the EU – is equally important. Yet as our analyses will show, the EU and metropole tend to play a greater role with respect to the OCTs than vice versa. While existential questions such as 'Are we a state or should we aim to become one?' are rarely raised in established states with formal sovereign status, such fundamental questions are real and crucial for the territories in question and brought up on a regular basis. The real-life impact of sovereignty games is very visible in these political entities and to their populations. Therefore they structure the political debate within the islands to a large extent – along with their relations (material and rhetorical) with the outside world. These debates are important for understanding postcolonial sovereignty games.

The book includes cases which are alike in terms of formal status, as they all have a self-governing arrangement with the metropole and OCT status with the EU,[23] but they inhabit varying political-cultural contexts. The contexts involve both different experiences with sovereignty and different experiences with empire. While each polity may have a unique experience with sovereignty, distinct clusters of perspectives may summarize how sovereignty is experienced in the EU; in a specific, regional, postcolonial setting; and in relation to a particular colonial empire. This volume covers micropolities whose next-door neighbours exhibit varying levels of prosperity, political stability, social conventions, and whose metropoles embody varying political-cultural and socio-economic traditions and have varying colonial histories.

More specifically, cases are analysed in the *Caribbean* (The Cayman Islands, the British Virgin Islands, and Caribbean Netherlands[24]), the *Pacific* (French Polynesia, New Caledonia), the *Indian Ocean* (Mayotte), and the *North Atlantic* (Greenland). All the relevant metropole member states are represented here (the United Kingdom (UK), France, the Netherlands, Denmark). Patterns are identified in the concluding chapter of how micropolities operate in order to gain agency by selectively and creatively articulating the concept of sovereignty.

Organization of the volume

Following this introduction, three theoretical chapters each review a distinct perspective on sovereignty (briefly introduced above): in Chapter 2, *Siba Grovogui* introduces *the postcolonial experiments aiming at sovereignty.* In Chapter 3, *Cormac Mac Amhlaigh* discusses the various attempts to theoretically grasp *continuity and change in sovereignty in the EU.* Finally, in Chapter 4, *Godfrey Baldacchino* evaluates the *micropolity sovereignty experience.*

The core of the volume consists of the case studies. In addition to eight individual OCTs, we have also included three 'meta-cases'. First, the *Brussels scene* of the OCT sovereignty games is introduced in Chapter 5, focusing especially on the European Commission and Overseas Countries and Territories Association (OCTA). Second, the UK and French cases are framed by brief introductions by *Ulf Hedetoft* and *Ulla Holm*, respectively, to British (Chapter 6) and French (Chapter 10) national identity as they are played out in their approaches to their (former) empires and to the EU.[25] Where the relations between the EU and British OCTs covered in this book all revolve around global financing, the games observed in the French OCTs covered in this book all relate directly to their positions in relation to sovereignty along the spectrum integration–autonomy–sovereignty.

In the chapters on the British OCTs, *Ronen Palan* adopts a historical perspective in Chapter 7, tracing how the relations between the British Overseas

Territories and another quasi-sovereign polity, the *City of London*, accounts for the present role of these entities in offshore financing. In Chapter 8, *William Vlcek* zooms in on the strategies pursued in relation to the *Cayman Islands'* reactions to the EU's current attempts to tax offshore savings. *Bill Maurer*, in Chapter 9 on the *British Virgin Islands*, focuses on the role of the colonial legacy in arguments for why offshore finance should not be regulated.

Turning to the French overseas in Chapter 11, *Bernard Poirine* examines the role given to the EU in debates in *French Polynesia* as an imagined alternative to the French connection. *Peter Brown* presents, in Chapter 12, the centrifugal politics of imperial victimhood in *New Caledonia* and its implications in terms of sovereignty games and for the relations with the EU. *Karis Muller*'s Chapter 13 interrogates the case of *Mayotte*, which voted to leave OCT status behind in order to integrate with/in metropolitan France as an overseas department and the EU as its first predominantly Muslim polity.

The last two case studies focus on the Dutch and Danish imperial remnants. Even if these two colonial powers have a parallel history of receding to small or medium state status in the EU – and lately in occasional euroscepticism – their respective relations to their OCTs are, at least when it comes to legal formalities, almost symmetrically opposed. In Chapter 14, *Geert Oostindie* details the failed Dutch attempts to make the constituent parts of the *Caribbean Netherlands* acquire their own sovereignty(/-ies) – departing from the framework of a constitution exemplarily facilitating 'free association'. In contrast, *Ulrik Pram Gad* demonstrates in Chapter 15 how Denmark in practice facilitates an independent *Greenlandic* agency in relation to the EU, even if it may have been more reluctant about formal devolution in the Danish empire. Finally, a concluding chapter discusses systematic patterns across the case studies – and on the basis of these new insights, it suggests more ways to cross-fertilize postcolonialism and EU studies in order to facilitate a better understanding of International Relations.

Notes

1 Hansen (2002) and Behr (2007) are among the very few granting attention to how the European integration process was and still is influenced by the European imperial legacy. Polat (2011) represents a rare example of applying postcolonial theory – particularly the concepts of mimicry and hybridity – as a theory of European integration. His analysis focuses, however, on Europe's relationship to its own past rather than the colonial relation. For a few – but valuable – meetings between IR and postcolonialism, see Paolini (1999); Barkawi and Laffey (2002); Ling (2002); Chowdhry and Nair (2002); cf. Chacko (2004).

2 In accordance with article 198 of the Treaty on the Functioning of the European Union. For a more detailed explanation, see Hannibal, Holst, *et al.* (this volume).

3 In national discourse, British overseas islands are invariably 'territories'; Greenland insists on being a 'country', while Denmark has some trouble using this designation; some parts of the Caribbean Netherlands are also 'countries', while other islands are now simply 'municipalities'; the French have experimented with a series of labels for various parts of its *Outre-Mer*: 'territories', 'regions', 'departments', and 'collectivities'.

4 The relative prosperity of the OCTs cannot be accounted for solely by the drop in the average GDP of the EU member states after the 2004 enlargement.

5 Kochenov (2011) provides a comprehensive overview of the legal constitution of the triangular relation – but does not provide for a broader understanding of the possibilities of agency opened up by this constitution and the broader impact on the international. Petersen (2006) analyses the Danish Commonwealth and the EU as parallel challenges to a traditional concept of sovereignty, but the relationship between Greenland and the EU is not dealt with. Loukacheva (2007: ch.7) compares Greenlandic and Nunavut relations to the EU in a legal perspective but does not use the analysis to complicate the concept of sovereignty explicitly. Baldacchino and Greenwood (1998) deal with the relationships between small, insular economies to sovereignty and the EU, but none of these economies are OCTs and the theoretical perspective is more socio-economic than political (cf. Hache 1998). Sutton (1991) covers a number of the (Caribbean) OCTs but does not problematize the concept of sovereignty as such.

6 Our tripartition of the debate is parallel to Browning's (2005).

7 For a detailed account of this so-called 'neo-medievalism' and its relevance for contemporary international relations, see Friedrich (2001). 'Polycentric' is another label which conveys a similar analysis of the EU; a set of interlocking legal orders with a constant battle for supremacy (MacCormick 2004: 14f).

8 A separate question in the literature on empires concerns whether imperial projects – as a radiation of an ordering project from a centre to a periphery – are necessarily universal in pretension (Wæver 1997: 65; cf. Zielonka 2006: 156f). This question need not detain us here.

9 If allowed for, a lengthier answer might involve Luxembourg, Strasbourg, and even a couple of member state capitals – Berlin and Paris spring to mind.

10 For a much more detailed and nuanced analysis of the genealogies and positions of postcolonialism, which nevertheless roughly agrees with our crude summary, see Paolini (1999: 49–126). For an alternative categorization of ways to provide a foundation for postcolonial identity and agency – performatively by revolution against oppression; by the recovery of indigenous cultural resources; and by invoking a practical relation to the land – see Kohn and McBride (2011).

11 Paolini finds the 'challenge to hegemony and scope for agency' opened by Bhabha's concepts of mimicry and hybridity 'trivial and marginal' (1999: 107) due to Bhabha's Lacanian debt when developing his concepts (1999: 74): 'The resistance involved [in mimicry] is strangely other-than-subjectivity. The colonized are necessary only to reflect back as not quite same . . . The process is mostly subjectless; mimicry resides in the symbolic order of language' (Paolini 1999: 78).

12 This represents a very different approach to games than that of game theory. For an exploration of the contrast between these two understandings of games, see Fierke and Nicholson (2001).

13 Grovogui, this volume, recalls how the idea that multiple regimes of sovereignty co-exist goes back to Hegel.

14 For an excellent overview over the microstate literature in International Relations, see Neumann and Gstöhl (2006).

15 In socio-economic research on micropolity, sovereignty is often treated according to a traditional conceptualization as a formal either/or question (Bartmann 2002; Stringer 2006), which must be cleared up for economic reasons (Streeten 1993).

16 The ambiguous position between independence and integration may combine a room for self-determinacy with a measure of economic support and security. These polities may even use the undecided question of political status as a resource in the negotiations with the metropole (Sutton 2008: 7) while instrumentalizing their autonomous status to facilitate development policies (Baldacchino and Milne 2006: 487).

17 These arrangements may not all fit any of the two UN-approved ways of decolonizing apart from full, formal sovereignty: equal integration or free association; see Hannibal, Holst, *et al.*'s contribution to this volume.

18 A series of categories of European polities appear parallel in different ways: the British

crown dependencies (Isle of Man, Channel Islands) and the Nordic self-governing areas (Faroe Islands, Aaland) might be as potentially sovereign as the OCTs. The post-Soviet breakaway entities (Transdnistria, Abkhazia, South-Ossetia) and the post-Yugoslav ones (Republika Srpska, Kosovo at least until recently) distinguish themselves by having claimed sovereignty with less than unconditional success. A handful of formally sovereign microstates (Liechtenstein, Andorra, San Marino, Monaco) have a relation to a significant (m)other state – or in a few cases: a couple of parent states – which is comparable with the relations of the OCTs. Even if the metropole relations of these polities involve submission and have been characterized in terms of (internal) colonization, the racialization and civilizational hierarchies involved in colonization are not as black and white – pun intended – as in the overseas cases.

19 There is no general consensus as to how a state, economy, or polity is most appropriately defined as 'micro' – should the defining criterion be the size of the territory, the economy, or the population? Most researchers, however, use population as the yardstick, and many draw the distinction at 300,000 residents (Armstrong and Read 2000: 290).

20 Yet another neighbouring category to the self-governing postcolonial OCTs singled out for analysis comprises entities which cannot be characterized as state-like in their own right since they do not have a permanent population or local government structure. Among the territories included in the EU's OCT arrangement are unpopulated Antarctic territories and military base areas with temporarily stationed personnel. The UK territory of Diego Garcia in the Indian Ocean is a special case, as it has an exiled population which nevertheless is 'permanent' in the sense that at least part of it wants to return. The smallest of the settler-colonies within the OCT framework would possibly also fit this category: as these entities do not have a state-like stratification of their local social structure – there is no local authority, the authorities are all far away in the metropole; 'we' identify 'us' not as 'Tinyremoteislanders' but as, for example, 'British' – they do not have formal sovereignty as a meaningful prospect. Therefore, they – contrary to the OCTs in focus for the book – do not qualify as postcolonial but only as colonial. We could also add the 'jurisdictions' under British military control – such as the Sovereign Base Areas of Akrotiri and Dhekelia; and the absence of the 'right of abode' on Ascension Island.

21 This is where our perspective differs from how Cornago (2010) develops a conception of the 'para-diplomacy' of sub-state entities in a contribution to Constantinou and Der Derian's (2010) efforts to recover 'sustainable diplomacies' as ways to mediate estrangement excluded from the Westphalian, state-monopolized diplomacy. The discourses and practices in focus for our analysis may, on the one hand, be counted as a sub-category of para-diplomacy. On the other hand, we focus particularly on the ways in which these practices do articulate the concept of sovereignty creatively.

22 The project has thereby been engaging with both 'the linguistic turn' within the social sciences and its notion that language is decisive for power relations and with the more recent 'turn to practice', which studies day-to-day human interactions and routines beyond or outside written texts (Schatzki *et al.* 2001).

23 The OCT populations vary from uninhabited islands to several hundred thousand residents. Among the polities included in the EU's OCT framework, the book covers all cases with a population of at least 20,000 (which allows the identification of an internal political debate documented in accessible written and oral sources) – only Bermuda has been omitted, as its government has insisted on not being included in the OCT arrangement, and the Turks and Caicos has been omitted as its self-governing arrangement is currently suspended.

24 The Netherlands Antilles and Aruba are analysed best as one case; Aruba was separated from the Antilles in 1986. The further break-up of the Antilles is currently implemented.

25 The legacies of the Dutch and Danish empires are covered by the case studies on Caribbean Netherlands and Greenland, respectively.

References

Aalberts, T.E. (2004) 'The future of sovereignty in multilevel governance Europe – a constructivist reading, *Journal of Common Market Studies*, 42(1): 23–46.

Adler-Nissen, R. (2009) 'Late sovereign diplomacy', *Hague Journal of Diplomacy*, 4(2): 121–41.

Anghie, A. (2005) *Imperialism, Sovereignty and the Making of International Law*, Cambridge: Cambridge University Press.

Appiah, K.A. (1996) 'Is the post- in postmodernism the post- in post-colonial?', in P. Mongia (ed.) *Contemporary Post-colonial Theory*, London: Arnold.

Armstrong, H.W. and Read, R. (2000) 'Comparing the economic performance of dependent territories and sovereign micro-polities', *Economic Development and Cultural Change*, 48(2): 285–306.

Baldacchino, G. and Greenwood, R. (eds) (1998) *Competing Strategies of Socio-Economic Development for Small Islands*, Vol. 2, Charlottetown: University of Prince Edward Island.

Baldacchino, G. and Greenwood, R. (eds) (2010) ' "Upside down decolonisation" in subnational island jurisdictions: questioning the "post" in postcolonialism', *Space and Culture*, 13(2): 188–202.

Baldacchino, G. and Milne, D. (2006) 'Exploring sub-national island jurisdictions: an editorial introduction', *The Round Table*, 95(386): 487–502.

Barkawi, T. and Laffey, M. (2002) 'Retrieving the imperial: empire and international relations', *Millennium*, 1(31): 109–27.

Barkin, J.S. (1998) 'The evolution of the constitution of sovereignty and the emergence of human rights norms', *Millennium: Journal of International Studies*, 27(2): 229–52.

Bartelson, J. (1995) *A Genealogy of Sovereignty*, Cambridge: Cambridge University Press.

Bartmann, B. (2002) 'Meeting the needs of the micro-polities', *The Round Table: The Commonwealth Journal of International Affairs*, 91(365): 361–74.

Behr, H. (2007) 'The European Union in the legacies of imperial rule? EU accession policies viewed from a historical comparative perspective', *European Journal of International Relations*, 13(2): 239–62.

Bhabha, H. (1994) *The Location of Culture*, London: Routledge.

Börzel, T.A. and Hosli, M. (2003) 'Brussels between Bern and Berlin: comparative federalism meets the European Union', *Governance*, 16(2): 179–202.

Briggs, Charles L. (1996) 'The politics of discursive authority in research on "the invention of tradition" ', *Cultural Anthropology*, 11(4): 435–68.

Browning, C.S. (2005), 'Westphalian, imperial, neomedieval: the geopolitics of Europe and the role of the North', pp. 85–101 in C.S. Browning (ed.) *Remaking Europe in the Margins: Northern Europe after the Enlargements*, Aldershot: Ashgate.

Browning, C.S. and Joenniemi, P. (2004) 'Contending discourses of marginality: the case of Kaliningrad', *Geopolitics*, 9(3): 699–730.

Browning, C.S. and Joenniemi, P. (2008) 'Gibraltar, Jerusalem, Kaliningrad: peripherality, marginality, hybridity', pp. 141–58 in N. Parker (ed.) *The Geopolitics of Europe's Identity: Centers, Boundaries, and Margins*, Houndsmills: Palgrave Macmillan.

Chacko, P. (2004) 'Postcolonial globalities', *Borderlands e-journal* 3(3). Online. Available at: http://www.borderlands.net.au/vol3no3_2004/chacko_postcolonial.htm (accessed 2 April 2012).

Chowdhry, G. and Nair, S. (2002) 'Introduction: power in a postcolonial world: race, gender and class in international relations', in G. Chowdhry and S. Nair (eds) *Power, Postcolonialism and International Relations: Reading Race, Gender and Class*, London: Routledge.

Constantinou, C. (2007) 'Aporias of identity: bicommunalism, hybridity and the "Cyprus problem"', *Conflict & Cooperation*, 42(3): 247–70.

Constantinou, C. (2008) 'On the Cypriot states of exception', *International, Political Sociology*, 2(2): 145–64.

Constantinou, C.M. and Der Derian, J. (eds) (2010) *Sustainable Diplomacies*, Houndsmills: Palgrave Macmillan.

Cornago, N. (2010) 'Perforated sovereignties, agonistic pluralism and the durability of (para)diplomacy', in C.M. Constantinou and J. Der Derian (eds) *Sustainable Diplomacies*, Houndsmills: Palgrave Macmillan.

Darby, P. and Paolini, A.J. (1994) 'Bridging international relations and postcolonialism', *Alternatives*, 19: 371–97.

Doyle, M.W. (1986) *Empires*, Ithaca, NY: Cornell UP.

Drake, H. (2000) *Jacques Delors: A Political Biography*, London: Routledge.

Emmott, B. (2008) *Rivals: How the Power Struggle between China, India and Japan Will Shape our Next Decade*, London: Penguin.

Espersen, O., Harhoff, F. and Spiermann, O. (2003) *Folkeret: De internationale retsforhold*, Copenhagen: Chr. Ejlers Forlag.

European Commission (2009) *Communication from the Commission to the European Parliament, The Council, The European Economic and Social Committee and the Committee of the Regions: Elements for a new partnership between the EU and the overseas countries and territories (OCTs)*, COM(2009) 623, Brussels, 6 November.

Ferguson, Y.H. and Mansbach, R.W. (2008) *A World of Polities: Essays of Global Politics*, London: Routledge.

Fierke, K.M. and Nicholson, M. (2001) 'Divided by a common language: formal and constructivist approaches to games', *Global Society*, 15(1): 7–25.

Friedrich, J. (2001) 'The meaning of new medievalism', *European Journal of International Relations*, 7(4): 475–502.

Gad, U.P. (2005) 'Dansksprogede grønlænderes plads i et Grønland under grønlandisering og modernisering', *Eskimologis Skrifter* no. 19, Copenhagen: Department for Eskimology and Arctic Studies, University of Copenhagen.

Gad, U.P. (2009) 'Post-colonial identity in Greenland?', *Journal of Language and Politics*, 8(1): 136–58.

Gad, U.P. (2010) '(How) can they become like us? Danish identity politics and the conflicts of "Muslim relations"', PhD thesis, Department of Political Science, University of Copenhagen.

Gammeltoft-Hansen T. and Adler-Nissen R. (2010) 'Disclaiming sovereignty', paper presented at the Annual ISA Convention, February 2010.

Gregory, D. (2004) *The Colonial Present*, Oxford: Blackwell.

Grovogui, S. (2004) 'The trouble with the evolués: French republicanism, colonial subjectivity, and identity', in P.M. Goff and K.C. Dunn (eds) *Identity and Global Politics: Theoretical and Empirical Elaborations*, New York: Palgrave Macmillan.

Hache, J.-D. (1998) 'Towards a political approach to the island question', in G. Baldacchino and R. Greenwood (eds) *Competing Strategies of Socio-Economic Development for Small Islands*, Vol. 2, Charlottetown: University of Prince Edward Island.

Hall, S. (1996) 'When was "the post-colonial"? Thinking at the limit', in I. Chambers and L. Curti (eds) *The Post-Colonial Question*, London: Routledge.

Hansen, L. (2006) *Security as Practice*, London: Routledge.

Hansen, P. (2002) 'European integration, European identity, and the colonial connection', *European Journal of Social Theory*, 5(4): 483–98.

Hooghe, L. and Marks, G. (2003) 'Unraveling the central state, But how? Types of multi-level governance', *American Political Science Review*, 97(2): 233–43.

Hout, W. (1996) 'Globalization, regionalization and regionalism: a survey of contemporary literature', *Acta Politica*, (31): 164–81.

Ikenberry, J.G. (2004) 'Illusions of empire: defining the new American order', *Foreign Affairs*, 83(2): 144–54.

Jackson, R. (1990) *Quasi-States: Sovereignty, International Relations, and the Third World*, Cambridge: Cambridge University Press.

Jepperson, R., Wendt, A. and Katzenstein, P. (1996) 'Norms, identity and culture in national security', pp. 33–75 in P. Katzenstein (ed.) *The Culture of National Security: Norms and Identity in World Politics*, New York: Colombia University Press.

Keating, M. (1998) *The New Regionalism in Western Europe: Territorial Restructuring and Political Change*, Cheltenham: Edward Elgar.

Keating, M. (2001) *Plurinational Democracy: Stateless Nations in a Post-Sovereignty Era*, Oxford: Oxford University Press.

Kochenov, D. (ed.) (2011) *EU Law of the Overseas: Outermost Regions, Associated Overseas Countries and Territories, Territories Sui Generis*, Alphen aan den Rijn: Kluwer Law International.

Kohn, M. and McBride, K. (2011) *Political Theories of Decolonization: Postcolonialism and the Problem of Foundations*, New York: Oxford University Press.

Ling, L.H.M. (2002) *Postcolonial International Relations: Conquest and Desire between Asia and the West*, New York: Palgrave.

Loukacheva, N. (2007) *The Arctic Promise: Legal and Political Autonomy of Greenland and Nunavut*, Toronto: University of Toronto Press.

MacCormick, N. (2004) *A Union of Its Own Kind? Reflections on the European Convention and the Proposed Constitution of the European Union*, Edinburgh: Neil MacCormick.

Manners, I. (2002) 'Normative power Europe: a contradiction in terms?', *Journal of Common Market Studies*, 40(2): 235–58.

Mbembe, A. (1992) 'The banality of power and the aesthetics of vulgarity in the postcolony', *Public Culture*, 4(2): 1–30.

Mbembe, A. (2002) 'African modes of self-writing', *Public Culture*, 14(1): 239–73.

Mongia, P. (1996) 'Introduction', in P. Mongia (ed.) *Contemporary Post-colonial Theory*, London: Arnold.

Morgenthau, H.J. (1948; 2nd edn 1956) *Politics Among Nations*, New York: Alfred A. Knopf.

Motyl, A.J. (2001) *Imperial Ends: The Decay, Collapse, and Revival of Empires*, New York: Colombia University Press.

Neumann, I.B. and Gstöhl, S. (2006) 'Introduction: Lilliputians in Gulliver's World? Small states in International Relations', in I.B. Neumann, C. Ingebritsen and S. Gstöhl (eds) *Small States in International Relations: A Reader*, Seattle, WA: University of Washington Press.

Nielsen, J.K. (2000) 'Kriterierne for Grønlands økonomiske bæredygtighed', *Politica*, 32(1): 22–32.

Palan, R. (2003) *The Offshore World: Sovereign Markets, Virtual Places, and Nomad Millionaires*, Ithaca, NY: Cornell University Press.

Paolini, A.J. (1999) *Navigating Modernity: Postcolonialism, Identity and International Relations*, Boulder, CO: Lynne Rienner.

Petersen, H. (2006) *Retspluralisme i Praksis: Grønlandske Inspirationer*, Copenhagen: DJØF Publishing.

Polat, N. (2011) 'European integration as colonial discourse', *Review of International Studies*, 37(3): 1255–72.

Ruggie, J.G. (1993) 'Territoriality and beyond: problematizing modernity in International Relations', *International Organization*, 47(1): 139–74.

Saïd, E. (1978) *Orientalism*, New York: Pantheon.

Schatzki, T.R., Cetina, K.K. and Savigny, E.V. (2001) (eds) *The Practice Turn in Contemporary Theory*, London: Routledge.

Sørensen, G. (2002) 'The global polity and changes in statehood', in M. Ougaard and R. Higgott (eds) *Towards a Global Polity*, London: Routledge.

Spivak, G. (1988) 'Can the subaltern speak?', in C. Nelson and L. Grossberg (eds) *Marxism and the Interpretation of Culture*, Urbana, IL: University of Illinois.

Spruyt, H. (2005) *Ending Empire: Contested Sovereignty and Territorial Partition*, Ithaca, NY: Cornell University Press.

Streeten, P. (1993) 'The special problems of small countries', *World Development*, 21(2): 197–202.

Stringer, K. (2006) 'Pacific island micro-polities: pawns or players in Pacific Rim diplomacy?', *Diplomacy & Statecraft*, 17(3): 547–77.

Sutton, P. K. (ed.) (1991) *Europe and the Caribbean*, London: Macmillan.

Sutton, P. K. (2008) ' "The best of both worlds": autonomy and decolonisation in the Caribbean', Working Paper No. 2, Centre for Caribbean Studies, London Metropolitan University, August. Online. Available at: www.londonmet.ac.uk/library/h16097_3.pdf (accessed 31 August 2012).

Tunander, O. (1997) 'Post-Cold War Europe: a synthesis of a bipolar friend–foe structure and a hierarchic cosmos–chaos structure?' pp. 15–42 in O. Tunander, P. Baev and V.I. Einagel (eds) *Geopolitics in Post-Wall Europe: Security, Territory and Identity*, London: Sage.

Turner, S. (2002) 'Sovereignty, or the art of being native', *Cultural Critique*, 51(3): 74–100.

Wæver, O. (1997) 'Imperial metaphors: emerging European analogies to pre-nation state imperial systems', pp. 59–93 in O. Tunander, P. Baev and V.I. Einagel (eds) *Geopolitics in Post-Wall Europe. Security, Territory and Identity*, London: Sage.

Wæver, O. (2002) 'Identity, communities, and foreign policy: discourse analysis as foreign policy theory', in L. Hansen and O. Wæver (eds) *European Integration and National Identity*, London: Routledge.

Wæver O. and Tickner, A. (2009) 'Introduction: geopolitical epistemologies', pp. 1–31 in O. Wæver and A. Tickner (eds) *International Relations Scholarship Around the World*, London: Routledge.

Walker, N. (2003) 'Late sovereignty in the European Union', in N. Walker (ed.) *Sovereignty in Transition*, Portland: Hart Publishing.

Walker, N. (2008) 'The variety of sovereignty', in R. Adler-Nissen and T. Gammeltoft-Hansen (eds) *Sovereignty Games: Instrumentalizing State Sovereignty in Europe and Beyond*, New York: Palgrave Macmillan.

Waltz, K.N. (1979) *Theory of International Politics*, New York: McGraw-Hill.

Whitman, R.G. (ed.) (2011) *Normative Power Europe: Empirical and Theoretical Perspectives*, New York: Palgrave Macmillan.

Wittgenstein, L. (1968) *Philosophical Investigations*; trans. G.E.M. Anscombe, Oxford: Blackwell.

Young, R. (2003) *Postcolonialism: A Very Short Introduction*, New York: Oxford University Press.

Zielonka, J. (2006) *Europe as Empire: The Nature of the Enlarged European Union*, Oxford: Oxford University Press.

2 Postcolonial sovereignty

Experimentation with statehood and self-determination

Siba N. Grovogui

Recently, a bundle of phenomena parsimoniously known as 'globalization', 'transnationalism', 'failure of states', 'ethnic cleansing and genocide', 'migration', 'global pandemic of diseases', 'global environmental degradation', and, more recently, the Arab Spring have brought into focus the practices of sovereignty. A number of problems associated with these phenomena have occurred in Africa and question the very idea of postcolonial sovereignty while fostering the notion of collective security and human solidarity through humanitarian intervention. This view is supported not only by military and security strategists but also among human rights activists and other humanitarians that promote democratic governance. For instance, the military and the humanitarian views came together in the settlement of the political dispute in Sudan to create a new state, Southern Sudan; as in other cases, the solution was to reinforce national unity, as in the Democratic Republic of the Congo. This is to say that there is not only a gap between the idea and concept of sovereignty and its practices but also variations in the conditions under which sovereignty or statehood is granted.

The first two sections in this chapter examine the gap between the abstract concept and the practices of postcolonial sovereignty with particular focus on Africa. Then the following two sections analyse how the various sovereignty regimes allowed for the articulation of postcolonial sovereignty and why this eventually did not live up to the postcolonial imaginaries of sovereignty. A final section calls attention to how the Africanist explanation has helped legitimize biases in the regimes of sovereignty, which led to disappointment.

Principles and practices of sovereignty

In revisiting the concept and practices of postcolonial sovereignty, I have reservations about the tendency to, first, blur the distinction between the concepts and practices of sovereignty and, second, project sovereignty on fixed and determinate grounds. Like any concept or institution, sovereignty has universal and particular dimensions. In the first instance, sovereignty has universal legal, moral, ethical, political, and ontological resonances that account for its emergence as the acceptable principle of organizing the international system, even to postcolonial entities. Legally, sovereignty represents a set of privileges and immunities intended to allow a body or juridical entity to reach for its destiny without the fear of interference from others, whether rival domestic agents or external actors. It confers upon the repository of the powers of sovereignty, or the sovereign, specific capacities and the obligations to render just laws, equal justice, and good (if not legitimate) governance. The sovereign retains a degree of subjectivity allowing it to act within a structure or world in interaction with other beings or things. In this regard, sovereignty does not infer or confer any specific moral quality on action. Nor does it necessarily intimate the representativeness of the agent and/or the legitimacy of the action. It does suggest, however, that the sovereign retains agency, with full faculties and capacities to act independently – even if it sometimes means that the sovereign act is to unite with another.

Analytically, therefore, it matters whether one focuses on the privileges and immunities of the sovereign (represented today by the state) or the capacities, attributes, and faculties conferred upon the body politic (the socio-political corpus seeking to enact its own moral and ethical ends) – or both. The notion of postcolonial sovereignty originates in the context as a rebuke to the inferences made by empire-builders and colonialists since the sixteenth century that human faculties, particularly cognitive faculties and human capacities, were so unevenly distributed across geography, culture, and race as to warrant depriving some non-European entities of the abilities to reflect, to generate useful knowledge, and therefore to envisage legitimate forms of (self)government. In this context, the idea and concept of agency crystallized into theoretical and institutional traditions that featured human faculties, knowledge, or science and rationalism, and power as necessary conditions of sovereignty. The related explanations and perceptions of the moral and cultural abilities of peoples defined civilization and, as such, allowed colonialists to establish hierarchies among human communities. The resulting idea that a fraction of humanity – defined by faith (Christianity), geography (Europe), and later progress (the West) – possessed the essential faculties of Man and therefore should reign as overlord over the rest became the focal point of the struggle of colonial populations and what we now call postcolonialism.

In this regard, colonial struggles were successful in dismantling the myth and practices of non-European sovereignty. In other regards, the exercise of postcolonial sovereignty has been wanting. To be sure, the symbols marking the end of colonialism included a transfer of administrative powers from the colonial rulers to the leaders of the newly independent entities. Considering a succession of autocratic, authoritarian, tyrannical, and repressive regimes in postcolonial Africa, one would be forgiven for mistaking the claims made by this plethora of unrepresentative rulers for the final axiom, jurisprudence, or metaphor of postcolonial sovereignty. Analytically, however, the symbol of sovereignty – in whatever iconography – should not be mistaken for the moral, ethical, and ontological foundation upon which the idea of postcolonial sovereignty was founded: that – whether by providence, law, or simply happenstance – postcolonial entities should be able to endow themselves with the constitutional means and the material and symbolic spaces to rule themselves, without fear of repression from within or aggression from without. Thus, the postcolonies were to envisage themselves as peoples with the right to enter into agreements with others with respect to the means and mechanisms of their own emancipation.

Sovereignty thus understood is a legal theology, a moral axiom, an ethical principle, constitutional requirement, or all of these together. From the above perspective, it is legitimate to accept the principles that constitutional law makes the sovereign; that the sovereign rules according to law that s/he is authorized by the people to make; and that the sovereign obeys the given law of the people that s/he herself made on behalf of the people. But these criticisms, often directed at rulers who run states into the ground, pertain nonetheless to governance – or the performance of individual sovereigns. Their authors also often mistakenly think that they do not pertain to the essence of postcolonial sovereignty: whether postcolonial entities make their own laws; whether this explicitly means that no other body but the postcolonies themselves make their own laws; and whether these entities retain the essential sovereign faculties and capacities regardless of the outcomes of self-government.

The best way to approach postcolonial sovereignty is therefore to dissociate the problems associated with individual performances from the general or central organizing principle of international life. It would thus be possible to contemplate limits to sovereignty in some circumstances of malgovernance. Questions related to these circumstances are warranted, especially when there is violence or confusion about the legitimacy of power (or how the presumptive sovereign came into being), the nature of the law to which the sovereign claims to be subordinated (public constitutional law, 'princely' privileges, or the like), and the laws that the sovereign makes for others (or whether they are just according to generally accepted standards of justice).

Most postcolonial theorists would not defend sovereign privileges if doing so means endorsing autocracy, dictatorship, and economic mismanagement. They would also object to the conflation of postcolonial dysfunctions with the more legitimate question of postcolonial sovereignty – often posed negatively as to whether there is something constitutively amiss with postcolonial polities or, to be precise, the African body politics that render them unqualified (because they are presumably unable) to self-constitute as distinct, autonomous, and self-governing entities; to make laws for themselves based on their own traditions, values, and aspirations; and to enter into agreements to form unions with others or secede when necessary, to bind themselves and others to, or to entertain any other obligations, duties, and expectations that flow from international norms, treaties, and conventions that carry with them requirements of reciprocity, non-discrimination, and equality.

As stated by Thomas Hobbes and generations of scholars since, sovereignty is to the body politic what the soul is to the body natural (Hobbes 1997). It is the medium through which modern political entities understand themselves as worthy members of the human community and thus worthy of the honour and dignity of recognition, on the one hand, and of the ability to live within secure borders, on the other. The status flowing from this worthiness does not confer any special privileges outside the universally accepted jurisprudence except to allow provisionally that the sovereign body politic is omniscient (that is, cognizant of its own needs and desires) and omnipotent (or able to find within its own faculties and capacities the resources to meet its expectations of self). These criteria do not imply that the person embodying the symbol of sovereignty on behalf of the body politic is infallible and incapable of injustice. Yet African and other postcolonial entities have elevated the central assumptions of sovereignty into jurisprudence, which appears to have shaped postcolonial interventions in international law and international relations from the 1955 Bandung Conference to the 1961 birth of the Non-Aligned Movement to the great UN debates on issues such as intervention, the law of the sea, demilitarization, and peaceful co-existence.

In short, the postcolonial aspiration to sovereignty cannot be reduced to a mere desire for an administrative franchise from former colonial rulers. Nor was the franchise necessarily predestined to effect separation. For instance, from the end of the Second World War to the mid-1950s, the vast majority of French colonies sought a modicum of union with the former metropole on grounds ranging from cultural affinities to the fear that the postcolonies would be deprived of their own economic inheritance; now entangled in the wealth of empire, it would be transferred to the metropole alone. The British Commonwealth was also a political form that enacted a union between the former colonial overlord and the former dependencies upon decolonization. Related events confirm the thesis advanced by Mac Amhlaigh (this volume) that international cooperation, or even a political or administrative union, does not necessarily undermine sovereignty. They also support Baldacchino's contention (this volume) that the postcolonial experience of sovereignty has had substantive economic dimensions. On the other hand, anti-colonialists were aware that the formal administrative separation between colonial powers and the colonized did not guarantee successful decolonization – and therefore full sovereignty. In actuality, the mechanisms of the franchise re-inserted the formerly colonized more firmly in the very structures leading to colonialism and the usurpation of domestic sovereignty. Nor should postcolonial sovereignty be assumed to be completed only when presumed universal institutions originating in the West have been fully implemented in the postcolonies. Historically, institutions and their base values and norms have reflected temporal concerns often delineated by space. In this sense, the tropes, rituals, symbols, iconographies, and ethical parameters of sovereignty may originate from local traditions, conventions, and jurisprudence without diminishing the dignity, honour, and virtues bestowed by the universal concept of sovereignty and all of the associated moral, ideological, and political implications.

Practices of sovereignty in postcolonial Africa

Decolonization undeniably expanded the spheres of freedom and the expression of sovereign will by Africans. Yet many erroneous conclusions have been derived from this fact. For instance, Crawford Young (1988) proposes that decolonization was the result of the constant interactions of three levels of agency: African, metropolitan, and international. This position initially appears legitimate and even demonstrable (Gifford and Louis 1988). As Young intimates, both the 'African' and the 'international' proceed and flow from the 'metropolitan': the West. The problem is that there is no space allotted to African ideas and imaginaries of decolonization and postcolonial freedom. The other problem is that the norms defined as Western practices do not have singular points of origins and, for this reason, could not be implemented or executed in the context of colonialism and decolonization according to uniform rationalities. Not only is it inaccurate to separate Europe from its colonies before independence, it is simply untrue that the implemented forms of freedom were solely the outcome of European reflections and dispositions without input from Africans. Even so, the African 'input' was uniformly given as complements and/or amendments to European ideas and institutions. They also assumed the form of contestations that compelled colonial powers to alter their initial positions (Grovogui 2006).

My contention is that the representation of sovereignty in the postcolonial era is an epistemological question of great import that seems to be absent in Africanist discourses; for instance, is decolonization to be equated with a transfer of power? Did sovereignty under post-war Western liberal constitutionalism enable political, legal, and ethical forms consistent with the aim of restoration of sovereignty in the postcolonies? Or was the form of postcolonial sovereignty already pre-figured in the greater institutional arrangements envisaged to ensure Western hegemony? Did the related political arrangements actually legitimize the political subordination of the postcolonial states and therefore foreclose the possibility of democratic sovereignty? In other words, did the implemented forms of postcolonial sovereignty erect legal and moral prohibitions against social experiments? Were there responsibilities for colonial powers flowing from the colonial act that were obscured by the language of transfer of power? Theorists also elided the facts that the African state inherited 'artificial' international boundaries; that the 'nation' was but merely political fiction with no real cultural foundations; and that the sovereignty of the state was fragile due to the composition of the nation and the inability of the state to defend itself against external subversion.

Ali A. Mazrui (1993) is categorical with regard to these questions. The ability of African leaders to shape their own destinies and those of their populations has been exaggerated by analyses that focus on the mere fact of the transfer of power. Such analyses often ignore or depreciate the effects of the Cold War, global capitalism, and the determination of former colonial powers to maintain their hegemonic positions within both (Mazrui 1993). Ali Mazrui points to dimensions of postcolonial governance that are often noted and yet not incorporated in the explanations of the ultimate outcome of postcolonial governance, including the Cold War. The operations of the Cold War manifested themselves at multiple levels in Africa, including the neocolonial interference and overthrow of democratically elected but 'disagreeable' African leaders by former colonial powers and superpowers acting in conjunction with domestic allies. Nkrumah (overthrown in 1966) was a victim of both interference and removal. He was preceded by Congo's Patrice Lumumba (1961) and Togo's Sylvanius Olympia (1963). All three were replaced by military dictators. It would be easier to ascribe these actions to Africans, and these coups were indeed in a sense African. Yet the 'Africanness' of these actions is mostly owing to the fact they took place on the African continent. Otherwise, the alliances that executed them, their mechanisms of implementation, and structures of legitimation were all commodities of global politics long before African independence. Foreign interference at independence and military coups in the early years of postcolonial rule show how considerable segments of the postcolonial state entertained views of postcolonial rule and international morality that conflicted with those of ruling elites in the former colonial metropoles. They also show that, depending on the alliances in place, domestic elites were either constrained and burdened by the regulatory and constitutive dimensions of Cold War politics or they benefitted politically from the their institutions, regimes of legitimacy, and political practices.

Multiple regimes of sovereignty

Sovereignty is grounded in both determinate and indeterminate sets of social relationships; and these social relations give form, intelligibility, and legibility to the social or moral order from which sovereignty arises. In short, sovereignty is an institution founded upon specific ethical conventions based on temporal understandings of the moral order. For instance, Christian doctrines, moral thoughts, and political philosophy tells us that, from the time of Carolus Magnus, or Charlemagne, to the Holy Roman Empire and throughout the Middle Ages, there subsisted contestations about the nature of the moral order and its constitutive elements. The subsequent political settlements generated specific organizing principles of the relationships among sovereign entities and resulting arrangements actualized a succession of regimes of sovereignty. Charlemagne and Pope Leo III, for instance, initiated a regime of sovereignty when they brokered the agreement instituting a co-dependency between them while affirming their common control of the realm. This initial regime was modified by Pope Nicholas II, who first declared his independence from the Emperor; Gregory VII, the first Pope elected by Cardinals and Bishops; and Innocent III, who formalized the Church structures by unifying the Church and the Flock under a centralized papal leadership and a disciplined and loyal clergy.

Since then, multiple sovereignty regimes have both competed and co-existed. For instance, while the Emperor remained otherwise central to the survival of Western Christendom, his relationships with popes, priests, kings, and lords continued to change until the advent of the Holy Roman Empire. Each new arrangement brought about a new regime of sovereignty or a modification of the political structures upon which sovereignty rested. Likewise, beginning in the sixteenth century, Western powers became determined to 'emancipate' themselves from the political chaos and anarchy generated by the antagonisms of the Reformation, Counter-Reformation, and subsequent political events. The peace treaties of Augsburg (1555), Westphalia (1648), and Vienna (1815) would establish consensual rules of mutual recognition and the principle of cooperation for the attainment of collective historical ends – cultural, ideological, economic, or otherwise. The resulting compacts created ethical realities: codes of rules, norms, and principles that created a juridical equality between states actually unequal in size, capacity, and legitimacy.

As it originated in Europe, sovereignty was therefore the most exalted form of authority in any society, the entity whose powers over its objects, subjects, and spheres are qualified only by the will that brings it into being: the sovereign. From the evolving relations between Sacerdotium (church) and Imperium (royals) in Latin Christendom to the Holy Roman Empire, Hanseatic League, and the Italian city-states, the office of the sovereign frequently remained vested in a person whose authority was abided within the realm. The will of the latter was thought to mystically constitute the moral foundation of sovereignty just as its ethical embodiment provided the foundations of politics. This is to say that from the ninth century coronation of Charlemagne to the eleventh century onset of the Investiture Struggle to the advent of secular dynastic regimes and empires, the identity of the officeholder, the sovereign, was indistinguishable from the function of the office: sovereignty. Sovereigns pretended to have hegemony over other social agents. They thus insisted on unilaterally framing the juridico-ideological context of the moral order; on charting the context of all relations within society; on defining the foundations and instruments of social interactions writ large; on defining time and social knowledge; and on assigning social roles and spatiality within their realms.

This situation lasted throughout the Middle Ages but could not withstand post-Renaissance formulations of politics and ethics. Upon Thomas Aquinas' speculations on law and natural rights, reason began to supplant faith as the chief support of Christian thought. The triumvirate of 'God, nature, and prescription', which had displaced 'God-Pope-Men', was itself no longer an acceptable basis of political authority. The rediscovery of Greece through Arab scribes, the revelation of the existence of beings beyond Shem, Ham, and Japhet in a world hitherto unknown, the spread of scientific knowledge, and the advent of the printing press undermined old orthodoxies. From the Renaissance onward, collective identity replaced the natural order; the foundation of political authority shifted from God to imperial claims; while theological prescription gave way to rationalism and necessity. The 'Enlightenment' was upon History when reason and free will prevailed as the ethical foundations of politics.

The Enlightenment ushered in political contestations that echoed the Investiture Struggles. The Renaissance mediated the relationship between Men and God through Nature (or Legacy) and Reason, which displaced the Papacy but made the Flock subservient to dynasts and kings. Still, the Renaissance did not conclusively elucidate key questions about the sovereign. Hence, during the eighteenth century, dynasts, kings, and princes once again confronted domestic political entities and subjects in epic battles over power, its foundations, and its symbols. These contestations were reflected in the French, American, and Haitian revolutions, which definitively held that the holder of the title of sovereign may be the symbol of sovereignty, but not the inherent repository of the sovereign will. In fact, these three revolutions separated the identity of the officeholder, who symbolically embodies sovereignty, from the locus of the sovereign will: citizens, individuals, and persons.

These three revolutions symbolized the quest by Man-as-political-subject of sovereign rights based on conceptions of human faculties as unalienable endowments – that is non-transferable and thus beyond the reach of the police powers of states or those holding the titles of sovereign. One thinks of Thomas Jefferson's opening act in the 'Declaration of Independence'. Indeed, the American, French, and Haitian revolutions claimed inalienable faculties and immunities for their subjects, but they differed on the capacities in which Man would claim such powers: the French revolution opted for Citizenship; the American revolution chose Individualism; and the Haitian revolution picked Personhood. Each of these revolutions established two inextricably linked sovereign entities, the governor and governed, both self-conscious agents, both endowed with specific capacities. These revolutions also envisaged parallel privileges and immunities for citizens, individuals, and persons, to be protected as means to the realization of a political and civil society. Each entity, in its context, was imagined as bearer of immutable rights parallel to those of the competing domestic sovereign. (Hence the concept of reserved rights in the US constitution.) Finally, even as they sought to regulate them under homogenous social contracts, the French, American, and Haitian constitutional orders implicitly exhibited the diversity of human faculties and capacities.

Postcolonial imaginaries of sovereignty

The discussion above provides multiple lessons for understanding postcolonial sovereignty. First, it demonstrates that sovereignty cannot be treated as objective or without reference; it is therefore not sufficient to point to the ordering principles of international life under the Charter of the UN as evidence of horizontal relations among UN member states. It is significant that the UN system also enables practices that subvert the principle of a singular mode of sovereignty as the basis of international morality. It matters therefore that hegemonic powers have established politically convenient rules and norms of behaviour as well as mechanisms for conflict resolution that re-inscribed colonial dynamics in different guises. The second lesson is that neither sovereignty nor sovereignty regimes can be properly understood without attention to the will of sovereigns. At the centre of historical disputes over sovereignty are arguments concerning the nature and ownership of sovereign powers within domestic and global politics and systems of association.

The third lesson, corresponding to a Westphalian moment, is that wholly contingent entities may assume determinate political identities for the purpose of historical struggles implicated in the design and organization of sovereignty. The actual events leading to postcolonial sovereignty necessarily flow from this (historical) logic. It is a logic that depends on the specificities of time (i.e. colonialism) and space. In other words, the colonies derived from Western imperialism contained historical forms of politics and bureaucratic and administrative organizations specific to each colonial order: British, French, Spanish, Portuguese, Dutch, and

Danish. These forms and modes of existence provided the basis and legitimacy for anti-colonial and postcolonial claims to sovereignty. The latter also ensured that anti-colonial imaginaries of sovereignty contained concurrent but dissimilar regional coordinates. The latter guided postcolonial designs and conduct or standards of behaviour corresponding to the need to guarantee access to the strategic resources of life: symbolic (e.g. self-determination and national recognition) and material (raw materials for industry, markets for manufactured products, and capital for investment). It follows therefore that postcolonial entities necessarily aspired to sovereignty regimes that superseded prior ones under colonial rule. This quest for sovereignty was not a matter for states alone. It involved populations that had emancipated themselves from colonial orders and their regimes of power and politics. Yet the context of decolonization was one of internal and external contestations and, therefore, of dynamics of conflict and negotiations among unequal actors, agents, and political subjects.

Viewed from this perspective, the goals of the anti-colonial struggle for self-determination were neither entirely happenstance nor necessarily given. At the outset, the former colonial powers simultaneously tolerated and assisted in the advent of particular forms of postcolonial polities and aspirations, while they strove to pre-empt postcolonial policies and orientations that run counter to Western aspirations to hegemony and/or domination in the guise of the preservation of 'national interests'. These practices, together with their legal and moral justifications, then specify the standings of African states in international relations and, by extension, the regime of sovereignty applicable to 'Africa'.

The idea that multiple sovereignty regimes may concurrently prevail in one epoch and in the same international order is not new. Friedrich Hegel, for instance, provides a compelling explanation of the necessary concurrence of multiple sovereignty regimes and their origins in the aspirations of the more powerful and politically significant actors of the international community (Taylor 1975). In Hegel's view, sovereignty reflects dynamics of conflict and negotiation among unequal agents across time and space. Specifically, the nineteenth century intra-European regime originated in wars and social conflicts, but also negotiations and political settlements among dynastic rulers, princes, and other rulers in competition and coalition with other politically significant actors: burghers, merchants, financiers, and later, industrialists and other capitalists. The wars reflected the conflicting wills and interests of presumptive sovereigns while political settlements echoed a common European desire to achieve an order ensuring its collective survival. This situation required a common understanding, a controlling ethos, of the mechanisms for reconciling conflicting wills and divergent interests. The result was a political ethos that uneasily accommodates the combination of autonomy and interdependence, antagonism and cooperation, exclusion and inclusion, and freedom and subordination.

Hegel's arguments, which are reprised by others, suggest that any international order may in fact countenance multiple ethical realities corresponding to its order of sovereignty. These are specified by distinct codes of rules, norms, and principles applicable with regularity to particular world regions based on the sentiments, desires, and wills of hegemonic powers in contestation with local aspirants or claimants of sovereignty (Bartelson 1995). These subjective factors occur even as the international (in this case the UN) formally proclaims a juridical equality between states actually unequal in size, capacity, and legitimacy. To wit, from the Concert of Europe, the Holy Alliance, and later the North Atlantic Treaty Organization, Western powers enacted structures and mechanisms that enabled the co-existence of powerful centralized states (e.g. France) alongside 'quasi-states' (Belgium), weak states (Switzerland), and microstates (Vatican, Andorra, and Liechtenstein) (cf. Duursma 1996). These structures and mechanisms ensure the capacity of smaller states – such as Belgium, Luxemburg, Denmark, and Switzerland – to survive intact as national entities and, thus, enable their governors and the governed to envisage the conditions of domestic reproduction. Indeed, the survival of such microstates depends even today on their insertion into structures of the international political economy and by their normative regime of power, privileges, and entitlements.

The above suggests that the material discrepancies among states are not sufficient conditions for inclusion or exclusion, leading to discrimination and/or subordination (Taylor 1975). Thus, while the West extended toleration and reciprocity to European microstates through treaties and associations, the former colonial powers never fully adapted to the fact that postcolonial entities could be the co-equals of their former masters. Here, therefore, material inequalities served as the justification for hierarchy and domination. In Africa, specifically since the 1884–5 Berlin Conference, European states and their agents translated the weakness of political institutions and political turmoil, first, into a licence to conquer and colonize and, second, into a duty to suppress postcolonial sovereignty – not merely the state. To this end, Western powers have consistently claimed the right to supplant the sovereign rights of Africans with other political arrangements and mechanisms that bestow ultimate authority over African affairs to Western entities, either incorporated, unincorporated, or both.

The resulting arrangements have corollaries in international law and morality. Hence, from the time of conquest to date, the regimes of sovereignty and law that have governed the interactions among European communities within the boundaries of Western Christendom have formed a particular body of law (*jus gentilis*) that seldom applied to others. Rather, by design, *jus gentium* differed from the rules and procedures that applied to Christian merchants, settlers, and other colonial adventurers. Further, these two sets of laws bore no resemblance to yet a third set, which governed the dynamics between Westerners and non-Europeans (Reynolds 1992). Each set of laws or each legal regime enacted specific rules of property, reciprocity, and justice that converged teleologically toward the expropriation and disempowerment of Africans and other colonial subjects in favour of Western entities (Reynolds 1992: 9–22).

The resulting regimes of law and institutions culminated in complementary sovereignty regimes, such that the survival of Western microstates depended on the suppression of 'native' sovereignty. For instance, while one regime contributed to today's 'resilience' of European 'quasi-states', another helped undermine the sovereignty of African entities and, later, assisted in the 'failure' of a number of Africa states. Specifically, the sovereignty regime applied by European powers to Belgium since its inception in 1830 to the present contrasted greatly with what was applied to the Congo from the Berlin Conference in 1884 to the end of Belgian colonial rule in Congo in 1960. This contrast is significant because Westphalian common sense has enabled many theorists to favourably compare Belgium as a successful 'quasi-state' to such 'failed' 'quasi-states' as Congo (Jackson 1990). A similar contrast has been made between Switzerland, a centrally weak European state, and weak African states such as Congo in order to posit presumed differences between the Westphalian model and African deviation.

These historical regimes of sovereignty played a role in engendering differences between such European quasi-states as Belgium and Switzerland and the African ones to which they are often favourably compared, such as Congo. For instance, although European powers competed with each other for hegemony in the nineteenth century, they concurred across national competition to establish institutions of global governance that set 'Europe' apart from other regions, including 'Africa'. In particular, the Great Powers instituted parallel practices of sovereignty that both regulated intra-European relations and allocated access to the strategic resources of the emergent global political economy. These juridico-political regimes allowed the sovereign and economic agents of Belgium, one of the smallest European states, to conquer the vast expanses of African lands to be known as Congo (Hochschild 1999). Likewise, at Congo's independence, a Western coalition destroyed Patrice Lumumba's ruling coalition and supported Mobutu Sese Seko's subsequent despotism. These events were later compounded by an ethos of permissiveness that enabled graft and the embezzlement of public Congolese funds and helped bring Zaïre to the brink of financial bankruptcy. Swiss banking institutions, which are shielded by state-enacted secrecy regulations, provided the channels for these transactions. The effect has been to allow a net transfer of power and wealth from places in Africa (Congo) to Europe (Belgium and Switzerland).

I do not seek to impute to Europe responsibility for the corruption of public life in postcolonial Africa and the resulting political violence. Nor do I seek to accuse Belgium or Switzerland of immoral practices and hold them up as the principal agents of the colonial enterprise and subsequent misery of Africans. Indeed, the constitutional and institutional make-up of the African state was undoubtedly problematic from the start, profoundly structuring the choices available to African leaders after independence. Rather, my first goal is to refute Westphalian common sense and to highlight the instrumentalities of sovereignty as means to rethinking the postcolonial African condition and potential solutions to it. In this context, my contention is that while one regime contributed to today's 'resilience' of European 'quasi-states', another helped undermine the sovereignty of African entities and, later, assisted in the 'failure' of a number of Africa states. Colonial Congo, it should be recalled, was among the most brutalized colonies of Africa, where forced labour, child labour, punishment by amputation, and other cruelties were introduced by colonial overlords as social control mechanisms. Congo is also where the US and USSR engaged in direct conflict in Africa over the objections of Ghana, Guinea, Egypt, and Tanzania; where the first elected African Head of Government was assassinated; where foreign agencies were first involved in such an assassination; and where the US backed the then most corrupt ruler in the history of postcolonial Africa. Only two years after Lumumba was assassinated, President Olympio was assassinated by the Togolese army; and three years later, Nkrumah was overthrown.

Conclusion: knowledge, objectivity, and the human interest

It may be a truism that the present forms of postcolonial sovereignty have alienated the citizenries of many states in Africa. This means that the instruments of power assumed by the state to bear on the postcolonial African condition do not approximate those embedded in anti-colonial imaginaries or those of contemporary Africans. However, when placed in the larger context of the external institutional regimes that give form to trans-territorial expressions of power, African alienation and state collapse cannot be dissociated from the involvements of external powers, their agents, and base-corporations. Indeed, according to Richard Falk (1992), contemporary sovereignty regimes remain rooted in 'forms of knowledge' that continue to depend upon colonial relationships and their psychic, ideological, and political dispositions. Mahmood Mamdani also deplores that some theorists perpetuate the notion that Africa is chronically engulfed in chaos. While some attribute this condition to an inherent antagonism of opposing 'tribes', others view in it the absence of civil institutions that can temper the obsessive pursuit of self-interests by domestic groups at the expense of the majority (Mamdani 1996).

The result is that analysts omit the most important lesson that may be obtained from the so-called failure of the African state: that the political arrangements that hampered Africans from positively exercising self-determination have originated both domestically from the state and externally from foreign entities. It must be recalled that, upon decolonization, postcolonial entities from around the world have consistently sought to restructure the terms of global politics; to bring about a new international economic order; to maintain neutrality in the Cold War; to institute equitable international regimes of the sea, air, and space; to reorient global resources from the arms race to human needs; to preserve the cultural heritage of humanity; to redefine the purpose of scientific and cultural activities in the human interest; and so on. This agenda came to a halt in the late 1970s, as Western powers opposed it on account of their own sovereignty. Indeed, there is an eerie coincidence between the final defeat of the Third World reform agenda in the late 1970s and the onset of the current African crisis. The policies put in place by Western powers in lieu of Third World ones promoted investment guarantees, financial deregulation, foreign aid conditionalities, and other neoliberal orthodoxies subtended by the need for immediate aggregate economic growth – and not social and human development. These policies contributed to the marginalization of Africa. The growing intrusion of Western-dominated financial institutions in the domestic African policy arenas also gained momentum during this time. The active support of Western powers for globalized private capital and finance further entrenched the shift of power away from financially-strapped states to global institutions.

Further, the insufficiency of Westphalian common sense becomes apparent when considering the effects of the historical coordinates of sovereignty instituted concurrently by European powers in Africa. Recall how sharply distinct juridico-political regimes allowed the sovereign and economic agents of Belgium, at the time a small quasi-state, to conquer vast expanses of African lands to be known as the Congo, and how, subsequent to 1885, European powers instituted dubious treaties and accords based on legal and political machinations, force, and deceit – all of which allowed individual and corporate European profiteers to legitimize their foothold in Africa. 'Africa' was thus subordinated to the requirements of the global political economy and an ordering of civilizations and human faculties such that European conceptions of community, religion, citizenship, and property took precedence over all others. This scenario did not change much after the eclipse of formal empires, thanks in part to Cold War geopolitics.

In sum, sovereignty takes form through multiple, complex, and differentiated institutions that congeal into formal and informal regimes of authority and practices. The mechanisms of differentiation are recognizable norms, rules, and ethical standards that guide collaborating, competing, or mutually unintelligible geopolitical entities. Together, the regional coordinates of sovereignty promote hierarchical systems among states and world regions. They modulate power transterritorially and across geopolitical regions to give form to international governance. Thus, sovereignty regimes reflect historical distributions of power and subjectivity within the international order and corresponding symbolic and material economies. These allotments depend upon the complementary processes of imposition, subordination, negotiation, and abjuration of interest and values by relevant actors. In short, sovereignty regimes define the place and role of each geopolitical region along with the range of sovereignty practices available to it.

References

Bartelson, J. (1995) *A Genealogy of Sovereignty*, Cambridge: Cambridge University Press.

Duursma, J. (1996) *Fragmentation and the International Relations of Micro-States*, London: Cambridge University Press.

Falk, R. (1992) *Explorations at the Edge of Time*, Philadelphia: Temple University Press.

Gifford, P. and Louis, W.R. (eds) (1988) *Decolonization and African Independence: The Transfers of Power*, New Haven: Yale University Press.

Grovogui, S.N. (2006) *Beyond Eurocentrism and Anarchy: Memories of International Order and Institution*, New York, Palgrave Macmillan.

Hobbes, T. (1997) *Leviathan*, R.E. Flathman and D. Johnston (eds) New York: W.W. Norton.

Hochschild, A. (1999) *King Leopold's Ghost*, Boston: Houghton Mifflin Company.

Jackson, R.H. (1990) *Quasi-States: Sovereignty, International Relations and the Third World*, Cambridge: Cambridge University Press.

Mamdani, M. (1996) *Citizen and Subject*, Princeton: University of Princeton Press.

Mazrui, Ali A. (ed.) (1993) *General History of Africa Since 1935*, Berkeley, CA: University of California Press.

Reynolds, H. (1992) *The Law of the Land*. Victoria, Australia: Penguin Books.

Taylor, C. (1975) *Hegel*, Cambridge: Cambridge University Press.

Young, C. (1988) 'The colonial state and post-colonial crisis', in P. Gifford and W.R Louis (eds) *Decolonization and African Independence: The Transfers of Power*, New Haven: Yale University Press.

3 Late sovereignty in post-integration Europe

Continuity and change in a constitutive concept

Cormac Mac Amhlaigh

International cooperation is not traditionally considered a threat to state sovereignty. It has been frequently argued that the ability to establish and maintain international relations is the very expression of sovereign status (Wæver 1995: 420). This is even the case where post-state institutions have been established, charged with formulating and executing policy decisions (Lake 2007). However, the process of European integration overseen by the institutions of the European Union (EU) as a form of international cooperation presents a challenge to conventional understandings of the continuing sovereignty of its constituent member states. This is due, it is argued, to two particular features of European integration which distinguish EU membership from more traditional forms of international cooperation: constitutionalism and majority decision-making.

Constitutionalism relates to the collection of legal doctrines developed by the judicial arm of the EU – the European Court of Justice (ECJ) – which resulted in its legal order evolving, through judicial fiat, from a treaty under international law to an autonomous hierarchical legal order such that EU law became the 'law of the land' (Weiler 1991: 2415) in every EU member state. From the point of view of the sovereignty of EU member states, perhaps the most significant feature of this development was the supremacy doctrine, which provides that national law, even national constitutional law, is subject to the provisions of EU law in cases of conflict (ECJ 1964). This doctrine poses a challenge to the legal supremacy of national constitutions as well as the political competence of national administrations, the activities of which are subject to the provisions of EU law as enforced by domestic courts.

The second significant feature of European integration that challenges conventional understandings of the sovereignty of EU member states is the loss of a veto by individual member state governments in the Council of the EU (the upper chamber of EU government representing the interests of member states) in relation to political decision-making by EU institutions (Keohane 2002: 748). From an early stage in European integration, the requirement of unanimity for voting in the Council, where each member state has equal representation, was dispensed with such that EU member states were bound by decisions of law and policy, even if they explicitly voted against the proposals.[1]

This chapter examines the state of sovereignty in contemporary Europe in the light of the particular challenges stemming from EU membership and how these challenges can offer insights into the trilateral relationship between Overseas Countries and Territories (OCTs) of EU member states, their respective metropoles, and the EU. Drawing on linguistic approaches to law and International Relations (IR), it examines the nature of sovereignty in the EU in terms of Neil Walker's 'late sovereignty' and particularly the constitutive and regulative rules of 'late sovereignty games' in the European context. The chapter goes on to track both continuity and change in the concept of late sovereignty in the EU and concludes by assessing the relevance of the concept of late sovereignty to the trilateral relationship between the non-continental territories of EU member states, the member states themselves, and the EU.

W(h)ither sovereignty?

Harbingers of the demise of sovereignty are hardly new.[2] Given the novelty and invasive nature of European integration as a form of international cooperation, however, it is perhaps unsurprising that the experience of European integration has resulted in the renewal of the prophecy of the death of sovereignty. Neil Mac-Cormick, for example, has forcefully argued in the European context that the continent has shifted from sovereignty to 'post-sovereignty' due to the European integration process (MacCormick 1999). However, it is arguably premature to conclude with MacCormick that some fundamental epistemic shift has taken place beyond understandings of sovereignty in legal and political practice in Europe. Such a position ignores the significance of sovereignty as the 'object language' (Walker 2003: 10) of domestic politics and its important role as a 'bargaining resource for transnational politics' (Keohane 1994), even in a post-integration space.[3] Moreover, completely abandoning the concept is unfeasible in the European integration discourse. Sovereignty is necessarily central to understanding European integration, even if only to emphasize its irrelevance in the EU context (Mac Amhlaigh 2009: 555).

Even if sovereignty can still be said to be relevant in the post-integration European context, however, it is also difficult to affirm with the liberal intergovernmentalists that European integration is simply another form of (sovereignty preserving) international cooperation (Moravcsik 1998). The sheer breadth of national policies which owe their origins to policy formulated at the EU level, combined with the considerable autonomy of EU institutions and the invasive nature of EU law, render the claim that European integration is simply 'business as usual', in terms of international cooperation, increasingly hollow.

Thus, rather than being redundant or remaining unchanged, sovereignty has evolved, where it still retains its purchase on law and politics (both national and supranational) if not, precisely, in the form which it took in the heyday of the Westphalian system of sovereign states. In order to explore the continuity and change in the concept of sovereignty in the European experience, it might be useful to engage in some conceptual ground-clearing to grasp what is a 'polysemous' concept (MacCormick 2011).

Sovereignty cannot be reduced to some rigid set of characteristics to be used as a measure for assessing whether or not an entity or institutional configuration qualifies for sovereign statehood. Such an approach entails:

> identifying a class of properties as 'essential' to statehood, thus demarcating 'sovereignty' from deviant cases and eliminating obnoxious borderline cases by searching for ever more fine-grained qualitative differences. The desired outcome is a clarified concept, evident in its logical purity and the by the empirical givenness of its referent.
>
> (Bartelson 1995: 27)

However, this approach falls foul of the 'descriptive fallacy' that sovereignty corresponds to some objective reality, 'out there', the meaning of which is fixed in all times and places. Rather, as a normative concept connoting legitimate governing authority (as opposed to raw power), sovereignty is a form of *normative discourse*. Thus, following the 'linguistic turn' in IR (Aalberts 2004a) and (notably earlier) in jurisprudence (Hart 1994), sovereignty, it is submitted, is better understood as a politico-legal concept which is an 'institutional' rather than a 'brute' fact (Searle 1969: 50).

The positing of sovereignty as a linguistically constituted institutional fact therefore precludes a rigid conceptual analysis of the fate of sovereignty in European integration, as its existence is contingent upon its usage or, more specifically, the rules governing its usage in discursive practice (Aalberts 2004a; Werner and de Wilde 2001). Moreover, these rules allow for the playing of 'sovereignty games'[4] the rules of which, like the rules of all language games, are subject to change and evolution. They are not inexorable but rather, in the Wittgensteinian sense, customary (Wittgenstein 1968: 198).

Furthermore, as with all language games, the rules of sovereignty games are central to the intelligibility of the practice *qua* sovereignty game (Wittgenstein 1968: §199). In this regard, following Searle's refinement of the rules of language games, sovereignty games can be understood as entailing both constitutive and regulative rules (Searle 1969).[5] On Searle's classic formulation, the former are constitutive of the practice itself in that they not only constitute the actors or participants in the practice, but also in the sense that they enable participants and observers to understand that a particular game, such as chess or football, is being played. The regulative rules, on the other hand, stipulate criteria for the execution of the practice constituted by the constitutive rules, such as prescribing how the practice can be undertaken and establishing criteria for a 'good' or 'plausible' performance of the practice (Lindahl and van Roermund 2000).

It is in this respect, it is argued, that the EU sovereignty experience is best understood. It is not irrelevant, as the post-sovereigntists claim, but nor has it remained fixed; rather, as with all linguistically-based concepts, it has evolved through the playing of sovereignty games from what can be termed 'high sovereignty',[6] as characterized by the Westphalian system of sovereign states, to what Neil Walker has dubbed 'late sovereignty' (Walker 2003, 2008a, 2008b, 2010).

From high sovereignty to late sovereignty

The form of sovereignty which has dominated international law and international relations in modern history, characterized as the Westphalian state system, can be described as 'high sovereignty', whereby sovereignty and statehood were synonymous. Krasner notes, the era of high sovereignty can be traced back to the mid-1700s.[7]

The constitutive and regulative rules of games played with high sovereignty are reasonably well understood. Following Searle's formulation of institutional facts in terms of 'X counts of Y in context C' (Searle 1969: 35), and emphasizing the constitutive function of the rules in constituting the actors in the game, Werner and de Wilde posit the constitutive rules of high sovereignty games in the following way: a 'political collective (X) counts as a state (Y) in the context of a sovereignty discourse (C)', where a claim to sovereignty 'attempts to establish a relation as an institutional fact . . . and a set of right and responsibilities' (Werner and de Wilde 2001: 292). These rights and responsibilities represent a combination of what Krasner has termed Westphalian and International Legal Sovereignty (Krasner 1999: 9) expressed in terms of internal ultimate authority over territory and people and external equality. Moreover, the regulative rules of these high sovereignty games evolved from the earlier justifications of absolute monarchy and imperial conquest to claims of nationhood, popular sovereignty and the right to self-determination (Werner and de Wilde 2001: 295).

If, as noted above, the European integration process has challenged the dimensions of the 'high sovereignty' games, the question is to what extent sovereignty has evolved from the era of 'high sovereignty' and what do 'late sovereignty games' look like?

In answering these questions by assessing the evolution of sovereignty in Europe from 'high sovereignty' to 'late sovereignty' period, the balance between continuity and change is crucial. The meaning of sovereignty from its 'high' period must retain some purchase in late sovereignty games such that they can be cognized as *sovereignty* games. As such, the practices of late sovereignty in European integration must be *intelligible* as a form of sovereignty game and not something else; that is, not, for example, *post*-sovereignty, where the practices can be understood as not-sovereignty games in the same way as throwing chess pieces around the room can be understood as not-chess playing. Late sovereignty games cannot constitute a negation of sovereignty.[8]

In his account of 'late sovereignty', Walker provides a comprehensive account of an evolved sovereignty in the European context (Walker 2003, 2008a, 2008b, 2010), which entails a number of features in the discursive career of the concept of sovereignty: 'continuity, distinctiveness, irreversibility and transformative potential' (Walker 2003: 19). The important element of *continuity*, which is central to the intelligibility of post-integration European late sovereignty games *qua* sovereignty games, features in Walker's account of late sovereignty in terms of the idea of *ultimate authority*. By retaining a 'focal meaning' (Finnis 1980: 9) of sovereignty as a form of ultimate authority, Walker argues, the 'deep conceptual structure of sovereignty' is preserved (Walker 2003: 23). With regard to the *change* side of the equation, the evolutionary element of *late* as opposed to high sovereignty is manifest in a number of respects in late sovereignty. First of all, the 'particularizing' element of the ultimate authority claim has evolved. While the ultimate authority claim in high sovereignty games relates to authority over territory and people, in late sovereignty the limiting element of sovereignty and the demarcation of one sovereign claim from another relates not to territory but rather to *function* (Walker 2003: 22). Thus in late sovereignty, autonomy does not imply territorial exclusivity.

A corollary of this is that in late sovereignty games the hegemony of states has been challenged. In late sovereignty games, the range of participants has expanded to include polities which do not fit the classic state model, such as the EU. This therefore allows for the mutual late sovereignty claims of the EU *and* member states over the same territory and people and does not result in a zero-sum resolution of sovereignty at either level, national or supranational.[9] In terms of a Searleian account of the constitutive rules of late sovereignty games, then, late sovereignty can be said to relate to an *institutional plausible claim* (X) to ultimate authority over a specific functional domain (Y) in the context of a multilevel political discourse (C).

Moreover, in late sovereignty games, the criteria stipulated by the regulative rules have expanded beyond the traditional canons of high sovereignty games. Whereas the tropes of high sovereignty remain present in late sovereignty games (see below), other justifications for sovereignty claims not based on ideals of popular sovereignty or constituent power have been added. Thus, the late sovereign claim to ultimate authority over a particular functional domain can itself be justified on functional grounds. Indeed, this is precisely what has happened at the EU level, where the late sovereignty claims of the EU over functional domains are themselves justified according to functionalist considerations in what Fritz Scharpf has termed 'output legitimacy' (Scharpf 1999).

EU late sovereignty games in practice

The evolution of the rules of sovereignty games from high to late sovereignty can be seen in the claims made at both the supranational and national levels in the context of the European integration process. For example, the ECJ's claims to the direct effect and supremacy of EU law, part of the 'constitutionalization' referred to above, are characteristic of late sovereignty claims both in the sense that they were made not by a traditional high sovereignty actor, i.e. a state, but a supranational institution; and in the sense that they constitute claims to ultimate authority over functional domains based on output legitimacy rather than more conventional, normative democratic considerations.

With regard to the claim to ultimate authority, in developing the constitutional doctrines of the EU Treaty system, the ECJ made a claim to ultimate authority over the functions governed by EU law by claiming that:

> the . . . Treaty is more than an agreement which merely creates mutual obligations between the contracting states . . . The Community constitutes a new

> legal order . . . for the benefit of which states have limited their sovereign rights, albeit within limited fields, and the subjects of which comprise not only their Member States but also their nationals.
>
> (ECJ 1963: 12)

This was complemented in the subsequent *Costa* judgment with a claim to the *autonomy* of the EU legal order, resulting in its primacy over national law (ECJ 1964: 594). In this case, the ECJ claimed that accession to the (then) Community constituted a 'permanent limitation' of EU member state sovereign rights (ECJ 1964: 594), the implication being that the EU enjoyed ultimate authority over the areas where the member state's sovereign powers had been limited. A more recent iteration of the EU's late sovereignty claims to ultimate authority is found in the ECJ's decision in *Kadi* (ECJ 2008). In this case, involving a clash between the United Nations (UN) and EU legal orders, the ECJ stressed the autonomy of the EU's legal order, finding that it constituted an '*autonomous* legal system which is not to be prejudiced by an international agreement' (ECJ 2008: 316). This rather robust claim to the autonomy (and therefore ultimate authority) of the EU legal order was made, not as against the legal orders of EU member states which was the case in *Van Gend* and *Costa*, but rather outwardly towards the legal order of the UN and the international community.

In terms of justifying these claims to ultimate authority by the Court, in developing the doctrines of the direct effect and primacy of EU law, the ECJ relied not on ideas of a constituent power nor on the right to the self-determination of an EU people, but rather, in true late sovereign fashion, on *functional* grounds. In *Costa*, the Court found that unless the legal system enjoyed ultimate authority over its functional domains, 'the realisation of the aims envisaged by the Treaty' would be endangered (ECJ 1964: 455) and the effectiveness of EU law would be impugned (ECJ 1964: 456). Moreover, the justification of this late sovereignty claim in *Kadi* was based not only on the achievement of the aims of the treaty, as in *Costa*, but also on the 'principles of liberty, democracy and respect for human rights and fundamental freedoms' embedded in, and protected by, the EU's (autonomous) legal order (ECJ 2008: 303).[10] This latter case illustrates a fluidity with regard to the justification of late sovereignty claims. Thus, they break new ground in terms of justifying sovereignty by including functionalist grounds within the acceptable criteria for ultimate authority claims, while at the same time allowing for a fluidity between justifications, according to context.

Even if EU member states engage in late sovereignty games qua sovereign actors, they have not remained unaffected by the passage from high to late sovereignty in the EU context. With regard to the claim to ultimate authority, unqualified, and categorical assertions of ultimate authority over territory and people by EU member states have tended to be replaced by more temperate claims to residual authority in late sovereignty games, which take into account the member states' commitments to European integration (Kumm 2005). In terms of the conventional justifications proffered by particular member states in high sovereignty games, moreover, these have undergone a transition from one form of high sovereignty justification to another form in the member state in question due to the integration process, a fluidity which characterizes these claims as late as opposed to high sovereignty claims. Two examples from EU member states illustrate this point: the German Federal Constitutional Court's (GFCC) 'Lisbon decision' of 2009 and the United Kingdom's (UK) European Union Act of 2011.

In June 2009, the GFCC handed down its decision on a challenge to the German ratification of the Lisbon Treaty of 2008 (GFCC 2009). The Court found that such ratification would not *per se* violate the German Basic Law (*Grundgesetz*). In doing so, however, it asserted German sovereignty at various junctures in the judgment accompanied by justifications of its sovereignty claims by reference to the classic tropes of high sovereignty such as constituent power, popular sovereignty, and self-determination (GFCC 2009: para. 204, 223, 310).

However, it is argued that such uses of high sovereignty justifications for German sovereignty by the GFCC constitute a shift from high to late sovereignty claims given the particular context within which they were made; namely the post-war German state. In the reconstruction of post-war Germany and particularly in the drafting of the Basic Law, the previously unhappy experiences with popular sovereignty were suppressed in favour of a strong assertion of the rule of law and supremacy of the Basic Law over the political process. This was copper-fastened in the Basic Law itself through an absolute prohibition on the holding of referendums or plebiscites (Mollers 2006). This was also explicitly recognized by the GFCC itself in the Lisbon decision, where it found that:

> The Basic Law . . . breaks with all forms of political Machiavellianism and with a rigid concept of sovereignty which until the beginning of the 20th century regarded the right to wage war – even a war of aggression – as a right due to sovereign state as a matter of course.
>
> (GFCC 2009: para. 199)

Thus, the post-war German constitutional landscape was marked by a prominent and well-respected constitutional court, which regularly struck down the laws of the *Bundestag* for violating the provisions of the Basic Law (Kommers 1997). As such, post-war German sovereignty was justified less according to constituent power and popular sovereignty and more on a 'constitutional patriotism' (Habermas 1998) with a 'sovereign' Basic Law.[11] Against this background, the justificatory claims of German sovereignty in the Lisbon decision, based on popular sovereignty, a German constituent power and self-determination mark a shift from the constitutional patriotism which has underpinned and justified German sovereignty in the post-war era, marking a late sovereign fluidity in the justification of ultimate authority claims by an EU member state.

Unlike the post-war German experience, the UK constitutional tradition prioritizes the political institution of Parliament over the written law through the foundational doctrine of parliamentary sovereignty, which has become both the claim and justification of UK sovereignty in the high sovereignty period (Goldsworthy 1999). Thus, the 'high sovereignty' claims of the UK have assumed the form of expressions of parliamentary sovereignty, justified by reference to its 'facticity' whether historical or political (Wade 1955: 157–8).

However, the justification of parliamentary sovereignty in UK constitutional discourse has undergone a shift in the past decade or so due, *inter alia*, to the European integration project, marking the passage from high sovereignty to late sovereignty in the UK. Judicial pronouncements, most notably from the UK's former highest court, the House of Lords,[12] have suggested that the justification of parliamentary sovereignty is not based on its (circular) 'facticity' but rather on its acceptance by the common law, which in turn means that it can be bounded by considerations such as EU membership (House of Lords 2005). Perhaps more significantly, however, the European Union Act 2011 illustrates the passage from high sovereignty to late sovereignty in the UK context.

There are two particular features of the Act that provide evidence of this. First, s. 18 of the Act, the 'sovereignty clause', states, in paradigmatic late sovereignty mode, that EU law 'falls to be recognised and available in law in the United Kingdom only by virtue of Acts [of Parliament]' (UK Parliament 2011: 18). Second, and more strikingly from the point of view of the transition from high to late sovereignty, are the series of referendum locks contained in the Act itself. For example, s. 2(2) of the Act provides that EU Treaties shall not be ratified by the UK unless a referendum has been held approving the reforms. The referendum locks mark an assertion of UK sovereignty claims in the sense that they require all Treaty amendments to be subject to a national referendum approving the changes. Constitutionally speaking, the referendum requirements appear to suggest a shift in conceptions of parliamentary sovereignty from a 'continuing' to a 'self-embracing' form (Hart 1994: 149), which would seem to be supported by recent judicial positions on parliamentary sovereignty. Perhaps more strikingly from the viewpoint of the regulative rules of UK sovereignty, however, the introduction of referendum requirements such as that of s. 2(2) seem to suggest a shift in justification of UK sovereignty from the *fact* of parliamentary sovereignty to popular sovereignty. This shift becomes all the more apparent given that popular sovereignty and constituent power as a justification of UK sovereignty has been virtually absent in UK constitutional discourse throughout most of the 'high sovereignty' period (Loughlin 2006). This fluidity, betrayed by the shift in justification of UK sovereignty, it is argued, makes these recent assertions of UK sovereignty late, rather than high, sovereignty claims.

In sum, the playing of late sovereignty games in the European integration context reveals how the constitutive and regulative rules of late sovereignty are followed by the participants in the language game. The late sovereignty claims of the EU reflect the evolution of the constitutive rules of high sovereignty games albeit that the focal meaning of sovereignty is retained in its sense of ultimate authority over particular functional domains. Moreover, the evolution of the regulative rules of late sovereignty games becomes apparent in the fluidity and in some cases novelty of the justification of ultimate authority at the member state level.

Late sovereignty games and OCTs

What light can European late sovereignty games shine on the OCT–metropole–EU trilateral relationship? As the introduction to the present volume explains, OCTs are non-continental colonial territories of EU member states which have resisted the urge to assert independence in the post-war era of decolonization for economic, political, and geographic reasons.[13] The EU itself has a stake in the governance of OCTs *qua* EU member states given that they enjoy special exemptions and provisions from, *inter alia*, the rules governing the single market.[14] These exemptions and concessions are regulated and patrolled by the EU level, rendering it a significant actor in the governance of these territories. This subsequently results in a trilateral relationship between the OCT, member state, and EU which has postcolonial relevance. So what role can sovereignty, or late sovereignty, play in this trilateral relationship?

In terms of the agency of the OCTs themselves, they are possibly best characterized by their reluctance to play *high* sovereignty games, that is, claiming ultimate authority over a particular territory (usually islands) and people based on regulative rules such as the right to self-determination.[15] The late sovereignty games paradigm in the EU context therefore may open up a space for OCTs to make *late* sovereignty claims regarding particular functions without resulting in independence (and therefore abandonment by the metropole), which would inevitably result from making high sovereignty claims. As discussed in the previous sections, the characteristics of late sovereignty games include the agency of actors as participants in late sovereignty games which do not fit the mould of sovereign statehood. Like the EU, OCTs can therefore play *late* sovereignty games as non-sovereign state actors, making claims to functional autonomy rather than territorial exclusivity.

As noted above, the disjunction between sovereignty and statehood in late sovereignty games is also accompanied by a broadening of the repertoire of justifications for late sovereignty claims such as the functional and normative justifications of EU sovereignty by the ECJ as well as fluidity in the usage of such justifications. This expansion of the repertoire of regulative criteria for late sovereignty claims as compared with high sovereignty claims means that there are more options available to OCTs to substantiate their late sovereignty claim to functional autonomy beyond the high sovereignty form of popular sovereignty and self-determination (providing the foundation for the undesired goal of independence). The functional autonomy of OCTs can thus be justified according to the 'special status' of these territories predicated on functional justifications including geographic, demographic and economic factors which have been formally recognized at the EU level, as in Articles 198 and 349 of the Treaty on the Functioning of the European Union.[16]

What results when applying the paradigm of late sovereignty games to the OCT–metropole–EU trilateral relationship, then, is a 'variegated federal landscape of governance' (Baldacchino, this volume) where ultimate authority claims based on functional autonomy are made at different levels of the trilateral relationship. In this way, the multilevel governance resulting from the playing of late sovereignty games in the trilateral relationship can be seen as a vindication, rather than negation, of the role and relevance of sovereignty in post-integration Europe (Aalberts 2004b), even if only one of the participants in these sovereignty games fits the typology of agency in high sovereignty games.

Conclusion

In this contribution, the EU sovereignty experience was analysed through the notion of late sovereignty. If 'high sovereignty' dominated the sovereignty games of the past 200 years or so, then the post-war experience of European integration can be said to mark the transition from high sovereignty to late sovereignty. Walker's account of late sovereignty was then unpacked in order to understand both how late sovereignty remains a conception of sovereignty and not post-sovereignty, as well as analysing precisely how the constitutive and regulative rules of late sovereignty games differ from those of high sovereignty. This late sovereignty paradigm was then illustrated by reference to sovereignty claims made within the EU context by EU member states as well as the EU itself. It was argued that the late sovereignty paradigm is also a useful way of understanding the complex trilateral relationship between OCTs, the metropole and the EU in sovereignty terms, as late sovereignty claims do not imply statehood and autonomy and can be asserted in ways which do not imply or lead to statehood. As such, sovereignty is alive and well in twenty-first-century Europe, albeit not in a form that the architects of the Westphalian system of sovereign states would necessarily recognize.

Notes

1 Majority voting was introduced in 1966 as part of the 'third stage' of the transitional development of the then European Economic Community. This development was not unproblematic and gave rise to the empty chair crises and the Luxembourg compromise (Teasdale 1993). Nonetheless, majority voting has been applied to ever-wider policy areas in the form of qualified majority voting such that it is now the primary method of decision-making at the EU level (Christiansen and Reh 2009).

2 Perhaps Marx was the original prophet of the demise of the state and therefore sovereignty. Carl Schmitt writing in the interwar period also prophesized the demise of sovereignty due to the rise of liberalism (Schmitt 2005[1922]). For a prominent recent account, see (Strange 1996).

3 This was clear from the ratification debates of the Constitutional Treaty in France and the Netherlands and the Lisbon Treaty in Ireland. It would be simplistic to conclude that concerns over national sovereignty were the sole cause of the majorities against ratification of the Treaty in these cases, but it was certainly a factor and featured prominently in political debate surrounding the referendums. For the Irish context, see Laffan (2008).

4 The notion of 'sovereignty games' is well defined in IR literature (Jackson 1990; Sørensen 1999). As Werner and de Wilde point out, however, much of the literature on sovereignty games presupposes the state as an immutable fact (Werner and de Wilde: 2001: 291–2). The notion of sovereignty as an institutional fact, however, presupposes the inverse, that the games qua discourse constitute the actors engaged in the game. As Aalberts puts it, 'the rules . . . constitute the fact – they are the

conditions of possibility of the very activity, which could not happen or 'be' except for the defining rules (as set out by language)' (Aalberts 2004a: 249).

5 'I want to clarify a distinction between two different sorts of rules, which I shall call regulative and constitutive rules . . . As a start, we might say that regulative rules regulate antecedently or independently existing forms of behavior; for example, many rules of etiquette regulate inter-personal relationships which exist independently of the rules. But constitutive rules do not merely regulate, they create or define new forms of behavior. The rules of football or chess, for example, do not merely regulate playing football or chess, but as it were they create the very possibility of playing such games' (Searle 1969: 33).

6 Following the periodization of history, in terms of the early, high and late middle ages.

7 Krasner attributes the introduction of the idea of the equality implicit in international legal sovereignty to Emmerich de Vattel and particularly his *Le droit de gens* of 1758. Westphalian sovereignty, on the other hand, relating to internal autonomy, has, Krasner argues, virtually nothing to do with the eponymous Peace of Westphalia of 1648. The principle of the internal autonomy of states was first articulated clearly in the eighteenth century by Vattel and Christian Freiherr von Wolff (Krasner 1999: 14–20).

8 In this regard, notwithstanding the evolutionary potential of all language games, particularly on Wittgenstein's scheme, the language game of late sovereignty must retain some basic idea of what sovereignty means such that it can be understood that sovereignty games are still being played. Thus, even if we accept that the meaning of language is conventional and not essential, as well as the fact that it is evolutionary, both with reference to its constitutive and regulative rules, if language is to perform its primary function, that of communication, then the meaning or intelligibility of speech acts must retain some sort of central or 'focal' meaning. If the meaning of concepts is constantly up for grabs, then communication through language becomes impossible. I understand Cavell to be making a similar argument (Cavell 1958).

9 A situation which Walker has developed in terms of constitutional pluralism (Walker 2002).

10 For discussion, see Mac Amhlaigh (2011).

11 This is perhaps most evident in the GFCC's 'battles' with the ECJ over fundamental rights protection in the EU legal system; the so-called 'Solange' case law, where the Court deferred to the jurisdiction of the ECJ as long as it deemed the protection of fundamental rights in EU law to be the equivalent of that of the German Basic Law. The assertion of sovereignty in this case, it is submitted, being the sovereignty of the German Basic Law over EU law. See Kumm (1999)

12 In 2009, the UK Supreme Court replaced the Judicial Committee of the House of Lords as the highest Court in the UK pursuant to the reforms of the Constitutional Reform Act 2005.

13 See the introduction and Baldacchino's contribution to the current volume.

14 For a clear example of this in the context of EU financial regulation, see Vlcek's contribution to the current volume. More generally, see Ziller (2000) and Kochenov (2009).

15 For discussion, see Baldacchino, this volume.

16 Article 198 of the Treaty on the Functioning of the European Union (TFEU), which anchors the OCT–EU arrangement, provides that 'the Member States agree to associate with the Union the non-European countries and territories which have special relations with Denmark, France, the Netherlands and the United Kingdom [listed in an Annex to the Treaty] . . . The purpose of association shall be to promote the economic and social development of the countries and territories and to establish close economic relations between them and the Union as a whole. In accordance with the principles set out in the preamble to this Treaty, association shall serve primarily to further the interests

and prosperity of the inhabitants of these countries and territories in order to lead them to the economic, social and cultural development to which they aspire'. Even more striking in this regard is Article 349 of the TFEU (quoted in Baldacchino's contribution to this volume), which lays out the special provisions for the Outermost Regions of the EU.

References

Aalberts, T. (2004a) 'The sovereignty games states play: (quasi-)states in the international order', *International Journal of the Semiotics of Law*, 17: 245–57.

Aalberts, T. (2004b) 'The future of sovereignty in multilevel governance Europe – a constructivist reading', *Journal of Common Market Studies*, 42(1): 23–46.

Bartelson, J. (1995) *A Genealogy of Sovereignty*, Cambridge: Cambridge University Press.

Cavell, S. (1958) 'Must we mean what we say?', *Inquiry*, 1: 1–4, 172–212.

Christiansen, T. and Reh, C. (2009) *Constitutionalizing the European Union*, Basingstoke: Palgrave Macmillan.

ECJ (1963) *Van Gend en Loos*, 26/62.

ECJ (1964) *Costa v. ENEL*, 14/64.

ECJ (2008) *Kadi v. Council of the European Union*, C-402/05 & C-415/05.

Finnis, J. (1980) *Natural Law and Natural Rights*, Oxford: Clarendon Press.

German Federal Constitutional Court (GFCC) (2009) Lisbon Case, BVerfG, 2 BvE 2/08.

Goldsworthy, J. (1999) *The Sovereignty of Parliament: History and Philosophy*, Oxford: Oxford University Press.

Hart, H.L.A. (1994) *The Concept of Law*, Oxford: Oxford University Press.

Habermas, J. (1998) *The Inclusion of the Other*, Cambridge, MA: MIT Press.

House of Lords (2005) *Jackson v. Attorney General*, UKHL 56.

Jackson, R.H. (1990) *Quasi States: Sovereignty, International Relations and the Third World*, Cambridge: Cambridge University Press.

Keohane, R. (1994) 'Hobbes' dilemma and institutional change in world politics. Sovereignty in international society', in H.-H. Holm and G. Sørensen (eds), *Whose World Order: Uneven Globalization and the End of the Cold War*, Boulder, CO: Westview.

Keohane, R. (2002) 'Ironies of sovereignty: the European Union and the United States', *Journal of Common Market Studies*, 40(4): 743–65.

Kochenov, D. (2009) 'Substantive and procedural issues in the application of European law in the overseas possessions of European Union Member States', *Michigan State Journal of International Law*, 17(2): 198–288.

Kommers, D.E. (1997) *The Constitutional Jurisprudence of the Federal Republic of Germany*, Durham, NC, and London: Duke University Press.

Krasner, S. (1999) *Sovereignty: Organized Hypocrisy*, Princeton, NJ: Princeton University Press.

Kumm, M. (1999) 'Who is the final arbiter of constitutionality in Europe?', *Journal of Common Market Studies*, 36: 351–86.

Kumm, M. (2005) 'The jurisprudence of constitutional conflict', *European Law Journal*, 11(3): 262–307.

Laffan, B. (2008) *Ireland and the EU Post-Lisbon, Notre Europe Note*. Online. Available at: www.notre-europe.eu/en/axes/visions-of-europe/works/publication/ireland-and-the-eu-post-lisbon (accessed 10 December 2008).

Lake, D. (2007) 'Delegating divisible sovereignty: sweeping a conceptual minefield', *Review of International Organizations*, 2: 219–37.

Lindahl, H. and van Roermund, B. (2000) 'Law without a state? On representing the Common Market', in Z. Bankowski and A. Scott (eds), *The European Union and Its Legal Order*, Oxford: Blackwell.

Loughlin, M. (2006) 'Constituent power subverted: from English constitutional argument to British constitutional practice', in M. Loughlin and N. Walker (eds), *The Paradox of Constitutionalism*, Oxford: Oxford University Press.

Mac Amhlaigh, C. (2009) 'Revolt by referendum? In search of a European constitutional narrative', *European Law Journal*, 15(4): 552–63.

Mac Amhlaigh, C. (2011) 'The European Union's constitutional mosaic: big 'C' or small 'c', is that the question?', in N. Walker, J. Shaw and S. Tierney (eds), *Europe's Constitutional Mosaic*, Oxford: Hart.

MacCormick, N. (1999) *Questioning Sovereignty*, Oxford: Oxford University Press.

MacCormick, N. (2011) 'Sovereignty and after', in H. Kalmo and Q. Skinner, *Sovereignty in Fragments*, Cambridge: Cambridge University Press.

Mollers, C. (2006) 'We are (afraid of) the people: constituent power in German constitutionalism', in M. Loughlin and N. Walker (eds), *The Paradox of Constitutionalism*. Oxford: Oxford University Press.

Moravcsik, A. (1998) *The Choice for Europe*, London: Routledge.

Scharpf, F. (1999) *Governing in Europe: Effective and Democratic?*, Oxford: Oxford University Press.

Schmitt, C. (2005[1922]) *Political Theology*, Chicago: University of Chicago Press.

Searle, J. (1969) *Speech Acts: An Essay in the Philosophy of Language*, Cambridge: Cambridge University Press.

Sørensen, G. (1999) 'Sovereignty: change and continuity in a fundamental institution', *Political Studies*, XLVII: 590–604.

Strange, S. (1996) *The Retreat of the State*, Cambridge: Cambridge University Press.

Teasdale, A. (1993) 'The life and death of the Luxembourg compromise', *Journal of Common Market Studies*, 31(4): 567–79.

UK Parliament (2011) *European Union Act 2011*, c. 12.

Wade, W. (1955) 'The basis of legal sovereignty', *Cambridge Law Journal*, 13(2): 172–97.

Walker, N. (2002) 'The idea of constitutional pluralism', *Modern Law Review*, 65(3): 317–59.

Walker, N. (2003) 'Late sovereignty in the European Union', in N. Walker (ed.), *Sovereignty in Transition*, Oxford: Hart.

Walker, N. (2008a) 'Europe at 50: a mid-life crisis? "democratic deficit" and "sovereignty surplus"', *Irish Journal of European Law*, 15(1 & 2): 23–35.

Walker, N. (2008b) 'The variety of sovereignty', in R. Adler-Nissen and T. Gammeltoft-Hansen (eds), *Sovereignty Games: Instrumentalizing State Sovereignty in Europe and Beyond*, New York: Palgrave Macmillan.

Walker, N. (2010) 'Surface and depth: the EU's resilient sovereignty question', University of Edinburgh Working Papers, 2010/10, 1–22.

Weiler, J. (1991) 'The transformation of Europe', *Yale Law Journal*, 100: 2405–83.

Werner, W. and de Wilde, J. (2001) 'The endurance of sovereignty', *European Journal of International Relations*, 7(3): 283–313.

Wittgenstein, L. (1968) *Philosophical Investigations*, G.E.M. Anscombe (trans.), Oxford: Blackwell.

Wæver, O. (1995) 'Identity, integration and security: solving the sovereignty puzzle in EU Studies', *Journal of International Affairs*, 48(2): 389.

Ziller, J. (2000) 'Flexibility in the geographical scope of EU Law: diversity and differentiation in the application of substantive law on Member States' territories', in G. de Burca and J. Scott (eds), *Constitutional Change in the EU: From Uniformity to Flexibility?* Oxford: Hart.

4 The micropolity sovereignty experience

Decolonizing, but not disengaging

Godfrey Baldacchino

On the tenth day of the tenth month of 2010, the Netherlands Antilles – consisting of four and a half islands – were formally dissolved; in their place, two territories, Curaçao and Sint Maarten, graduated to autonomy status, joining another, already autonomous territory (Aruba); while the remaining three – Bonaire, Saba, and St Eustatius – were realigned as 'special municipalities' of the Netherlands. None of the five erstwhile colonies opted for independence, although that option was manifestly available (see Oostindie, this volume). We should not be surprised.

The active and dogged pursuit of extended colonial relationships has been aptly described by Dutch scholars observing the Netherlands Antilles as 'upside-down decolonization': a situation in which the metropolis presses the former colony to accept independence, but to no avail (Hoefte and Oostindie 1989, 1991: 93). This is described as 'an unusual situation' (Allahar 2005: 132) whereby the mother country seemed willing, even anxious, to free itself from the responsibilities of empire, but the colonies in question would demur, not letting the mother country off the hook (Oostindie and Klinkers 2003: 116, 145). The persisting seven colonial powers – Australia, Denmark, France, the Netherlands, New Zealand, the United Kingdom (UK), and the United States (US) – find themselves in an '*enforced* colonial condition', while their wards '*opt* for dependency status' (Skinner 2006: 185; italics added).

This behaviour is neither unusual nor paradoxical. The politics of 'upside-down decolonization' are the norm in today's small, non-independent territories. With some exceptions – Bougainville, Scotland, Greenland and New Caledonia (Gad, and Brown, this volume) – sovereignty no longer appears to be the obviously desirable trajectory of peoples who see themselves as dispossessed political entities or at the losing end of federalist developments (e.g. Trompf 1993: xxv; Baldacchino and Milne 2006). In the contemporary world, there may be solid definitive advantages in *not* being independent. Yet the value-laden discourse of mainstream political science, along with the scrutiny of the United Nations Special Committee on Decolonization, belie an enduring obsession with the mantra of sovereignty as an intrinsically laudable, and almost historically unavoidable, evolutionary route. The flexing of domestic jurisdictional muscle for strategic gains and leverage is an important resource for small autonomous territories. But this need not be coterminous with independence and sovereignty.

Indeed, the main thrust of this chapter is that sovereignty, in the guise of independent statehood, is not necessarily an asset: many jurisdictions today deliberately refrain from becoming sovereign in order to better pursue their interests. This is important, at least for two main reasons: First, it flies in the face of conventional expectations that every polity would desire and aspire to become sovereign and independent if it could; moreover, it obliges us to take a closer and more nuanced look at some of the power dynamics in international political economy.

Mainly for these reasons, this chapter reviews the alternatives, origins, economic performance, behaviour, and overall 'experience' of small island developing states (SIDS) and non-independent, sub-national island jurisdictions (SNIJs) that have considerable degrees of autonomy and self-determination. The argument also critiques the concept of small as applied to both these clusters. While self-determination remains a valuable goal, a strong case remains to be made for non-independent territories to craft and nurture dynamically contoured, negotiated, constitutional arrangements with a larger, richer, and stronger metropolitan player rather than the nationalist and anti-colonialist-driven pursuit of full independence, as in the heyday of decolonization.

Customizing sovereignty – customizing alternatives

Four decades of failed independence referenda have confirmed that various smaller – mainly island – jurisdictions have remained largely unperturbed by the grand wave of decolonization that has swept the world, creating over 100 new sovereign states in its wake. As colonization retreated after 1945, it left behind puddles of jurisdiction, with the largest territories obtaining sovereignty first, the smallest territories following last, and the *very* smallest units stubbornly refusing to budge.

That the smallest colonies took the longest to achieve independence was also due to the serious doubts of their colonial masters regarding their viability and stability as independent states (Diggines 1985; Pirotta *et al.* 2001; Plischke 1977: 9–10). It has been argued, for example, that 'independence is an extravagant and improvident recipe for the remaining small territories' (Wainhouse 1964: 133); and that 'in the 1980s, Britain was left with a few colonies, mainly islands, too small by any standards to become independent nations' (Chamberlain 1985: 51). Indeed, the presumed non-viability of small countries was so ingrained that initial attempts at decolonizating small territories were geared towards federative solutions: the West Indies Federation, Malaysia–Singapore and, indeed, the Netherlands Antilles. All these experiments are now consigned to history.

For the most part, however, the very smallest territories have not sought or achieved independence at all. These have been 'decolonizing without disengaging' (Houbert 1986) over the past century, with the earliest examples possibly being the so-called 'insular cases' where, after 1899, Cuba, Guam, the Philippines, and Puerto Rico were 'territorially incorporated' into the United States (e.g. McKibben 1990). These were followed much later by the 'departmentalization' of four French overseas island territories in 1946, and dramatized by the secession of Anguilla, which refused independence as part of St Kitts and Nevis in 1979 and remains a British Overseas Territory (BOT). The 2010 dissolution of the Netherlands Antilles continues this pattern. Historical practice and/or international provisions have secured over time the autonomy of such territories as Åland, the Channel Islands, and the Isle of Man. Military interventions and/or sectarian strife have led to *de facto* autonomous jurisdictions in Northern Cyprus, Southern Mindanao, and Taiwan (the latter remains somewhat unique in being recognized as a sovereignty country by some two dozen states). Constitutionally or legally entrenched provisions secure and frame the autonomy of island provinces like Hawai'i, Jeju, Mwali, Prince Edward Island, and Tasmania. 'First nations' enjoy self-determination in locations such as Nunavut and Haida Gwaii/Queen Charlotte Islands (both in Canada), Rotuma (in Fiji), and the Torres Strait Islands (in Australia). There are the various territories and former colonies, not interested in outright, full, or quick routes to independence (as stubbornly confirmed in various plebiscites), which are engaged in evolving relations with Amsterdam, Canberra, Copenhagen, London, Paris, Washington, or Wellington, as well as with such supranational entities as the European Union (EU). Specific sub-national arrangements treat the Azores, Corsica, Kish, Labuan, Madeira, Nevis, Sardinia, Sicily, Scotland, or Zanzibar differently from the rest of their respective state, often with respect to cultural differences and distinct histories, or as an outcome of a deliberate, central government strategy. There are also special island (or mainly island) regions which enjoy a specifically different autonomy portfolio, *de jure* or *de facto*: Hong Kong, Macao, Sakhalin, and Shetland – thanks to recognition of the prudent management of resources (investment finance, human capital, fossil fuels) that might be threatened by a loss of autonomy. The contemporary political map is strewn with cases of small (often island) jurisdictions, and the non-sovereign examples vastly exceed the sovereign ones.

The legal and political creativity employed to facilitate non-sovereignty is considerable; Watts has identified five categories of 'forms of political relations which combine autonomy [read: self-rule] and partnership [read: shared rule] within federal political systems' (Watts 2000: 23–9, 2008: 33–8). Moreover, non-sovereignty does not equal powerlessness: Pitcairn is not a sovereign state; it is, however, the world's smallest recognized sub-national jurisdiction, the only remaining BOT in the Pacific, and whose citizens (some 47 of them) have been deemed fit to submit complex legal challenges to Britain's administration of the island in the context of widely reported child-sex abuse trials (e.g. Trenwith 2003; Middleton 2005).

On the other side of the fine line between sovereignty and non-sovereignty, the presumed smallness of states also creates ambiguity and flexibility in relation to what sovereignty means. The three most recently independent states in the Pacific, each of which is a member of the United Nations (UN) – the Federated States of Micronesia, the Marshall Islands, and Palau – have been defined as 'hybrid jurisdictions' (Levine and Roberts 2005), since their status represents attempts at exploiting the advantages of *both* conventional sovereignty *and* an autonomy supported by a benign and affluent patron state (in this case, the US). When possible, it is far better to have your cake and eat it too (Palan 1998).

Such observations 'on the ground' inspire a robust challenge to conventional wisdom: sovereignty is often treated as indivisible; a country is either sovereign or it isn't, with absolutely no room for dithering in between. And yet this rule of thumb is increasingly found wanting in the twenty-first century (Mac Amhlaigh, this volume). Lake (2003: 310) suggests acknowledging a gradation or 'a continuum of increasing hierarchy in international relations'. He adds (2003: 314) that 'anomalies may be more commonplace than we often realize'. Likewise, Kerr (2005) postulates a pecking order of sovereignty, one including both non-sovereign jurisdictions with considerable powers of self-determination (e.g. the Cook Islands) as well as sovereign jurisdictions with limited room for manoeuvre (e.g. Cyprus). When Krasner (2001) speaks of 'problematic sovereignty', he attributes this to both a difficulty of classification – 'Is Somalia a state? Is Somaliland a state?' – as well as the nebulosity surrounding the workings of such jurisdictions in international relations (IR).[1]

Enter the 'small state' – risk or chance?

But what exactly is a 'small state' or a 'micropolity'? How small does it have to be to qualify? Discourse is power: the labels used to define our subjects are themselves highly charged and instrumentalized, the consequences of clear power dynamics. Across disciplines and concerns, small states have been rendered synonymous to chronically vulnerable and problematic territories for which aid, assistance, and especially favourable deals are therefore quite legitimate. This strident 'deficit' discourse surrounding small states has found fertile ground, both in the vocabulary of small state policy makers (who tend to believe their own rhetoric), as well as some mainstream neo-classical economic advisors (Briguglio and Kisanga 2004; but see Easterly and Kraay 2000; Shaw and Cooper 2009).

References to 'small states' – and later 'microstates' and even 'ministates' (Harbert 1976; Srinivasan 1986; Lewis 2002) – become more systematic in the 1960s after US-based or trained political scientists in particular voiced concerns as to how these newly independent entities would (allegedly) be both unable to even minimally execute their international obligations, as well as being pesky and unreliable players in the context of strategic, big-stakes, Cold War superpower politics (Baker Fox 1959; Rothstein 1966, 1968; Vital 1967; Keohane 1969; East 1973; Plischke 1977). Their UN membership – which in itself has become a cherished signifier of sovereign status – was considered a 'problem' to the extent that a scientific status report was commissioned (Rapaport *et al.* 1971) and an appointed Committee of Experts sought (unsuccessfully, as it turned out) to develop language and protocol that would have treated small states to what amounted to second class status in the UN (Gunter 1977).

That a small or micro state is considered weak, vulnerable, and even an unreliable and stunted version of a larger, somewhat more appropriate state, is a paradigm that has gripped the imagination of many policy makers, even before the arrival of dozens of small states onto the world stage, but especially since the final decades of the twentieth century, when many small states could look at their independence experience with some measure of disappointment. Susceptibility to natural disasters, remoteness, insularity, limited institutional capacity, limited commodity diversification, and a high degree of openness to price fluctuations, along with the whims of aid donors, tour operators, and foreign investors . . . these are the main component factors of economic vulnerability, factors which tend to be exogenous to small states and over which they have little, if any, influence or control (Alford 1984; Bray 1987; Bray and Packer 1993: 20; Commonwealth Consultative Group 1985; Commonwealth Secretariat/World Bank 2000; Diggines 1985; Harden 1985; Lyon 1985). The composite conditions of openness, a high trade-to-GDP ratio, and dependence on very few export commodities are claimed to render small states highly vulnerable to 'external shocks' (e.g. Briguglio 1995; Dolman 1985: 42; Dommen 1980: 936; Doumenge 1985: 86; Kaminarides *et al.* 1989; Wood 1967: 2). Championed by the Commonwealth Secretariat, adopted by the UN and the World Bank, leading to landmark international meetings like the SIDS conference in Barbados in 1994 and the follow-up in Mauritius in 2005, the rhetoric has become so pervasive and predictable that small states have possibly come to expect and believe it to be true. Diplomatic resources are deployed to (try and) convince the various powers that be that small states cannot survive without special measures, long transitional periods, exemptions, and fiscal and other bailouts.

The outcome of this international campaign remains mixed. The UN Conference on Trade and Development (UNCTAD) has developed a specific programme dedicated to SIDS since 1994 (Hein 2004). Most of the SIDS – the UN currently recognizes 38 – are remote, small in land area and population (less than 2 million), with a very narrow resource base, and fragile land and marine ecosystems that are highly vulnerable to natural disasters. Their economies are open and depend heavily on trade for national income. In contrast, the World Bank has only 'noted' the alleged vulnerability of small states; the World Trade Organization will not accept it, since it would open the floodgates for other requests for exemption; passionate arguments about the devastating impact of rising sea levels (especially on low-lying atoll archipelagos) have not led to policy changes (Baldacchino 2009). The most that can be realistically expected from international diplomatic efforts is support for 'capacity building' in order to nurture a domestic 'resilience' intended to combat or mitigate this inherent and chronic weakness (e.g. Briguglio *et al.* 2006). Titles of texts discussing the predicament of small states frequently feature ominous terms and phrases. Apart from 'vulnerability', these include: 'problems', 'dilemmas', 'small is dangerous', 'paradise lost' (Easterly and Kraay 2000: 2013), as well as 'sinking' or 'disappearing' (e.g. Markovich and Annandale 2000).

Small states have often been seen as synonymous to weak or failed states in political science literature, lumped in the same category as many larger developing countries. Even today, the definition of a 'small state' in politics and IR can include countries that are, or have felt, threatened by much larger neighbours such as Costa Rica, Cuba, Finland, Israel, Jamaica, Singapore, and Taiwan (e.g. Gayle 1986; Ingebritsen 2006). While the EU does not officially refer to small states, all EU member states except the 'Big Six' (France, Germany, Italy, Poland, Spain and the UK) have been considered small in the political science literature (e.g. Thorhallsson 2000). The 53-member British Commonwealth, which can be credited with definitely putting the small state in the focus of international and regional policy, was galvanized into such action after the US military intervention in one of its members, the island state of Grenada, in 1983. Its concern with the vulnerability of a small but sovereign state to external intervention or invasion (Commonwealth Consultative Group 1985; Diggines 1985; Harden 1985; Lyon 1985; Bray 1987; Bune 1987; Charles 1997) has not really abated since, instead evolving to consider issues of economic and environmental sustainability (e.g. climate change and rising sea levels) as well as capacity building and good governance (e.g. Nath *et al.* 2011). Small, often island, states have also been increasingly seen as frontline zones in the struggle against arms trafficking, money, and drug laundering as well as illegal migration, requiring assistance to beef up their human, material, and technological infrastructure to adequately police their territorial lands and seas (e.g. Bartmann 2007; Sutton and Payne 1993).

Such widespread prejudice signals a tendency in the literature to consider 'large states' as 'normal', apart from preferable. And yet this is hardly the case in practice. Out of 266 jurisdictions listed in the 2011 edition of the Central Intelligence Agency (CIA) *World Factbook* (CIA 2011), only 11 have populations exceeding 100 million; while 160 have populations of less than 10 million (of which 41 have a resident population of under 100,000). Moreover, there is 'no widely accepted definition of a small state' (Crowards 2002: 143), nor is there any sharp or self-evident dichotomy or cut-off point between 'small' and 'large' states (Baehr 1975: 466). Indeed, cut-off points tend to shift and change on the basis of expediency in order to catch up with the population growth of outliers.[2]

Prejudiced nomenclature aside, there is a different, and much more optimistic, approach to the small polity. It is perhaps less self-evident and more subdued because it does not thrive on strident diplomacy. This is a pragmatic positioning which opines that smallness can provide a flexibility and adaptability that larger states cannot wield. The assumed logic of scale economies is questioned, especially where this is applied to political systems. The undercurrent leitmotifs here are self-reliance, authenticity, self-management, popular democratic participation, and a plausible reaction against mass anonymity and insignificant peripherality. This approach connects easily with ideas dating back to Plato and Rousseau that small is beautiful, practical, and 'possible' (Schumacher 1973: Chapter 5; Kohr 1973; Berreman 1978: 235; McRobie 1981; Max-Neef 1982). This suppleness can be deployed both strategically and opportunistically. Against a global context of dynamism and uncertainty, it is argued that small polities are more vibrant, smart, versatile, and flexible; they stand a better chance of coping and surviving rapid change than do larger, monolithic, more staid, and complex systems (Blazic-Metzner and Hughes 1982: 86; Srinivasan 1986: 211; Sutton 1987: 18; Chiew 1993). Smaller countries are also claimed to practise more benign politics and to enjoy higher degrees of social cohesiveness (Kuznets 1960: 28; Knox 1967: 44; Dommen 1980: 942; Srebrnik 2004; Baldacchino 2005; but see Baldacchino, 2012a).

Political status and economic scorecards

Talking about economic strategy highlights the proactive qualities that a small polity, be it an SIDS or an SNIJ, has by virtue of being a polity, with a slate of jurisdictional and regulatory instruments at its disposal. Nevertheless, in a world where 'the strong do what they can and the weak suffer what they must' (Thucydides 1972[431bc]: 402), we must temper our analysis with the realization that small states cannot and do not always plan their future. Just as they are reluctant price takers in the open market of goods and services, they are also reluctant policy takers in the open world of international political economy. Indeed, small states typically spend more time and effort exploiting opportunities that may arise – and for which they may not have planned at all. While meant to be supple and flexible, since they are in principle expected to regularly accommodate to changes at any point in time, small states may appear fragile and threatened by exogenous change. They may suffer large swings and lurches in economic wealth, however measured (e.g. Cali *et al.* 2011).

The economic development trajectory of many small polities is, after all, not typically an outcome of a well-laid out plan. It may look so in retrospect; it may be presented so by the media and government spin doctors who may see, and hence establish, a method to the madness. It also looks good on microstate governments and their leadership who are, after all, meant to govern and thus exercise some control over their economic destiny. Instead, when the development trajectories of small economies are profiled from the vantage point of the strategic flexibility used by small states (at multiple levels as individuals, household units, corporate entities, and complete jurisdictions), one sees these actors seeking to exploit opportunities and maximize economic gains in a turbulent and dynamic external environment with which they must engage. These actors keep alive and nurture a portfolio of skills and revenue streams which enables them to migrate inter-sectorally and trans-nationally (Baldacchino and Bertram 2009; Baldacchino 2011). It is in relation to these opportunities that one should plausibly rationally and critically address the benefits or otherwise of full independence versus sub-national autonomy for the world's smallest polities.

Meanwhile, we are confronted with two clusters of small, mainly island territories that provide living experiments of not just the pliability of sovereignty but also of the manner in which independence can or cannot translate into citizen affluence and economic development. Indeed, it is somewhat ironic that while the analysis of one of these clusters – the SIDS – still remains driven by vulnerability considerations, an analysis of the second cluster – of the SNIJs – suggests a markedly different set of endowments. When McElroy and Sandborn (2005) compare socio-economic and demographic data from 19 SIDS with that of 16 SNIJs, both sets hailing from the Caribbean and the Pacific, the difference in the results is statistically significant (to 0.025 or 0.001 levels) for no less than 17 of 25 distinct variables. This warrants the authors to claim, somewhat daringly, that 'the dependents . . . have come to represent a new, successful, insular development case' (ibid.: 11). This empirical realization is supported by the political economy of small jurisdictions, which is patterned in such a way as to suggest two broad 'economic developmental' routes. Both models apply to SIDS and SNIJs alike.

(a) MIRAB

The MIRAB model (Bertram and Watters 1985, 1986) remains the most popular for explaining the predicament of most SIDS. The key hypothesis states that a class of economies and societies now exists in which the combined effect of MIgration, Remittances, Aid and Bureaucracy (hence MIRAB) '*determines* [rather than supports] the evolution of the [economic] system' (Bertram and Watters 1985: 497; emphasis in original). The notion of 'autonomous economic growth' in specific contexts is simply 'false' (Watters 1987: 33). The MIRAB concept remains appealing (Bertram 2006) and may have even assumed the stature of a self-fulfilling prophecy, especially in the South Pacific.

The MIRAB route reveals itself as a standard 'regional development' tactic for peripheral regions and territories the world over. In cases with metropolitan cores and stagnant peripheries – and where aren't there? – the MIRAB cluster of features constitutes the classic response to assuage the ailments of those on the edge, particularly if accompanied by a dominant ideology of professed redistribution and equalization; that is, unless the central power 'is prepared to see living standards slide' (Bertram and Watters 1985: 513). After all, the standard measures used by the core to support the periphery include an element of workfare (bureaucracy within MIRAB) and transfer payments (aid within MIRAB). Meanwhile, migration, internal this time, is also likely from the periphery to the centre, as people – particularly the young, the skilled, the educated, the ambitious – search for work and an even better education, occasionally visiting relatives back home or sending them gifts in cash/kind (migration in MIRAB). The novelty of MIRAB, other than the fancy yet meaningless acronym, lies in identifying uncannily similar patterns operating *between* states as well as *within* them.

MIRAB comes across as a pragmatic, welfare-maximizing strategy in line with the theory of competitive advantage (Poirine 1998: 91); it now may, or may be seen to, legitimize, justify, and lock into place such an 'economic-development strategy' in the long term (Treadgold 1999). As long as sources of revenue (a combination of remittances and/or aid) remain secure and as long as the shifting fortunes of any such 'external' source are adequately compensated for by similar 'external' alternative sources, then that is all that really matters. This is an unorthodox, parasitic, perhaps perverse manner of earning one's keep in the world; but nevertheless effective and in its own way sustainable (Bertram and Watters 1985: 512; Bertram 1993: 257; Poirine 1998). The basis of acute dependency can change; but not dependency itself. The art of politics becomes the securing and locking in of such a dependency mechanism. Politicians secure domestic support on the basis of how strongly and effectively they are seen in procuring aid and other rentier income from external sources.

The SNIJs that are most exemplary of locked-in dependency are the current nine 'outermost regions' of the EU (of which only one is not an island) whose predicament is enshrined in Article 349 of the Treaty on the EU. Such language assures the permanence of the development constraints and stifles initiatives towards escaping or reducing dependency. It simply cannot get better than this:

> Taking account of the structural social and economic situation of Guadeloupe, French Guiana, Martinique, Réunion, Saint-Barthélemy, Saint-Martin, the Azores, Madeira and the Canary Islands, which is compounded by their remoteness, insularity, small size, difficult topography and climate, economic dependence on a few products, the permanence and combination of which severely restrain their development, the Council . . . shall adopt specific measures . . . [These measures concern such areas] as customs and trade policies, fiscal policy, free zones, agriculture and fisheries policies, conditions for supply of raw materials and essential consumer goods, State aids and conditions of access to structural funds and to horizontal Union programmes. [They are] aimed, in particular, at laying down the conditions of application of the Treaties to those regions, including common policies.[3]

There are examples of MIRAB economies amongst both SIDS and SNIJs. When conceived in 1985, Bertram and Watters applied the label to just five Pacific island micro-territories, two of which were recently independent states (Kiribati, Tuvalu), with the other three being semi-autonomous, subnational jurisdictions (Cook Islands, Niue, Tokelau). Twelve years later (Bertram 1999), Western Samoa (now Samoa), Tonga, French Polynesia, Federated States of Micronesia, other small US-associated Pacific Territories, and Rapa Nui – as well as the outlying islands of so-called 'non-MIRAB' island states, such as Fiji, Papua New Guinea, and the Solomon Islands – were added to the pioneering five or noted to have been added by other researchers. By 1998, the US Virgin Islands, Saint Helena, St-Pierre et Miquelon, and Mayotte had been added to the list from beyond the Pacific basin (Poirine 1998). McElroy and Morris (2002) identify and confirm four African island polities as MIRABs: Cape Verde, Comoros, and São Tomé e Príncipe (all SIDS), and Mayotte (an SNIJ). We have been told that 'all SPINs [South Pacific Island Nations] match to a greater or lesser degree the model of rent-dependent MIRAB' (Fleming 2002: 6). Connell (1991: 252, 270) had argued that the model is applicable, to a greater or lesser degree, to most SIDS, since most of them have moved 'from subsistence to subsidy' (ibid.). It is not merely the economic system described, but the model itself, which appears to be durable and persistent.

(b) PROFIT

The MIRAB approach is well aligned to the vulnerability thesis: small states and territories would have no other way to survive were it not for regular financial transfers from other countries. But one can conceptualize economic and political strategies for small states and territories that are *not* driven by the siphoning of aid (by governments) and remittances (by households). These strategies are more proactive and depend much more on the nurturing of specific, local, jurisdictional capacities, or powers. They comprise the management of external relations but, unlike in the MIRAB case, this is done 'by means of domestic policies and governing institutions' (Warrington 1998: 101). There is evidence that a few policy areas have been especially targeted by small states and territories for the flexing of their jurisdictional powers as an economic resource: 'people considerations' affecting citizenship, residence, and employment rights (P); resource management (R); overseas engagement and ultra-national recognition (O); finance (FI); and transportation (T). The resulting acronym is PROFIT. PROFIT economies therefore differ from their MIRAB counterparts by being more interested in a shrewd immigration and cyclical migration policy; engaging in tough external negotiations concerning the use of local mineral, natural, political, environmental, and other 'imaginative' resources; securing and controlling viable (possibly subsidized) means of transportation; and luring foreign direct investment via low tax and other attractive finance regimes. They flex their jurisdictional powers to affect the international flows of financial and human capital, cargo, and tourism (Baldacchino 2006, 2010b).

Both the MIRAB and PROFIT models constitute approaches towards tapping externally generated wealth that goes beyond agricultural, manufacturing, industrialization, and commodity production strategies. Both are as likely to exhibit 'bureaucratic dominance' (Watters 1987: 50), given structural diseconomies of scale. And both are likely to depend substantially on 'rent income' which accrues by virtue of identity and location (Bertram and Watters 1985: 510). The one key difference between MIRAB and PROFIT lies in the priority given to substantive as against procedural interests. The first – when successful – is an end in itself; the second is a means to a further end. The first relegates the MIRAB territory to a regime of subsidy, of 'aid with dignity' (Connell 1998), of consumer-led growth without development, of seeking the responsibility for economic benefits in exogenous, extraterritorial policy fora. The second – when successful – is a jurisdictional or constitutional tool, an endogenous instrument for public policy which local 'governing wits' (Warrington 1998: 105) can usually transform into economic prosperity. Attitude matters. Likely island candidates to be lauded for the (thus far) successful use of the PROFIT approach would include both small island states (which have graduated beyond SIDS) and SNIJs: Åland, Aruba, Bermuda, Barbados, Cyprus, Malta, Mauritius, and the Seychelles.[4]

Dyadic, mainland–island relations: what's in it for the island?

Whether dealing with SIDS or small, non-independent polities that have considerable degrees of autonomy and self-determination (SNIJs), what I hold to be crucial is the flexing of sovereignty, understood as domestic jurisdictional power, for strategic gain and leverage.

This is a 'game' that can be played with very different intentions in mind. Each set of actors would have its dynamics nested in a particular configuration of geography, history, culture, and politics. Moreover, the contested jurisdictional terrain would appear differently, depending on the perspective of either party. Nevertheless, one can hypothesize that each set of such actors is likely to consist of two unequal players: a smaller, less powerful, less populated entity and a larger, stronger, more populated entity. The stage is set for the deployment of some 'imaginative geographies' (Saïd 1979).

For the smaller player, the purpose of extra-territorial deals would mainly be to secure, for example, pecuniary gain, military protection, currency stability, and welfare supports via the drawing of rent and other surpluses from other jurisdictions directly, or from the citizens thereof (Fabri and Baldacchino 1999: 48; Palan 1998: 630; 2002: 154; 2003: 59; Poirine, this volume). Also important is access to diplomatic channels via direct international representation (Gad, this volume) and access to the labour markets and citizenship rights of larger richer states (particularly Oostindie, and Muller, this volume). For those considering or boasting an offshore finance or electronic gam(bl)ing industry, extra-territorial links allow (at least a semblance of) international oversight and regulatory supervision (Maurer, this volume). Autonomous governments 'choose' to use some of their sovereignty-derived regulatory powers in order to encourage non-local transnational actors – be they individuals, corporations, or other governments – to make use of, invest in, or simply to transfer funds to their own regulatory environment (Baldacchino 2012b; Hudson 2000: 270; Maurer, and Vlcek, this volume). The smaller faction, of course, never completely relinquishes the potential resort to the metropole, if and when dire straits (e.g. budgetary shortfalls, economic recessions, environmental disasters, over-population, labour surpluses, or labour shortages) so determine or suggest. No wonder, therefore, that few of these smaller territories have struggled *for* independence; most have waged intense diplomatic struggles to maintain or extend benign colonial links with their overseas *patron*, at times going so far – as demonstrated by Mayotte in a 2009 referendum – as to press for integration, the very antithesis of sovereignty (France 2011; Muller, this volume). Various small states and territories today may not have just deployed but actually traded in their sovereignty, or part thereof, in exchange for economic largesse by exploiting this limbo granted by peripherality. Palan (2002: 172) argues that such polities have gone so far as to have prostituted their sovereign rights.

Non-sovereign, sub-national units may exercise their own right and ability to make laws – which, granted, *may* have been devolved or bestowed formally or constitutionally by sovereign states – in order to perform this task. Many 'dependencies' of sovereign states have resorted to their own 'actorness' (e.g. Vlcek 2008: 3) to develop strategy games precisely because they *can* do so given that they have the right to make their own laws within their territories: a crucial attribute of sovereignty that can also be claimed by, or accorded to, such subnational non-independent units (Palan 2003: 21). These candidates may have actually perfected the skill to a higher level, since their own, often fuzzy and ambiguous, political status allows them to exploit more nimbly, selectively, and securely the spaces afforded by going after rents, or 'jurisdictional shopping', for other purposes. Many of these places embody the broad personalities of federal or confederal cultures: a combination of self-rule and shared rule; of 'leave us alone' along with 'let us in' on major decisions affecting the national or collective whole (Duchacek 1986: 296).

Small sub-national jurisdictions have managed to extract concessions, either *within* the ambit of a larger, sovereign state and/or (typically in alliance with their patron state) within the ambit of a confederate super-state such as the EU. Key areas where such unequal arrangements have been secured to date include citizenship rights (with associated rights of residency, property purchase, and work permit – Oostindie, and Poirine, this volume); indigenous self-government (Brown, and Gad, this volume); paradiplomacy (Maurer, Vlcek, Brown, Poirine, and Gad, this volume); and economic sovereignty. All four areas question the strict definition of sovereignty and its imputed exclusive powers and obligations: regarding single citizenship; equal rights for all citizens; the rights of international representation; and local government transactions, respectively.

The view from the larger, richer, patron is markedly different. From there, small sovereign states or autonomous sub-units within the purview of the state could simply be seen as troublesome upstarts, to be suffered (Oostindie, this volume) and perhaps occasionally appeased (Gad, this volume). They could also be seen as objects of design, however; regulatory spaces that can be crafted and deliberately engineered by central governments (or their elites), eager to exploit these spaces as distinctly (and preferably discreetly) 'managed' zones for economic, commercial, military, or security-related activities in a globalized economy (Palan, and Muller, this volume) – perhaps to the chagrin or despair of any local inhabitants. Small jurisdictions, often islands surrounded by large swathes of ocean territory which they can hardly patrol or exploit, also make ripe and willing targets for soft and 'politically correct' imperialism.

Thus, from the perspective of small island territories, there are very plausible reasons to aspire to an 'arms' length' relationship with a larger, benevolent 'mainland' patron. McElroy and Mahoney (2000) explain how the smaller players in these unequal dyads derive substantial economic advantages from the arrangement. These include free trade with, and export preference from, the parent country; social welfare assistance; ready access to external capital through special tax concessions; access to external labour markets through migration; aid-financed infrastructure and communications; higher quality health and educational systems; natural disaster relief; and provision of costly external defence. Autonomy without sovereignty may also facilitate tourism development because of easier terms of access and security.

Meanwhile, the rationale for these metropole–island arrangements is scarcely one-sided. The logic for 'mainland–island relations' becomes clearer when seen in the context of states requiring unique offshore spaces outside the straitjacket of the increasingly restrictive, 'level-playing field' rules of international law, human rights, and free trade among sovereign states in the contemporary neo-liberal age. Islands provide bounded spaces for the emergence of ingenious new species of asymmetrical economics and governance practices. The pattern repeats itself over and over again, where typically large states make creative use of their small, far-flung, and remote island jurisdictions to facilitate activities that would be simply anathema on home ground. Being entrepreneurial about sovereignty is a task not restricted to the world's small and micro polities (Baldacchino 2010).

Sovereignty in flux

The relationships among most mainland–island dyads are far from smooth or settled. Asymmetrical federalism is by definition perpetually subject to negotiation. In 2005, Jeju Island became a 'special administrative province' of South Korea, enjoying even more autonomous powers (Chosun Ilbo 2005), while the Bermuda Independence Commission visited London for high-level talks (Sanders 2005). In 2006, Tokelau rejected a move to independence in free association with New Zealand following a referendum (Scoop Independent News 2006). A non-binding referendum on Greenland's extended autonomy was held in 2008 and was approved by 75 per cent of voters. And Mayotte, the French overseas territory, became the 101st *département* of France (and its 5th *département d'outre-mer*) on 29 March 2011 following a 2009 referendum approved by over 95 per cent of voters (Muller, this volume).

The fluidity of the mainland–island arrangement is enhanced precisely because it is both federal (and thus involves multilevel governance, which presents competing claims for legitimacy and policy competence) and asymmetrical (where the striking of idiosyncratic or special deals and outcomes is often preferred). The relationship is liable to perpetual shifts, nuances, and changes; and 'full sovereignty' (whatever that phrase may imply in the twenty-first century) remains a viable option and vision, should it be impossible to work out decent terms for a subnational solution. Suitable examples of this critically fluid nature of governance would include Bougainville (Ghai and Regan 2009), with the recent changing nature of that island's status towards autonomy either within, or possibly independent from, Papua New Guinea. In such and similar cases, the issue of renegotiation may be fractious: the terms of the relationship may be the subject of civil strife, guerrilla movements, or other forms of internal warfare, diplomatic tension and independence leaning political parties (Baldacchino and Hepburn 2012). These may take the guise of 'infra-nationalism', which is a political and institutional structure beyond the constitution, a *de facto* island (or sub-island) state apparatus existing in a taunting defiance of the main state, with which relations are not harmonious. This has also occurred in recent decades in such diverse places as Aceh, Corsica, Cyprus, Irian Jaya, Mindanao, New Caledonia, and Sri Lanka (Weiler 1991).

This state of variability is often represented in an expression of an ambivalent, 'love–hate' nationalism. The smaller (island) player is often demonstrably proud of its own (sub?-)national identity, captured also by explicitly showcased cultural differences (in language, religion, history, ethnic composition, political ideology, and other identity symbols such as flags, anthems, currency, monuments, and emblems) from its larger player. Yet it may refer to a benign, special relationship with the larger player for the purpose of defending its prized autonomy and self-determination (from the threat of international piracy, general insecurity, or irredentist neighbouring states; Muller, this volume). If the relationship lies in discord, local political movements and the public at large are likely to see, and play upon, the image of the larger player in a colonial or imperialist light, whether as blissfully ignoring its legitimate appeals; or (worse), unfairly and insensitively pushing its weight around, swamping their fundamental rights to self-determination. The larger player, in contrast, would tend to react (if at all) by invoking obligations towards order, national equity and fairness, social cohesion, and regional stability as well as against renegade, destabilizing, and quirky politics. The situation 'on the ground' is usually far more complex, with different political parties, social classes, and other social groupings on the island, on the mainland, elsewhere (as in interested regional and international powers), and in between (the influential island diaspora and the expatriate island community), championing and expressing their preference for one or more of what could be a bewildering range of relational solutions (e.g. Ramos and Rivera 2001: 1–21).

Agitating for full sovereign status

What becomes evident from these dynamics is that sub-national units can target specific functions and powers which they then seek to secure: *de facto*, *de jure*, or any which way in between. While always dependent on context, all of the functions and powers typically associated with sovereignty can present themselves for negotiation. But this is not to neglect the drive and achievement of full independence from the equation. Admittedly, the drive by former colonies pressing for, and achieving, full sovereignty has stalled somewhat since Brunei Darussalam achieved its independence in 1984. Were it not for Kosovo, Montenegro, and East Timor, along with the three special cases of the Federated States of Micronesia, Marshall Islands, and Palau, the latest decades would have seen no examples of newly independent small states. And yet there is no shortage of potential candidates: the UN Special Committee on Decolonization still monitors 16 'non self-governing territories' (of which 14 are islands). Meanwhile, various other territories have decided that they would rather retain or enhance some aspects of autonomy while remaining or seeking integration with their colonial power rather than seek to secede from it, at times after holding independence referenda.

It may sound ironic that such an autonomy arrangement is also more likely to be gained and secured where there are movements or political parties agitating for full independence in these sub-national territories. Quebec has had two dramatic 'independence referenda' (in 1980 and 1995) and is now (November 2012) again run by a sovereigntist (albert minority) government. In some cases, territories are bracing for eventual independence referenda (Bougainville, New Caledonia, Scotland) or may entertain fresh referenda for the same purpose (Tokelau, Nevis). There are independence-leaning parties or movements in places like Åland, Bermuda, Bougainville, Corsica, the Balearics/Catalonia and the Basque Country (Spain), Faroes, French Polynesia, Greenland, Guam, Hawai'i, Nevis, New Caledonia, Okinawa/Ryukyus, Padania (Northern Italy), Puerto Rico, Québec, Rodrigues (Mauritius), Sardinia, Scotland, Sicily, Taiwan, Tobago, Wales, and Zanzibar.

Such initiatives may appear surprising at a time when there are clear economic and security advantages in being associated with a larger, richer, metropolitan patron. For all its benefits, sovereignty may prove powerless in stemming fiscal collapse: recent fiscal crises in Iceland, Ireland and Greece offer cases in point. Strong arguments – cultural, fiscal, economic, and political – in favour of full independence remain. Many can arise out of sheer frustration with existing autonomy arrangements. The presence and activities of independence-leaning political parties and movements can also contribute significantly to the successful negotiation and securing of even more generous measures of autonomy from (sometimes hesitant, sometimes accommodating, otherwise indifferent) metropolitan powers. Peoples with a distinct history and culture, often a distinct language – and often psychologically facilitated by islandness – can claim an equally distinct ethnic/national identity, which then develops into what are seen as rightful claims towards self-government or decolonization, as supported by the international community. This awareness and mobilization can be facilitated by the existence of autonomy arrangements which enable the territory to flex its capacity and potential for even more self-government.

Yet for the very same reasons, identifiable ethnic, cultural, or linguistic minorities *within* sub-national units can become concerned with and militate against movements towards secession. The aboriginal peoples of Northern Québec (primarily the Cree and Inuit) vehemently resisted the possibility of having the province break away from Canada, organizing their own referenda on independence (and heavily rejecting the independence option). The Shetland Islands are not supportive of an independent Scotland; the Marquesas are not keen on an independent French Polynesia; and the citizens of the island of Suðuroy are the least keen on an independent Faroes (Baldacchino and Hepburn 2012). The presumed divisibility of potential new states can become a major political issue in itself, liable to be exploited by the federalist camp. Unlike small and single island territories, sprawling archipelagos and large continental masses are more likely to harbour diverging sentiments and views on full independence. Such episodes have been played out in places like Anguilla (see above), Mayotte (Muller, this volume), and Tuvalu (which refused independence as part of larger Kiribati and secured its own independence) (McIntyre 2012).

A wealth of diversity

The assorted and dynamic examples of federal 'self-rule' and 'shared-rule' arrangements between SNIJs and their metropoles, as described above, are a continuing testament to the rich governance systems, with all their anomalies and asymmetry, remaining after the retraction of the Western empires. Moreover, these delicate arrangements between metropoles and their maritime dependencies have in turn been absorbed and 'grandfathered' at the supranational level within the EU. In their vast majority, then, these examples from the world's sub-national (mainly island) jurisdictions show a remarkable pattern of mutual accommodation and convenience between large (often metropolitan) states and their offshore islands. It is usually not in the interests of either party to push these islands into straightforward sovereignty, as was so often the case in the decades immediately following the Second World War, even if such a path was realistically feasible. Now, both seem to prefer a negotiated bilateral partnership that can take its place within the highly variegated 'federal' landscape of governance within the modern world. 'Sovereignty association' appears to be a more savoury and palatable moniker than stark sovereignty (e.g. Béland and Lecours 2006; Lecours 2011). Of course, the metropolitan state may also harbour an evident embarrassment over these remnants of empire and the continuing burden that they may present.

The patterns and motivations on each side for current non-sovereign constitutional arrangements are messy and do not always move in the same direction or remain constant from one case to the next. In any event, the contemporary global political and legal geometry is more complex than it has ever been and obliges the rethinking of older notions of sovereignty and the international state system. Upholding and distinguishing strict 'sovereign' from 'non-sovereign' entities in international practice was never consistently followed in the past and is even less tenable today, as power is increasingly pooled among and across states and reconfigured and redistributed from and within national territories. This practical spirit increasingly animates the arrangements of many offshore islands with their metropolitan partners, where small sovereign states would seek special deals that allow transfers of sufficient rentier income from richer nations; while non-sovereign island jurisdictions would wish to preserve, or even enhance, their asymmetrical status and autonomous powers rather than take the risk of joining the ranks of sovereign states themselves. The latter position, of course, appears somewhat timid and self-defeating from the perspective of those who grew up in the heady days of colonial emancipation following the Second World War; but it is no longer so. Opting for non-sovereign jurisdictional status is a highly rational, strategic choice that can result in substantial net material and security gains for the smaller jurisdiction. Such judgements should not be lightly or ideologically dismissed, particularly at a time when security concerns are real and when sovereignty for most islands has largely failed to deliver relatively high levels of economic prosperity (McElroy and Parry 2012). Being a sub-national island jurisdiction typically bestows a solid safety net supported by a metropolitan patron while granting enough discretion to safeguard national identity, local culture, and the general exercise of local power. McElroy and Pearce (2006) refer to a 'superior level of performance' by sub-national island jurisdictions. Meanwhile, the metropolitan player can exercise 'soft imperialism' (which does not typically raise eyebrows among the members of the UN Committee on Decolonization), keep a watchful eye for potentially lucrative geostrategic military or economic rents, and lavish its munificence upon its small island beneficiaries.

Conclusion: ignoring the siren call

Contemporary island territories would therefore appear wise to ignore the siren call of sovereignty *à la vingtième siècle* and cut their arrangements more pragmatically and creatively. Such pragmatism manifests itself clearly, for example, in the muddy but lucrative waters of paradiplomacy, no longer the exclusive preserve of sovereign states (Bartmann 2009; Kelman *et al.* 2009). There are obviously many circumstances where sovereignty will prove itself to be the most logical or compelling course of action: such would explain the independence of East Timor, Montenegro, and Kosovo (e.g. Bahcheli *et al.* 2004) and Southern Sudan in 2011. And there are many examples of (often small) island sovereign states succeeding beyond all expectations and where the tools of sovereignty have been a vital element in this success. A good case study would be Iceland; but even here, as Kristinsson (2000) argues, the continued utility of undiminished sovereignty together with non-membership of the EU will depend on circumstances. Surely this is the point: the appropriate political architecture and jurisdictional status for any small island polity can preferably only be known after careful review of all its options – current and likely in the foreseeable future – undertaken in a clear-sighted and level-headed spirit (e.g. Le Rendu 2004). For our purposes, there certainly appears to be every reason to expect small islands making this kind of review to continue to opt for contoured, negotiated, constitutional arrangements in the future (e.g. Dodds 2002), and weighing carefully how and what kind of sovereignty would benefit or hinder such a quest. In the context of Europe, potential EU membership – a possibility which only exists for overseas territories via a European metropole state – would be an important consideration in this context.

I started this chapter with a reference to the Dutch Antilles; it appears fitting to end with another episode drawn from the same region. When the Dutch colony of Suriname was making preparations to achieve full independence in 1975, the Surinamese premier, Henck Arron, contacted his counterpart in the Dutch Antilles, Juancho Evertsz, and asked him whether he would lead his islanders to join Suriname into full sovereignty. The blunt answer: 'If you allow yourself to be hung, it does not mean that I will do the same' (quoted in Hoefte and Oostindie 1991: 75). So far, at least, history has proved Evertsz right.

Notes

1 Somalia, a widely recognized sovereign state, independent since 1960, with a population of over 9 million and a seat in the UN, has very much been a failed state since its 1991 implosion. Meanwhile, Somaliland (population 3.5 million), an as yet undeclared independent state, effectively broken away from Somalia in 1991 and has been administering itself and democratizing since (Srebrnik 2003; The Economist 2005). It 'actually feels like a proper country' (The Economist 2010).

2 For many years, the cut-off point for 'small states' was a population of 1 million; this was raised to 1.5 million and later to 2 million due to the growing populations in small African states such as Botswana, Lesotho, Mauritius, Namibia, and Swaziland.

3 Consolidated versions of the Treaty on European Union and the Treaty on the Functioning of the EU, http://eur-lex.europa.eu/LexUriServ/LexUriServ.do?uri=OJ:C:2010:083: FULL:EN:PDF.

4 A third cluster of variables that may explain small state economic strategy posits tourism as the key industry. Tourism comes with 'genuine comparative advantages' for many small, and especially island, states (Connell 1991: 265). Tourism may help graduate jurisdictions out of a MIRAB mould; however, tourism is in itself a rent-accruing activity bearing its own 'geo-strategic' (that is sun, sea, sand – and sex?) services,

which hardly vest jurisdictional muscle in the provider; the industry remains fickle and vulnerable, mainly to economic uncertainty and local and regional political instability. Small island tourism economies (SITEs) were originally proposed as a distinct, small state development syndrome (McElroy 2006), but have been re-labelled more recently as a subspecies of the PROFIT syndrome (Oberst and McElroy 2007; Parry and McElroy 2009).

References

Alford, J. (1984) 'Security dilemmas of small states', *The Round Table: Commonwealth Journal of International Affairs*, 73: 377–82.

Allahar, A. (2005) 'Identity and erasure: finding the elusive Caribbean', *Revista Europea de Estudios Latinoamericanos y del Caribe*, 79: 125–34.

Baehr, P.R. (1975) 'Small states: a tool for analysis', *World Politics*, 27: 456–66.

Bahcheli, T., Bartmann, B. and Srebrnik, H.F. (eds) (2004) *De Facto States: The Quest for Sovereignty*. London: Taylor & Francis.

Baker Fox, A. (1959) *The Power of Small States: Diplomacy in World War II*. Chicago IL: University of Chicago Press.

Baldacchino, G. (2005) 'The contribution of social capital to economic growth: lessons from island jurisdictions', *The Round Table: Commonwealth Journal of International Affairs*, 94: 35–50.

Baldacchino, G. (2006) 'Innovative development strategies from non-sovereign island jurisdictions: a global review of economic policy and governance practices', *World Development*, 34: 852–67.

Baldacchino, G. (2009) 'Governance in small places: the unleashing of asymmetrical federalism', in G. Baldacchino, R. Greenwood, and L. Felt (eds) *Remote Control: Governance Lessons for and from Small, Insular and Remote Regions*. St John's NL: Memorial University of Newfoundland: ISER Press.

Baldacchino, G. (2010) *Island Enclaves: Offshoring, Creative Governance and Subnational Island Jurisdictions*. Montreal, Canada: McGill-Queen's University Press.

Baldacchino, G. (2011) 'Surfers of the ocean waves: change management, inter-sectoral migration and the economic development of small island states', *Asia Pacific Viewpoint*, 52: 236–46.

Baldacchino, G. (2012a) 'Islands and despots', *Commonwealth and Comparative Politics*, 50: 103–20.

Baldacchino, G. (2012b) 'Governmentality is all the rage: the strategy games of small jurisdictions', *The Round Table: Commonwealth Journal of International Affairs*, 101: 235–51.

Baldacchino, G. and Bertram, G. (2009) 'The beak of the finch: insights into the economic development of small, often island, economies', *The Round Table: Commonwealth Journal of International Affairs*, 98: 141–60.

Baldacchino, G. and Hepburn, E. (eds) (2012) 'Island independence movements and parties', special issue, *Commonwealth and Comparative Politics*, 50(4), December.

Baldacchino, G. and Milne, D. (2006) 'Exploring sub-national island jurisdictions', *The Round Table: Commonwealth Journal of International Affairs*, 95: 487–502.

Bartmann, B. (2007) 'War and security' in G. Baldacchino (ed.) *A World of Islands: An Island Studies Reader*. Charlottetown, Canada and Luqa, Malta: Institute of Island Studies, University of Prince Edward Island and Agenda Academic, pp. 295–322.

Bartmann, B. (2009) 'In or out: sub-national island jurisdictions and the antechamber of para-diplomacy', in G. Baldacchino and D. Milne (eds) *The Case for Non-Sovereignty: Lessons from Sub-National Island Jurisdictions*, London: Routledge.

Béland and Lecours, A. (2006) 'Sub-state nationalism and the welfare state: Québec and Canadian federalism', *Nations and Nationalism*, 12: 77–96.

Berreman, G. (1978) 'Scale and social relations', *Current Anthropology*, 19: 225–245.

Bertram, G. (1993) 'Sustainability, aid and material welfare in the small South Pacific island economies: 1900–1990', *World Development*, 21: 247–58.

Bertram, G. (1999) 'The MIRAB model: twelve years on', *Contemporary Pacific*, 11: 105–38.

Bertram, G. (2006) 'Introduction: the MIRAB model in the 21st century', in G. Bertram (ed.) *Asia Pacific Viewpoint*, 47: 1–13.

Bertram, G. and Watters, R.F. (1985) 'The MIRAB economy in South Pacific microstates', *Pacific Viewpoint*, 26: 497–519.

Bertram, G. and Watters, R.F. (1986) 'The MIRAB process: earlier analysis in context', *Pacific Viewpoint*, 27: 47–59.

Blazic-Metzner, B. and Hughes, H. (1982) 'Growth experience of small economies', in B. Jalan (ed.) *Problems and Policies in Small Economies*. London: Croom Helm.

Bray, M. (1987) 'Small countries in international development', Review Article, *Journal of Development Studies*, 23: 295–300.

Bray, M. and Packer, S. (1993) *Education in Small States: Concepts, Challenges and Strategies*. Oxford: Pergamon.

Briguglio, L. (1995) 'Small island developing states and their vulnerabilities', *World Development*, 23: 1615–32.

Briguglio, L. and Kisanga, E.J. (eds) (2004) *Economic Vulnerability and Resilience of Small States*, Malta: Formatek.

Briguglio, L., Cordina, G. and Kisanga, E.J. (eds) (2006) *Building the Economic Resilience of Small States*, Malta and London: Islands and Small States Institute and Commonwealth Secretariat.

Bune, P. (1987) 'Vulnerability of small states: the case of the South Pacific region and Fiji', *Courier* (UNESCO), 104: 85–7.

Cali, M., Razzaque, M. and Te Velde, D.W. (2011) *Effectiveness of Aid for Trade in Small and Vulnerable Economies*, Economic Paper No. 91, London: Commonwealth Secretariat.

Chamberlain, M.E. (1985) *Decolonization: The Fall of the European Empires*. Oxford: Basil Blackwell.

Charles. E. (1997) *A Future for Small States: Overcoming Vulnerability*. London: Commonwealth Secretariat.

Chiew, J. (1993) 'Smallness of scale: obstacle or opportunity? Reframing the issue of scale', in K.M. Lillis (ed.) *Policy, Planning and Management of Education in Small States*. Paris: International Institute for Educational Planning, UNESCO.

Chosun Ilbo (2005) 'Jeju Island to become special autonomous province'. Online. Available at: http://english.chosun.com/site/data/html_dir/2005/05/22/2005052261011.html (accessed 22 March 2011).

CIA (2011) *CIA World Factbook*. Online. Available at: www.cia.gov/library/publications/download (accessed 22 March 2011).

Commonwealth Consultative Group (1985) *Vulnerability: Small States in the Global Society*, London: Commonwealth Secretariat.

Commonwealth Secretariat/World Bank (2000) *Small States: Meeting Challenges in the Global Economy*, London and New York: Commonwealth Secretariat/World Bank,

Joint Task Force on Small States. Final report, mimeo. March. Online. Available at: www.thecommonwealth.org/Shared_ASP_Files/UploadedFiles/03D192ea-ccf2-4fa2-96b3-f7da64ad245b_taskforcereport.pdf (accessed 22 February 2011).

Connell, J. (1988) *Sovereignty and Survival: Island Microstates in the Third World*, Research Monograph, 3, Sydney: University of Sydney, Department of Geography.

Connell, J. (1991) 'Island microstates: the mirage of development', *Contemporary Pacific*, 3: 251–87.

Crowards, T. (2002) 'Defining the category of "small" states', *Journal of International Development*, 14: 143–79.

Diggines, C. (1985) 'The problems of small states', *The Round Table: Commonwealth Journal of International Affairs*, 74: 191–205.

Dodds, K. (2002) *Pink Ice: Britain and the South Atlantic Empire*, London: I B Tauris.

Dolman, A.J. (1985) 'Paradise lost? The past performance and future prospects of small island developing countries', in E.C. Dommen and P.L. Hein (eds) *States, Microstates and Islands*, London: Croom Helm.

Dommen, E.C. (ed.) (1980) 'Islands', *World Development*, special issue, 8: 929–1059.

Doumenge, F. (1985) 'The viability of small inter-tropical islands', in E.C. Dommen and P.L. Hein (eds) *States, Microstates and Islands*. London: Croom Helm.

Duchacek, I.D. (1986) *The Territorial Dimension of Politics: Within, Among and Across Nations*, London: Westview Press.

East, M. (1973) 'Size and foreign policy behaviour: a test of two models', *World Politics*, 25: 556–76.

Easterly, W. and Kraay, A.C. (2000) 'Small states, small problems? income, growth and volatility in small states', *World Development*, 28: 2013–27.

The Economist (2005) 'Trying to behave like a proper state', 29 September. Online. Available at: www.economist.com/node/4466050 (accessed 4 September 2012).

The Economist (2010) 'Not so failing', 1 July. Online. Available at: www.economist.com/node/16488840 (accessed 4 September 2012).

Fabri, D. and Baldacchino, G. (1999) 'The Malta Financial Services Centre: a study in microstate dependency management?', in M.P. Hampton and J.P. Abbott (eds) *Offshore Finance Centres and Tax Havens: The Rise of Global Capital*, Basingstoke: Macmillan.

Fleming, E. (2002) 'Strategic paths to competitiveness in agriculture in South Pacific island nations', Geneva: UNCTAD. Online. Available at: http://r0.unctad.org/infocomm/diversification/nadi/study_ver2.PDF (accessed 22 February 2011).

France (2011) 'On 31 March 2011, the "lagoon island" of Mayotte will officially become France's 5th overseas department and the 101st French department'. Online. Available at: www.france.fr/en/knowing/geography/overseas-departments-and-territories/article/mayotte-becomes-101st-french-department (accessed 22 March 2011).

Gayle, D.J. (1986) *The Small Developing State: Comparing Political Economics in Costa Rica, Singapore and Jamaica*, Aldershot: Gower.

Ghai, Y.P. and Regan, A.J. (2009) 'Unitary state, devolution, autonomy, secession: state building and nation building in Bougainville, Papua New Guinea', in G. Baldacchino and D. Milne (eds) *The Case for Non-Sovereignty: Lessons from Sub-National Island Jurisdictions*, London: Routledge.

Gunter, M. (1977) 'What happened to the United Nations ministate problem?', *The American Journal of International Law*, 71: 110–24.

Harbert, J.R. (1976) 'The behaviour of the ministates in the United Nations, 1971–1972', *International Organisation*, 30: 109–27.

Harden, S. (ed.) (1985) *Small Is Dangerous: Micro-States in a Macro-World*, London: Frances Pinter.

Hein, P.L. (2004) 'Small island developing states: origin of the category and definitional issues', in *Is Special Treatment of Small Island Developing States Possible?* Geneva and New York: UNCTAD.

Hoefte, R. and Oostindie, G. (1989) 'Upside-down decolonization', *Hemisphere*, 1: 28–31.

Hoefte, R. and Oostindie, G. (1991) 'The Netherlands and the Dutch Caribbean: dilemmas of decolonisation', in P.K. Sutton (ed.) *Europe and the Caribbean*, London: Macmillan.

Houbert, J. (1986) 'Decolonizing without disengaging: France in the Indian Ocean', *The Round Table: Commonwealth Journal of International Affairs*, 75: 145–66.

Hudson, A.C. (2000) 'Offshoreness, globalization and sovereignty: a post-modern geo-political economy?', *Transactions of the Institute of British Geographers*, 25: 269–83.

Ingebritsen, C. (2006) 'Conclusion: learning from Lilliput', in C. Ingebritsen, I. Neumann, G. Stöhl, and J. Beyer (eds) *Small States in International Relations*. Seattle, WA and Reykjavik, Iceland: University of Washington Press and University of Iceland Press.

Kaminarides, J., Briguglio, L. and Hoogendonk, H.N. (eds) (1989) *The Economic Development of Small Countries: Problems, Strategies and Policies*, Delft: Eburon.

Kelman, I., Davies, M., Mitchell, T., Orr, I. and Conrich, B. (2009) 'Island disaster paradiplomacy in the Commonwealth', in G. Baldacchino and D. Milne (eds) *The Case for Non-Sovereignty: Lessons from Sub-National Island Jurisdictions*, London: Routledge.

Keohane, R. (1969) 'Lilliputians' dilemmas: small states in international politics', *International Organization*, 23: 291–310.

Kerr, S.A. (2005) 'What is small island sustainable development about?', *Ocean and Coastal Management*, 48: 503–24.

Knox, A.D. (1967) 'Some economic problems of small countries', in B. Benedict (ed.) *Problems of Smaller Territories.* London: Athlone Press.

Kohr, L. (1973) *Development without Aid: The Translucent Society*, Swansea: Christopher Davies.

Krasner, S.D. (2001) 'Problematic sovereignty', in S.D. Krasner (ed.) *Problematic Sovereignty: Contested Rules and Political Possibilities*, New York: Columbia University Press.

Kristinsson, G.H. (2000) 'From home rule to sovereignty: the case of Iceland', in G. Baldacchino and D. Milne (eds) *Lessons from the Political Economy of Small Islands: The Resourcefulness of Jurisdiction*, Basingstoke: Macmillan.

Kuznets, S. (1960) 'Economic growth of small nations', in E.A.G. Robinson (ed.) *The Economic Consequences of the Size of Nations*, London: Macmillan.

Lake, D.A. (2003) 'The new sovereignty in international relations', *International Studies Review*, 5: 303–23.

Le Rendu, L. (2004) *Jersey: Independent Dependency? The Survival of a Microstate*, London: Ex Libris Press.

Lecours, A. (2011) 'Sub-state nationalism in the Western World: Explaining continued appeal', *Ethnopolitics*, 11: 1–19.

Levine, S. and Roberts, N.S. (2005) 'The constitutional structures and electoral systems of Pacific island states', *Commonwealth and Comparative Politics*, 43: 276–95.

Lewis, P. (2002) *Surviving Small Size: Regional Integration in Caribbean Ministates*, Kingston, Jamaica: UWI Press.

Lyon, P. (ed.) (1985) *Small States and the Commonwealth*, London: Butterworth.

Markovich, V. and Annandale, D. (2000) 'Sinking without a life jacket? Sea level rise and the position of small island states in international law', *Asia Pacific Journal of Environmental Law*, 5: 135–55.

Max-Neef, M.A. (1982) *From the Outside Looking In: Experiences in Barefoot Economics*, Uppsala: Dag Hammerskjöld Foundation.

McElroy, J.L. (2006) 'Small island tourist economies across the lifecycle', *Asia Pacific Viewpoint*, 47: 61–77.

McElroy, J.L. and Mahoney, M. (2000) 'The propensity for political dependence in island microstates', *INSULA: International Journal of Island Affairs*, 9: 32–5.

McElroy, J.L. and Morris, L. (2002) 'African island development experiences: a cluster of models', *Bank of Valletta Review* (Malta), 26: 38–57.

McElroy, J.L. and Parry, C.E. (2012) 'The long term propensity for political affiliation in island microstates', *Commonwealth and Comparative Politics*, 50: forthcoming.

McElroy, J.L. and Pearce, K.B. (2006) 'The advantages of political affiliation: dependent and independent small island profiles', *The Round Table: Commonwealth Journal of International Affairs*, 95: 529–40.

McElroy, J.L. and Sandborn, K. (2005) 'The propensity for dependence in small Caribbean and Pacific islands', *Bank of Valletta Review* (Malta), 31: 1–16.

McIntyre, D.W. (2012) 'The partition of the Gilbert and Ellice Islands', *Island Studies Journal*, 7: 135–46.

McKibben E.L. (1990) 'The political relationship between the United States and Pacific island entities: the path to self-government in the Northern Mariana Islands, Palau and Guam', *Harvard International Law Journal*, 31: 257–64.

McRobie, G. (1981) *Small is Possible*, London: Cape.

Middleton, J. (2005) 'Picking up the pieces on Pitcairn Island', *New Zealand Herald*, 22 March. Online. Available at: www.nzherald.co.nz/section/story.cfm?c_id=2andobjectid=10116489 (accessed 24 September 2012).

Nath, S., Roberts, J.L. and Madhoo, Y.T. (eds) (2011) *Saving Small Island Developing States: Environmental and Natural Resource Challenges*, London: Commonwealth Secretariat.

Oberst, A. and McElroy, J.L. (2007) 'Contrasting socio-economic and demographic profiles of two, small island, economic species: MIRAB versus PROFIT/SITE', *Island Studies Journal*, 2: 164–76.

Oostindie, G. and Klinkers, I. (2003) *Decolonizing the Caribbean: Dutch Policies in a Comparative Perspective*, Amsterdam: Amsterdam University Press.

Palan, R. (1998) 'Trying to have your cake and eating it: how and why the state system has created offshore', *International Studies Quarterly*, 42: 625–43.

Palan, R. (2002) 'Tax havens and the commercialization of state sovereignty', *International Organization*, 56: 151–76.

Palan, R. (2003) *The Offshore World: Sovereign Markets, Virtual Places and Nomad Millionaires*, Ithaca, NY: Cornell University Press.

Parry, C.E. and McElroy, J.L. (2009) 'The supply determinants of small island tourist economies', *ARA: Journal of Tourism Research*, 3: 13–22.

Pirotta, G.A., Wettenhall, R. and Briguglio, L. (2001) 'Governance of small jurisdictions: guest editors' introduction', *Public Organization Review*, 1: 149–65.

Plischke, E. (1977) *Microstates in World Affairs: Policy Problems and Options*. Washington, DC: American Enterprise Institute for Public Policy Research.

Poirine, B. (1998) 'Should we hate or love MIRAB?', *Contemporary Pacific*, 10: 65–107.

Ramos, A.G. and Rivera, A.J. (eds) (2001) *Islands at the Crossroads: Politics in the Non-Independent Caribbean*, Kingston, Jamaica: Ian Randle.

Rapaport, J., Muteba, E. and Therattil, J.J. (1971) *Small States & Territories, Status and Problems*, United Nations Institute for Training and Research Study, New York: Arno Press.

Rothstein, R.L. (1966) 'Alignment, nonalignment, and small powers: 1945–1965', *International Organization*, 20: 397–418.

Rothstein, R.L. (1968) *Alliances and Small Powers*, Institute of War and Peace Studies of the School of International Affairs of Columbia University, New York: Columbia University Press.

Saïd, E. (1979) *Orientalism*, New York: Vintage.

Sanders, R. (2005) 'Bermuda: independence or not?', *Caribbean Net News*, 8 March. Online. Available at: www.caribbeannetnews.com/2005/03/08/sanders.shtml (accessed 22 February 2011).

Schumacher, E.F. (1973) *Small Is Beautiful: Economics as if People Mattered*, London: Blond and Briggs.

Scoop News (2006) 'Tokelau referendum does not produce two-thirds majority', Media release, New Zealand Government, 16 February. Online. Available at: www.scoop. co.nz/stories/PA0602/S00232.htm (accessed 22 February 2011).

Shaw, T.M. and Cooper, A.F. (eds) (2009) *The Diplomacies of Small States: Between Vulnerability and Resilience in the Global Political Economy*, Basingstoke: Palgrave Macmillan.

Skinner, J. (2006) 'Formal and informal relations on colonial Montserrat and Gibraltar', in J. Skinner and M. Hills (eds) *Managing Island Life: Social, Economic and Political Dimensions of Formality and Informality in Island Communities*, Dundee, Scotland: University of Abertay Press.

Srebrnik, H.F. (2003) 'Can Clans form Nations? Somaliland in the Making', in T. Bahcheli, B. Bartmann and H.F. Srebrnik (eds) *De Facto States: The Quest for Sovereignty*, London: Taylor and Francis.

Srebrnik, H.F. (2004) 'Small island nations and democratic values', *World Development*, 32: 329–42.

Srinivasan, T.N. (1986) 'The costs and benefits of being a small, remote, island, landlocked or ministate economy', *World Bank Research Observer*, 1: 205–18.

Sutton, P.K. (1987) 'Political Aspects', in C.G. Clarke and T. Payne (eds) *Politics, Security and Development in Small States*, London: Allen and Unwin.

Sutton, P.K. and Payne, A. (1993) 'Lilliput under threat: the security problems of small island and enclave developing states', *Political Studies*, 41: 579–93.

Thorhallsson, B. (2000) *The Role of Small States in the European Union*, Farnham: Ashgate.

Thucydides (1972[431BC]) *History of the Peloponnesian War*, Translated by Rex Warner, London: Penguin Classics.

Treadgold, M.L. (1999) 'Breaking out of the MIRAB mould: historical evidence from Norfolk island', *Asia Pacific Viewpoint*, 40: 235–49.

Trenwith, A. (2003) 'The empire strikes back: human rights and the Pitcairn proceedings', *Journal of South Pacific Law*, 17(2). Pacific Islands Legal Information Institute. Online. Available at: www.paclii.org/journals/jspl/042003Volume7Number2/EmpireStrikes. html (accessed 22 February 2011).

Trompf, G. (ed.) (1993) *Islands and Enclaves: Nationalisms and Separatist Pressures in Island and Littoral Contexts*, New Delhi: Sterling.

Vital, D. (1967) *The Inequality of States: A Study of the Small Power in International Relations*, Oxford: Oxford University Press.

Vlcek, W. (2008) 'Competitive or coercive? The experience of Caribbean offshore financial centres with global governance', *The Round Table: Commonwealth Journal of International Affairs*, 97: 439–52.

Wainhouse, D.W. (1964) *Remnants of Empire: The United Nations and the End of Colonialism*, New York: Harper & Row for the Council on Foreign Relations.

Warrington, E. (1998) 'Gulliver and Lilliput in a new world order: the impact of external relations on the domestic policies and institutions of micro-states', *Public Administration and Development*, 18: 101–05.

Watters, R.F. (1987) 'MIRAB societies and bureaucratic elites', in A. Hooper (ed.) *Class and Culture in the South Pacific*, Suva, Fiji Islands: Institute of Pacific Studies.

Watts, R.L. (2000) 'Islands in comparative constitutional perspective', in G. Baldacchino and D. Milne (eds) *Lessons from the Political Economy of Small Islands: The Resourcefulness of Jurisdiction*, Basingstoke: Macmillan.

Watts, R.L. (2008) 'Island jurisdictions in comparative constitutional perspective', in G. Baldacchino and D. Milne (eds) *The Case for Non-Sovereignty: Lessons from Sub-National Island Jurisdictions*, London: Routledge.

Weiler, J.H.H. (1991) 'The transformation of Europe', *Yale Law Journal*, 100: 2403–83.

Wood, D.P.J. (1967) 'The smaller territories: some political considerations', in B. Benedict (ed.) *Problems of Smaller Territories*, London: Athlone Press.

5 European Union

Facilitating the OCTs in Brussels

Ida Hannibal, Kristine Holst, Ulrik Pram Gad, and Rebecca Adler-Nissen

Exploring the relations between the European Union (EU), the Overseas Countries and Territories (OCTs), and the metropole member states, this chapter zooms in on the European corner of the triangle. More specifically, it investigates the sovereignty games played out on what we call 'the Brussels scene'. This 'scene' is a physical place: Brussels as the centre of the EU. Yet it is also a symbolic space for agency and interaction between the European Commission, member states and OCTs.

The EU–OCT association is currently up for renegotiation, and the European Commission has proposed reform that could fundamentally change the OCTs' relationships to the EU. Since the establishment of the European Community (EC) in 1957, the OCTs have belonged to a peculiar category bringing together remnants of European colonialism, entitling them to EU aid and benefits. During the last two decades, the OCTs have gradually gained a degree of subjectivity in Brussels by participating in meetings and discussions between the European Commission and the metropole member state. This subjectivity entails room for manoeuvre for the OCTs in order to act strategically and articulate their own views on the EU–OCT relationship. Until recently, whether or not the OCTs should also somehow pay back to the EU was not on the agenda. In 2008, however, the European Commission launched a Green Paper, *Future relations between the EU and the OCTs*, which marks a more strategic approach to the OCTs. This possibly signals the end of an era in which the OCTs underwent continued improvement in terms of their opportunities to act as players in Brussels. Since the Lisbon Treaty came into effect in 2009, the EU has been re-organizing its foreign policy apparatus and strengthening its strategic focus on its foreign policy. This may imply that the OCTs will be asked to serve as 'strategic outposts' for Europe, but it is yet to be seen *if* and *how* the OCTs will adapt to this situation.

In the following, we analyse the past, present, and future of the EU–OCT relationship using the three analytical strategies outlined in the Introduction to this book. The chapter proceeds with a section on the historical development of the OCTs' status as it has been institutionalized in the Treaty and the consecutive EU–OCT Association Decisions. Drawing on legal texts, official papers, and interviews, this *institutional* analysis shows how the OCT category includes a diverse group of islands, which never underwent the formal decolonization process, that is, they never acquired sovereignty. While opting neither for formal sovereignty nor full integration into the metropole member state, the OCTs had their own clause in the Treaty for decades without much attention from the EU. However, this changed in the 1990s and onwards. The OCTs and the metropole member state used the Treaty text to enhance the OCTs' benefits and possibilities in relation to the EU. Today, the OCTs' close linkages to the EU offer them unique opportunities for strategic interaction in Brussels. In this way, the EU impacts on the relations between its member states and their former colonies.

The second section is a *praxis* analysis of how the OCTs utilize their increasing room for manoeuvre. More particularly, the section analyses how the OCTs and their counterparts articulate the limitations which the micropolities find with respect to their strategic agency in Brussels. This section is based on 19 interviews conducted between 2009 and 2011 with officials currently or previously working with EU–OCT relations for an OCT, for one of the metropole member state, or for the European Commission. The interviews have been analysed with a view to uncovering the practices, strategies, and tacit understandings of the officials participating in the triangular relation. The section points out the OCTs' scarce resources and their perception of the Commission as a monolithic counterpart as the main *limitations*, which the OCTs use to explain why they do not fully utilize the room for manoeuvre opened up in Brussels. Conversely, it also points out the activation of metropole resources and the pooling of efforts in the OCT Association (OCTA) as realized or potential *levers* for acting strategically in Brussels. While the metropole member states were initially the OCTs' only leverage in relation to the EU, the OCTA collaboration offers a means for the OCTs to articulate common interests and make use of their somewhat arbitrary legal category.

The third section presents a textual discourse analysis of how the OCTs have responded to an invitation from the Commission to (re)define the rationale of their future relationship with the EU: As part of the current initiative to reform the EU–OCT relation, the Commission published a Green Paper in 2008 and invited the OCTs, member states and others to comment and elaborate on their visions. The analysis of the OCT responses to the Green Paper consultation and the embedded strategies for the future EU–OCT relations reveals how the OCTs generally fail to perform the subjectivity that the Green Paper invites. Whereas the Commission envisions a reciprocal, late sovereign pooling of responsibilities and resources, the OCTs appear to prefer a (post)colonial self-presentation and insist on the continuation of an asymmetrical dependency relation. Finally, a concluding section considers the prospects of the OCTs' relations with the EU in the light of the attempts to strengthen the EU foreign policy apparatus.

From European colonies to OCTs

Why does the EU care about these former colonies scattered around the world? This section tracks the historical ties between the EU and OCTs and shows how the succinct answer to the question is simply – *because it is in the Treaty*. The rationale of the EU–OCT relationship based on poverty reduction has, as described below, been maintained quite uncritically since its conception in the Rome Treaty and until the present day. At the same time, the OCTs have seen their position towards the EU enhanced by incremental steps over the last 20 years or so. In recent years, however, questions are being raised as to whether the relationship with the rather wealthy OCTs can be continued based on the classic approach to development aid (European Commission 2008: 4–5). The Green Paper on the future relations between the EU and the OCTs also raises this criticism and can thus be seen as a first step towards defining a new rationale for the EU–OCT relationship in the twenty-first century.

Remnants of European empires

The OCT category was established during the Treaty of Rome negotiations. The conventional version of European history explains this in terms of the outcome of give-and-take negotiations: the French Parliament was highly sceptical towards the notion of a common European market, which would impair the national protection of French industries. A compromise was reached that offered France concessions, including the favourable treatment of French overseas possessions (Dinan 2005: 32–4). Postcolonial critics demonstrate, however, that the inclusion of the colonies resonated with ideas of 'Eurafrica' providing a *Lebensraum* for Europe, which was particularly present in Germany (Hansen and Jönsson 2011). In any case, the idea of mentioning the overseas territories in the Treaty was highly debated, because most of the founding member states – with the exception of Belgium – were worried about the prospect of becoming involved in neocolonial politics (French Government 1957). The preamble to the Treaty of Rome accommodated this concern by referring explicitly to a more legitimate reference point, namely the UN principles of development cooperation and poverty reduction. In this way, a dual purpose was enshrined in the association with the OCTs from the outset: the French interest in catering to their overseas possessions and development concerns with broader international legitimacy.

The decolonization process transformed many OCTs into sovereign states, which subsequently withdrew from the OCT association. These newly independent African states instead became associated with the EC under development agreements for the 'African, Caribbean and Pacific states' (ACPs) (European Commission 1999).

Even if most (large) colonies became sovereign (ACP) states, not all of them did. And not all of the colonies that did not gain sovereignty remained in the OCT arrangement, as a series of small territories were formally integrated in the metropole state. To facilitate this group of territories, the EU has organized certain derogations from the *acquis* for what is categorized as *outermost regions*.[1] Integration – in the metropole and in the EU – therefore appears as a possible alternative to the remaining OCTs: the outermost regions are – for a number of the OCTs – their neighbours. They are faced with comparable economic challenges. And the Treaty offers opportunity for an OCT to change its status to an outermost region without amending the Treaty.[2]

The OCT association with the EC is in many ways parallel to the ACP association, simply due to the historical connection: OCTs became ACP states upon gaining their independence. This parallelism includes a classic approach to development aid focused on poverty reduction (as a 'legitimate' approach to former colonies). Today, however, the remaining OCTs differ dramatically from the original group of French possessions and include islands, which would not normally be considered developing countries. Meanwhile, the Treaty text on the EU–OCT association remains unchanged as a 'frozen' statement of the strategic compromise concluded at the birth of the Community and still constitutes the point of departure for the interaction between the OCTs and the EU. Since 1991, however, the OCTs appear to have been moving away from the ACP parallelism while shifting closer to the outermost regions.

From trailing ACP to having an independent voice

The reconfigurations of the OCT arrangement beginning in 1991 have rendered it possible to talk about a room for manoeuvre for the – non-sovereign – OCTs in Brussels. In the 1990s, the first steps were taken towards the actual involvement of the OCTs, and this development has continued since 2001 with increased rights and benefits. The last decade has meant an increase and institutionalization of the OCTs' interactions with the EC. This is due partly – but not exclusively – to lobbying on the part of the OCTs. After a relatively passive relationship to the EU for four decades, the OCTs are invited to have a say.

Until 1991, the Council's association decisions on the relations with the OCTs were mainly 'light versions' of the agreements with the ACP countries including more or less the same provisions. The OCTs basically 'inherited' the terms from the EU's agreements with the ACP countries and received the same privileges regarding development assistance and trade agreements. The OCTs were not included in the ACP negotiations, however, and the OCT–EC relationship went almost exclusively through the metropole member state (European Commission 1999: 13–14). The EU–OCT relationship was almost completely unknown in Brussels, and according to one former Greenlandic official, it was only by accident that Greenland was made aware of the possibility of being associated with the EU as an OCT when Greenland withdrew from the EU in 1985.[3]

In 1991, however, the Council adopted an association decision[4] including terms for the OCTs that deviated from those concerning the ACP relation. The Council decision established the principle of a *partnership* between the Commission, the OCTs, and the metropole member state (European Commission 1999: 14). This was the first recognition of the OCTs as *independent actors* that could be part of the negotiations concerning the relation to the EU instead of merely being passively represented by their metropole member state. In 1997, the association decision from 1991 was reviewed mid-term.[5] On this occasion, the OCTs, despite not being part of the EU, gained access to some of the EU's internal funding programs. Being able to apply for EU funding from different programmes, for example within research, has increased the potential contact points of the OCTs with the Commission as well as the possibility of achieving funding by other means than the European Development Fund. It thus offers the OCTs an alternative entrance to the EU system and could be viewed as a step away from the classic approach to development aid. In preparation for the negotiations regarding a new association decision for the OCTs in 2001, the Commission again chose to consult not only the metropole member state but *also* the OCTs at a common conference in 1999 (European Commission 2002: 20). This increased interaction led to the establishment of organized cooperation between the OCTs in the OCT Association (OCTA) formally established in 2002. The first step towards an OCT organization was taken in 2000 when some of the OCTs met for the first time on their own initiative to coordinate positions on the new draft association decision.[6] Hence, OCTA and the cooperation between the OCTs can be seen as a result of the constitution by the EU of the OCTs as *like units* in a common category. Although the OCTs are very different from each other and spread around the world, they are motivated to join forces and find mutual strategies due to their special institutional position in the EU system. The 2001 association decision[7] ultimately set the path for a more institutionalized *trilateral* dialogue with OCT participation. The decision established an annual political summit (OCT–EU Forum) as well as two fora for technical dialogue. The tripartite meetings where the Commission, metropole member state and OCT officials meet in Brussels have been hosted by the Commission 4–6 times annually since 2002. The Partnership Working Parties conceived for a more technical dialogue were held regularly in 2005–8 but then halted due to limited OCT participation.[8]

The revisions in the association decisions since 1991 imply a radical expansion and formalization of the OCTs' possibilities for interaction in Brussels. As illustrated in Figures 5.1 and 5.2, all communication between the OCTs and the EU before 2001 went through the metropole member state (5.1), while the new association decision created fora on three levels with independent OCT participation (5.2). Importantly, however, this expanded room for manoeuvre is still only an *informal* one, as the OCT association decisions are agreed on by unanimity in the Council. As one former OCT official describes, the OCT association decision is *not* an agreement between parties but a *unilateral beneficial* decision offered by

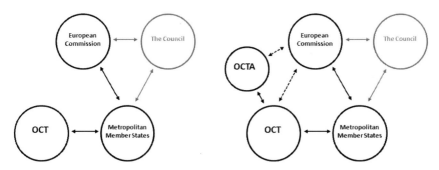

Figure 5.1 Communication between the OCTs and the EU

Figure 5.2 Communication between the OCTs and the EU after OCTA

the member state to these island communities.[9] This makes the ability of OCTs to exploit these informal channels all the more important, which we further explore in the next section.

The Green Paper marks the culmination of the increased involvement of the OCTs, as they are invited to have a say on a unilateral Council decision. Furthermore, the upcoming reform of the EU–OCT relation has strengthened the OCTs' access to the Commission. An OCT taskforce was created in the Directorate General (DG) Development of the European Commission[10] in relation to the preparation of the renegotiation of the EU–OCT association. The creation of the taskforce marks a considerable upgrading of the OCT focus within the European Commission, increasing the staff dealing with OCTs from one to three employees and a head of unit referring directly to the Director General.[11] Moreover, the taskforce is staffed by national experts with a background in working either in one of the metropole member state or in an OCT. They have generally been positively attuned to the OCTs and attempted to speak their case. The Green Paper consultation could be seen as a window of opportunity for the OCTs as they are invited to prove their value to the EU. Conversely, failing to do so could end up hampering their favourable relations to the EU.

Utilizing the growing room for manoeuvre

The previous section showed that the OCTs have gained room for manoeuvre in Brussels, as they have been gradually included in the (informal) negotiations on OCT policies as well as everyday interactions between the Commission and the metropole member state. This section explores how the OCTs utilize this room for manoeuvre in practice and finds that the OCTs are increasingly portraying themselves as independent players. The section further investigates the perceived limitations and potential levers that the OCTs appear to face in relation to their metropoles, other OCTs, and to the Commission. The OCTs use both metropole resources and join forces in OCTA. However, the OCTs miss possibilities for influence because they reduce the Commission to a monolithic entity.

OCT resources

The OCTs are consistently portrayed – by themselves and others – as having very scarce human resources. Arguably, this restrains their room for manoeuvre in Brussels. The OCTs are small economies and often geographically isolated (European Commission 2008: 3), meaning that the practical possibility of participating in Brussels-based meetings is limited. For officials from Saint Helena in the South Atlantic, for example, simply getting to and from Brussels can take several months.[12] Consequently, a permanent presence in Brussels or in the capital of the metropole member state is crucial, making participation in meetings possible. In fact, only OCTs with a representation in Europe participate in the meetings during the year.[13] With small populations, the OCTs have limited human resources and are controlled by small administrations with very few employees with a higher education. The lack of trained staff in the OCTs reduces the effective participation of the OCTs in EU matters.[14] Furthermore, any given OCT official dealing with the EU – whether based in Brussels, in the metropole capitals, or in the OCTs – usually also have other portfolios. The Falkland Islands, for example, only have one person hired on a part-time basis to deal with the EU.[15]

What the OCTs achieve depends on the representing officials' initiatives, networking skills, and understanding of how the EU works. For any initiative to bear fruit, however, it must be followed up by the local authorities on the OCTs. One Brussels-based official notes that the communication between the representatives and staff on the islands does not always suffice. The island authorities might even be a barrier to achieving results in Brussels if they do not prioritize EU issues. This may be due to other priorities, but possibly also to a lack of knowledge and understanding of the importance of the Brussels-based initiatives. Moreover, the OCTs allocate their resources to addressing immediate challenges such as the financing of concrete projects, which leaves less room for long-term strategic planning.[16] In sum, EU politics – especially locally in the OCTs – is often neglected in favour of other tasks.[17]

As outlined in the previous section, the OCTs' channels to the EU system are informal. At the same time, it is not a high-priority area for the Commission and some of the metropole member states. The tripartite meetings might therefore fade out again like the Partnership Working Parties have done if the OCTs do not show an interest and engagement.[18] The informal room for manoeuvre in Brussels is thus directly affected by the OCTs' resources, as a low utilization can make things come to a halt. The limited resources of the OCTs may, however, also be used as a lever for extracting further subsidies from the EU – as will become clear below.

Metropole resources

To compensate for their limited resources, the OCTs often attempt to use the metropole member state. The OCTs use the metropole member states' privileged access to the EU by either getting them to obtain information otherwise not available to non-EU partners or even getting them to speak their case in the Council. In fact, our interviews with OCT officials reveal a surprisingly close and non-controversial coordination with the metropole. This is anything but a relation of direct colonial domination (or at least the domination is not explicit). Instead, the OCTs act *through* and not around the metropole member state in their dealings with the EU. OCTs find that the metropole member states are often willing to advocate OCT interests.[19]

For example, in the negotiations on a new trading regime as part of the 1991 Overseas Association Decision, the Netherlands Antilles and the Netherlands played together in an intimate, hitherto unseen manner. The trade regime giving the OCTs free access to a non-reciprocal duty-free export of their goods to the EU was very controversial and subject to month-long heated discussions in the Council (Commission 1999: 13). Even though the Netherlands Antilles formally had no access to Council meetings, the representative from the Netherlands Antilles, against common practice, sat with the Netherlands at the negotiation table (European Commission 1999: 38). The Netherlands and the Netherlands Antilles succeeded in changing the OCT association decision by pointing out the historical progression of the trade rules among the EU member states and claiming that, according to the Treaty, these rules should also be applied to the OCTs.

Joining forces in OCTA

The OCTs present their joint organization (OCTA) as a source of representation, visibility, and a better handling of their interests towards the metropole member states and the Commission. In that sense, OCTA is a potential lever for greater influence, and the organization has strengthened the identity of the OCTs as legitimate players in the political game. Still, the organization is far from realizing its potential as a political lobbying apparatus.

Officially, OCTA represents a forum for the exchange of ideas, information, and best practices; for the development of effective working relations; for defending the collective interests of the members; and for making policy recommendations.[20] OCTA provides a platform for the self-representation of the OCTs as actors in their own right. For the representatives of French Polynesia and Greenland, which are both very engaged in OCTA, the organization is seen as a means of gaining 'an independent voice'.[21] For the president of OCTA, one of the most important gains of the OCTs' participation in the meetings is the very fact that the OCTs participate: it is of symbolic importance that knowledge is exchanged not just about the OCTs but with the OCTs. Moreover, if important cases should appear, the continuous contact is reminding the Commission and the metropole member states that the OCTs are *partners* that must be informed and consulted.[22]

The tripartite, bi-annual high-level OCT fora have a special role: they secure institutionalized face-time – and even leisure time, when fora are held annually in one of the OCTs – with high-level Commission officials, including the Commissioner.[23]

As the OCTs are non-sovereign entities, OCTA's success as a 'para-diplomatic'[24] forum depends on the extent to which the metropole member states and the Commission see this as a legitimate role for the OCTs and are willing to cooperate with OCTA. The Commission has taken OCTA's self-representation somewhat seriously. Although OCTA cannot be characterized as an international organization and is not recognized as a counterpart for the Commission, the OCT taskforce has chosen to step up the cooperation with OCTA as an actor in its own right, although still on a loose and informal basis.[25] As for the metropole member states, there are various perceptions of the extent to which the OCTs and OCTA can play an independent role. However, most are happy to let the OCTs and OCTA take the lead at tri-partite meetings.[26] This gives the OCTs some leeway but has also meant less consistent metropole attendance. While OCTA is thus being recognized by relevant partners to some extent, it has yet to begin acting as an interest organization. A Commission official expresses slight disappointment with OCTA's depth because of lack of staff: 'the quality in what comes out is till low, partly because they do not have enough time, and partly because they do not have enough knowledge of the [EU procedures]'.[27]

OCTA's lacks are generally explained by the demanding task of applying for and managing EU funding. OCTA's work in aiding the OCTs on these bureaucratic necessities takes up almost all of the organization's time and resources whose manpower consists of already-busy OCT officials based in Brussels or other European capitals. It is generally agreed that a permanent secretariat in Brussels would strengthen OCTA.[28] According to one former OCT official, a permanent secretariat would make OCTA less dependent on individual representatives and make it work more like a proper interest organization.[29] However, negotiations on such a secretariat have stranded due to disagreements on financing[30] as well as ambition.

The Commission as monolith

While the OCTs use OCTA and the metropole member state as gateways to influence, they are less inclined to view the EU as a source of influence. In fact, the OCTs predominantly view the Commission as an opponent and do not appear to differentiate between the sections of the Commission that are friendly-minded to the OCTs and those who are less so. This limits the informal contacts between OCT officials and Commission staff.

Coordination with the Commission mainly concerns funding. Here, the OCTs feel that they are met with unreasonable and at times even absurd demands. For example, one official underlines the absurdity in the Commission's demands on offers from three different suppliers of copy machines if there *is* only one supplier on the island.[31] Mistrust leads to conflicts between the OCTs and the Commission. One Commission official perceives this to be a lack of cooperation and initiative on the part of the OCTs,[32] whereas the OCTs lament the lack of understanding from the Commission. One example is the permanent financing of the OCTA secretariat, where a solution has yet to be found. Another example is the Partnership Working Parties that have been put on hold because the OCTs cannot send technical experts to Brussels for the meetings. Video conferencing might offer a solution to this problem, and while all of the parties have suggested as much, it has not yet been instigated.[33]

Whereas the OCTs portray the Commission *as such* as a counterpart, the OCT taskforce within the Commission partly portrays itself as a potential strategic alliance partner that could speak for the OCTs when represented at Council meetings and internally in the Commission: the OCT taskforce can – and already does to some extent – promote the OCTs to other, less positively attuned, parts of the Commission. One taskforce official thus explains that, due to their peculiar *inbetweenness* and general higher level of wealth, the OCTs have been under-prioritized in DG Development, which has focused on traditional poverty eradication.[34] According to this official, some colleagues in the Commission are unconvinced that there should even *be* an OCT policy. This signals how parts of the Commission are sceptical towards the OCTs and that the taskforce must continually justify the OCT policy to colleagues. Another taskforce official states that not only does the taskforce require the help of the metropole member states and the OCTs to 'explain' the value of the OCTs to the EU, it also needs the help of other Commission branches with specific knowledge concerning the policy areas where the OCTs might be of value to the EU. The OCT taskforce may thus act as an advocate when pitching OCT policies to the rest of a more sceptical Commission bureaucracy. And the OCT scepticism within the Commission makes it pertinent for the OCTs and metropole member states to help the taskforce justify and substantiate the EU–OCT association.

According to both OCT, metropole, and Commission officials, the OCTs face certain limitations on the 'Brussels scene'. However, they might use the metropole member state as a strategic ally if the member state accepts acting as a policy advocate. There are also increasing opportunities for collective action through OCTA. Particularly noteworthy is how the OCTs present the Commission as a monolith, whereas one part of the Commission – the OCT taskforce – presents itself as strategic partner for the OCTs to cooperate with in order to smooth the relation to the rest of the Commission bureaucracy. This may have repercussions when the revised OCT arrangement meets the Council of Ministers, as most member states do not have overseas countries or territories.

Colonial legacies and unused possibilities

As mentioned, the OCTs have gradually been casted – by themselves and by others – to play a more active role in shaping their relationship with the EU. The process has culminated with the Commission Green Paper on the Future relations between the EU and the OCTs (European Commission 2008). In this paper, drafted by the OCT Task Force, the Commission invites the OCTs to contribute with their own ideas on how to modernize the EU–OCT relationship.[35] Notably, even if the Commission launched the reform early on by stating that there were 'no precooked answers' (Director General Stephano Manservisi quoted in an EU–OCT Forum Press Release 2007), the Green Paper poses its questions in a manner implying that a change in the relation is needed and that this requires the OCTs becoming more responsible. The changes envisioned for the OCTs can be conceptualized as a change in sovereignty games. Hitherto, a (post)colonial dependency game has been played focusing on aid to the dependent part, which is not awarded a very pronounced independent subjectivity – and hence the not-very-post colonial character of the relation signalled by the brackets.

The increasing institutionalization of OCT subjectivity throughout the 1990s and 2000s has not been coupled with increased responsibilities. The OCTs have thus succeeded in negotiating a greater say and more benefits while avoiding more responsibility. In the Green Paper, the Commission describes the current partnership between the EU and the OCTs as one of traditional development cooperation: a non-reciprocal relationship with very limited responsibilities on the part of the OCTs. This present (post)colonial relation is not of 'mutual interest' (European Commission 2008: 10), and it does not activate 'the potential of OCTs as strategically important outposts, spread all over the world, as proponents of the EU's values' (European Commission 2008: 2). The Green Paper indicates that this non-reciprocal relationship will not be acceptable in the future and instead suggests the possibility of developing what might – as described in the introductory chapter of this volume – be called a 'late sovereign' game modelled on the relation between the EU member states and based on the pooling of interests, responsibility, and sovereignty. The Commission portrays the OCTs as more than just third countries due to 'the OCTs' and the EU's membership of the same family' (European Commission 2008: 2). The OCTs are said to share values and history with Europe, and they are 'part of its ultimate frontiers' (European Commission 2008: 6).[36] But if the OCTs are part of the community, they must assume obligations to the community:

> How could the partnership between the OCTs and the EU become more active and reciprocal, in the mutual interest of both partners? Which *actual responsibilities* should this entail for the OCTs or the Member States to which they are linked?
>
> (European Commission 2008: 13)

The Green Paper asks about the strategic significance, duties, and regional role of the OCTs (European Commission 2008: 10). The questions in the Green Paper may be read as a direct request for the justification and substantiation of a future late sovereign relation. It marks new rules if the OCTs wish to play on the 'Brussels scene'. The OCTs clearly must come up with some kind of answer if they want to maintain the privileges granted to them by the EU. The Commission views this as important in order to convince increasingly sceptical member states in the Council to continue the financial support to some of the member states' former colonies, which happen to be rather wealthy as measured in terms of GNP per capita.[37]

A (post)colonial subject in continued dependency

Most of the OCT responses to the Green Paper argue or imply that the OCTs have a 'right' to assistance from the EU, arguing for the continuation of the asymmetrical (post)colonial relationship. Some responses consist only of a 'wish list' specifying the needs of the OCT in question.[38] However, the responses from a number of OCTs do include various arguments for *why* the OCTs have a *right* to assistance from the EU. These arguments revolve around the 'development needs' (Saint Helena 2008: 8; cf. Cayman Islands 2008: 1–2) of the OCTs and their inability to sustain modern societies with a European standard of living without EU assistance. The argument here is that this situation is at least partly owing to the past colonial activities of the EU member states and that the EU therefore has a historical responsibility for showing solidarity with the OCTs (see Netherlands Antilles 2008: 7). The EU ought to display 'solidarity' with the OCTs and stand by their historical and legal recognition of the development needs of the OCTs.[39]

Other OCTs refer to concrete wrongs perpetrated by the EU member states against the OCTs, arguing that the EU has a continuing (moral) responsibility to support the OCTs. French Polynesia tacitly refers to the colonial past by asking France and the EU to help the islands to become less economically dependent on France (French Polynesia 2008: 3). The *Conseil Economique, Social et Environnemental* of French Polynesia explicitly refers to colonial injustices by claiming that France – and the EU – are historically indebted to Polynesia because the islands have endured French nuclear testing on its territory (French Polynesian CESE 2008: 1), thereby *involuntarily* contributing to French and European security. There is a bond which obliges the EU to contribute to the development of French Polynesia.

The British Virgin Islands brings this historical 'shaming' up-to-date by highlighting that the OCTs are especially vulnerable to the negative impacts of climate change:[40]

> This is the result not of their own actions but of the activities of polluting countries, which include numerous medium-sized and large EU Member States . . . *There is a strong moral case for EU countries as a whole to maintain the tradition of solidarity* by helping OCTs become more resilient to the potential damage of climate change to their long-term sustainability.
> (British Virgin Islands 2008: 13, italics added)

So even if some EU member states find that the EU should cease payments on the colonial debt of a few imperial states, they are nevertheless morally obliged to help the OCTs due to their CO_2 emissions making them co-responsible for climate change and its adverse effects on the OCTs.

These arguments basically run parallel with the rationale behind the postcolonial relation between the EU and the ACP states: the OCTs – like the ACP states – require assistance, and the EU has an historical and/or moral responsibility to assist its former colonies. The only differences are – or should be – that the OCTs should be met with fewer bureaucratic demands than the ACP countries[41] and that the OCTs, due to their closer relation to the metropole member states (i.e. their non-sovereignty) have the right to a closer relationship to the EU:

> [T]he Community's relationship with ACP countries has been improved to such a degree that in some cases they are better than those between OCTs and the Community. *As a recognised part of the European family and not independent countries, OCTs should be able to enjoy a preferential relationship with the Community.*
> (Falkland Islands 2008: 4, italics added)

A number of the OCTs position themselves close to the outermost regions of the EU by stressing how the OCT shares their conditions and challenges (e.g. New Caledonia 2008: 2; Anguilla 2008: 2; Greenland 2008: 6). However, a future status closer to that of the outermost regions has only been envisioned in terms of *rights* and not in terms of *obligations* (i.e. to implement EU regulations). In fact, the obligations of the outermost regions are precisely what makes most French OCTs prefer a unique position in-between the ACP and the outermost regions (Groupe de l'Outre-Mer 2008: 1; French Polynesia 2008: 3; Saint-Pierre et Miquelon 2008: 1).

Generally, the OCTs do not answer the central question asked by the Commission in the Green Paper of how the OCTs might be of value to the EU. Nor do they acknowledge the need for a modernization of the relationship, instead insisting on a continuation of the current relationship and thereby the familiar rules of a (post)colonial sovereignty game maintaining OCT dependency on the EU.

A postcolonial subject in late sovereign robes

In their responses, a number of the OCTs do seek to meet the request from the Commission to provide substance to a more equal partnership between the EU and the OCTs in the future. The envisioned equality, however, pertains to the decision-making process rather than any contributions to the EU.

Some OCTs ask for better information, increased involvement, and recognition in Brussels. New Caledonia suggests that the involvement of the OCTs in policy-making is further formalized (New Caledonia 2008: 6–8), whereas the Cayman Islands suggest that the OCT delegation should have weight and recognition at the negotiating table vis-à-vis the EU (Cayman Islands 2008: 2). Greenland finds a need to develop a common strategy for how political ownership and 'empowerment' may be secured for each OCT (Greenland 2008: 7).[42]

The Commission Green Paper suggests that OCTs may be of value for the EU by acting as 'outposts' for European values and as 'centres of experience and expertise' (European Commission 2008: 11). The OCTs, however, fail to provide substance to this loosely defined vision.

A number of the OCT responses stress that the OCTs share European values on democracy, human rights, rule of law, good governance, and sustainable environmental policy.[43] This could serve as the ticket to a 'late sovereign' relation known from the relation between the EU member states, which pool their sovereignty and responsibilities:

> These values which the EC seeks to promote to third countries are already part of our society . . . [We] are direct links into otherwise remote areas of the globe enabling the EU to influence policies, values and standards.
>
> (Falkland Islands 2008: 1, 5)

The OCTs present themselves as assisting in spreading European values (French Polynesia 2008: 8) by serving as 'centres of excellence' in relation to their neighbouring countries.[44] Yet none of the OCTs specify how they can actually do so. Rather, as the case of Mayotte implies, the role as outpost is in itself so valuable for the EU that it justifies additional funding – and the role as a centre of experience and expertise is to be financed by the EU through the European Development Fund (Mayotte 2008: 5). Generally, it is explicitly left to the Commission to describe and facilitate this role for the OCTs (Saint Helena 2008: 14; Anguilla 2008: 2). The Netherlands Antilles indirectly recognize that they may need to take responsibility in meeting 'European norms and standards',[45] but immediately proceed to emphasize that this must be a 'voluntary' process and that the Commission must take the initiative to help the OCTs assume responsibilities (Netherlands Antilles 2008: 2). The Falkland Islands even formulate their possible potential as a question to the Commission (2008: 2).

Only one OCT – Greenland – makes a strategic move in its response which differs significantly from those outlined above in its presentation of itself as – at least partially – on equal terms with the EU and emphasis on the geo-political importance of Greenland in relation to the EU's influence in the Arctic region (see Gad, this volume.)

The OCTs substantiate the notion of a more mutual partnership based on greater OCT *involvement* rather than increased OCT *responsibilities*. Whenever a greater role for the OCTs is implied, it is left to the Commission to investigate the potential. What begins as an argument for a 'late sovereign' relationship involving the pooling of sovereignty for mutual benefit ends instead with an asymmetrical dependency relationship referring to the past. A certain disappointment with the results of the consultation process can be sensed in the Commission's subsequent analysis, stating that 'Only a few contributions provide input on the actual responsibilities this should entail for the OCTs themselves' (European Commission 2009: 3).

Conclusion: perspectives for the OCTs in Brussels

The OCTs have a unique position in Brussels, as they make up a peculiar category of colonial remnants maintaining a privileged position in the EU. Their position is privileged in the sense that it allows them access to more resources from the EU than accorded to the ACP countries – mostly former European colonies with significantly lower average GDP than the OCTs (see Broberg 2011). Even though the OCTs have very limited resources, they have gained a presence in Brussels, they have strong policy advocates in their metropoles, and the OCT taskforce in the Commission is also eager to present itself as their facilitator. The EU's treatment of the OCTs contributes to their enhanced subjectivity and room for manoeuvre in Brussels. Furthermore, there seems to be a potential for the OCTs to gain further influence in relation to EU–OCT policies by joining forces in OCTA and working out long-term strategies.

Yet the OCTs are asked to engage in a more reciprocal relationship with the EU. Instead of the (post)colonial game of dependency hitherto played, which have let the OCTs maintain their privileged access to the EU while other ex-colonies gradually lose such privileges – the Commission asks the OCTs to play along in the EU's late sovereign game by pooling resources and sovereignty.

The OCTs respond by insisting on a continued (post)colonial game. The OCTs do not attempt to evade the colonial legacy by opting for independence; nor do they (generally) take responsibility for late sovereign cooperation. This, notably, does not imply that they do not employ an independent subjectivity: when invited to participate, they show up – and when asked about their preferred future, they answer. But most OCTs independently refrain from claiming independence – thereby dodging the associated responsibilities. Instead, they rely on the metropoles to act as their strategic advocates.

This continued (post)colonial strategy is likely to run into trouble, however, at least when pursued in relation to the EU. First, the reformed OCT arrangement – and the budget set aside for OCTs – must be passed by the decision-making bodies of the EU (Council and Parliament), where many have no relation to OCTs. The OCTs (and their metropoles) have thus far only met with a branch of the Commission (the OCT taskforce) especially attuned to the needs of the OCTs and their metropole member states.

Second, the Lisbon Treaty marks ambitions to develop a common foreign policy. Consequently, the OCTs should expect the Commission to mean business when it proposes a more reciprocal relationship in the future. There is also a clear interest in Brussels to simplify the various associations that the EU has to countries such as Norway and Switzerland, the outermost regions, and the ACP countries. This is especially relevant for the OCTs, because the more these different associations are compared and discussed, the greater the risk of attention on and criticism of the privileged position of the OCTs. How Brussels will deal with this question of special treatment will be of vital importance to the future of the EU–OCT association. Dodging the responsibilities of independent, postcolonial sovereignty might be a continued option. But dodging the responsibilities of late sovereignty may not.

Notes

1 The outermost regions were created as a category in 1991 and include the French overseas departments, the Spanish Canary Islands and the Portuguese islands, the Azores, and Madeira (see Kochenov 2008: 208).
2 Article 355(6) of the Treaty on the Functioning of the European Union.
3 Interview with former official representing Greenland conducted in Copenhagen, 2 October 2009.
4 Council Decision 91/482/EEC of 25 July 1991 on the association of the overseas countries and territories with the European Economic Community (OJ L 263/1, 19 September 1991).
5 Council Decision 97/803/EC of 29 November 1997 amending at mid-term Decision 91/482/EEC on the association of the overseas countries and territories with the European Economic Community (OJ L 329, 29 November 1997).
6 See the OCTA website http://octassociation.org/public.asp?id=9&pid=9&level=2&l ang=en&pnode=1&bn= introduction&pbranch=about&domain=public (accessed 21 March 2010).
7 Council Decision 2001/822/EC of 27 November 2001 on the association of the overseas countries and territories with the European Community (OJ L 314, 30 November 2001).
8 Interview with Commission official.
9 Interview with former OCT official.
10 Now DG EuropeAid Development and Cooperation (DG DEVCO) after the merger with DG EuropeAid (DG AIDCO).

11 Interview with Commission official from the OCT taskforce conducted in Brussels, 4 November 2009.

12 Because they have to wait for a monthly cargo ship to take them from Saint Helena to South Africa and back. Two different OCT officials drew attention to this rather absurd circumstance, which can be confirmed by the cargo ship's schedules on http://rms-st-helena.com/schedules-fares/, accessed 17 March 2011. Recently, however, the UK government announced the construction of an airport on the island (www.fco.gov.uk/en/news/latest-news/?view=News&id=686561982, accessed 7 March 2012).

13 According to the OCTA secretariat, the following OCTs had representations in Brussels in 2009: Aruba in the Hague; British Virgin Islands, Cayman Islands, Falkland Islands and Montserrat in London; Greenland, French Polynesia, The Netherlands Antilles, Wallis and Futuna Islands in Brussels; and Saint-Pierre and Miquelon and New Caledonia in Paris.

14 Interview with former OCT official.

15 Interview with official representing the Falkland Islands, conducted in London, 3 November 2009.

16 Interview with Commission official. A similar point is underlined by Greenland in its written reply to the green paper (Greenland 2008: 4).

17 Interview with metropole official working with OCT issues.

18 Interviews with OCT officials and Commission official.

19 As one official who formerly represented the OCT explains, 'One has to say that the relations are good for all four mother countries. It's not a battle field. Of course there is disagreement but nothing severe.'

20 The OCTA mandate, www.octassociation.org/public.asp?id=10&pid=10&level=2&lid=en&pnode=1&bn=mandate&pbranch=about&domain=public (accessed 5 December 2010). On a daily basis, OCTA has a number of different functions: OCTA participates in tripartite meetings (represented by the president and/or the secretariat assistant), draft newsletters, send meeting summaries to the OCTs, and assist with information and fund applications.

21 Interviews with OCT representing officials; see Croes (2008).

22 Interview with the then OCTA president conducted in Brussels, 5 November 2009.

23 Interview with Commission official conducted in Brussels, 24 March 2011.

24 Para-diplomacy defined as 'all those external activities by non-sovereign jurisdictions that stimulate and approximate the formal, legal and recognized diplomatic practices of sovereign states' (Bartmann 2006: 544).

25 Interview with Commission official from the OCT taskforce.

26 Interviews with three different metropole representatives.

27 Interview with Commission official from the OCT taskforce.

28 According to a Commission official from the OCT taskforce.

29 Interview with an official who formerly represented an OCT. Studies also show that actors with fewer resources in international politics – such as the OCTs, but also small states and developing countries – can benefit from a pooling of resources in order to obtain a better use of international organizations (Drahos 2003: 93).

30 At the OCT–EU forum in 2008, the OCTs agreed to contribute to the financing of a secretariat (Smith 2008: 2), but not to the extent demanded by the Commission. From the Commission's point of view, it is partly a question of whether such expenses can be justified to other member states and partly a result of a poor track record with a similar ACP secretariat that has not been working according to the intent (interview with Commission official from the OCT taskforce).

31 Interview with metropole official.

32 Interview with Commission official from the OCT taskforce.

33 Interview with Commission official from the OCT taskforce and interview with an official representing an OCT.

34 Interview with Commission official from the OCT taskforce. DG Development is now merged with DG Aidco and called DG Devco.
35 The Green Paper consultation (1 July–17 October 2008) was open to all relevant stakeholders, and responses were submitted by member states, OCTs, non-government organizations, and others. This chapter concentrates exclusively on the OCTs' response to the green paper.
36 Furthermore, it is noted that the OCTs have their own chapter in the Treaty and that OCT citizens hold EU citizenship (European Commission 2008: 6–7).
37 Interview with Commission official from the OCT taskforce.
38 See Anguilla 2008: 1.
39 The preamble of the Treaty of Rome confirms 'the solidarity which binds Europe and the overseas countries and desiring to ensure the development of their prosperity, in accordance with the principles of the Charter of the UN' (Identical formulation in the Lisbon Treaty), cf. article 182 TEF, today article 198 TEUF.
40 Primarily natural disasters such as floods and hurricanes.
41 See Greenland (2008: 6), British Virgin Islands (2008: 5, 14) and Netherlands Antilles (2008: 7).
42 See also French Polynesia (2008: 4). The British Virgin Islands also request more information and representation but only envisage this via the UK as opposed to increased OCT inclusion in Brussels (British Virgin Islands 2008: 6).
43 See French Polynesia (2008: 9), Saint Helena (2008: 13), Mayotte (2008: 3), and British Virgin Islands (2008: 1–3).
44 In relation to environmental protection and biodiversity (French Polynesia 2008: 5) or food security (Mayotte 2008: 2). In less 'soft' areas than values and standards, Greenland envisions itself as a 'stepping stone' to North America (Greenland 2008: 2), but 'The EU will . . . have to decide how to make advantage of this . . . and enter into bilateral dialogue' (ibid.: 7), whereas the Netherlands Antilles presents itself as a possible bridgehead for 'the European business model' (Netherlands Antilles 2008: 3) with a role in the fight against international terror and crime – especially if they are awarded a role as a transportation hub for Caribbean goods and persons to the EU (ibid,: 4). French Polynesia claims that the Pacific OCTs could strengthen the EU in its competition with the US, China, and Japan (2008: 4).
45 See British Virgin Islands (2008: 2, 7).

References

Anguilla (2008) 'Anguilla's response to Green Paper questionnaire', *Response to COM(2008) 383* (All responses to COM(2008) 383.
Bartmann, B. (2006) 'In or out: sub-national island jurisdiction and the antechamber of para-diplomacy', *The Round Table*, 95(386): 541–59.
Broberg, M. (2011) 'The EU's legal ties with its former colonies: when old love never dies', *DIIS Working Paper* 2011: 01. Online. Available at: www.diis.dk/graphics/Publications/WP2011/WP2011-02%20til%20tryk.pdf (accessed 30 March 2011).
British Virgin Islands (2008) 'Response by the government of the British Virgin Islands, 30 October 2008', *Response to COM(2008) 383.*
Cayman Islands (2008) 'Cayman Islands response', Leader of Government Business, Hon. D. Kurt Tibbetts, JP, *Response to COM(2008) 383.*
Croes, F. (2008) *Speech of the Minister Plenipotentiary of Aruba in The Hague*, Frido Croes, in representation of the Prime Minister of Aruba, at EU–OCT forum 25–29 November 2008 in Grand Cayman. Online. Available at: www.octassociation.org/old-site/oct_ministerial_conference.asp (accessed 27 March 2011).

Dinan, D. (2005) *Ever Closer Union: An Introduction to European Integration*, 3rd edn, New York: Palgrave Macmillan.

Drahos, P. (2003) 'When the weak bargain with the strong: negotiations in the World Trade Organization', *International Negotiation*, 8: 79–109.

EU–OCT Forum Press Release (2007) *Press release: A more European OCT – EU association*. 2007 OCT–EU Forum. Brussels, 27–28 November 2007. Online. Available at: http://ec.europa.eu/development/icenter/repository/2007-OCT-EU-Forum.pdf(accessed 9 March 2010).

European Commission (1999) *Communication from the Commission: The Status of OCTs Associated with the EC and Options for "OCT 2000". Volume I*. COM (1999) 163, Brussels, 20 May 1999.

European Commission (2002) 'The Overseas Countries and Territories: renewed partnership with the Community', *The Courier ACP–EU*, January–February, pp. 19–20. (Author Gail Sutton, Trainee, Regional Matters and OCTs, DG Development, European Commission).

European Commission (2008) *Green Paper. Future relations between the EU and the Overseas Countries and Territories* COM (2008) 383, Brussels, 25 June 2008.

European Commission (2009) *Communication from the Commission to the European Parliament, The Council, The European Economic and Social Committee and the Committee of the Regions: Elements for a new partnership between the EU and the overseas countries and territories (OCTs)*, COM (2009) 623, Brussels, 6 November 2009.

Falkland Islands (2008) 'Political considerations for the Falkland Islands', The Falkland Islands Government, 16 October 2008, *Response to COM (2008) 383.*

French Government (1957) 'Territoires d'outre-mer et Marché commun', *Note de la Direction des Affaires économiques et financiers*, Paris, 5 February 1957. Online. Available at: www.ena.lu/note_directorate_economic_financial_affairs_paris_february_1957-2-1273 (accessed 16 March 2011).

French Polynesia (2008) 'La réponse du gouvernement de la Polynésie française', Le Président, 15 October 2008, *Response to COM (2008) 383.*

French Polynesian CESE (2008) 'L'avis du Conseil Economique, Social et Environnemental (CESE) de la Polynésie française', *Response to COM (2008) 383.*

Greenland (2008) 'Greenlandic response to the Green Paper, 17.10.2008', *Response to COM (2008) 383.*

Groupe de l'Outre-Mer (2008) 'Réactions de Groupe de l'Outre-Mer du Conseil Economique, Social et Environnemental au Livre Vert de la Commission', 6 October 2008, *Response to COM (2008) 383.*

Hansen, P. and Jönsson, S. (2011) 'Bringing Africa as a "dowry" to Europe. European integration and the Eurafrican project 1920–1960', *Interventions*, 13(3): 443–63.

Kochenov, D. (2008) 'Substantive and procedural issues in the application of European law in the overseas possessions of European Union Member States', *Michigan State Journal of International Law*, 17(2): 195–289.

Mayotte (2008) 'Délibération de la séance plénière du 29 Septembre 2008', *Response to COM (2008) 383.*

Netherlands Antilles (2008) 'Standpunt Regering van de Nederlandse Antillen', *Response to COM (2008) 383.*

New Caledonia (2008) 'Contribution de la Nouvelle-Calédonie', *Response to COM (2008) 383.*

Saint Helena (2008) 'Response to the Green Paper', *Response to COM (2008) 383.*

Saint-Pierre et Miquelon (2008) 'Réponse de Saint-Pierre-et-Miquelon'. Le Président, Conseil Territorial, 5 November 2008, *Response to COM (2008) 383.*

Smith, N. (2008) *Closing remarks by Mr Neil Smith OCT–EU Forum 2008*, Financial Secretary/TAO, British Virgin Islands, 28 November 2008. Online. Available at: www. octassociation.org/oldsite/forum_2008/final_declarations/BVI_Final_TAO_Neil_ Smith.doc (accessed 22 February 2010).

6 British conceptions of state, identity, and sovereignty

Shifting global contexts

Ulf Hedetoft

Applying a historical perspective, the British conception of state identity, sovereignty, and national interests has fairly consistently played itself out among four different nodes: (1) the United Kingdom (UK) as a composite state – that is, the perspective of internal colonization and shifting power relations between England, Scotland, Wales, and Northern Ireland; (2) the UK as a (post-/neo-)colonial power – that is, the perspective of British colonial relations, both in the classical age of imperialism and during and after decolonization; (3) the UK's 'special relationship' with the United States (US) after the Second World War – that is, the UK as the US's hegemonic lieutenant and a 'third force' in global affairs after the imperial decline; and (4) the UK's difficult and often strained relations with Europe – that is, Britain as the 'island nation', cut off from the Continent and happily situated in the mid-Atlantic as an Anglo-Saxon bridge to North America.

In this context, if we ignore the first of these four, the remaining three have – in varying patterns of interaction – been instrumental in imagining, defining, and construing Britain's international identity, power ambitions, and perceptions of sovereignty for several centuries. Winston Churchill possibly best captured these imperial imaginings during the Second World War (Deighton 1995), when he set forth his vision of Britain as positioned at the centre of three concentric and interlocking circles: the Transatlantic (Special) Relationship; Commonwealth; and finally (also in his order of priorities) Europe. Where the first two were, and to some extent remain, invested with emotional attachment and symbolic significance in Britain – and thus are not *only* viewed through the prism of hard-nosed *realpolitik* – the latter has never been more than at best a pragmatic *mariage de convenance*, at worst an object of conflict and disdain.

That said, it must also be admitted that the British, largely due to their economically utilitarian approach to the outside world, have always displayed a general, although never consistent, knack for pragmatism, both in their approach to sovereignty and to methods for maintaining an influence on world affairs. *Colonization* never took place according to a theoretical or philosophical template (unlike France; see Holm, this volume), instead assuming a variety of forms, from highly formal to quite informal variants, and was never based on the idea that colonies were supposed to develop into faraway versions of the Home Counties. *Citizenship* was initially imagined as a very British prerogative of descent, but was slowly, although also here inconsistently, extended to many (former) colonial subjects; it subsequently created problems in connection with early migration to Britain after the Second World War; and it finally assumed three distinctly different forms in 1981, when the *ius soli* principle of British nationality was partially abandoned through the introduction of three forms of citizenship: British Citizenship, British Dependent Territories Citizenship, and British Overseas Citizenship (1981 Act).

Likewise with sovereignty: on the one hand, a dominant vision (influenced by Bodin 1955[1606] and Austin 1832; see also Lakin 2008) has argued that sovereignty – understood in semi-feudal terms as 'Crown-in-Parliament' – is indivisible and absolute (a vision still very much alive in the Thatcher years); on the other, sovereignty in imperial/colonial practice was a more variegated thing, and the British propensity for muddling through as regards authority and gradations of independent rule proved itself both in India (e.g. dyarchy), the Middle East (e.g. mandate territories), Africa (e.g. tribal rule), and of course the Dominions (extensive self-government) – not to mention the age of decolonization and further down the road, when in the late 1980s/early 1990s Britain was finally compelled to come to terms with a radically altered global position. The period bracketed by Dean Acheson's famous statement (1962) that 'Britain has lost an empire and not yet found a role' and Geoffrey Howe's less famous, but no less representative phrase, 'sovereignty is not virginity which you either have or you don't' (Howe 1991) conceals a process of a sometimes very reluctant and painful national self-awareness, a process during which pragmatism gradually overrides historical pride, emotionalism, and 'Little Englandism', and begins to accept new international rules of the game – including reformed relations with the European Union (EU) (see further, Mac Amhlaigh, this volume).

In different terms, the end of this process marks the final recognition that, although it might still hold both true and be politically compelling that Britain would need to focus on America, Europe, and erstwhile colonial relations to maintain some modicum of global influence as a mid-sized power, neither was Britain at the centre of the circles nor was it possible to ignore a radical shift in the relative significance of the three nodes. The game had changed. The importance of Europe was growing, the Special Relationship was less special, and the former colonies (most of which still symbolically recognize the British monarch as their ceremonial Head of State) were either independent players in their own right or, as British Overseas Territories (BOTs), still tied to the UK, but, particularly since the *2002 British Overseas Territories Act* (2002 Act), within an asymmetric structure, enjoying real autonomy without formal sovereignty, including independent relations with the EU, and striving to take advantage of their freely chosen relations of dependence to the Mother Country, which is still responsible for security and foreign policy.[1]

As far as Europe goes, Britain has been a reluctant member from the start in 1973 (George 1990), after a few failed attempts blocked by President de Gaulle. This interest in membership in itself reflects that the costs of non-membership even then (in the 1960s and early 1970s) were seen to exceed the benefits both of more traditional sovereignty and of trying to outbalance the European competitors by means of overseas and transatlantic alliances. That illusion had been pursued and found wanting during the 1950s, when most colonies claimed independence and were abandoned one by one (tumbling like domino pieces after the 'Sceptered Isles' had lost India, 'the Jewel in the Crown'), and when the Americans had made it clear – first in the Suez Crisis, later in the turmoil surrounding the British purchase of US Skybolt and Polaris Missiles (on both, see for example Dobson 1995) – that they much preferred a Britain with few if any colonial possessions and little independent nuclear clout.

So Britain caved in and entered a political condominium that it would much have preferred to avoid – something that Lady (then Mrs) Thatcher made no bones about. And although things have now changed considerably, New Labour's European policies having since the late 1990s shown more commitment to the European project, the UK is still in some ways the odd one out (outside the euro zone, outside the Schengen Agreements, outside key parts of the Freedom, Security and Justice pillar, and deeply dissatisfied with the Common Agricultural Policy). In Blairite discourse, Britain's revised position and strategy have often been formulated as a wish to become a key power in EU politics alongside Germany and France. This ambition has undoubtedly been prompted by greater economic interdependence between Britain and the continental countries than previously (at times having led to serious consideration of membership of the euro zone), but also by a realization that the American connection is not strong enough to carry Britain's ambitions forward. Balancing between the EU and the US in security-related and military policy areas (viz. collaboration between the two in the 'War on Terror') undoubtedly remains a high priority, but Britain's active engagement in efforts to build up an independent military capacity at the EU level has been considerable in recent years. In general terms, political and business elites have thus realized particularly the economic benefits of membership and over time warmed somewhat to the European idea. Nevertheless, there is little doubt that political euro-scepticism remains quite strong in the UK, not least in these times of euro zone turbulence, and governments are adept at playing the card of popular reluctance (2011 EU Act; see Mac Amhlaigh, this volume).

This realization takes place within a political and strategic configuration of forces that shrewdly calculates the national benefits of increased European commitment in the context of older networks and linkages. Because of the UK position as one of the world's key financial centres (London is the only serious European rival to Frankfurt – one of the most important legacies of empire; see below) and as a nuclear power, a permanent member of the UN Security Council and G8 member, it is well situated to manoeuvre within a unique configuration of sovereignty dimensions: the endogenous abandonment of traditional sovereignty vis-à-vis the EU in favour of economic and political benefits is modified by various opt-outs and opt-ins, while the maintenance of traditional, *de jure* sovereignty vis-à-vis states external to Europe remains prominent, and the effects of globalization threatening to erode even those kinds of sovereignty games can be impacted, because the UK enjoys a modicum of direct influence on the leading world power, in former colonies, and in key global institutions. This does not mean that the gravitational pull of EU forces can be ignored, but rather that the autonomy and room for manoeuvre allowed by this configuration requires a delicate balancing act on the part of British political leaders in order to optimize British interests in shifting contexts (Hedetoft 2008).

In sum, this balancing act reflects how Britain, having developed from a global colonial Empire to a normalized, mid-sized state, nevertheless still actively attempts to avail itself of the advantages, connections, and networks which derive from the colonial legacy and which significantly shape and help explain much of its foreign policy today, as regards, for example, financial policy, military missions, nuclear policies, diplomatic leverage, European relations, and development and trade strategies. Britain has lost an Empire but is beginning to find a role whereby age-old colonial relations can be put to advantage in a new way.

As already indicated, this is true not least as regards the policy domain of trade, economic relations, and finance; the Empire would have been nothing without the dependence on the City of London on colonial trade relations – starting with mercantilism and the early currency and banking system, developing into the gradually more state-controlled extraction of wealth and resources in foreign lands, and resulting in huge corporate monopolies basing their operations not on trade with but setting up shop in forcefully acquired colonial possessions. The global strength and status of the British currency until 1931 was founded on this basis, and the financial networks that still survive today owe their existence to this period.[2] It therefore makes sense that a spate of the mutual relations that we can identify between Britain and a number of the BOTs today are financial by nature and pragmatically facilitated by the citizenship regulations. This also explains why the UK Government's *1999 White Paper on Britain and the Overseas Territories* (UK Government 1999) as well as the *Response of the UK to the European Commission Green paper on the 'Future Relations Between the European Union and the Overseas Countries and Territories'* (United Kingdom 2008) have elaborate and detailed observations regarding good governance in relation to the financial sector and the significance of financial behaviour and financial relations in particular.[3]

The mental rearrangement accompanying the transition from colonial power to mid-sized state is reflected in the internal composition of Britain. No longer a white enclave, solely inhabited by a 'superior race', Britain is now a postcolonial ethnic mix of 'colonizers' and 'colonized' – and their descendants. Some of the colonized hail from the Overseas Territories (OTs) and have no, or at least very few, problems entering Britain, obtaining British Citizenship (as it is their right) and taking up full residency there – although the reverse does not hold: Britons cannot enter, live, and work in the OTs without enduring the bureaucratic hassle of applying as ordinary immigrants and running the risk of being turned down. This is an example of the current asymmetric relationship between the UK and these 14 erstwhile colonial micro-possessions. In microcosm, it reveals how colonial relations in the contemporary global sphere contain new rules of the game, new spaces of autonomy and room for manoeuvre, less formally conspicuous interactions of dominance, and more complex calculations of costs and benefits on both sides.

It also displays new history lessons and opens a laboratory for studying a radically new form of pragmatism in international relations. When Britain willingly accepts asymmetries seemingly weighted in its own disfavour when it might have otherwise avoided them, it is a relatively safe bet that other advantages, new levers, and different channels of interest have opened up – mostly in the financial sphere (off-shore finance, tax havens, money-laundering, international harbour functions, etc.). For their part, the OTs do their utmost to reap the benefits of this modernized space of dependency, priding themselves, like Bermuda, on being 'a British Overseas Territory with more self-government than Scotland, Wales and Northern Ireland' (Forbes 2011). This is a world that can no longer be conceived in terms of the White Man's Burden, with the UK projecting itself as the benevolent civilizer. Not that the BOTs no longer need development aid, but the UK does its best to shift this economic (and moral) burden onto the EU as a European obligation while itself harvesting maximum benefits from the relationship, for example, by insisting on the maintenance of an elaborate system of preferential trade agreements (United Kingdom 2008: 3, 7–8). This is increasingly a globalized interactive game, where the dynamics between (former) colonies and (former) colonial powers (with the EU playing the role as moderator) offer a reasonable chance for a successful outcome for both parties.

Notes

1 For the reader's reference, the remaining Overseas Territories of the UK are, in the Caribbean, Anguilla, British Virgin Islands, Cayman Islands, Montserrat, and the Turks and Caicos Islands; and elsewhere Bermuda, British Antarctic Territory, British Indian Ocean Territory, Falkland Islands, Gibraltar, Pitcairn Island, St Helena (including Ascension Island and Tristan da Cunha), South Georgia and South Sandwich Islands, and the Sovereign Base Areas on Cyprus. See www.fco.gov. uk/en/about-us/what-we-do/overseas-territories.
2 For an account of the more recent history of the relations between the City of London and the BOTs, see Palan's contribution to this volume.
3 The central role of finance for both the sovereignty games played between Brussels, London, and the BOTs in question is clear from Palan's, Vlcek's and Maurer's contributions to this volume.

References

1981 Act: *British Nationality Act 1981*. Online. Available at: www.legislation.gov.uk/ukpga/1981/61/contents (accessed 23 February 2011).
2002 Act: *British Overseas Territories Act 2002*. Online. Available at: www.legislation.gov.uk/ukpga/2002/8/contents (accessed 23 February 2011).
2011 EU Act: *The European Union Act 2011*. Online. Available at: www.fco.gov.uk/en/global-issues/european-union/003-EU-act (accessed 23 February 2011).
Acheson, D. (1962) 'Great Britain has lost an Empire and has not yet found a role', speech at West Point (5 December). See for example Douglas Brinkley (1990) 'Dean Acheson and the "Special Relationship"', *The Historical Journal*, 33(3): 599–608.
Austin, J. (1832) *The Province of Jurisprudence Determined*, London: John Murray.
Bodin, J. (1955[1606]) *Six Books of the Commonwealth (selections)*, Oxford: Blackwell.

Deighton, A. (1995) 'Britain and the three interlocking circles', in A. Varsori (ed.) *Europe 1945–1990: The End of an Era?*, Basingstoke: Macmillan.

Dobson, A.P. (1995) *Anglo-American Relations in the Twentieth Century*, London: Routledge.

Forbes, K.A. (2011) *Bermuda and Great Britain*. Online. Available at: www.bermuda-online.org/colonial.htm (accessed 23 February 2011).

George, S. (1990) *An Awkward Partner: Britain in the European Community*, Oxford: Oxford University Press.

Hedetoft, U. (2008) 'Sovereignty revisited: European reconfigurations, global challenges and implications for small states', in L.W. Pauly and W.D. Coleman (eds) *Global Ordering: Institutions and Autonomy in a Changing World*, Vancouver: UBC Press, 214–34.

Howe, G. (1991) 'Sovereignty and interdependence. Britain's place in the world', *International Affairs*, 66(4): 675–95.

Lakin, S. (2008) 'Debunking the idea of parliamentary sovereignty: the controlling factor of legality in the British Constitution', *Oxford Journal of Legal Studies*, 28(4): 709–34.

UK Government (1999) *White Paper on Britain and the Overseas Territories 1999*. Online. Available at: www.ukotcf.org/pdf/charters/WhitePaper99textOnly.pdf (accessed 23 February 2011).

United Kingdom (2008) 'United Kingdom's response to Green Paper questionnaire', *Response to COM(2008) 383*.

7 Symbiotic sovereignties

The untold story of the British Overseas Territories

Ronen Palan

A decade or so into the twenty-first century, it became clear that some of the more outlandish predictions about globalization have failed to materialize. Not so long ago, the favourite subject among academics and journalists alike was the end of everything: the end of the state, the 'end of geography' (as one popular book boldly claimed), even the end of history, no less. Today's talk is about the rise of new powers: China, India, Brazil, and possibly Russia (the BRIC) countries. Yet globalization includes another puzzle: while the very large states appear to be faring well, perhaps even more intriguing is how this also appears to be the case for the very small states, the micropolities, that are by and large anachronistic survivals of time passed by.

The surprising success of a string of small Overseas Countries and Territories (OCTs) in the era of globalization cannot be explained unless we pay attention to a scantly studied phenomenon: the emergence of symbiotic sovereignties. The concept of symbiotic sovereignties refers to cases whereby a *de facto* sovereign authority presents itself as two separate entities, often one of which is considered a sovereign authority and the other a suzerain authority. In this symbiotic relationship, the two authorities may appear to clash on occasion. The smaller claims a degree of 'relative autonomy' from its mother; however, the successful development of the dependent OCT must ultimately be sought in its symbiotic links with its sovereign partner.

Sovereignty games are at the heart of the relationship between Britain and many of its leading Overseas Territories (OTs). I should stress that this chapter specifically discusses the OTs, such as the Cayman Islands and British Virgin Islands, that have developed flourishing Offshore Financial Centres (OFCs). The concept also presents us with a useful framework for analysing what happens when a third authority enters the game, in this case, the European Union (EU). The nice little symbiotic understanding that was constructed over the years between Britain and its OTs is increasingly placed under strain although, as argued below, the EU, which has a long-standing fraught relationship with Britain and in particular with its financial sector, has yet to establish a clear and unambiguous policy towards the British OTs.

My analysis of the symbiotic relationship at the heart of these sovereignty games draws on a tradition of thought that Gad and Adler-Nissen describe in the

Introduction to this volume as institutional analysis. I analyse the various strategies that have developed around what they describe as 'frozen formalized sovereignty arrangements institutionalized in the form of legal texts'. In one tradition of thought, institutionalized relationships and rules of law are seen as constraining action, defining a narrow space of what is allowed and what is not allowed. In my reading, however, formal rules and institutions are not only delineating spaces of acceptable behaviour, they also structure areas of possibilities. Any types of rules and norms, whether explicit or implicit, while serving to restrict and prescribe behaviour, simultaneously also serve as pointers for transgression, change, and evolution. In other words, institutions and norms account for what is not allowed, but also structure the evolution of patterns of transgression. Change therefore takes place not only within the boundaries of institutional path-dependency but also by re-imagining the very same boundaries (Palan 2006).

Following a very rapid process of de-colonization, few remaining scattered polities remained of the once glorious British Empire by the late 1970s. Importantly, they tended to be very small and their ability to survive as independent states in the world is highly questionable. Today, the United Kingdom (UK) continues to hold responsibility for the three Channel Islands, the Isle of Man and 14 OTs (11 of which are permanently populated). Of these territories 11 have OFCs of varying size and significance to their economies.

Some of these polities, like the Channel Islands, were either geographically too close to Britain and too proud of their 'Britishness' to contemplate true independence. Others, such as the Falkland Islands and Gibraltar, suddenly found themselves at a point in history where they had to make a choice – in the case of the former, this choice was about remaining British or joining a junta-led Argentina; in the case of the latter, the alternative to remaining British was joining Franco's Spain. They both chose Britain. The Falklands War in 1982 sealed the Britishness of the Falkland Islands, and by the time Spain began transitioning to democracy after the death of Franco in 1975, Gibraltar had already dealt with the very unique dilemma that all remaining small British polities had to face. They were caught in a widening net cast by the fledgling offshore financial market that emerged in London in 1957. Curiously, the origins of the market are also related to the British postcolonial experience. Many of these small island economies were recast as mini-City of London outposts, known today as offshore financial centres. They take a place of pride among those OCTs that Gad and Adler-Nissen describe as having 'done extremely well in recent decades, possibly due to their peculiar status as 'almost sovereign but not quite''. In the case of the British outposts, 'almost sovereign' meant that they have become experts in what I have described elsewhere as the technique of commercialization of sovereignty (Palan 2002). Small polities have learned to take advantage of their independent status to craft their tax and financial laws so as to attract largely virtual residencies of banks, corporations, and even rich individuals in their territories. At the same time, the absence of 'full' sovereignty is perceived as an advantage for a good many reasons: these polities guaranteed the political and legal stability that financiers demand; they are also subsidized by the British state, which provides them with currency stability, diplomatic and military service, and sometimes adds real money subsidies to the mix.

The chapter describes how City of London financiers sought to incorporate these polities into an expanding global network of OFCs, centred around the City. The chapter demonstrates how close institutional affinities between the City and these polities were one of the important reasons for the close integration between them. The City created a symbiotic sovereignty in this case. The chapter concludes by examining how this relationship between Britain and its dependencies is changing in light of EU policies towards tax havens generally, and Britian and its dependencies specifically.

The rise of the Euromarket

Britain's relationship with some of its OTs dates back to the medieval period. Yet despite the long historical association between the UK and the dependencies that survived the collapse of the British Empire, the relationship between Britain and the polities that serve as OFCs is surprisingly new, the result of a development that took place in 1957; September 1957 to be exact.

The Euromarket emerged in late 1957 in London, most probably by accident and for reasons having very little to do with its subsequent development. It was the last great rear-guard battle of a disintegrating British Empire, the Suez Crisis, which led to the development of this unregulated financial market (Burn 2005; Altman 1969; Hanzawa 1991). On 26 July 1956, Egyptian President Gamel Abdel Nasser announced his decision to nationalize the Suez Canal. British and French forces, joined by Israelis, recaptured the canal in an operation in the end of October that year. The operation was opposed by others, however, including the United States (US). The US mounted strong diplomatic and financial pressure, the latter crucial from the perspective of the processes that shaped future relationship between Britain and its OTs, on the UK to persuade it to withdraw from Egypt.

The impact of the US financial pressure was harsh. The Bank of England had lost $50 million between 30 October and 2 November of 1956. In response to US pressure, Saudi Arabia started an oil embargo against Britain and France, while other NATO countries, including the US, refused to fill the gap until Britain and France withdrew from Egypt. Britain sought assistance from the International Monetary Fund, but this was also denied by the US. Eisenhower in fact ordered the US Treasury to prepare to sell off the US Government's Sterling Bond holdings. (The US Government held these bonds in part to aid post-war Britain's economy and as partial payment of Britain's enormous Second World War debt.) Had the US carried out the threat, Britain's foreign exchange reserves simply could not have sustained the devaluation of the pound that would come after the US actions – at least that was the view in the Cabinet. Faced with mounting speculation against the pound, the British government responded by raising interest rates from 5 to 7 per cent, and imposed strict restrictions on the use of sterling in trade credits with non-residents.

This latter decision proved to be a problem. City banks, which evolved for more than a century as specialists in international lending, particularly to British Commonwealth countries and the so-called British informal empire in Latin America, thus saw their core business disappear overnight. They responded by using US dollars in their international dealings, arguing, presumably,[1] that such transactions have no bearing on the British balance of payments. What followed remains murky to this date, but it appears as though the Bank of England decision to allow these sorts of transactions was interpreted in the context of the English common law to imply that banks' intermediation between non-resident parties undertaken in foreign currency (US dollars at the time) would be deemed by the Bank of England to have taken place outside the UK. As these transactions were taking place in London, they could not be regulated by any other regulatory authority and ended therefore in a regulatory vacuum. This new market was called the Euromarket, or alternatively the Eurodollar market, subsequently also known as the offshore financial market.

Kenneth Boulding maintains that evolutionary change is strongly affected by the existence of 'empty niches' in existing ecosystems, which can be filled by either genetic mutation or migrations of species. He uses the introduction of rabbits to Australia as an example: 'it is very clear that Australia had an empty niche for rabbits, which because of the isolation of the continent genetic mutation had not filled, but once humans introduced rabbits, they expanded very rapidly into a very large niche' (Boulding 1991: 13).

In line with the analogy, then, the development of offshore financial markets as a pragmatic solution to the City commercial banking problem represented such an 'evolutionary mutation' that revealed an ecological 'empty niche' in the global financial markets. Although the Euromarket remained small and practically unknown for about three or four years, US banks, hemmed in by New Deal financial legislations, discovered the market in the early 1960s and began setting up branches in London specializing in Euromarket operations. It soon became clear that the market could be utilized not only to circumvent Bank of England regulations but also the very strict capital control regulations that were imposed under the Bretton Woods regime as well. American banks flocked to the market and to London, because they could avoid Regulation Q, which was introduced in the 1930s. Regulation Q placed an interest rate ceiling on time deposits in US banks.[2] It kept bank interest rates on time deposits very low, a situation that met with little objection from the banks for a long time, but American banks found themselves at a disadvantage when the world economy began to flourish in the late 1950s. In other words, the Euromarket has attracted banks and financial institutions that were interested in escaping their national regulations.

British Overseas Territories

The Euromarket proved a boon to the City of London. The City of London remained a major financial centre in the post Second World War era despite the great weaknesses of the British economy because it served as the financier of the large sterling area. The sterling area was established in the 1930s, and re-established in 1946 following Britain's disastrous flirtation with fixed exchange to the dollar (which was agreed to as part of the 1946 loan agreement with the US). While many may no longer remember this to be so, about 40 per cent of international trade was denominated in sterling as part of the sterling area all the way up until the early 1960s (Schnek 1994). The City was therefore faring relatively well as an 'imperial' financial centre. Known for its air of gentlemanly capitalism, the City remained a powerful, if somewhat conservative, force of British imperial ambitions.

The Euromarket, which was a mutation at the very heart of the British Empire, would change all that; it changed the course not only of the City of London, but also its relationship to its remaining imperial outposts.

The British Empire, the largest empire the world has ever seen, disintegrated very rapidly after the Second World War. By the late 1970s, only a few scattered polities remained. This motley crew of small islands, Hong Kong, and the Rock of Gibraltar were drawn into the last imperial project of the dying British Empire, orchestrated by one of its core constituencies, the City of London. In the process, many British-held OTs have joined the ranks of the world's premier offshore financial centres.

The argument I am forwarding here – and it may or may not apply to other European OCTs – is that many of the better-known British OTs are in effect extensions of the City of London; they are mini-Cities strewn around the globe.

The City of London

The interpretation presented here suggests that the sovereign games discussed in the introduction to this book are a learned behaviour that was subsequently developed by British OTs. They like to claim that they were the authors of their own transformation into flourishing offshore financial centres and that they have learned to take advantage of their sovereign prerogative to create wealth in their territories. The best available historical evidence – which is rather scant to be truthful – suggests otherwise; British OTs were recast as offshore financial centres by City lawyers and financiers seeking to establish mini-City outposts for a number of good reasons.

Why did the final act of the British Imperial project take the form it did? One argument can be dismissed from the outset, namely, that the British state has created a new role for these outposts. By the 1970s, the financial affairs and relationship between Britain and the dependent territories were subject to a number of reviews, including an important internal review conducted by the Department for International Development (DFID). DFID came up with proposals to develop these polities as 'offshore financial centres'. As I will show below, however, DFID came late to the game. The successful (for the time being) development of British suzerainties into OFCs was not a government-driven policy, but rather development prompted by the City of London.

In my view, the last Imperial city state projects had to do with the nature of institutional affinities. The City of London is a unique political entity, described invariably as quasi-feudal or quasi-democratic. The City of London, which used to be called the Corporation of London, describes itself rather modestly as the oldest local authority in England. It plays the role of a local authority within the Square Mile and is responsible for services such as housing, refuse collection, education, social services, the environment, health, and much, much more. In fact, the Corporation of London runs its own police force as well as two of London's most beloved parks, Epping Forest and Hampstead Heath, which are outside the Square Mile. Most importantly, the voting structure in the City is dominated by what is referred to as the non-residential business vote. The City of London Corporation has not undergone the same reforms as other British municipalities since 1835. Consequently, eligible voters in the borough are either residents who are 18 years old and British, Commonwealth or EU citizens, or – and this is where the difference with other boroughs comes to light – are sole traders or partners in an unlimited partnership or appointees of qualifying bodies. Each body or organization with premises in the City, whether incorporated or unincorporated, can appoint a number of voters based on the number of workers it employs. In effect, qualified voters can vote twice, while residents of the City can only vote once. For all intents and purposes, the City of London is therefore run more like a guild in the control of the financial and business interests located within the Square Mile.

It is noteworthy that the City shares many attributes with other remnants of the British Empire, such as the Channel Islands, the Caribbean British possessions, Hong Kong (until 1997), and the British Pacific Islands. This proved important in light of certain 'deficiencies' of London itself, as part of the UK, as a financial centre. First and foremost, while the market in the City was largely unregulated, banks were subject to relatively high level of corporate taxation compared with either pre-Second World War or by today's standards. Before 1965, British companies were subject to income tax on their profits at the same rate that was levied on individuals as well as a profits tax. The standard rate of income tax in the early 1950s stood at 50 per cent, while the additional profits tax was more complex and changed over time. Combined corporate taxation could easily reach 60 and 70 per cent of profits – and often did! As the international financial markets began developing in the early 1960s, taxation unsurprisingly became a sore point for British banks. Moreover, British banks and corporations, as opposed to foreign banks, were paradoxically at a disadvantage vis-à-vis foreign institutions in having limited access to the Euromarkets because they could not pose as non-residents for the purpose of Euromarket transactions.

London bankers had an incentive to shift Euromarket operations outside the UK for tax reasons. The spill-over from London to other centres began in the early 1960s and followed what appears to be the proverbial path of least resistance. It began most naturally with the British polities adjacent to the UK. They shared British law and their political and institutional organizations shared many of the unique political attributes of the City. Jersey seemed an obvious stepping stone for the establishment of low-tax Euromarket operations – it shared British common law, was protected under the UK security umbrella, and used the British pound. Yet the Channel Islands were not ideal places for Euromarket transactions, as they were subjected to a Special Statuary Instrument, the 1947 UK Exchange Control Act. Companies were regarded as residents for exchange control purposes unless specifically designated as non-residents by the Bank of England, and hence barred from accessing the fledgling Euromarket. Companies had to apply to the Bank to obtain 'non-resident' status and provide detailed information regarding the proposed share structure and other financial matters (Johns and Le Marchant 1993). The situation had changed with the introduction of the little-known Sterling Rescheduling Act of 1972. From then on, the Channel Islands developed as full-fledged OFCs.

Mark Hampton notes that 'in the official narrative of the Jersey OFC, the story goes that the island's government – the States of Jersey – showed great foresight and leadership and actively created the OFC from the early 1960s' (Hampton 2007: 4). He demonstrates very clearly, however, that 'the emerging offshore centre was driven by international financial capital, merchant banks, which set up in the island to service certain wealthy customers' (2007: 4). London banks took the lead and began setting up subsidiaries in Jersey, Guernsey, and the Isle of Man in the early 1960s. By 1964, the three big American banks – Citibank, Chase Manhattan, and the Bank of America – arrived on the scene as well (Toniolo 2005: 454).

The Channel Islands also proved attractive due to their unique semi-feudal type of politics, more akin to the politics of the Corporation of London than modern democracy.[3] Austin Mitchell and Prem Sikka described Jersey as a 'town government writ large, with all its intimacies and inefficiencies' (2002: 4). The island became a British Crown possession in 1204, the last of the French possessions retained by the British Crown. Executive authority resides with the Lieutenant-Governor, who acts as the Crown's representative on the island. In reality, the Lieutenant-Governor consults with the States of Jersey and both executive and legislative powers lie primarily with the States of Jersey. In that sense, it is largely autonomous.

There is democracy on the island but (as in the City of London) no party system, no real choice between programme and policies, and no independent civil service. Elected politicians are members of both the legislature and the executive. 'In this sense it appears that in the Jersey States there is the nearly complete fusion of the legislative and executive powers' (Le Hérissier 1998: 170). Again, this is reminiscent of the role of the Mayor and the committee of aldermen in the City of London. Additionally, there were strong personal links between the City and Jersey. In this context, and lacking any effective mechanism for critical discussion, once the Islands' legislatures were convinced of the merits of establishing OFCs, Jersey's secrecy and lack of oversight allowed for even greater freedom and experimentation with financial instruments than was possible on the mainland and was possibly the principle cause of its extraordinary success. What is of little doubt is that the Jersey and Guernsey financial centres developed as satellites of London Euromarket operations.

The development of the Channel Islands in the 1960s as OFCs demonstrates the importance of institutional affinities, personal linkages, and geographical proximity; otherwise, it is unclear why London banks would choose these polities for their ancillary Euromarkets transactions.

Second, third, and fourth wave expansion of the Euromarket

We also know from various reports that, faced with the high infrastructural costs of a London base, some of the smaller American and Canadian banks 'realized that the British Caribbean polities offered a cheaper and equally attractive regulatory environment – free of exchange controls, reserve requirements, and interest rate ceilings, and in the same time zone as New York' (Hudson 1998: 541). Furthermore and crucially, the Caribbean booking centres were not subject to the 1947 UK Exchange Control Act. They were developed by the North American banking community to serve as conduits for Euromarket transactions.

The OFCs in question were British-held territories. In contrast to the Channel Islands, the early spill-over into territories such as the Bahamas and Cayman Islands, reckons Sylla, 'was, like the London Euromarket, not motivated by tax advantages, but because it was cheaper to set up branches in these locations' (Sylla 2002: 53, see also Bhattacharya 1980).

Three Caribbean centres – the Cayman Islands, Bahamas, and initially Panama – benefited in particular from the rapid expansion of the Euromarket, while Bermuda chose an alternative developmental path for reasons described in Palan *et al..* (2010) and developed into the world's premier captive insurance centre. In time, Bermuda also developed as an important conduit for American foreign direct investment. These conduits are rather different, however, from the 'holding company' structures that the Benelux countries, Ireland, and to a lesser extent Switzerland specialize in. Panama declined as a centre for Euromarket operations commensurate with the rise of British-held Caribbean polities. By the late 1970s, the Caribbean basin accounted for one-fifth of the gross size of total Eurocurrency operations. By the 1980s, US bank branches in the Caribbean comprised more than one-third of the assets of all US foreign bank branches in the American region.

The theory of institutional affinities may also help explain the development of the Asian OFCs with strong British links. As the widening Indo-China war in the mid-1960s increased foreign exchange expenditures in the region, tightening credit in 1967 and 1968 contributed to rising interest rates in the Eurodollar market. Tapping existing dollar balances in the Asia-Pacific region became attractive for many banks. The Bank of America was the first to hit on the idea of establishing a specialized facility for Eurodollar operations in East Asia.

Initially, the Bank of America approached the one jurisdiction that shared many of the characteristics described above, namely, Hong Kong. The Hong Kong colonial government, however, was not particularly forthcoming. It had placed restrictions on the financial sector as far back as the early 1950s. Having failed to persuade the Hong Kong government, the Bank of America sounded out the next available jurisdiction that shares many of the above characteristics. Singapore proved more accommodating. It responded by setting up a facility in 1968 called the Asian Currency Unit to encourage Euromarket activities. The moratorium on the establishment of new banks in Hong Kong was lifted in 1978, and this change proved a great success. In February 1982, the interest withholding tax on foreign currency deposits was abolished. In 1989, all forms of tax on interest were abolished as well. With the government becoming more proactive, by 1995–96, Hong Kong had soon become the second largest OFC in the Asia-Pacific region and between the sixth and seventh largest International Finance Centre in the world (Jao 1979). In the late 1960s, a fourth wave of expansion into small Pacific polities, such as Nauru, Vanuatu, and Palau, had begun, but they never managed to leverage their tax advantages into a flourishing OFC.

Enter Europe

British OTs have a complex yet symbiotic relationship with the British state. A report to the Commonwealth office warns, 'Whilst the UK faces the ultimate risk should any financial malpractice occur, it is the responsibility of Territory governments to develop the necessary regulatory arrangements' (National Audit Office 2007: 7). The report, written before the outbreak of the financial crisis, works on the assumption that the relationship between Britain and its OTs is an unequal relationship benefiting the smaller partners in particular. In other words, the report assumes that the British OTs proved much more adept than the British state in these sovereignty games.

   The argument above challenges some of the predicates of the report (and others like it). The relationship between the British state and its successful OTs is based on finance; it is a symbiotic relationship that strengthened the City's hold on global finance. But the 'official' narrative that is repeated again and again in British government reports is of an asymmetrical relationship that supposedly benefits the smaller partners. Such narrative serves a useful purpose: intentionally (or not, the authors of these reports may not be entirely aware of the true situation) minimizing the City's role in these centres, as long as such narrative persists, the symbiotic relationship between Britain and its OTs is played down. It is a narrative that demands no radical change in the relationship between the UK and its dependent territories. The politics of reform (a useful agenda that suggests ongoing improvement) is aimed primarily at handling the risk and subsidy issues between the two parties in these symbiotic relations while protecting the essence – the power of the City of London.

   However, the cosy relationship between Britain and its territories is coming under strain from other quarters, as the EU is a powerful force with its own 'imperial ambitions' (as Gad and Adler-Nissen describe it in the Introduction). The key players in the fledgling EU, Germany and France, were traditionally opposed to tax havens as well as the extreme forms of financial deregulation espoused by the City. The British OTs are therefore caught in the cross-fire between British imperial interests and the EU imperial ambitions; the fate of that clash is not as yet clear – which also means that the fate of the British OTs is not clear either.

   The series of treaties that established the European Community (EC) and the EU offered little in terms of tax coordination. It was broadly accepted, however, that a single market requires tax neutrality on international business operations. The Commission established a fiscal and financial committee which published a report in 1962 calling for tax harmonization across the EC. Unsuccessful attempts at tax code harmonization followed in 1975 and 1985. But as the Organisation for Economic Cooperation and Development (OECD) was preparing its report on harmful tax competition, the EU council was agreeing, on 1 December 1997, to a package of measures to tackle harmful tax competition within the Union as well (ECOFIN 1999). Thus began a new phase in EU policy towards tax havens. More than other EU policies, this new policy defines the relationship between the EU and British OTs.

The 1997 Code of Conduct on Business Taxation has the potential to change everything. The code does not have the status of a legal instrument, but it provides an informal approach to regulation, which proved surprisingly effective (Radaelli 2003). In adopting this code, member states work to eliminate numerous harmful tax competition practices and avoid new ones. Whereas the OECD campaign is limited to financial and other services, the EU Code looks at business activities in general, with greater emphasis on mobile activities. To avoid charges of imperialism, the code does not elaborate a principle of 'just taxation' nor imposes it on recalcitrant states. Instead, taking a line adopted by the OECD, the code accepts the principle of tax competition, allowing states freedom of choice in this matter. However, the EU insists that the tax regime's rules be applied equally on all businesses in the jurisdiction, domestic and foreign. The code therefore targets the practice whereby non-residents are provided a more favourable tax treatment than that which is generally available in the member state concerned – which is precisely what tax havens do. Citing the code, for example, in 2006 the Commission forced Luxembourg to abandon its 1929 holding companies. Similarly, the adoption of new tax regimes by Jersey, Guernsey, and the Isle of Man since 2008 (notably the 0 per cent tax rate on business profits) may be taken to task for not respecting the code. Ireland adopted a 12.5 per cent rate for active income; a revised regime for Madeira has been approved as well, and a new tax regime has been proposed for Gibraltar, which intends a zero corporate tax rate. Malta and Cyprus have also submitted their tax rules to the Commission. The Code is therefore generally viewed as a success.

The EU is also pushing for the harmonization of corporate taxation across the continent. Multinational companies with subsidiaries in more than one European country pay taxes in the countries in which they operate, but they tend to shift profits to the lowest-tax country through complex systems of transfer pricing. The EU forwarded a clear set of proposals to deal with other abuses as well. In 1989, a first draft proposed a pan-European withholding tax of 15 per cent for all savings income, including investments by non-residents of the EU. It was abandoned under pressure from Luxembourg, which was reluctant to give up its bank secrecy laws. A second draft was presented in 1998 and subsequently re-launched in June 2000 as part of the great international mobilization against tax havens. A European directive was introduced in July 2001 and finally implemented in July 2005. Since July 2005, all member states are required to exchange information with the relevant national authorities. Austria, Belgium, and Luxembourg retained their bank secrecy rules (Austria later abandoned them) but are required to impose a withholding tax on earnings from deposits starting at a rate of 15 per cent from 2005 to 2007, rising to 20 per cent from 2008 to 2010, and to 35 per cent thereafter. Crucially, the EU insisted that a series of micro-states and OCT jurisdictions outside the EU proper will comply with the scheme. Andorra, Liechtenstein, Monaco, San Marino and the British OTs (including the Channel Islands, Isle of Man, and the Caribbean dependencies) also comply.

Moreover, the European Court of Justice (ECJ) was also instrumental in the reform of European taxation from the mid-1980s on. An important court ruling in 1985 left direct taxation to the responsibility of each member state, but it called on states to devise their tax laws to respect treaty obligations. In the 20 years thereafter, the ECJ has delivered more than 50 judgments along these lines. The ECJ has adopted a far more aggressive attitude since 2005. It had previously tended to side with individuals and corporations and not with member states seeking to protect their revenues. However, in a landmark judgment in April 2005, the Halifax case, the Court ruled that European law forbids transactions if the sole purpose is to create a tax advantage. This interpretation was reaffirmed in a case involving Cadbury Schweppes in May 2006, when the court condemned what it called 'wholly artificial' subsidiaries in tax havens. In another important judgment delivered on 13 March 2007 (the so-called thin-cap affair), the Court ruled that states could restrict freedom of establishment of wholly artificial structures devoid of economic reality and having tax avoidance as their principal objective. The Court reaffirmed its position again in July of that year.

The battle has shifted recently to the area occupied by offshore hedge funds. Germany and France are pushing hard for a so-called 'European Passport', registration requirements for managers with assets over €100 million that will allow funds to be marketed in member states to professional clients. The UK, of course, opposes the idea. Many insiders believe that, if implemented, these rules will spell the end of the Cayman Island hedge fund industry (there is also talk of a separate Asian passport) (see also Vleck, this volume).

The EU is therefore taking a strong position on the issues of tax avoidance and evasion, a position which is in fact stronger than either the UK or US is taking towards financial regulation.

Conclusion

The suggestion here is that the success of British dependent and overseas territories is due, in part, to the fact that the British state has its own 'internal' micropolity jurisdiction in the City of London. Unlike a typical borough or municipal government in Britain, which most business people find difficult to work with, the City of London Corporation has been constructed by, and works well, for these financiers. It is not entirely surprising to discover that financiers who were groomed in the unique political conditions characterizing the City of London would be attracted to fairly similar polities throughout the British Empire. They sought to develop diplomatic and economic relationships with the polities that are most akin to the City, the British dependent and overseas territories. The evidence that such was the thinking in London and the OTs is somewhat anecdotal and draws largely on personal accounts from the individuals involved in these processes – although to date no systemic academic study of these relationships has been conducted. The relationships between Britain and its overseas tax havens have neither the character of traditional colonial relations, nor are they the standard relation of postcolonial dependency seemingly characterizing most of the other territories described in this volume. Rather, it is a symbiotic relationship that underpins the position of the City of London in global finance.

The second theme running through this chapter is the unique postcolonial experience of Britain. The City of London was at the heart of the rise, and subsequent fall, of the British Empire. The relationships between Britain and its OTs are largely determined, it is interesting to note, not only by the imperial past, but also by the attempt of the City to survive post-imperial Britain by constructing a new 'informal empire' of its own.

The conclusion of this discussion is that the relationships between the EU and its British-held OTs are mediated through the City. Whether British OTs will remain British Imperial outposts, as all of the signs suggest they wish to be, or will become, in Gad and Adler-Nissen's terminology, the last European colonial outposts, which is what the EU wishes them to be, is in essence a major issue concerning the future and place of finance in the EU.

Notes

1 The arguments were taking place behind closed doors between the banks and the Bank of England; we have only retrospective verbal accounts from some of the participants interviewed many years later (see Burn 2005).
2 Regulation Q prohibits member banks from paying interest on demand deposits. See Electronic Code of Federal Regulations (e-CFR). The National Recovery Administration, which was set up under the New Deal, sought to fix prices in industry in order to eliminate 'ruinous' competition, and Regulation Q attempted to do the same in the banking sector.
3 A House of Commons report describes the Island of Sark in these terms: 'Until 2008, Sark's government was based on a feudal system. The Seigneur, a hereditary position, was the head of government. Chief Pleas was made up of the feudal landholders – the Tenants – and twelve deputies of the people. The Seneschal was the presiding officer and Chief Judge' (House of Commons Justice Committee 2010: 18). The report provides a detailed description of the legislative arrangements in the Channel Islands.

References

Altman, O.L. (1969) 'Eurodollars', in E.B. Chalmers (ed.) *Reading in the Euro-Dollar*, London: W.P. Griffith.

Bhattacharya, A. (1980) 'Offshore banking in the Caribbean', *Journal of International Business Studies*, 11(3): 37–46.

Boulding, K. (1991) 'What is evolutionary economics?', *Journal of Evolutionary Economics*, 1: 1–19.

Burn, G. (2005) *Re-Emergence of Global Finance*, London: Palgrave.

ECOFIN (1999) Code of Conduct Business Taxation Council of the European Union. Brussels. Online. Available at: http://ec.europa.eu/taxation_customs/resources/documents/primarolo_en.pdf (accessed 12 March 2012).

Hampton, M. (2007) *Offshore Finance Centers and Rapid Complex Constant Change*, Kent Business School, Working Paper No. 132.

Hanzawa, M. (1991) 'The Tokyo offshore market', in *Japan's Financial Markets*, Foundation for Advanced Information and Research, Japan Fair.

House of Commons Justice Committee (2010) Crown Dependencies, Eighth Report of Session 2009–10. Ordered by the House of Commons to be printed 23 March.

Hudson, A.C. (1998) 'Reshaping the regulatory landscape: border skirmishes around the Bahamas and Cayman offshore financial centers', *Review of International Political Economy*, 5(3): 534–64.

Jao, Y.C. (1979) 'The Rise of Hong Kong as a Financial Center', *Asian Survey*, 19(7): 674–94.

Johns, R.A. and Le Marchant, C.M. (1993) *Finance Centres: British Isle Offshore Development Since 1979*, London: Pinter Publishers.

Le Hérissier, R. (1998) 'Jersey: exercising executive power in a non-party system', *Public Administration and Development*, 18: 169–84.

Mitchell, A. and Sikka, P. (2002) 'Jersey: auditors' liabilities versus people's rights', *Political Quarterly*, 70: 3–15.

National Audit Office (2007) *Managing Risk In The Overseas Territories*, Report by the Comptroller and Auditor General, HC 4 Session 2007–8, 16 November 2007, Foreign and Commonwealth Office, London: The Stationery Office.

Palan, R. (2002) 'Tax havens and the commercialisation of state sovereignty', *International Organization*, 56(1): 153–78.

Palan, R. (2006) 'Norms, sovereignty and the American Empire' in K. Giesen and Van Der Pijl (eds) *Global Norms for the 21st Century: Political, Science, Philosophy, Law*, Newcastle: Cambridge Scholar Press.

Palan, R., Murphy, R. and Chavagneux, C. (2010) *Tax Havens: How Globalization Really Works*, Ithaca: Cornell University Press.

Radaelli, C.M. (2003) 'The code of conduct against harmful tax competition: open method of coordination in disguise?', *Public Administration*, 81(3): 513–31.

Schnek, C. (1994) *Britain and the Sterling Area: From Devaluation to Convertibility*, London: Routledge.

Sylla R. (2002) 'United States banks and Europe: strategy and attitudes', in S. Battilossi and Y. Cassis (eds) *European Banks and the American Challenge: Competition and Cooperation in International Banking Under Bretton Woods*, New York: Oxford University Press.

Tonilo, G. (2005) *Central Bank Cooperation at the Bank for International Settlements, 1930–1973*, Cambridge: Cambridge University Press.

8 Sovereignty games and global finance

The Cayman Islands

William Vlcek[1]

The Cayman Islands are home to a world-leading offshore financial centre (OFC) and are the domicile for a significant number of hedge funds (Z/Yen Group Limited 2010). It is this position as an important financial centre that makes the Cayman case particularly interesting, because the outcome from any sovereignty game under play among the Cayman Islands, the United Kingdom (UK) and the European Union (EU) may produce externalities affecting other major financial centres and global finance more generally. This study casts light on the complex interplay over human rights and international taxation engaged between the postcolonial citizens of Britain's imperial past in the Caribbean with a postmodern Europe.

The following analysis situates the Cayman OFC as the central element in both the triangular relationship with the UK and the EU and examines the position of the Cayman Islands in the world economy. The imposition of the EU Savings Tax Directive on the Cayman Islands serves as the case study, contextualized by the preceding experience for British-imposed legislation decriminalizing homosexuality. The latter human rights issue remains a very contentious topic for Caymanian society, and it was revisited during the constitutional reform process introducing a Bill of Rights in the new Cayman Islands Constitution. Before developing this case study for sovereignty games involving the Cayman Islands, the next section provides a brief historical background for the Cayman Islands and its OFC.

Background for sovereignty games in the Cayman Islands

An overseas territory

The Cayman Islands (Grand Cayman, Little Cayman, and Cayman Brac), with an estimated population of 51,384 in 2011, are located 240 km south of Cuba and 268 km northwest of Jamaica. Formally recognized as a British colony in the seventeenth century, they were not environmentally suitable for the plantation economy prevalent on the other Caribbean islands and instead became the home to escaped slaves and Europeans (some with slaves), because the islands were relatively ungoverned. The lack of a formal government also permitted pirates and privateers to use the Cayman Islands as a source for supplies, an historical legacy that has been applied on occasion to its financial services sector (e.g. Mortished

2004).[2] Because of its small size, the Cayman Islands were structured as a 'colony of a colony' under Jamaica until 1962, when Jamaica headed down the path to sovereign independence while the Cayman Islands resolved to retain a formal relationship with the UK (Bodden 2007).

The conflicting desires over decolonization that were present in the Cayman Islands, Jamaica and the UK helped to shape this outcome. In the UK, a perception dominated the decolonization process in the late 1950s and early 1960s that there was some indeterminate minimum size (population, territory, economy) required in order to establish a viable independent, sovereign state. For example, a UK government report in 1957 noted that some territories were 'of no material value and could not hope to maintain themselves with a stable administration if the British left' (as cited in McIntyre 1996: 259–60). An earlier UK government report raised concerns in 1951 over the potential for what today would be called a 'lack of democratic governance', and its authors suggested that a political 'status short of independence' was needed.

> To hand over unrestricted control in internal affairs in small territories where the bulk of the population is economically weak and politically immature might, in practice, involve the abandonment of the people to the dictation of a dominant group which would be free to indulge in tyranny and corruption without let or hindrances.
>
> (as cited in McIntyre 1996: 253)

Believing that a number of small islands in the British West Indies could not succeed on their own as independent states, the UK pursued the construction of a West Indies Federation, such that the combined capabilities of the various island territories could support independence. Jamaica was viewed as an anchor for the Federation, while most politicians across the prospective member islands for this Federation were more interested in autonomy than in shifting the central government authority from Westminster to Kingston. As Baldacchino notes (this volume), federated solutions involving islands remain 'in flux', a situation also reflected by the deconstruction of the Netherlands Antilles (Oostindie, this volume). Bodden (2010: 57) suggests that there were further concerns in the Cayman Islands among politicians regarding the Federation; economically, the loss of the special visa regime with the United States (US) that permitted Caymanians to work on US merchant vessels, and culturally, concern that the white elite-dominated Caymanian society would be 'overrun' by the more populous black-dominated society of Jamaica. The remedy was separation from Jamaica-the-colony and exclusion from the proposed Jamaica-led West Indies Federation, with the Cayman Islands 're-established' as a colony under direct rule from Westminster.

The pivotal point, however, concerning an agreement in the UK to restructure its political relationship with the Cayman Islands was the fact that Cayman was not 'aid dependent', a situation that continues today. Here, the Cayman Islands represent an exception to the concern with the viability of a small territory as an independent sovereign state, because the Caymanian economy in the late 1950s benefitted from the influx of US dollar remittances sent by the men serving in the US merchant fleet (hence, the concern over the status of the US visa regime). The subsequent development of the offshore financial centre continued to negate any need for direct financial support from the UK.[3] 'One thing seems crystal clear and that is the United Kingdom's willingness to entertain the Cayman Islands' request was primarily based on the fact of the islands' financial independence' (Bodden 2010: 85). Consequently, the UK government had no problem with the Cayman Islands remaining a dependent territory because such a relationship would incur little direct financial cost. It is only in more recent years that the concept of 'contingent liability' has emerged to suggest that the Cayman Islands' OFC poses the risk of a financial liability on the UK Treasury (National Audit Office 1997, 2007). This concern has become central to the sovereignty games played between London and the Cayman Islands.

An offshore financial centre

Historically, the Cayman Islands have never collected income taxes, government revenue being collected from import tariffs and duties. Economic independence and development as a British territory no longer intermediated by Jamaica would be pursued by emulating the financial services industry under development in the Bahamas and Bermuda, initially via the enactment of legislation to attract foreign capital. This strategy was outlined by the British Governor of Jamaica in 'Extract from Jamaican Governor's Intelligence Report for November–December 1960', archived in the Colonial Office collection CO 1331/4271, 'Attitude of the Smaller Dependencies of the West Indies Towards the Federation', a copy of which is on deposit with the Cayman Islands National Archive. Recall that Jamaica's colonial governor was also the executive for the Cayman Islands, as the islands were subordinate to Jamaica until 1962. Moreover, this situation should be understood in the context of a 1961 population of approximately 8,000 residents for all of the Cayman Islands, not exactly a large number of people from which to develop a world-leading financial centre.

Correspondence from the Governor General of the West Indies dated 5 April 1960 (in Colonial Office file CO 1331/4271) covered the 'Resolution and Statement of Aims from the Cayman Islands Legislative Assembly' provided by the Legislative Assembly. The essential logic of the case it made for continued minimal taxation (no income taxes) in the Cayman Islands was the intention to attract 'free capital seeking a statutory home for general investment elsewhere with a minimum of obstruction and control'; and as such, the argument remains essentially the same today.[4] The rationale for the proposed companies legislation to attract this 'free capital' was compared to the situation of Delaware in the US, which was already operating as a centre for corporate registrations as a means of raising revenue for the state government. In a letter dated the following day, the Governor General observed:

But the links of the Cayman Islands with the United States are very close, and the Influence of the American (and Canadian) businessman is great through tourism. (Indeed the recent proposal to pass a special Companies Law based on the American and Bahamian models so as to attract 'brass plate' companies as in the Bahamas, emanates mainly from two very prominent Canadians who have recently visited the Caymans for a holiday).

(Cayman Islands National Archive 1960–1)

Consequently, and in contrast to the case made by Palan (2010), UK government documents indicate the direct involvement of Canadian and American businessmen in the initial construction of the Cayman offshore financial centre, modelled after the example of the financial services industries emerging at the time in the Bahamas and Bermuda. Thus, the narrative told in Cayman is that rather than US firms relocating from London to the Cayman Islands, the formative capital and initial firms involved in establishing the OFC came directly from North America in the 1960s. The Cayman OFC subsequently attracted firms and expatriate employees from the City of London to Cayman for its expansion into Euromarket operations in the 1970s (Palan, this volume). Before considering the imposition of the EU Savings Tax Directive in the Cayman Islands, it is useful to understand the environment in which the sovereignty game took place.

Legislating moral conduct – human rights in the Caribbean

Citizens in the British West Indies territories possess an identity separate from that of society in the metropolitan state while retaining a belief that complete independence could be worse than their current semi-sovereign status. A comparative assessment with neighbouring independent jurisdictions (e.g. GDP per capita, living standards, crime statistics, etc.) suggests to many that the benefits afforded by maintaining the connection with the metropolitan state facilitate a better quality of life. Yet the distinct Caribbean identity includes beliefs for a society/social structure that is not necessarily consistent with the social structure of the metropolitan state, and by extension the EU. Consequently, the British Caribbean Overseas Territories (OTs) resisted changes proposed for their constitutional structure abolishing capital punishment and decriminalizing homosexuality (Clegg 2006). There is, however, a significant feature characterizing the relationship between the government in Westminster and its OTs that is different from that of the other EU metropolitan states with their OTs: the 'Order in Council'. An Order in Council is a special form of legislation in the UK made under the Royal Prerogative, a common law power that remains with the Crown and operates through the Privy Council. It is thus legislation that is not subject to Parliamentary debate and 'is normally subject to less judicial scrutiny than other types of legislation' (Antoine 2008: 233). In those instances where an OT government is unwilling to legislate, as with capital punishment and homosexual conduct, an Order in Council can be used to impose legislation against local wishes. And, as will be seen with the case of the EU Savings Tax Directive, the government in Westminster is also willing to use the threat of one as a coercive negotiating tactic. The death penalty was abolished in 1991 and homosexuality decriminalized in 2000 via Orders in Council. While the resistance to change was attributed to 'cultural differences', the use of the Order in Council demonstrates more fundamentally the persistent presence of power in the metropolitan–OT relationship – and consequently its presence in the background of any sovereignty game (Bodden 2007: xv, 115). This colonial remnant of Imperial power is viewed by some as the UK's 'nuclear option', and as such it limits the range of manoeuvre available to an OT in any sovereignty game.[5]

For human rights, the triangular relationship between the Cayman Islands, the UK and EU is less clear because the direct involvement of the EU, as an actor, is somewhat nebulous. It is a binary relationship, and a Foreign and Commonwealth Office White Paper in 1999 explicitly tied human rights in the OTs to 'good government', stating that those that 'choose to remain British should abide by the same basic standards of human rights, openness and good government that British people expect of their Government'. Consequently, the OTs are expected to comply with the same 'international obligations' of the UK, including the European Convention on Human Rights and the United Nations (UN) International Covenant on Civil and Political Rights (Foreign and Commonwealth Office 1999: 20). The White Paper identified three issues that it felt needed to be reformed, because they placed the UK government in a position where it risked 'being in breach of important and fundamental international agreements'. The UK was 'exposed' to a 'contingent liability of costs and possibly damages' where, in the event of a lawsuit against an OT government that it lost and was unable to pay, Westminster would be left with that financial obligation. The conclusion then was simple; these OT laws must be changed, and because the British government was committed 'to a modern relationship with the Overseas Territories based on partnership and responsible self-government', the preferred solution was legal reform undertaken by each respective OT government. Nonetheless, failing local action, the White Paper stated that the UK would legislate change with an Order in Council to accomplish the necessary legal revision (Foreign and Commonwealth Office 1999: 20). For the Cayman Islands in 1999, the only human rights issue identified was the decriminalization of homosexual acts.

Naturally, the White Paper attracted extensive debate in the Legislative Assembly of the Cayman Islands. As already noted, the UK legislated the end of capital punishment in the Cayman Islands with an Order in Council in 1991, a fact which one Member of the Legislative Assembly (MLA) addressed:

> In that case there were many in the Cayman Islands who felt that the death penalty should remain on our books. But as long as we were a territory of the UK we had to comply with the same standards the UK set for itself.
>
> (Cayman Islands Legislative Assembly 1999: 287)

A similar statement of diverging attitudes between the Cayman Islands and the UK was noted from the White Paper and raised in legislative debate; that 'some Caribbean communities' continued to be strongly opposed to homosexuality 'based on firmly held religious beliefs' (Foreign and Commonwealth Office 1999: 21). This observation was received approvingly by some MLAs; for example, 'I am glad to say that Cayman is one of those jurisdictions based firmly on our religious beliefs' (Cayman Islands Legislative Assembly 1999: 322). All legislative debate occurred in an atmosphere fully cognizant of the UK's stated intention to legislate by Order in Council should the territories fail to act as desired on the specified human rights issues. Nonetheless, this MLA (and Minister for Community Affairs, Sports, Women, Youth and Culture) further stated her belief that when the matter came to a vote in the Assembly, it would be a 'conscience vote' (Cayman Islands Legislative Assembly 1999: 323).

Given the local feelings on this subject, the UK's desire for legislative change to take place under 'principles of partnership' (as understood by the government in Westminster) would not occur for the case of Cayman and the decriminalization of homosexuality. As explained to me in one interview, 'homosexuality has connotations in the Caribbean very different than in Europe'; and as a politically charged issue in the Cayman Islands, no politician could be seen as supporting it.[6] Consequently, there was no public support to change the domestic legislation, which in turn meant the UK promulgated an Order in Council – there was no alternative. As Peter Clegg observed, 'British action highlighted the determination to enforce basic standards of human rights, but it is interesting to observe that although the law was changed the view of many in the Overseas Territories has not' (Clegg 2006: 140). Changing a law does not at the same time change social attitudes, and the issue of homosexuality remains a contentious topic in Caymanian society. Its decriminalization has been framed as the first step down a slippery slope towards the legalization of same-sex marriages and the further corruption of Cayman's (Christian) culture. Consequently, it was referred to repeatedly throughout debate over constitutional reform and the inclusion of a Bill of Rights in the new Cayman Constitution. For example, a court ruling in Aruba that a Dutch same-sex marriage certificate must be recognized as valid and legal by the government of Aruba provided evidence for Caymanian activists that the UK could force the legalization of same-sex marriage on the Cayman Islands in the future with an Order in Council (Cayman Net News 2007).

Yet, regardless of the public proclamations made in the Legislative Assembly and the creation of public interest groups professing to speak on behalf of citizens, the attitude of the public at large is not necessarily opposed to homosexuality. In the course of conducting fieldwork, the question was posed informally to a range of different individuals. As to be expected in a diverse, modern society, the full range of possible responses was encountered. One interviewee noted, with regards to the media reports of local reactions to blatant homosexual conduct in public, that homosexual visitors coming to Cayman in order to make a statement might encounter problems.[7] The suggestion offered was that simple discretion and respect for local mores and customs on the part of gay couples would avoid such problems or confrontations between tourists and residents.[8] One attempt at preempting efforts to stir up local sentiment was a Private Members Motion (12/01) in 2001, directing the government to conduct a review of the Penal Code to determine that it contained 'adequate provision . . . for the maintenance of appropriate standards of public behaviour and public decency in the Cayman Islands'. Debate moved beyond public displays of affection by same-sex couples to highlight other forms of conduct that MLAs found inappropriate in public spaces as well as the inclusion of a Bill of Rights in the new Constitution (Cayman Islands Legislative Assembly 2001: 730–5, 46–60).

Interestingly, the word 'sovereignty' is rarely used in Cayman legislative debate. When it does appear in the Hansard, it is normally as part of the concept of 'financial sovereignty'. Specifically, the concept involves the determination of the local government budget and the management of government finances in Cayman. In the context of the discussions underway in 2002–03 over constitutional modernization in the Cayman Islands, it also involved the separation of responsibilities between the locally elected government and the Governor (and the retained powers of that office) such that,

> No more should people be able to go off to London to set up plans while we pay for it here and have a Governor who will pay for it even when we say, as elected representatives of the people, do not pay.
>
> (Cayman Islands Legislative Assembly 2003: 904)

The argument was 'that the United Kingdom Government should not have control of our financial affairs through Orders in Council, that is, the Privy Council, or by legislation in the Commons'. Furthermore, the Cayman Islands sought to have its OFC kept in mind when the UK negotiated international agreements that might impact its operation, expecting in fact that the Cayman Islands should be consulted by the UK government in advance of any agreement (Cayman Islands Legislative Assembly 2003: 796). The new Constitution reflects this position in part in §32, 'Exercise of the Governor's functions', where the Governor is directed to keep the Cabinet informed of any matter that 'may involve the economic or financial interests of the Cayman Islands' (Privy Council 2009: 24). The extent to which this consultation may occur in practice remains to be seen, however, as the desire for consultation may be understood as one outcome from earlier events involving the EU Savings Tax Directive.

Making a case of it – the Cayman Islands at the Court of First Instance

The imposition of the EU Savings Tax Directive on the Cayman Islands and the tactic pursued by Cayman to challenge its application to the Caymanian financial sector provides an interesting study for a sovereignty game by a European micropolity. Moreover, subsequent to the accusations that either the OFCs, the so-called 'shadow' banking system, financial derivatives, and/or the bond rating agencies were responsible for the international financial meltdown in 2008, a multitude of regulations, legislation and EU Directives have been proposed in order to prevent a recurrence. Consequently, this case may indicate the nature for ongoing sovereignty games among the EU, UK and British Caribbean OTs with regard to financial regulations proposed by the European Parliament and Commission, for example, to restrain investment (hedge) funds (Tait 2010). And certainly the point was made in one interview in the Cayman Islands that there is a perception in the Cayman government for the need to 'have an ear' in Brussels in order to become aware of any EU proposals with a potential impact for the Cayman Islands while still in the proposal stage.[9]

The background for this case is situated in the fact that taxation has been a contentious issue in the process to create a single market in Europe. In 2003, agreement was finally reached concerning the taxation of interest paid on the foreign savings accounts of individual EU citizens (natural persons); the Directive came into effect on 1 July 2005 (European Council 2003).[10] This Directive for the 'taxation of savings income in the form of interest payments' was structured with two options (exchange taxpayer account details or collect a withholding tax) in order to satisfy the competing interests between the member states with a significant financial sector and the member states concerned by the tax avoidance practices of their citizens. Because 'capital travels light – with cabin baggage only' (Bauman 2000: 58), the Directive also was predicated on the cooperation of six non-member jurisdictions (Andorra, Liechtenstein, Monaco, San Marino, Switzerland, and the US) to implement its procedures. Beyond these named non-member jurisdictions, the European Council was concerned that deposits would simply relocate to other convenient locations beyond the scope of the Directive. Hence, Article 17, paragraph 2(ii) states that the member states 'shall apply these provisions . . . [in] all relevant or associated territories (the Channel Islands, Isle of Man, and all dependent or associated territories in the Caribbean)' (OJ L/157, p. 45). A geographic weakness in the Directive in this specific paragraph is the fact that Bermuda, a British OT located in the North Atlantic, is not included in the scope of the Directive; further, as noted by the editors in their introductory chapter to this volume, 'Bermuda resists any association with the EU' (Gad and Adler-Nissen, this volume). Additional geographic weaknesses in the Directive include the absence of Hong Kong and Singapore, the destinations for significant financial flows from Europe at the time the Directive went into force (Parker *et al.* 2006; Taylor and Prystay 2006).

The government and financial industry in the Cayman Islands were worried about the potential impact on the industry should Cayman be forced to implement the EU Directive. In November 2002, the Leader of Government Business (the title for the Premier at that time) stated to the Legislative Assembly that the Directive, 'if implemented, would ring the death knell for Cayman's financial industry'. Throughout this period, he repeated that the Cayman government understood 'the position of the UK and other EU members in relation to their domestic economies' and declared the willingness of the Cayman government to discuss the Directive with them; nonetheless, the interests of the Cayman Islands came first (*Caymanian Compass* 2002b; see also, Cayman Islands Legislative Assembly 2003: 625). One week later, the *Caymanian Compass* reported that the Leader of Government Business had declared that 'Cayman has no intention of committing to the UK on the EU Savings Tax Initiative' and in fact the government was willing to go to the

European Court of Justice (ECJ) or even to the UN on the matter. This declaration was made on 15 November 2002, the deadline set by the UK Secretary of State for Overseas Territories in a letter requesting that the Cayman Islands 'reconsider its position of not being willing to commit' to the EU Directive (*Caymanian Compass* 2002a).

The intransigence expressed by the government of Cayman was matched by the government in Westminster. As reported by the *Caymanian Compass*, citing an article published in *The Times*, UK Chancellor Gordon Brown had given the European Council 'his "unequivocal assurance" that automatic exchange of information would be introduced in Britain's Caribbean territories. "If necessary we will legislate directly," he said' (*Caymanian Compass* 2002c; see also, Cayman Islands Legislative Assembly 2003: 765). The position of the UK Chancellor was framed by the Leader of Government Business as a 'conflict of interest', because on the one hand the Chancellor was responsible for representing the interests of the UK and its 'political constituency in the United Kingdom's financial services industry' while on the other hand the UK is responsible for the OTs and hence responsible for looking after their interests. The financial services industry in London is viewed as a competitor for the Cayman financial services industry in the islands (while a different picture is presented by Palan, this volume). Moreover, the Leader of Government Business declared to the Legislative Assembly:

> The fact remains, however, that all European Union Member States, including the United Kingdom, also have obligations both national and international to take into consideration the interests of the Caribbean Overseas Territories including these Cayman Islands.
>
> (Cayman Islands Legislative Assembly 2003: 765)

This latter statement suggests a view for continuing 'colonial' responsibilities, or it may be understood as expecting that interaction with the OTs would treat them as sovereign jurisdictions, at least with respect to financial sovereignty as devolved to the OTs by the UK. Nonetheless, the issue raised (as viewed from the Caribbean) concerned the lack of representation in the creation of a Directive that was to be imposed on them, as well as being a simple matter of 'fairness and equity'. It was, moreover, an issue for 'how Europe treats its colonies in the 21st century' (Cayman Islands Legislative Assembly 2003: 765). Essentially, the discourse in the Cayman Islands accepts the notion of national interests on the part of the UK with respect to the EU Savings Tax Directive and its role as administering jurisdiction, while emphasizing that the Cayman government expects that its national interests, specifically the financial services and tourism sectors, will be similarly acknowledged. It is basically a sovereignty game masked behind the alternate term, national interest.

As a move to resist the implementation of the EU Savings Tax Directive in the Cayman Islands, the government lodged a case at the Court of First Instance in the ECJ in March 2003. Essentially, the legal case was intended to force the European Commission to establish a 'Partnership Working Party' in keeping with the

European Council's 27 November 2001 Decision on 'the association of the over-seas countries and territories with the European Community' (OJ L/314 2001, p. 1). The agenda for the proposed Partnership Working Party was to address the potential impact of implementing the Directive on the Cayman financial services sector, the cost figure noted in the findings of the court was anticipated to be between 30 and 70 million US dollars annually (Court of the First Instance of the European Communities 2003: paragraph 69).[11] The ECJ dismissed the case, in part because it found that

> if the proposed directive is adopted, to take the necessary domestic (munici-pal) measures to ensure that, once the directive is implemented in the United Kingdom, the same measures will be applied to the territory of the Cayman Islands, this consequence, if it comes to pass, will not flow legally from the directive itself.
>
> (Court of the First Instance of the European Communities 2003:
> paragraph 67)

As such, the position of the Court was that the implementation, or not, of this specific EU Directive in the OTs was subject in this case to the constitutional agreement in place between the UK and the Cayman Islands. The Caymanian per-spective expressed in the *Caymanian Compass* was that the Court of First Instance found in favour of Cayman's position on the Directive, specifically 'that the EU cannot directly impose any obligation on the Cayman Islands to implement the EU savings tax directive' (*Caymanian Compass* 2003: 1).

Nonetheless, there should be little doubt as to how the scenario played out between Westminster and George Town with respect to the Directive because, as already observed, power remains a potent presence in the metropolitan-OT rela-tionship. As Sharman observed with regard to this ECJ case, 'since all the arm-twisting was being done by London rather than Brussels, this [Court decision] did not materially improve the Caymans' situation' (Sharman 2008: 1060–1). The UK Chancellor had already stated to his EU counterparts that the UK would 'legislate directly'; in other words, the UK government would use an Order in Council to enforce the demands of the metropolitan state on the reluctant or recalcitrant over-seas territory. Threats are a useful inducement to encourage negotiations when the power relations between parties are inherently uneven. At the same time, there appears to have been a quid pro quo such that to some extent this case represents a 'negotiated' settlement for the sovereignty game. As indicated by a letter from the UK Paymaster General Dawn Primarolo, in exchange for Cayman's cooperation on the Directive, she confirmed that 'the UK government will now take forward the undertakings in the fleshed out agreement'. The initial undertaking involved the official recognition by the UK's Inland Revenue of the Cayman Islands Stock Exchange 'as a recognized stock exchange for tax purposes' (Cayman Islands Legislative Assembly 2003: 1313).

The government of the Cayman Islands agreed in February 2004 to implement the information exchange procedures of the EU Savings Tax Directive, although the actual impact on the financial centre was quite nominal. As described by interviewees in the Cayman, the situation was that there were few individual account holders from EU member states with accounts paying interest in the Cayman Islands. This fact is underscored by the reports from the Tax Information Authority (TIA) created to deal with the collection, management and reporting of account holder data as requested by the EU Savings Tax Directive. In the first full year of reporting to the EU, there were 2,868 reported accounts with aggregate assets of 22.6 million US dollars (Tax Information Authority 2008). The most recent available report, for the 2009 calendar year, provided statistics for 7,397 reported accounts with aggregate assets of 12.2 million US dollars (Tax Information Authority 2010). The concern with the Cayman case lodged at the ECJ in 2003 was the costs that would be incurred by the Cayman government to create and maintain the reporting structure, in particular given the low number of affected accounts and the absence for any direct domestic benefit from collecting the data. Nonetheless, the creation of the TIA has served Cayman in good stead, as it is now the competent authority for the growing network of Tax Information Exchange Agreements that Cayman is party to as a result of the April 2009 G20 request to the OECD for a white/grey/black list of 'tax havens' (Organization for Economic Co-operation and Development 2009). What was initially an excessive cost to comply with the Directive's requirements may now be viewed as an investment that facilitated the Cayman Island's continued exemplary compliance structure to address the ever-growing multitude of international initiatives in which it has no voice in defining.

Future sovereignty games

This chapter considered the triangular relationship between the Caribbean jurisdiction of the Cayman Islands, the UK and the EU. The EU is an actor, to be sure, in the form of rules and regulations transmitted to Cayman, via the UK government in Westminster; however, it is not widely recognized as an independent actor directly engaged with the Cayman Islands. And when the role of the EU was raised in interviews with Cayman officials, their remarks tended to be framed in terms of the difficulty working with a massive bureaucracy located thousands of miles away that possessed little understanding of the Caribbean.

The nature of the relationship between the UK and the Cayman Islands is framed by the use of the Order in Council – the Constitution of the Cayman Islands is itself an Order in Council (Privy Council 2009). Part of the 'sovereignty game' aspect to the UK–Cayman (and more generally UK–OT) relationship for much of the past decade involved the production of a new constitution. In the specific instance of the Cayman Islands, the 2009 Constitution is a product of a process initiated in February 2007 (following unfinished previous reform processes begun in the 1990s and in 2001), and motivated in part by the objective to incorporate a Bill of Rights (Hendry and Dickson 2011: 151–2). The approved Bill of Rights includes a definition of the right 'to marry a person of the opposite sex' (§14), which is somewhat at odds with the trend found among developed states towards same-sex relationships but, once again, reflects the nature of society in Cayman (Kollman 2007). While the Constitution provides the framework in which future sovereignty games between Cayman and the UK will be played out, it retains the Royal Prerogative 'to make laws for the peace, order and good government of the Cayman Islands' (§125). However, one interviewee stated that there was a 'side letter' to indicate increased coordination with Cayman over the content of future Orders in Council.[12] According to the archived 'Cayman Constitution' website, there is a Letter of Entrustment from the UK government to the Cayman Islands promising to consult with the Cayman government on the content of future Orders in Council and constitutional change; however, these documents do not appear to be publicly available.[13]

The ECJ decision in 2003 suggests that the EU will remain an abstract player in any future sovereignty game involving the transmission of an EU directive or regulation to the Cayman Islands. These formal EU actions will be mediated by the UK, itself frequently engaged in sovereignty games with the EU. In these games, the UK's sovereignty over the Cayman Islands might initially appear to be a liability. Behind the scenes, however, the action can play out differently, because the option to legislate directly with an Order in Council remains available. As appropriate, the Cayman government is now interacting directly with the EU with the full knowledge of the UK government in areas such as financial services and economic development. One interviewee expressed frustration with the process, however, because EU rules require the use of a specific EU travel agent, EU common carrier or EU supplier of goods and services when EU funds are used, even though the Cayman Islands already has more convenient access to goods and services via its nearer large neighbour, the US.[14] From the Cayman perspective, the essential aspect in a triangular relationship between the Cayman Islands, the UK, and the EU is the recognition that political ideologies drive political actions in the EU, actions which are not necessarily in the best interests of a small Caribbean jurisdiction. Consequently, the desire expressed in the Cayman Islands for a relationship governed by mutual respect and a recognition that the needs and interests of those living in the Caribbean will not be identical to the needs and interests of those living in Europe.

Notes

1 Fieldwork for this research was generously funded by the Carnegie Trust for the Universities of Scotland; confidential interviews were conducted during November 2010 in George Town, Grand Cayman, with a number of government officials. Out of respect for the anonymity requested by many interviewees, even those that agreed to be on the record will not be identified.

2 The Cayman Islands also seek to profit from this heritage with an annual celebration of 'Pirates Week' every November.

3 In fact, it may be noted that even after the massive damage inflicted on the Cayman Islands by Hurricane Ivan in 2004, the UK government provided no aid and very little material support (Tonner 2005: 128–32).

4 For example, the registration of hedge funds in the Cayman Islands is justified by an argument that Cayman provides 'tax neutrality' for the operation of the fund. In other

words, transactions made by a hedge fund producing taxable income would not be taxed in the Cayman Islands. Taxes owed on income generated at source would be paid by the fund, while the remaining income would be distributed to investors (who would be responsible for income tax in their tax domicile). The fund itself achieves a higher return on investment due to the lower aggregate tax wedge achieved by using the Cayman Islands as its home jurisdiction. In 2010, there were 9,438 mutual funds licensed or registered in the Cayman Islands. See http://www.cimoney.com.ky.

5 Multiple interviews, 9–10 November 2010, Grand Cayman.
6 Interview, 9 November 2010, Grand Cayman.
7 Examples for media reports about the Cayman Islands from a different perspective are available at: Pink News: Europe's Largest Gay News Service, www.pinknews.co.uk.
8 Interview, 9 November 2010, Grand Cayman.
9 Interview, 10 November 2010, Grand Cayman.
10 A short history of the creation of the EU Savings Tax Directive is provided in Holzinger 2005: 481–7.
11 The Partnership Working Party was designed to provide a technical forum between EU and OT representatives, which failed to achieve its potential due to resource constraints; see Hannibal, Holst, *et al.*'s contribution to this volume.
12 Interview, 10 November 2010, Grand Cayman.
13 See www.constitution.gov.ky/portal/page?_pageid=1961,4660113&_dad=portal&_schema=PORTAL (accessed 8 July 2011).
14 Interview, 9 November 2010, Grand Cayman.

References

Antoine, R.-M. B. (2008) *Commonwealth Caribbean Law and Legal Systems*, 2nd ed., London: Routledge-Cavendish.

Bauman, Z. (2000) *Liquid Modernity*, Cambridge: Polity Press.

Bodden, J.A.R. (2007) *The Cayman Islands in Transition: The Politics, History, and Sociology of a Changing Society*, Kingston: Ian Randle Publishers.

Bodden, J.A.R. (2010) *Patronage, Personalities and Parties: Caymanian Politics from 1950–2000*, Kingston: Ian Randle Publishers.

Caymanian Compass (2002a) 'Cayman won't agree to savings tax plan', *Caymanian Compass* (George Town, Grand Cayman), 15 November, 1.

Caymanian Compass (2002b) 'Savings tax initiative: EU tax plan a threat, warns LGB',, 8 November, 1–2.

Caymanian Compass (2002c) 'UK: OTs will comply with tax plan', *Caymanian Compass*, 6 December, 1.

Caymanian Compass (2003) 'EU court backs Cayman challenge on savings tax', *Caymanian Compass*, 31 March, 1–2.

Cayman Islands Legislative Assembly (1999) *Official Hansard Report*, 1999 Session. Online. Available at: www.legislativeassembly.ky (accessed 15 December 2010).

Cayman Islands Legislative Assembly (2001) *Official Hansard Report*, 2001 Session. Online. Available at: www.legislativeassembly.ky (accessed 15 December 2010).

Cayman Islands Legislative Assembly (2003) *Official Hansard Report*, 2002 Session. Online. Available at: www.legislativeassembly.ky (accessed 15 December 2010).

Cayman Islands National Archive (1960–1961) *Attitude of the Smaller Dependencies of the West Indies Towards the Federation*, London, UK PRO reference CO 1031/4271.

Cayman Net News (2007) 'Gay marriage law imminent?' Cayman Net News. Online. Available at: www.caymannetnews.com/cgi-script/csArticles/articles/000141/014156.htm (accessed 26 August 2010).

Clegg, P. (2006) 'The UK Caribbean overseas territories: extended statehood and the process of policy convergence', in L. De Jong and D. Kruijt (eds) *Extended Statehood in the Caribbean: Paradoxes of Quasi Colonialism, Local Autonomy and Extended Statehood in the USA, French, Dutch & British Caribbean*, Amsterdam: Rozenberg Publishers.

Court of the First Instance of the European Communities (2003) *Government of the Cayman Islands v. Commission of the European Communities (T-85/03)*, Court of the First Instance of the European Communities. Online. Available at: www.curia.eu.int/en/content/juris/index.htm (accessed 30 September 2004).

European Council (2003) *Council Directive 2003/48/EC of 3 June 2003 taxation of savings income in the form of interest payments*, Official Journal of the European Communities (hereinafter OJ) L series 157.

Foreign and Commonwealth Office (1999) 'Partnership for progress and prosperity: Britain and the overseas territories', HMSO. Online. Available at: www.fco.gov.uk (accessed 17 August 2004).

Hendry, I. and Dickson, S. (2011) *British Overseas Territories Law*, Oxford: Hart Publishing.

Holzinger, K. (2005) 'Tax competition and tax co-operation in the EU: the case of savings taxation', *Rationality and Society*, 17: 475–510.

Kollman, K. (2007) 'Same-sex unions: the globalization of an idea', *International Studies Quarterly*, 51: 329–57.

McIntyre, W.D. (1996) 'The admission of small states to the Commonwealth', *The Journal of Imperial and Commonwealth History*, 24: 244–77.

Mortished, C. (2004) 'Pirates of the Caribbean refuse to play ball on tax havens', *The Times Online*. Available at: http://business.timesonline.co.uk/article/0,,8210-996741,00.html (accessed 26 March 2004).

National Audit Office (1997) *Foreign and Commonwealth Office: Contingent Liabilities in the Dependent Territories*, London: The Stationery Office.

National Audit Office (2007) *Foreign and Commonwealth Office: Managing Risk in the Overseas Territories*, London: The Stationery Office.

Organisation for Economic Co-operation and Development (2009) *A Progress Report on the Jurisdictions Surveyed by the OECD Global Forum in Implementing the Internationally Agreed Tax Standard*, Paris: OECD Publications. Online. Available at: www.oecd.org (accessed 5 April 2009).

Palan, R. (2010) 'International Finance Centers: The British-Empire, City-States and Commercially Oriented Politices', *Theoretical Inquiries in Law*, 11: 149–76.

Parker, G., Gimbel, F. and Burton, J. (2006) 'EU tax officials set sights on Asia', *Financial Times*, 3 September.

Privy Council (2009) *The Cayman Islands Constitution Order 2009*, Statutory Instruments, 2009 No. 1379, At the Court at Buckingham Palace.

Sharman, J.C. (2008) 'Regional deals and the global imperative: the external dimension of the European Union savings tax directive', *Journal of Common Market Studies*, 46: 1049–69.

Tait, N. (2010) 'Deal likely on draft EU hedge fund rules', *Financial Times*, 9 May, sec. Brussels.

Tax Information Authority (2008) *Reporting of Savings Income Information Statistics – European Union, Reporting Period 2005–2006*, Cayman Islands. Available at: www.tia.gov.ky (accessed 18 October 2010).

Tax Information Authority (2010) *Reporting of Savings Income Information Statistics:*

European Union, Reporting Period 2009, Cayman Islands. Available at: www.tia.gov. ky (accessed 18 October 2010).

Taylor, E. and Prystay, C. (2006) 'Swiss fight against tax cheats aids Singapore's banking quest', *Wall Street Journal*, 6 February, sec. A, 1.

Tonner, D. (2005) *Ivan: The Full Story: The Storm that Changed a Nation Forever*, George Town, Grand Cayman: Focus Communications.

Z/Yen Group Limited (2010) *Global Financial Centres 7*, London: City of London. Online. Available at: www.cityoflondon.gov.uk (accessed 8 July 2011).

9 Jurisdiction in dialect

Sovereignty games in the British Virgin Islands

Bill Maurer[1]

[T]here is little enthusiasm in the territory for changing our constitutional status.
(Government of the British Virgin Islands 2008: 10)

You are speaking in a West Indian court in what is in effect a foreign dialect.
(Eastern Caribbean Supreme Court justice, to an English solicitor)

The first epigraph comes from the response from the British Virgin Islands' (BVI) government to the European Commission's Green Paper on Europe's remaining Overseas Countries and Territories (OCTs), of which the BVI, a British overseas territory (OT), is one among many discussed in this volume (British Virgin Islands 2008). It sums up the nearly universal opinion in the BVI that there is no reason to change the territory's political status. The only people who are possibly willing to broach the topic of full independence and sovereignty are often, ironically enough, British nationals or other expatriates who implicitly hold onto a modernist teleology of political development inevitably culminating in independence. Occasionally, one will hear a 'down-islander', a migrant or the descendent of a migrant from the other now-independent eastern Caribbean Commonwealth countries, speak disparagingly of BVIslanders' continued colonial disposition. This occurs in moments of heated argument or conspiratorial tones with which a person deemed 'not to belong' to the territory (the legal and now popular expression applied to non-citizens) confides in the visiting anthropologist. The colonial status of the BVI is not an issue in elections nor is it part of any party platform. Many will still say, as they have at least since the 1980s, 'we have the best of both worlds: the US dollar, and British law and order'.[2]

But to conclude that sovereignty is not an issue in the BVI would be to oversimplify the situation dramatically, not to mention to distort the concept of sovereignty itself. The second quotation comes from a Jamaican justice in the Eastern Caribbean Supreme Court (ECSC) during its January sitting in the BVI. The BVI court system shares an appellate court with the other Commonwealth countries and territories of the Caribbean. Based in St. Lucia, the ECSC is an itinerant entity that travels from island to island throughout the year, hearing appeals to local High Court judgments. The next higher level of appeal beyond the ECSC is the Privy Council and/or British Supreme Court in London. In its jural structure, then, the BVI, its Caribbean neighbours and many other Commonwealth countries still reflect the legacy of British imperialism through the plurivocality of the common law. Unlike in an American appellate court, it is routine in a Commonwealth court to hear references to cases decided in faraway lands by foreign judges. There is considerable imperial nostalgia in such proceedings, as judges, barristers and solicitors dressed in ribbons and robes (although powdered wigs are no longer worn) debate case law from Malaysia, Hong Kong, Gibraltar, Papua New Guinea, and other exotic locales, all before a symbolic representation of the Crown. In this case, a large photograph of the Queen hangs (just slightly crooked) behind the bench. All who enter and leave the courtroom bow or curtsy before it.

The young English solicitor was making an argument before the justices of the ECSC, West Indians from all over the Caribbean. A judge from Jamaica – himself a member of the Jamaican elite, a fact not merely evident from his station but also from his very light skin-tone – interrupted the clearly nervous Englishman. 'Your accent is very difficult for us to understand', he stated. 'You need to speak slowly and clearly.' He interrupted him several times, in fact, before finally commenting, the irritation in his voice quite distinct, 'You are in effect speaking in a foreign accent'.

Together, these quotations embody how the BVI both 'refuses to be decolonized' (Gad and Adler-Nissen, Introduction to this volume) and wants to have it both ways, acting in some fora or in some social and political contexts as a sovereign entity or a polity possessed of sovereign authority. Of course, that sovereignty is further complicated by the pan-Caribbean (post-)colonial context. It is a Jamaican representative of a regional Caribbean court, here affirming the BVI's distinction from Empire. The 'almost sovereign but not quite' character of the BVI benefits it enormously in a game to attract international financial capital in the form of trust and corporate subsidiary formations that have turned the BVI into one of the largest international domiciles for corporations worldwide.

The BVI is a zone of overlapping and multiple jurisdictionalities and nested, partial sovereignties that find form in formal sovereignty arrangements, identity discourses, and diplomatic practices. It is a question of looking at different levels of scale and listening to the different registers with which the BVI speaks at those levels of scale. Gad and Adler-Nissen (this volume) convincingly argue that sovereignty is not a 'thing' but rather unfolds in a series of multiple, sometimes discrete and sometimes overlapping games. These are not to be understood as games of deracinated rational actors but rather as language games of 'meaning production and praxis' (Gad and Adler-Nissen, this volume). In the case of the BVI, the *accent* and *register* of the language games crucially inflects the territory's ongoing relationship to the United Kingdom (UK) and European Union (EU). Between the most local-level scale of legislative autonomy and the highest-level scale of international governance, one finds the BVI speaking as a consolidated, sovereign entity to other sovereign states and to global institutions: the BVI enters into treaties with sovereign nations, for example, around the exchange of tax information. It does so in the context of the international effort to combat money laundering and tax evasion, thus placating higher-level organizations like the EU and the

Organization for Economic Cooperation and Development (OECD). It also plays other international organizations against the OECD and EU in an effort to maintain its place as a centre for international incorporation. Most notably, the International Monetary Fund declared in 2008 that the distinction between 'onshore' and 'offshore' finance was meaningless, arguing that it is the activities not the places that ought to come under scrutiny. Indeed, the BVI made special note of this in its reply to the European Commission's Green Paper on the OCTs.

If we understand sovereignty games as *language* games, as discussed by Gad and Adler-Nissen (this volume), then the BVI provides a case in which accent, dialect, and register matter very much in the meaning-making and practical unfolding of such games. This is the chief claim of this chapter. The mild inflection of accent, indicating origin; the more developed distinction of dialect, creating a distinct speech community; the hierarchical relationships evident in register, marking politeness, disdain, or merely rank, generate a structured cacophony. As discussed below, they do so in the BVI in specific fora, where the history of slavery and colonization intersect with more recent labour migrations and the recent international and legal ramifications of the offshore financial services sector.

If the concept of polity can be used to describe such not-quite-sovereign entities as the BVI, 'those entities with a measure of identity, a degree of organization and hierarchy, and a capacity to mobilize persons and their resources for political purposes' (Ferguson and Mansbach 2008: 61, as discussed in the Introduction to this volume), then the BVI poses the question of how to understand a self-reflexively *involuted* polity. Here, the polity finds articulation through a plurality of accents, dialects, and registers, a multiplicity of sources of authority and formal and informal political mobilization. Those voices occasionally align in paradoxical ways. A Jamaican judge, speaking below a picture of the Queen and under the authority of *that* sovereign, castigates an Englishman for speaking in a 'foreign dialect'. In doing so, he echoes the pan-Caribbean nationalism of an advocate for the expulsion of the British from the BVI.

The plurality of voices also renders it difficult to interpret local-level questions, contests, and controversies, some with life-and-death consequences. I outline five main developments in the following that help to explain sovereignty games in the BVI at the local level which simultaneously reach out to other levels of scale: shifts in the memorialization of history; changes in labour migration, and, especially, the return of BVIslanders who had left for greener pastures elsewhere in the mid- to late twentieth century; an international crackdown against offshore finance and popular and professional reactions to it; and new patterns of incorporation that have brought Chinese companies to BVI shores. The chapter first outlines the distinctions among sovereignty, polity, and jurisdiction before taking each of these five developments in turn.

Jurisdiction, sovereignty, polity

The distinction between sovereignty and jurisdiction is important, both descriptively and analytically. It is descriptively important for understanding a place like the BVI: the BVI is a British OT with legislative autonomy and the ability to enter into international treaties with sovereign states; a jurisdiction subject to the ECSC, which exists under the British appellate court system; the home of the new Eastern Caribbean Commercial Court (ECCC), which has taken all commercial cases off the ECSC docket and consolidated another form of jurisdiction – over commercial cases heard 'at equity' and 'at law'. It is also a destination point for migrants from around the Caribbean, many of whom do not or cannot obtain citizenship and many of whose children born in the BVI have ambiguous legal status in that territory. For many years, there has been a small number of truly stateless residents, hapless victims of circumstance, colonial wars, and political reconfigurations that took place while they were crewmembers on sailing ships or otherwise in transit. Some of these people have finally obtained legal status, after many years of making an effort consciously to contribute to the life and livelihoods of the territory. Examples include the small Syrian merchant community, which maintains cramped, dusty shops full of everything you can possibly imagine, and a handful of doctors, lawyers, and other professionals. The BVI is also a place where people are constantly on the move, while at the same time there are deep eddies and side-currents of social relationships and histories keeping some people quite contentedly in place.

As regards the theoretical importance of the distinction between sovereignty and jurisdiction, I am indebted to an anthropologist of the Hopi (Native American) tribal court and literary historian. Justin Richland shows how Hopi tribal sovereignty is an effect of the everyday, pragmatic unfolding of activities before the tribal court that invoke 'tradition' as jurisdiction – a moment when 'Hopi juridico-political authority speaks to itself about itself' (Richland 2011: 206) and thereby constitutes 'sovereignty' as an effect of that metadiscursive practice. These are moments in the court where, for example, 'tradition' is explicitly invoked and discussed, and, in the unfolding of a series of linguistic acts, Hopi comes to be 'sovereign', even as the invocation of tradition in this manner points out the limits of that sovereignty. Richland echoes Bradin Cormack's work on the consolidation of the common law in early modern England. Noting the plural field of sometimes competing, sometimes overlapping, and sometimes semi-autonomous courts (common law courts, ecclesiastical courts, equity courts, Duchy courts, Admiralty courts, municipal courts, guild courts, market courts; Cormack 2007: 3), Cormack enquires about the importance of the 'mundane process[es] of administrative distribution and management' (2007: 9) among these courts that delimit the field of 'law' and juridical power in a manner that reveals the impossibility of 'sovereignty'. These courts operated according to spatial-territorial jurisdictionalities (maritime courts, municipal courts), temporal jurisdictionalities (market days; referring to the immediate past or to time immemorial), and generic jurisdictionalities (for 'matters spiritual or matters temporal' (Cormack 2007: 3)). From the point of view of a post-Second World War order of sovereign nation-states, it is difficult to grasp hold of this cross-cutting and overlapping field of jurisdictionality in time, space, and social relationships. However, this field is also utterly commonplace, if not banal. One can simply spend time in the city, where school boards, zoning ordinances, and a host of other entities maintain jurisdiction over time, place, or activity (see Valverde 2008).

Jurisdiction directs our attention to 'technical application' rather than ontological investigation' (Richland 2011: 232) of the sort that questions of sovereignty tend to suggest. It also opens up sovereignty to the notion of the polity developed in this volume, and does so by emphasizing the various authorities from whom the saying of the law emanates. These may or may not mobilize different groups of people in different circumstances. The technical application of diverse and plural jurisdictionalities sheds light on the layering and overlapping of what had heretofore been deemed sovereign authority.

History, memory, politics

The past decade has witnessed increasing attention to the 'founding fathers' of BVI legislative autonomy. Commemoration has included a postage stamp commemorating members of the Legislative Council signing the International Business Companies Ordinance of 1984 launching the BVI's successful vehicle for offshore incorporations. There are new parks, statues of past leaders, and public holidays. Some of these past leaders – mocked in their day for their connection to pan-Africanism or the anticolonial movement – are now remembered for preventing the leasing out of the entirety of the island of Anegada and most of Road Town (Wickam's Cay) to a foreigner.

But nothing is ever simple here: those who spearheaded the commemoration of these leaders themselves left the BVI for education at the University of the West Indies or elsewhere abroad. They are the people 'who gone to come back'. Those who stayed behind regard them as not-quite-true BVIslanders. There is a nascent battle for nostalgia in the BVI: those who 'gone to come back' remember a BVI connected to legacies of slavery, colonialism, and important anti-colonial leaders, and seek to articulate their own trajectories (of 'exile') to those leaders. Those who 'stayed behind' and actually helped build the territory take pride in their own accomplishments make fun of some of the more ostentatious efforts at commemoration, and organize instead things such as a celebration of the horse races at Sea Cow's Bay.

The distinction between these two loosely defined groups of BVIslanders maps onto political party affiliation. Those who gone to come back tend to affiliate with the National Democratic Party (NDP), also a party historically seen as a party of intellectuals and advocates for immigrants. It held power once, from 2003–7, and in addition to launching some of the commemorative activities like the placing of statuary around town, it also sought to 'modernize' the BVI through things like city planning, youth services and an e-governance project. The Virgin Islands Party, the counterweight to the NDP, is a political organization that has existed since the origin of legislative autonomy and traces its roots to the founding of the territory in its modern political form. It is tied to established BVI families who have long been economic and political elites yet not had as many off-island connections. It has represented the interests of the civil service.

And while those who had left are recalling the historical memory of pan-Africanism or pan-Caribbean anti-colonial movements, they are also perceived as backed by a couple of extremely wealthy expatriates, often discussed in hushed tones. In an especially tragic affair during a recent political campaign, a person carried about in a mock coffin became a living effigy of a longstanding expatriate resident. The poor young 'actor' himself wound up dead under mysterious circumstances shortly thereafter, found in an alleyway.

The position of 'those who gone to come back' represents one inflection of sovereignty games in multiple accents and registers. Speaking with a less West Indian accent, yet addressing each other, the BVI, powerful elites, and an underclass through the register of pan-Caribbean nationalism and the African-American politics of commemoration more associated with the United States (US) than the Caribbean, those who might articulate a conventional 'sovereignty' discourse do so in a gradient of registers, none standing sovereign over the others, none speaking from a place of unambiguous 'BVIslander' authority. They also provoke responses assuming the form of political shenanigans (and a mysterious death) in the register of still other histories.

Immigrant labourers and professionals

In the early 1990s, BVIslanders were up in arms about large numbers of immigrants from other Caribbean places: 'down-islanders' from the other Lesser Antilles, Guyanese of South Asian descent, and especially Dominicans who often claimed BVI ancestry as the descendants of cane workers in the Dominican Republic in the early part of the twentieth century. The legal categories 'belonger' and 'non-belonger' dominated discussion of immigration and worked their way into common parlance ('Him na belong here!'). Calypsonians sung against restrictive immigration and work permit policies. One, Benji V, himself an immigrant, won the crown of Calypso King with a song titled, 'Where we born is where we from', proclaiming US-style citizenship by place of birth preferable to the BVI's then descent based system (Maurer 1997).

Immigration remains a hot issue. But as more and more 'down-islanders' have married into BVI families, as the Guyanese have become more established and visible (through cricket matches next to the new Government Administration Building and other activities), and as the ubiquity of the mobile phone has fostered an equal ubiquity throughout Road Town of spoken Spanish (which was only whispered in public up until the 1990s), BVIslanders have grown accustomed to other Caribbean migrants.

Old stereotypes die hard, but even newer arrivals garner attention now: over the past five years, Filipino labourers, nurses, and accountants have arrived in the BVI. BVIslanders sometimes call them 'Chinese' or 'Chinee'. Some also use the term 'coolie' and draw distinctions between three groups of 'coolies': Guyanese Chinese (of which there are a couple of families who have been in the territory for over 30 years), Filipinos, and Chinese businessmen and women who come to the BVI either for real estate and tourism investment opportunities or on matters related to offshore incorporation. This last set is small but visible. Road Town is tiny. If you are on foot, even walking from your car to your office, you are visible. If you are a Filipina or Chinese woman and carrying a parasol to shade your skin, you are even more so.

There is yet another group of new arrivals: predominantly white expatriates from the UK and Canada (and some continental Europeans) coming to work in the offshore sector. There are now night spots and a restaurant or two catering specifically to these arrivals. They do not mix much socially with the yachting contingent – another large and longstanding group of white expatriates in the BVI – and they maintain some social distinctions among themselves. The lawyers and accountants tend not to mix with the 'trust company' people. This may have to do with occupational segregation, as the lawyers and accountants providing corporate services to the trust companies also become involved in regulatory or investigatory functions vis-à-vis those same clients. Some professionals in trust services are Panamanians who have had a longer history in Caribbean offshore finance. There have been some marriages among the lawyers and accountants between expatriate whites and expatriate West Indians. Still, one informant from England bemoaned the fact that most of his colleagues consider August Festival time, which commemorates Emancipation, as 'just a three-day holiday' and an excuse to get off-island.

Popular responses to the effort against tax havens

Even among the rank and file, there is a great deal of pride in the BVI's 'success' as a global offshore centre. Among laypeople, offshore finance is generally assumed to be 'offshore banking', despite the fact that the BVI is primarily a centre for trust formation and corporate registration. Indeed, among members of the political class and financial services professionals, the fact that the BVI is a centre for incorporations, not banking like the Cayman Islands, is important in BVIslander assessments of themselves vis-à-vis their Caribbean cousins. Offshore incorporation is seen as 'cleaner' than banking. This is one reason why the financial services regulator is very interested in increased effort concerning public education about the territory's role in international finance: He deplores the fact that students will say that the territory is famous for 'banking' and worries that this lack of understanding may one day hinder the territory's development. The distinction between banking and incorporation matters when the BVI speaks to the EU, US and international organizations, since offshore banking generally sounds shady to government regulators and EU bureaucrats, whereas incorporation raises fewer hackles.[3]

Although many BVIslanders have only a dim sense of what is taking place in the office buildings throughout Road Town, they also want their children to get law degrees or accounting credentials and to work in the 'trust company business'. People may joke that they think the trust company business is essentially a cover for money laundering but at the same time aspire to jobs in offices where you can wear nice clothes in air conditioning and – crucially – not have to serve tourists. As in many tourist destinations, the BVI tourism industry has tried to instil the feeling that 'service does not equal servile', but the legacies of colonialism and racism – and the ongoing presence of 'ugly tourists' – makes this a difficult sell.

BVIslanders are also proud of being 'top' in something. One BVIslander of Dominican Republic descent whom I have known for years pointed to the recent construction of the expanded Peebles Hospital and told me that the BVI was 'number one in finance' and would soon be 'number one' in health care, too. The offshore sector, meanwhile, directly contributes 56 per cent of government revenue and likely 80 per cent indirectly.

So, it is hardly surprising that people react strongly to efforts to rein in offshore finance. Palan's and Vlcek's respective chapters in this volume provide the broader context. Since 1998, a variety of international organizations have attempted to spotlight unfair tax competition and create sanctions against territories deemed not in compliance with emerging international norms on global fiscal policy. These organizations include the OECD, EU, Financial Action Task Force, Financial Stability Forum, and non-governmental organizations (NGOs) such as Oxfam and the Tax Justice Network. I will not review the debate here (see Maurer 2008; Sharman 2006; Palan, Murphy and Chavagneux 2010), but I will give you a sense of how BVIslanders responded.

After the US Senate Finance Committee held hearings on offshore tax evasion in the summer of 2008, local websites were abuzz:

> They STOLE us from our home land, CHAIN us like dogs in the bottom of their ships, THREW over the ship those of us who were to weak and sick, BRANDED us with hot iron when they sold us to the highest bidder, WIP and BEAT us to death for free labour, LEFT us to die after they made their wealth on these islands but GOD was on our side and we SURVIVE now the GREAT USA the one that we help built with force free labour [i.e. slavery, forced labor 'got for free'] is at it again.
>
> Now they trying to take away our daily bread, like they did with caribbean banana, so many travel restriction into their land for us and none for them into our land, the same money we make all goes back to them as we produce notting and have to import all from them, so to all in the SENATE/CONGRESS who want to now kill the caribbean islands for the WEALTH they now have because of OFFSHORE BANKING and IBC [International Business Corporation], REMEMBER GOD DON'T LIKE UGLY AND HE IS THE ONE AND ONLY ONE WHO PROVIDES FOR ALL OF US.
>
> God have his waY ["Y" capitalized to indicate Yahweh] to make those that benifited from free labour [i.e. slavery, labor got 'for free'] to now pay those that work for notting so caribbean islands reap your sweets.

Hastily, just a few days after the hearings, low-level British Virgin Islander staffers of the Financial Services Commission, the regulatory agency created to comply with OECD standards, created an impromptu float for the August Festival commemorating emancipation to promote their efforts.

Six months later, shortly after US President Barack Obama took office and the OECD stepped up its crackdown against tax havens, the echo of historical memory was heard again: ' "Why is it that we now in the colonies, because we are still a colony, can't have a financial center?" [BVI Premier Ralph] O'Neal told The Associated Press in an interview in his office overlooking the slate-blue Sir Francis Drake Channel. "If you're doing something and you're saying I can't do it, are you saying that I'm inferior?" ' (Fox 2009).

And a cynical commentator on the BVINews.com website, soon after the G20 summit had concluded, posted the following: 'Pack ya bags back to cutting sugar cane. Imagin we could be heading to work in the dr [Dominican Republic] like our grand parents' (BVINews.com, 3 April 2009).

This comment is interesting because of its reference to the history of labour migration to the Dominican Republic, a history that was often denied or denigrated in the early 1990s, when large numbers of Dominicans were coming 'back' to the BVI. It also invokes the history of labour extraction for plantation agriculture and a nod to slavery.

Slavery is so present not just because of the politics of race and colonialism but also because of kinship and corporate linkages to Panama, the Dominican Republic, and the remembered history of labour migration throughout the Caribbean basin in the aftermath of emancipation. Marshall (2002) writes about the region's circulatory and merchant elites. In the BVI, these include families who harnessed capital in the form of fishing boats and equipment to create regional trading networks in the late nineteenth and early twentieth centuries. They then became import/export businessmen who are now connected to the offshore sector by providing office space or actually offering corporate services. There is now an autochthonous cadre of trust company professionals with last names like Penn, O'Neal, Lettsome, and Fahie – all prominent BVI families. Also relevant in the context of the post-emancipation period is the circular migration to Panama when the Canal was being constructed. That migration became important around the time of the fall of Manuel Noriega, when Panamanian offshore services sought other shores and some washed aground in the BVI, where they remain.

This dense historical memory, these intertwined social relationships and meanings – this is why trust companies make some measure of sense in the BVI. A prominent Registered Agent in Road Town is a Panamanian by birth and related by oblique kinship connections to West Indian families. She has become a patron of the arts, and heralded in the press as a 'business diva'. An elderly woman I visited in the summer of 2008 would say to me both, 'I think there's money laundering going on there', and yet still be able to emplace and embrace this Panamanian and her company and its activities in terms of the long post-Emancipation Caribbean story.

In the bureaucratic register of its relationship to the EU, the BVI simply asserts its desire for a level playing field: 'The Commission has a responsibility not to seek to impose higher standards in the OCTs than in EU member states and to ensure it is properly aware of what the OCTs themselves want rather than deciding this for them' (British Virgin Islands 2008: 5). The statement both gestures towards a desired position of equality with EU member states and a recognition of enduring colonial relations in the post-emancipation period. The implicit message is not to change that relation but simply to apply the same standards to the BVI as to EU member states.

Professional reactions

BVIslanders also imagine themselves as the good – or at least, less bad – part of the offshore world. This has come about because of the recent crackdowns. 'With more than 800,000 regulated entities [here], things are bound to happen', I was told by a forensic accountant who was involved in busting one of the biggest fraud cases the BVI had ever seen. For those in the regulation and investigatory community, the BVI is a far better place to nab fraudsters because the new compliance regime has made the work easier and because the lack of international attention to 'onshore' jurisdictions – particularly Delaware, Oregon, and Kentucky – has made investigating activities booked in those states difficult. One accountant rolled his eyes when describing the futility of pursuing any cases involving these US states.

The new compliance regime, I was told, makes things 'easier'. One fraud investigator used to seek out 'show assets' – the fancy yacht, which would lead to the mistress, which in turn would convince the wife to open up about matters such as her husband's business affairs. Today, so much information is on the record that the investigator can usually forego the cloak and dagger aspects of his work.

As noted earlier, the BVI is not a banking centre but an incorporation centre. This also makes things 'easier', I was told, from a regulatory compliance and investigatory perspective: no anonymous accounts, just difficult-to-track incorporations, all interconnected in fantastically complex ways. People are still doing bad things with these structures, but the ethical issues are bracketed in the industry. I am often given a 'compared to what?' response when enquiring after the effects of tax havens on financial stability, revenue policies, or social welfare. Most people I have interviewed – who almost always talk off the record – express unease with the mobility of capital and its attendant moral valences but do not see what the BVI is providing as any worse than anything elsewhere. Some adopt a harm-mitigation perspective: better to have it (whatever 'it' is) take place in a 'well-regulated' jurisdiction (their terms) than somewhere completely off the map.

In 2008, BVI investigators cracked a massive fraud case involving a Russian telecommunications minister. The government confiscated $45 million and fined three funds $2.5 million each. It was seen as a major demonstration of the solidity and soundness of the BVI's new regulatory regime. The newspapers noted the irony that, in the same week that the UK had issued a report criticizing the BVI as vulnerable to fraud, BVI investigators succeeded in bringing criminals to justice and landed the biggest recovery of assets and fines in the Commonwealth's history. The BVI and Bermuda split the funds, representing a windfall for the BVI amounting to roughly 10 per cent of the territory's entire budget. Some of these funds, appropriately, were used to construct the new Eastern Caribbean Commercial Court building.

But local politics intervene. BVIslanders not directly involved in the offshore sector did not remember much about the case just one year later, except that there had been a whiff of scandal about the disposition of the funds and allegations that they benefited an NDP politician (although no one could really say how).

This is upsetting to the investigatory community: 'this was a major, major victory for fraud detection and investigation and criminal proceedings in the BVI and the offshore generally . . . They should have made a much bigger deal of it'. This interviewee's sense is that the media and government downplayed the victory because it might suggest that the BVI is full of criminals.

> People have this attitude of, oh no! There's nothing untoward going on here. But of course there is! There are a million companies here. There's nothing wrong with saying that there may be bad things going on, but the point is to show that you can do something about it.

The larger questions about the offshore world and financial globalization are bracketed here. The technical matters more than the ontological: big questions get deferred while a legal and accounting victory is celebrated by those directly involved. Still, they feel that the general public remains uninformed about the magnitude of what happened: 'People should be justifiably proud that they have an amazingly well-regulated system here and it worked.' In this instance, what could have been cause for a 'national' celebration or the consolidation of the polity around the offshore misfired. Instead, people recall party politics and elite infighting and questions about the disposition of a lot of money. In this case, it is expatriates who feel pride in the BVI. The BVI in which they invest their sentiments here is a regulatory apparatus in which they directly participate.

The new regulatory regime depends on the adoption of Tax Information Exchange Agreements (TIEAs) with other countries. One indicator of compliance with the new international regime is the signing of 12 such treaties. However, this is seen to have created a conflict between the regulatory officials and the government officials who negotiate these treaties and market the jurisdiction. Gregory Rawlings (2007) has argued that the role of international law through TIEAs represents a reassertion of sovereignty for offshore jurisdictions. This is true. At the same time, however, TIEAs have revealed a fracture of jurisdictional authority between the regulator and the government. In the BVI, these are lexicalized as such: 'the regulator', 'the government', and 'the industry'. As the government seeks to create these treaties, the regulator worries that things are moving too fast. The industry, meanwhile, lives with the uncertainty about the agent who speaks the law – the regulator or the government. This instability in the locus of *juris dictum* could be said to characterize the formal sovereignty of the BVI today, even as local meaning-making and identity discourses more complexly infold and involute that locus.

In addition, the establishment of the ECCC in the BVI is already having a number of symbolic effects. It harmonizes with existing local understandings of the BVI as a place of 'law and order'. It places the BVI on the map of chancery courts or courts of equity globally, next to Delaware and, more recently, Qatar and Bahrain. Indeed, the BVI court was always explained to me as being 'like Delaware's Chancery Court' and sometimes as potentially entering into a field of competition with the Gulf States.

The ECCC is also leading some in the regulatory community to imagine a world 'after' the offshore. The BVI could become a centre for arbitration rather than a centre for incorporation. The fact that the financial crisis that began in 2008 has led to an increased number of offshore insolvencies will – people believe – fill the docket of the new court and provide fee income for lawyers for at least a decade. In that time, according to this particular future fantasy, the BVI will have been able to diversify beyond trusts and 'asset protection' and towards being a 'beacon' for private international law; which incidentally is all about jurisdiction.

New patterns of incorporation

The ECCC is state-of-the-art. It is in a modern building in the heart of Road Town featuring new furnishings, high-end telecommunications, and teleconferencing capabilities. It contrasts with the old Supreme Court chambers, which are in the original Legislative Council building, a colonial-style structure somewhat in disrepair, nestled at the end of a busy road adjacent to a high school. The Queen watches over sittings in the old building. A large, flat screen monitor takes her place in the new building. Said one informant, 'It's like you're transported to England' when you sit in on a case at the ECCC. Said a staff member of the ECCC, while giving me a tour and gesturing to the monitor, 'We had Beijing here last week'. The ECCC itself embodies the complexity of space, polity, and jurisdiction in the BVI.

Observers of the offshore situation have noted new forms and patterns of incorporation in the Caribbean centres. About 10 per cent of Chinese companies registered with the US Securities and Exchange Commission, including some of the leading lights in China's new telecommunications and energy industries, are actually incorporated in the BVI or Cayman Islands. Observers initially assumed that these incorporations were vehicles for 'roundtripping' of capital: routing through the Caribbean offshore in order to reinvest in a Chinese enterprise as 'foreign direct investment' (FDI) and thereby subject to more favourable treatment by the Chinese authorities.

In 2008, however, China removed the FDI tax preferences. And yet Chinese companies continue to make use of Caribbean offshore shell corporations. Adding to the puzzle is the fact that most of the architectures they create in the Caribbean appear to be utterly straightforward: a Chinese company is owned by a BVI company is owned by a Cayman Islands company. For forensic accountants and financial fraud investigators working in the Caribbean, there is nothing to disentangle here, none of the complex relationships of part-ownership or interlocking subsidiaries that loop back upon one another that have characterized offshore incorporation for tax evasion or 'asset planning' purposes to which they have become accustomed. Said one such professional, given the straightforwardness of the offshore structures being set up: 'You have to wonder why they bother'.

William Vlcek has shown how this pattern of Chinese incorporation re-centres the Caribbean as a semi-peripheral mediator between traditional 'core' European and North American countries and an emerging China (Vlcek 2010). Sutherland,

Matthews, and El-Gohari (2009) find that both institutional arbitrage and the quest for American investment capital may propel Chinese offshore incorporations. Tax minimization through the Caribbean offshore thus seems to be less a motivating factor than property rights, investment seeking, and institutional arbitrage. Chinese incorporations in the Caribbean also confound assessments of FDI into China, a fact that has important political and economic implications in China itself.

Let me add two other possibilities. First, people are drawn to the 'brand' of the British Virgin Islands for the simple reason that the name of the territory includes the word British. This confers stability, legitimacy, and not a little bit of imperial nostalgia (Rosaldo 1989). The businessmen and women behind these structures – and their lawyers and accountants and the international contacts of their lawyers and accountants – began seriously exploring the Caribbean offshore centres immediately before the transfer of Hong Kong to China. The British Virgin Islands provides the Union Jack. And – not to put too fine a point on it – imperial whiteness. This represents another involution of the already-complicated racial politics and sovereignty games of the BVI and the wider Caribbean, an involution indexed in BVIslanders' talk about the 'Chinee' on-island today.

In addition to the symbolics of empire, there is also the pragmatics. As Vlcek argues, Chinese entrepreneurs and their agents are also drawn to the BVI and Cayman Islands for the protection of property and legal flexibility afforded by the common law. They also want the chance to have any legal proceedings that might result from their affairs heard before a court that will entertain arguments of equity. With the establishment of the Eastern Caribbean Commercial Court in Road Town, Chinese businesspeople can engage in a kind of institutional arbitrage for access to an equity court like Delaware's Court of Chancery but outside of the jurisdiction of the US.

One final note: a survey of trust company service businesses and offshore law firms in the BVI today reveals connections to Singapore, Hong Kong, the Gulf States, and the UK. A 1990 snapshot reveals a different pattern: a dense network of linkages, via Panama, into South America, and via the Channel Islands and Bermuda, the UK, and continental Europe. The geography – and jurisdictionality – of the offshore is being reconfigured. 'India will be big', said one informant. This new geography of offshore flows may represent a shift from tax evasion and estate planning by wealthy Latin Americans and Europeans to agents from the BRIC countries (Brazil, India, Russia, and China) playing a slightly different game: a new class of super-rich hiding money offshore, but also a new trajectory of global incorporation seeking access to law, seeking the *jurisdiction of equity*. The BVI offers just such jurisdiction.

Conclusion

The sovereign voice, the sovereign register that the BVI uses when speaking to the EU or multilateral organizations, is one among several in a set of language games that has other points of gravity, some local, some connected more to the Commonwealth, others to pan-Caribbean nationalism or the US. The fact that the BVI adjusts the register of its sovereignty games in relation to these different centres of gravity – and that sovereignty as such does not always have the greatest pull – precludes the analytical understanding of sovereignty as an either/or. As noted earlier, there is a productive (and now lucrative) instability in the locus of *juris dictum* in the BVI: much like the medieval polities described in the Introduction to this volume, the BVI participates in 'non-exclusive forms of territoriality' (Ruggie, as quoted in the Introduction to this volume) and overlapping authorities that crisscross the islands, like the cross-cutting currents that swirl around them. Local meaning-making adds to the impossibility of pinpointing that locus.

The BVI appears as a set of overlapping, never-quite meshing jurisdictions, each experienced by different people differently, for different purposes, according to different temporalities and different contexts. These different jurisdictions also render open-ended the congealing of any sort of polity – understood by Ferguson and Mansbach as an entity 'with a measure of identity, a degree of organisation and hierarchy, and a capacity to mobilize persons and their political resources for political purposes' (2008; see also the Introduction to this volume). While the BVI might speak with one voice to the EU, it does so – as in its response to the Green Paper – by touting the efforts of a super-wealthy expatriate to promote environmentally sustainable tourism or by demanding a level playing field in the domain of international financial regulation.

The meaning-production and praxis of the polity (see the Introduction to this volume) operate in the BVI in the domain of jurisdiction – not as spatial jurisdiction or the geographical boundary of sovereignty, but literally as the ability to speak the law, in which language, on whose terms, in what accent, dialect, or register it can be spoken. As is evident in the judge's comment to the lawyer, this is a specific kind of language game in which multiple modalities of speaking vie with one another, often in the same mouth: in register of strategic essentialism located in the BVI itself; in register of pan-Caribbean anti-colonial nationalism; in register of Englishness, of the Crown, of the stability and solidity of the Union flag and British law and order – and finding that this polyglot can be a good business proposition for the Chinese.

Notes

1 Research has been supported by the US National Science Foundation (SES-0516861). Any opinions, findings, and conclusions or recommendations expressed here are those of the author and do not necessarily reflect the views of the National Science Foundation. I thank Michael O'Neal, Janice Nibbs Blyden, and many other interlocutors in the BVI who remain anonymous. I also thank the editors for their comments on earlier drafts and the participants in the conferences that gave rise to this volume, especially Ronen Palan and William Vlcek. I thank Sylvia Martin and Nanao Akanuma for research assistance on Chinese incorporations in the BVI.
2 This comment was made to me during fieldwork in the early 1990s.
3 There is more moral opprobrium towards individuals who seek to evade taxes through offshore bank accounts than to corporations seeking the same through offshore incorporation but in the name of 'competitiveness' or in the name of getting out from under 'oppressive' regulatory 'burdens' in their home country.

References

British Virgin Islands (2008) 'Response by the Government of the British Virgin Islands, 30 October 2008', *Response to COM(2008) 383*.

Cormack, B. (2007) *A Power to Do Justice: Jurisdiction, English Literature, and the Rise of Common Law, 1509–1625*, Chicago: University of Chicago Press.

Ferguson, Y.H. and Mansbach, R.W. (2008) *A World of Polities: Essays of Global Politics*, London: Routledge.

Fox, B. (2009) 'Islands resent crackdown of tax havens by G-20', *Guardian* (UK). Online. Available at: www.guardian.co.uk/world/feedarticle/8438767 (accessed 5 March 2012).

Marshall, D. (2002) 'At whose service? Caribbean state posture, merchant capital and the export services option', *Third World Quarterly*, 23(4): 725–51.

Maurer, B. (1997) *Recharting the Caribbean: Land, Law and Citizenship in the British Virgin Islands*, Ann Arbor: University of Michigan Press.

Maurer, B. (2008) 'Re-regulating offshore finance?', *Geography Compass*, 2(1): 155–75.

Palan, R., Murphy, R. and Chavagneux, C. (2010) *Tax Havens: How Globalization Really Works* (Cornell Studies in Money), Ithaca, NY: Cornell University Press.

Rawlings, G. (2007) 'Taxes and transnational treaties: responsive regulation and the reassertion of offshore sovereignty', *Law & Policy*, 29(1): 51–66.

Richland, Justin B. (2011) 'Hopi tradition as jurisdiction: on the potentializing limit of Hopi sovereignty', *Law & Social Inquiry*, 36(1): 201–34.

Rosaldo, R. (1989) 'Imperialist nostalgia', *Representations*, 26: 107–22.

Sharman, J.C. (2006) *Havens in a Storm: The Struggle for Global Tax Regulation*, Ithaca, NY: Cornell University Press.

Sutherland, D., Matthews, B. and El-Gohari, A. (2009) *An Exploration of How Chinese Companies Use Tax Havens and Offshore Financial Centres: 'Round-Tripping' or 'Capital-Augmenting' OFDI?* Oxford Department of International Development, Program for Technology and Management for Development working paper SLPTMD-WP-42.

Valverde, M. (2008) 'The ethic of urban diversity: urban law and local norms', *Law & Social Inquiry*, 33(4): 895–923.

Vlcek, W. (2010) 'Development – great and small: "greater China", small Caribbean islands and offshore finance', in B. Guo and S. Guo (eds) *Greater China in an Era of Globalization*, Lanham, MD: Lexington Books.

10 French concepts of state

Nation, *patrie*, and the Overseas

Ulla Holm

France has no equal because the Overseas are part of France.
(President N. Sarkozy's New Year's speech to
the Overseas, 9 January 2011)

Commemorating the centennial of the conquest of Algeria in 1831, a huge colonial exposition was held in Paris in 1931 which glorified the French position as the world's second largest overseas empire. The event represented the zenith of the concept of *la plus grande France* (Greater France). The image of a France of 100 million inhabitants, spread across five continents was represented as forming the national republican conscience – the hexagon constituted a mere twenty-third of this empire. The French empire was thought of within the frame of the nation-state, thus expanding the principle of the indivisibility of the national territory to the entire empire (Girardet 1972: 186). At the same time, however, the copy of the beautiful temples of Anghor Vat and the exotic clothing of people from the Overseas should demonstrate that the enlargement of the French nation-state also left room for different cultures. Hence, the diversity of the empire and unity of the enlarged nation-state were represented as living peacefully together.

The concept of 'Greater France' (Aldrich 1996; Wilder 2001) thus had a built-in ambiguity regarding the relationship between the French state-nation and its empire. On the one hand, the concept pointed to the colonies as integral parts of the nation-state and as necessary in order to maintain the French position amongst the great colonial powers of Europe – especially Great Britain, which was the world's premier maritime power. On the other hand, the exclusion of the natives from the French political order established the empire as something outside France. Hence, 'Greater France' epitomized 'the distinction between metropole and colony, modernity and tradition, subject and citizen' (Wilder 2001: 218–19).

Eight decades have passed between the colonial exposition in 1931 and 'the Year of the Overseas' in 2011 (see below). Wars, decolonization, and the foundation of the European Community (EC) and European Union (EU) have marked the complicated French relationship to the Overseas in this span of time. A gradual French loss of influence on the European arena has taken place due to the waves of EU enlargement. France needs the Overseas in order to demonstrate that France is still a great power. At the same time, France needs the EU in order to being able to project itself – via the EU – onto the global scene and thereby to the Overseas. Thus, France looks to the EU as a multiplier of power in relationship to the Overseas.

French policy is about state policy, about a powerful, welded-together actor aiming to coin 'great' projects to structure consciousness, culture, the economy, and security policy. It is therefore hardly surprising that the dominant French concept of Europe is imagined on the basis of the French state model. The European concept is wrapped in the *Tricolore*. The European concept thereby becomes an enlarged, doubled French state possessing the same features as the French state. Via this concept of Europe, French civilization, the French message of political universalism and French politics is extended in actions towards the global arena. This universalism requires an external dimension of the political state-nation that might be represented in European, African or Overseas politics and global actions. The universalism of the French message allows for a representation of France possessing 'something extra' which is *grandeur* and *rayonnement* (Holm 2002).

However, the state-like Europe is challenged in French discourse by the Gaullist concept of Europe of the states, which means that Europe is lying outside the French state-nation. Under this concept, France acts in Europe by demarcating a line between France and Europe, which is considered an arena for French diplomatic manoeuvres. Politics of shifting alliances amongst the most important regional and global powers will be the outcome of the concept. Such politics might occur in relation to the Overseas if the EU starts to unravel. The outcome of this would be a quest for relative gains that will render France a very unstable actor towards the Overseas and the other EU member states.

The state-like Europe and Europe of the states have been challenged since the 1990s by a concept of differentiation combining the two former concepts. The concept of differentiation points both to the particularity of each overseas island and to the regionalization of the islands of the four oceans.

Since the late 1800s until after the Second World War, the specific French nationalization of imperialism (*Greater France*) has played out in the debates over how to reconcile *assimilation* and *association*. The first concept annuls specific cultural features of the colonized people by subsuming the colonized into French political republican values. The second makes way for the right to differences alongside the adherence to republican values. The acknowledgement of cultural disparities allows for greater flexibility in the administration of the colonies. Contrary to the concept of the right to differences, however, is the fact that the natives were largely considered so different from the 'real' Frenchman that they were not included in the nation-state as political citizens. This occurred even though the French revolutionary message has always been a call for political equality – for full political citizenship.

The uneasy balance between the political republican values (*assimilation*) and cultural diversity (*association*) is rooted in the French political culture, marked as it is by the revolution of 1789. The revolutionary message was that the French chose to join 'project France' on the basis of a political contract, entered into voluntarily. The individual citizen would sign the contract with the republican state, which in turn guaranteed equality and liberty. According to this discourse, only the republican state could guarantee that the French were *active* political citizens and that the nation fused completely with the state.

The need for a strong 'state-roof' to avoid fragmentation into particular interests entails a concept of an indivisible and unified Republic. However, since decolonization[1] and the foundation of the EC/EU, the changing relationship between the metropolitan state and the Overseas has challenged the concept of the indivisible and uniform Republic. Especially the rewriting of Article 73 of the Fifth Constitution in 2003 made possible an increasingly differentiated institutional evolution – one more respectful of political autonomy. This evolution is a consequence of the impact on French law of the EU law that draws a distinction between Outermost Region and Overseas Country and Territory (OCT). Hence, the Europeanization of French law-making is proceeding discretely.

A pattern of variable geometry in the relations between the metropole, the Overseas and the EU has become ever more visible. This has resulted in a debate in France on the future unity of the indivisible Republic. Critics have warned against the dissolution of the Republican unity (Roger 2009). A struggle over semantics has occurred regarding whether it is necessary to 'pluralize' or 'singularize' the notion of the Overseas. The current deputy minister of the Overseas, Mme Marie-Luce Penchard, declared that she prefers the notion *les Outre-mers* (the Overseas*)* to *l'Outre-mer* (the Oversea) (Penchard 2011). By using the plural instead of the singular, the minister is underlining that the islands do not constitute a singular unity. As Sarkozy stated: '[T]he unity of the Republic is not equivalent to the uniformity of the institutions' (Sarkozy 2009). Two years later, Sarkozy established that 'the Overseas are an element of the entire Republic and the French state as guarantor of the unity of the Nation' (Sarkozy 2011). Despite the emergence of the concept of differentiation, the concept of the indivisible Republic continues to constitute a central building block of the republican state-nation discourse.

A central message of the fused French state-nation is that all mankind should follow the 'universal French message'. It is universal because it is neither linked to a territory or a social category nor to any ethnic, cultural, or biological criteria.

Due to the concept of individual universalism implied in this construction, France is proud to be able to transform foreigners/immigrants into citizens. Giving special rights to ethnic or religious groups is therefore to revolt against the ideals of the 1789 Revolution. The ethnic or religious citizen does not exist or rather does not have to exist.

This mistrust of ethnic and religious communitarization is challenged by the culturally defined concept of *patrie*, which is an emotional and cultural container. *Patrie* relates to the non-institutionalized affiliation of a particular group to a defined territory on the basis of common history, habits, language, culture, and religion.

The concept of *patrie* was at work in the launching of *l'Année des outre-mer* (the Year of the Overseas) in February 2011. Minister of Culture Fréderic Mitterrand declared that the purpose of that 'year' was 'to demonstrate how cultural diversity enriches French culture' (Mitterrand 2011). At the same time, however, Mitterrand praised the inhabitants of the Overseas for their participation in the French Revolution and in the Resistance during the Second World War (Mitterrand 2011). A linkage was thus established between the Overseas being inside the political state-nation as political citizens because of the common heroic and political past and being outside because of the Overseas' own cultural *patries*, which are rooted in their cultural past and projected into the future.

The colonial exposition of 1931 represented the Overseas 'others' as exotic, loyal, and *passive* French citizens linked to France by the French educational project of *mission civilisatrice*, whereas 'The Year of the Overseas' represents the Overseas citizens as *active* and on equal footing with the hexagon in their common quest to have a strong voice in a globalized world.

The former French empire has been scattered like confetti-like outposts in the Atlantic, the Caribbean, the Indian Ocean and the Pacific since decolonization in the 1950s and 1960s (Guillebaud 1976).

Even if the remnants of the former colonial empire consist only of small outposts and pose an economic burden for France, the Overseas are still represented as an important element of the French vision of itself as a major actor at the global level.

French State Secretary for the Overseas Yves Jégo's 2009 statement bears witness to this vision: 'The Overseas make France the world's second maritime power. The Overseas' trump cards are also French trump cards' (Jégo 2009). The Overseas are thus geostrategically included in France. The purpose of this inclusion is to demonstrate that France still counts as a global power. In order to maintain its perceived status as a global power, France requires the EU as a multiplier of power in relationship to the Overseas. The question is how France conceives of the relationship between the EU and the Overseas in its quest to be an important global power.

The French response to the European Green Paper on the future of the relationship between the EU, the member states and the Overseas declares that '(t)he challenge of the future relations between the EU and the OCT is the emergence of a differentiated European strategy' (France 2008). It is indeed a challenge for the EU but also for France as for upholding French influence in the four oceans. The above-mentioned French response therefore emphasizes that 'the OCTs possess some specificities that might be trump cards for the EU because the OCTs are present all over the globe . . . (t)he OCTs are called to participating fully in the EU's role at the global level because of their geostrategical position' (France 2008). France obtains added European and global value by 'possessing' the OCTs, which '(a)re integral parts of the French Republic' (France 2008).[2]

'Europeanization' is linked to the regionalization of the Overseas. French Deputy Minister of the Overseas Marie-Luce Penchard has testified to this conception by declaring: 'The Overseas constitute poles of French influence and they can serve as regional support for French influence' (Penchard 2011). Regionalization thus represents one way of strengthening the French position on the global scene.

The inclusion of the Overseas in regional cooperation linked to the EU is coupled with 'departementalization' and 'Francification'. The Overseas are seen '(a)s an element of the entire Republic and the French state as guarantor of the unity of the Nation' (Sarkozy 2011).

In relationship to the official announcement of la Mayotte becoming the 101st French department on 31 March 2011, Sarkozy stated: '*La Mayotte, c'est la France*' (Sarkozy 2011). The concept of the indivisible Republic thus still continues to constitute a central building block of the republican state-nation discourse.

Departementalization, 'Francification', regionalization, and 'Europeanization' are simultaneously at play. All of these concepts have come to the political fore in an attempt to 'save' France from being a mid-range state (*puissance moyenne*) in relation to the Overseas.

Conclusion

The expansion of the French state-nation to include the Overseas still does its job. It points to the representation of France as a 'confetti empire-state' that 'reproduces distinctions among collectivities while subordinating them to a greater or lesser degree to the ruling authority' (Cooper 2005: 27). To a certain extent, one might hold France to be an 'old fashioned' empire from 'whose centre power radiates and fades towards the periphery by construction of concentric circles' (Tunander 1997: 32). As French researcher Jean-Francois Bayart writes, however: 'It is mistaken to compare the empires to wheels whose spokes go back to the centre and whose peripheries do only communicate with the centre' (Bayart 2009: 39).

The political geography of the remnants of the French Empire defies the concept of concentric circles. Some islands are integral parts of the French Republic. Others, such as New Caledonia, are possibly splitting completely away from France. The French notion of cultural diversity (*patrie*) might result in the Overseas breaking away from the hexagon because they prefer being a sovereign *Kulturnation*. Still others are in between French integration and full-fledged state sovereignty. A network of different political relations – scattered all over the four oceans – are established between France and its Overseas. An institutional political variable geometry is constituted that might change the status of the islands in relationship to France.

The ongoing regionalization of the Overseas and the concept of the doubling of France at the EU level might also change the geopolitical position of the islands. Being drawn closer to the EU and being still more regionalized might result in a displacement of the Overseas as an elongation of France. If this happens, France will no longer be France, having lost its confetti empire, which is represented as part and parcel of the French quest for being considered an important global power.

Notes

1 After the Second World War, France tried to 'save' its colonies from independence by inventing a new institutional framework. The 4th Constitution of 1946 inaugurated a new constellation of borders that turned the French Empire into 'a differentiated unit of belonging, in which all people were now considered rights-bearing citizens, but with a range of political relationships to the state' (Cooper 2005: 29). The preamble to the 4th Constitution of 1946 states that: 'France shall form with its overseas peoples a Union founded upon equal rights and duties, without distinction of race or religion . . . the French Union shall be composed of nations and peoples who agree to pool or coordinate'. The Constitution of 1958 declares that: 'The Republic shall recognize the Overseas populations with the French people in a common ideal of liberty, equality and fraternity' (Constitution of 1958: article 72–73).
2 The French OCTs represent nearly 60 per cent of all the EU's OCT populations.

References

Aldrich, R. (1996) *Greater France: A History of French Overseas Expansion*, London: Macmillan Press.

Bayart, J.F. (2009) 'Les études postcoloniales, une invention politique de la tradition?', *Sociétés politiques comparées. Revue européenne d'analyse des sociétés politiques*, nº14.

Cooper, F. (2005) *Colonialism in Question. Theory, Knowledge, History*, Berkeley, Los Angeles, London: University of California Press.

France (2008) The French 'Response to Green Paper Questionnaire', *Response to COM (2008) 383*. All responses to COM (2008) 383.

Girardet, R. (1972) *L'idée coloniale en France de 1871–1962*, Paris: La Table Ronde.

Guillebaud, J.C. (1976) *Les confettis de l'Empire: Martinique, Guyane française, la Réunion, Nouvelle-Calédonie, Wallis-et-Futura, Polynésie française, territoire française des Affars et des Issas, Saint-Pierre-et-Miquelon, Terres australes et antarctiques françaises, Nouvelles-Hébrides, Archipel des Comores*, Paris: Éditions du Seuil.

Holm, U. (2002) 'Det franske Europa: et retrospektivt perspektiv' ['The French Europe: A Retrospective Perspective'], PhD thesis. Aarhus: Aarhus University Press.

Jégo, Y. (2009) *L'Outremer fait de la France la deuxième puissance maritime du monde.* Online. Available at: www.zinfos974.com/Yves-Jego-L-Outremer-fait-de-la-France-la deuxieme-puissance-maritime-du-monde_a7541.html.

Mitterrand, F. (2011) Online. Available at: www.2011-annee-des-outre-mer.gouv.fr/actu-alites/192/edito-de-m-frederic-mitterand.html (accessed 11 June 2011).

Penchard, Marie-Luce (2011) Déclaration de Mme Marie-Luce Penchard, ministre char-gée de l'outre-mer, Paris, 25 August. Online. Available at: http://discours.vie-publique. fr/notices/113001906.html (accessed 1 September 2011).

Roger, P. (2009) 'Peut-on accorder l'outre-mer au pluriel sans menacer l'unité de la Répub-lique?', *Le Monde*, 10 April 2009.

Sarkozy, N. (2009) Online. Available at: http://outre-mer.gouv.fr/?2011-année-des-outre-mer-une-manifestion-pour-aller-au-dela-des.html (accessed 15 April 2009).

Sarkozy, N. (2011) 'La Mayotte, c'est la France', *Le Parisien*. Online. Available at: www. elysee.fr/president/les-dossiers/toutes-les-actions/temps-forts/voeux-aux-francais-pour-l-annee-2011.10332. html (accessed 18 January 2010).

Tunander, O. (1997) 'Post-Cold War Europe: a synthesis of a bipolar friend-foe structure and a hierarchic cosmos-chaos structure?' in O. Tunander, P. Baev and V.I. Einagel (eds) *Geopolitics in Post-Wall Europe: Security, Territory and Identity*, Oslo: PRIO/London: Sage.

Wilder, G. (2001) 'Framing greater France between the wars', *Journal of Historical Sociology*, 14(2): 198–225.

11 Will the EU and the euro lead to more sovereignty?

French Polynesia

Bernard Poirine

This chapter deals with French Polynesia, a French overseas territory, and how its relationship with the metropole state and the European Union (EU) is perceived as a means towards increasing its room for manoeuvre and its degree of sovereignty.

French Polynesia is a group of 118 South Pacific islands, scattered across an oceanic zone approximately the size of Europe (5,500,000 km²), while the total land area of the archipelago (3,600 km²) is about half the size of Corsica. Many of these islands, in the Tuamotu and Gambier archipelagos, are atolls, with a maximum altitude of less than three metres, making them potentially prone to suffer from the global climate warming and related rising sea levels. French Polynesia is a very remote place: by plane, it takes almost 24 hours to travel from Paris, 8.5 hours from Los Angeles, and 12 hours from Tokyo.

This chapter consists of three analytical sections. The first section, 'Europe as a tool for decolonization', shows how France and the local autonomist and separatist parties use Europe as a political tool to achieve their aims. The second section, 'Paying for colonialism', analyses the sovereignty games about how to share the cost of running French Polynesia between the French government, the local government, and the non-French members of the EU. The third section, 'The euro debate', deals with the debate about possibly replacing the Pacific Franc with the euro in the three French South Pacific territories: French Polynesia, New Caledonia, and Wallis and Futuna. What will the benefits be? For whom? Who will take (or not take) the responsibility and pay the costs? A concluding section sums up the analyses.

To understand the strategies employed in the triangular sovereignty games between Papeete, Paris, and Brussels, however, it is useful first to have an historical overview of how Tahiti became a French colony in the first place, of the most significant events of the colonial and postcolonial history, and of the current political, economic, and social situation in the islands.

The colonization of the Society Islands by France[1]

Tahiti became French almost by chance. Until 1830, Tahiti was mostly under British influence, because the English missionaries of the London Missionary Society had succeeded in converting the people and royal family (the Pomare family) to Christianity. A former English missionary turned businessman, George Pritchard was the British consul and a very influential counsellor to then Queen Pomare Vahine IV.

France had failed to establish colonies in New Zealand and wanted a greater presence in the Pacific Ocean. French Rear-Admiral Abel Aubert Dupetit-Thouars first took possession of the Marquesas Islands for France in May 1842 with the help of the French Catholic missionaries who had Christianized those islands. But he soon realized that the Marquesas had very little strategic or economic interest. He then proceeded to Tahiti and, with the assistance of French Consul J.A. Moerenhout, he managed to convince four of the Tahitian chiefs to sign a request for a French protectorate on 9 November 1842 while the British consul was travelling abroad. Queen Pomare herself later signed the same letter to King Louis Philippe. Dupetit-Thouard had no orders to do these things from the French government and was therefore acting on his own initiative. Before returning to France, he established an interim government.

Back in France, King Louis Philippe ratified the Act of Protectorate, while a similar request made in England by the British Consul Pritchard was turned down by the Foreign Office. The British government finally accepted the French protectorate in the name of *Entente Cordiale*, judging that the Queen had signed by her own will.[2]

On November 1843, Dupetit-Thouard gave Queen Pomare King Louis Philippe's letter accepting her request for the French protectorate. The French had returned with several warships under Captain Armand Bruat. On the pretext that the Queen would not take down her own royal flag and display the flag of the protectorate, Bruat decided, on his own, to annex the kingdom, to depose Queen Pomare, and to expel the British Consul Pritchard. The Queen wrote a letter of complaint to King Louis Philippe. The King decided not to ratify the annexation and ordered that Queen Pomare and the protectorate be re-established as before on 24 February 1844 (De Deckker 1997: 290).[3] In the meantime (the decision of King Louis Philippe would be known only on 12 July in Papeete), however, a small war had broken out between the French soldiers and the Tahitian 'rebels' loyal to the Queen. This war lasted three years (March 1844 to December 1846). The French finally won despite 50 casualties on their side and probably many more on the Tahitian side. At the end of this period, the war and a series of three deadly epidemics had decimated the population of the *Iles du Vent* (Tahiti, Moorea, Maiao) to the point where only 9,969 inhabitants (including foreigners) were left by 1848.

Under heavy pressure from the protectorate administration King Pomare V, son of Queen Pomare IV, who lacked his mother's strength of character, surrendered his kingdom to France on 29 June 1880. Yet the French did not succeed in bringing many settlers to this new colony. Most of the early rich colonists who established plantations were English, Scottish, or German, and married to the Tahitian aristocracy who owned most of the land. Their descendants (with names such as Salmon or Bambridge) still belong to the local Tahitian political, administrative, and business elite.

In 1944, the status of the islands was formally altered from 'colony' to 'territory', and the Tahitians became French citizens who, as such, elected their representatives at the French Assembly in 1945. The first separatist party (*Rassemblement démocratique des populations tahitiennes*, RDPT) was established in 1949. Its leader, Pouvana'a a Oopa, was elected as representative to the French Assembly. He was also elected vice president of the first autonomous government in 1957 (the president was the French High Commissioner). In 1957, a referendum was organized by France: 16,279 people voted in favour of remaining in the French Republic, while 8,988 people voted for independence. In 1964, President Charles de Gaulle decided to transfer France's atomic experiments from the Sahara Desert in Algeria to the Tuamotu Archipelago. This meant that French Polynesia had become of very high strategic importance to France. In 1992, President Mitterrand decided to suspend atomic experiments. In 1995, President Chirac resumed them for one year before stopping them forever. Consequently, French Polynesia has now much less strategic value to France than before 1995, and the French naval and military forces there have been greatly reduced.

The current political, economic, and social situation of French Polynesia

Nowadays, under the 1984 autonomy statute, French Polynesia is a French *collectivité d'outre-mer* (the word *territoire* is no longer used) with an autonomous assembly and government, president, flag, and anthem. The French government has jurisdiction over money, credit, international relations, higher education, national defence, police forces, and justice. All other matters fall under the jurisdiction of the local government, including fiscal law and the social security system.

The 260,000 residents are French and European citizens and hold EU passports. They vote in European elections as French citizens (in practice, however, the turnout rate is very low, since local politicians are uninterested in this election), and they elect three representatives (for all French territories and departments) to the European Parliament. In that sense, they belong to 'the European family' (European Commission 2009), but are not members of the EU. Instead, they are associated to the EU (because they are territories of member states) and belong to the group of Overseas Countries and Territories (OCTs).

The local political parties are divided between the autonomists, who had a majority until 2004 under President Gaston Flosse (the 'father' of the 1984 statute of 'full' autonomy), and the separatists led by Oscar Temaru. Since 2004, when Flosse lost the elections for the first time, Temaru and Flosse, together with a dissident autonomist, Gaston Tong Sang, have each held the presidency several times. The majority is now constantly changing, with some surprising alliances (Flosse struck an alliance with Temaru in 2007 to oust Tong Sang after the latter had won the elections). In 2011, Temaru returned to office – by November 2012 he still commands a very fragile majority.

The local currency, the Pacific Franc (*franc CFP*), is common to France's three Pacific territories: French Polynesia, New Caledonia, and Wallis and Futuna. It is issued and guaranteed by France and linked by a fixed exchange rate to the euro. Compared to many independent island nations, French Polynesia is relatively wealthy. The per capita GDP was equal to 17,216 euros in 2005, and French public transfers amounted to 5,378 euros per capita in 2008 (Haut commissariat de la république française en Polynésie française 2009). It must be pointed out that the cost of living is 51 per cent higher than in metropolitan France, according to a recent study, for which reason this apparently high GDP per capita is probably misleading in terms of the real standard of living. Moreover, this 'average' conceals the vast inequalities between a small political, administrative, commercial, and professional elite and the majority of the population.

The welfare state in French Polynesia is not as developed as in the French overseas departments, as the French social security system does not apply. There is much less redistribution of income than in France: no income tax, no wealth tax, no capital gains tax, no inheritance tax, but heavy import and corporate taxes, as well as a value added tax. There are no unemployment benefits and no minimum income scheme for poor families. Expatriate and local state civil servants are paid 84 per cent more than in France, and local civil servants obtained a similar pay scale in the 1970s. In the private sector, the wages for unskilled labour are lower than in France, and the minimum wage is similar. One recent study (Herrera and Merceron 2010) finds that income inequality is much higher than in France and is comparable to that of South American countries. Let us now turn to the sovereignty games between France and the local political autonomist and separatist parties in French Polynesia.

Europe as a tool for decolonization

This section analyses how France and the local autonomist and separatist parties use Europe as a political tool to achieve their aims. The analysis shows that, first and foremost, the French government has repeatedly stated that it is not ready to relinquish its special relationship with its overseas departments and territories, whatever the cost and benefits of this relationship may be (see Nicolas Sarkozy's quote below). In each of the overseas entities, however, separatist movements exist and may even succeed in gaining power in local governments, as is the case in French Polynesia and New Caledonia. In Polynesia, this gives rise to three different roles for Europe in the games played between autonomists and separatists. I will deal with these in turn.

First, the official France wants to keep the overseas departments and territories in the French Republic. In exchange for its aid, however, it would like to retain privileged access to its market. On a recent visit to the Caribbean department of Guadeloupe, then French President Nicolas Sarkozy stated:

> For me, the French State will always keep its role of control; it is the referee,
> and the safeguard of the Nation's unity. And to those who want you to believe

that we are preparing to abandon the French overseas departments and territories, I can answer clearly that it will never happen as long as I shall be president of the republic. It is a fundamental and personal pledge that I take before you.

(Sarkozy 2011)

French Polynesia is much less a strategic asset now than during the period of the atomic experiments in the Tuamotu Archipelago (1964–95). Consequently, even if it is not stated in official speeches, France expects to receive economic benefits in exchange for the high level of aid it continues to send to its overseas territory since the end of the atomic experiments.

Even though it is not stated officially, the French officials feel that the cost of aid given to the French overseas territories is increasingly difficult to bear for the French taxpayer and vastly outweighs the economic benefits that the French companies obtain from their ties with them, since the territory increasingly imports from Asia (Japan, South Korea, China, Taiwan) and less and less from France. Since France pays the costs, it feels entitled to receive most of the economic and strategic benefits: French companies ought to have an (unofficial) privileged access to the public works contracts.

There is no official way to discriminate in favour of French companies, but import duties are higher on goods originating from outside the EU, and public works contracts are rarely given to non-French companies. Examples can be cited such as the building of the new hospital in Tahiti, awarded to French construction company Bouygues (which subsequently opted out of the contract), and the new communications cable between Hawai'i and Tahiti, awarded to Alcatel-Lucent.[4]

Another way of discriminating indirectly in favour of French companies is the tax exemption program (*loi de défiscalisation outre-mer*), whereby French companies and individuals can receive a tax credit in proportion to the amount invested in the overseas departments and territories.

In sum, when it comes to the economic aspect of the relationship to Polynesia, keeping others out has been a French priority – including other European interests. Let us now analyse the separatists' view of Europe as a tool for decolonization.

Second, the separatists are seeking closer ties with Europe as a tool for decolonization. Oscar Temaru, who has recently succeeded in forming a new majority with some former autonomist representatives from the outer islands, has again been president of French Polynesia since 6 April 2011, ousting former President Gaston Tong Sang, an autonomist. On 19 August 2011, this majority passed a resolution demanding the inclusion of French Polynesia on the United Nations (UN) list of territories to be decolonized (New Caledonia is already on this list; see Brown, this volume).

The separatists see closer ties to Europe as a means to increase their room of manoeuvre when dealing with the French state. They prefer a multilateral relationship with the EU to a bilateral relationship with France. They see Europe as a non-colonialist political entity. In private, they admit they would rather become a European territory than remain a French territory (however, the official public discourse is still one of becoming independent, not a European territory). To quote Louis Savoie, a former foreign affairs advisor for Oscar Temaru: 'Oscar Temaru pins his hope upon the construction of a European overseas' (Louis Savoie, personal communication, 10 June 2010).

However, the separatists see France (and the other European metropole states) as an obstacle to this kind of multilateral European relationship with the OCTs, because France is keeping all of the economic and strategic benefits for itself (use of oceanic space, fishing rights, military bases, and restricted competition to French firms for public works such as the new hospital and the transoceanic Internet cable mentioned above) while asking other European states to share the costs of providing aid to its overseas territories.

> In order to be interested in helping the OCTs, the other European countries should share the economic and strategic benefits in return for the assistance of the European aid (for instance: the public works contracts), in other words, the OCTs should become European OCTs.
>
> (Louis Savoie, personal communication, 10 June 2010)

But are the European institutions interested in the economic and strategic benefits of small islands or archipelagos in the very remote Pacific Ocean? The only instance of such a European economic and strategic interest outside Europe is the Ariane European Space complex in French Guyana (a French overseas department on the east coast of South America): it is the only European Overseas Region to be close to the equator, the best position for launching satellites.

Now let us turn to the autonomists and their relationship to Europe.

Third, the autonomists are seeking increased aid from Europe but are unwilling to adopt European regulations limiting their hard-won autonomy from France. The autonomists want to increase their room for manoeuvre in their relationship with Europe. They want more aid from Europe but also want to retain their autonomy in matters of fiscal policy, import restriction, immigration, real estate investments made by non-French European citizens,[5] and the rules regarding the awarding of local public works contracts to private companies.

The Polynesian autonomists seek the help of France to promote a renewed partnership with the EU, including a separate fund, distinct from the European Development Fund (EDF) (see Hannibal, Holst, *et al.*, this volume), to finance development aid to the OCTs. They agree with France that the French OCTs are a strategic asset that the EU overlooks: 'Europe needs us as much as we need Europe', said former President Gaston Tong Sang at the 2010 Overseas Countries and Territories Association (OCTA) conference (*Les Nouvelles de Tahiti*, 25 March 2010).

Tong Sang expressed his expectations from the negotiations: 'a set of negotiated agreements enabling us to get a little closer to the Outermost Region' (*Les Nouvelles de Tahiti*, 25 March 2010). He stresses that 'it is time to consider the OCTs as a category different from the ACP (African, Caribbean and Pacific states)' (*Les Nouvelles de Tahiti*, 26 March 2010).[6]

At the same time, however, the autonomists want to preserve their privileged relationship with the EU. For example, they do not welcome the free entry of European citizens seeking work in French Polynesia, and they do not favour free competition from European firms and European regulations regarding public works contracts: 'The president of French Polynesia Gaston Tong Sang wishes that the local public works rules continue to be applied in French Polynesia, instead of the European rules' (*Les Nouvelles de Tahiti*, 26 March 2010).

The autonomists and separatists both agree that there should be limits to the free entry of EU citizens to work in French Polynesia. This is the case, since French Polynesia has been allowed to regulate immigration and work permits through its own *lois de pays*, in accordance Article 45 of the European Council Decision of 27 November 2001 regarding association of OCTs.

In so doing, French Polynesia discriminates against non-French EU citizens in order to protect local employment. The rationale behind such an exception to the rule of reciprocity is that the very small labour market could become unbalanced by a sudden influx of European immigrants.

This illustrates the *asymmetrical relationship* that OCTs tend to obtain from Europe and their mother state. As Godfrey Baldacchino aptly states, 'they can get away with it because they are small'.[7] In other words, Europe can tolerate exceptions to the rules as long as they concern only a very small part of the European population (i.e. non-French EU citizens migrating to French Polynesia to find work).

Fourth, both separatists and autonomists want to be treated as a quasi-state when dealing with the EU: they want to negotiate directly with Brussels. The government of French Polynesia would like to be able to negotiate directly with the EU on a number of topics of common interest, including tuna fisheries, the free entry of European citizens, and aid. It would then be able to negotiate points specific to French Polynesia in the treaty of free association without French mediation. In other words, French Polynesia would like to increase its sovereignty status when dealing with the EU by being treated as a quasi-state independent of France:

> . . . the Economic and Social Council recommends that an OCT may negotiate individual protocols associated with the Treaty aiming on the one hand, to have the specific situation of the relationship between the OCT and the EU recognized, and on the other hand, to primarily enforce the competences specific to an OCT in case of need and if that usefulness is recognized.
>
> (Conseil économique et social de la Polynésie française 2008: 6)

When asked about the possibility for such an arrangement, one European Commission official, speaking on the condition of anonymity, grants that it is possible – but only with the consent of the metropole member state in question:

> It's very much up to the OCTs themselves, and the Member States . . . it's a discussion between the member states. A lot of this is not Commission

decisions. It is member states and OCTs finding out how we progress in the most favourable way.

(Commission official, interviewed in Brussels, 24 March 2011)

To sum up this section, France wants to keep the Overseas while retaining economic benefits in return for aid; Polynesian autonomists seek European aid without submitting to the *acquis communautaire*; Polynesian separatists envision a direct relationship to the EU as a way of shedding their colonial link to France. In the meantime, both separatists and autonomists want Polynesia to act in a sovereign-like way – that is, without the detour around Paris – in relation to the EU. The EU, on its part, would accept a direct link to Papeete – but, eager to avoid interfering in the constitutional affairs of a member state, only if France takes the initiative and agrees that Polynesia is playing games with French sovereignty.

Paying for colonialism

This section analyses the rhetorical strategies which comprise a sovereignty game over who should pay the costs and who gets the economic and geostrategic benefits from the fact that French Polynesia belongs to the 'European family'.

As mentioned, French public transfers amounted to 5,546 euros per capita in 2009 (Institut de statistique de la Polynésie française 2011). The French state pays all military personnel, teachers, professors, judges, and policemen, as well as state public service pensions (61 per cent of the total public expenditure). The local government pays for all other expenses (39 per cent of total public expenditure).

The territory's most important resource is the French public transfers (1.4 billion euros in 2009), next comes tourism (roughly 315 million euros in 2009), and the third most important resource is Tahitian pearls (70 million euros) (IEOM 2011). French Polynesia finds European aid (about 600 million Pacific Franc annually) almost negligible compared to French transfers (175 billion Pacific Franc in 2009).

The section proceeds by analysing; first, how French Polynesia rhetorically employs its marginality, its size, and its colonial past as arguments for increased EU aid; second, the French position that the EU should share the French cost of aid; third, the position of the other EU member states.

The French OCTs' views on the EU aid debate

French Polynesia has employed a number of arguments for increased aid from the EU. First, it argues that it is part of the European family, therefore French Polynesia should receive as much aid per capita as the small Outermost Regions of the EU, including the French overseas departments (*départements d'outre-mer*, DOMs). The French overseas territories (and other OCTs) receive much less funding per capita from the EU than the DOMs, which are EU Overseas Regions (ORs).

According to Bruno Peaucellier (head of the Bureau of Foreign Affairs at the Presidency of French Polynesia), the OCTs receive 15–20 times less aid per capita than the French DOMs/Outermost Regions. One of the reasons why

Mayotte recently voted to become a DOM was the additional aid it expects to receive from France and Europe by becoming an OR. On the contrary, Saint Barthélémy is switching from DOM/OR status (part of Guadeloupe) to OCT status because it is rich, does not need European aid, and does not want to apply European custom and fiscal regulations.

In this instance, the marginal position of the OCTs is tilted towards inclusion in Europe – while other arguments tilt the marginality to the outside. One of the arguments goes like this:

Please help us as much as the ORs but do not apply the same European rules to us.

The French Polynesian government seeks more aid from the EU, but in a way that would not limit the self-government rule obtained from France regarding taxes on imports, import quotas, the local labour market protection, and the local fiscal regime on income from savings (no income tax). A newspaper explains:

> [Headline]: Brussels: At the EU–OCT forum, Gaston Tong Song made a request to make it easier for the OCTs to receive grants from Europe and to strengthen relations, while keeping the normative autonomy for the OCTs.
>
> [Subtitle]: Yes to the European currency, no to its standards.
>
> The French OCTs want more Europe and funding, but without the constraints, i.e. without the imposition of European standards, for instance in tax matters. They value their autonomy.
>
> *(Les Nouvelles de Tahiti*, 26 March 2010)

So marginality allows a strategic, rhetorical movement across the distinction between inside and outside.

Polynesia also employs its size – relative as well as absolute – as an argument for more favourable conditions. The aid to Polynesia, the argument goes, is 'a mere drop in the bucket'. The European OCTs want to be considered as a separate group: they find it unfair to be treated as the ACP countries because they belong to the 'European family'. They are asking for special treatment, that is, to obtain aid from a separate development fund dedicated specifically to the OCTs. According to Louis Savoie, the late Alexandre Leontieff (French Polynesian president in 1987–8) is reported to have once said: 'It is better to receive a large ladle of aid out of a separate small pot (for the OCT), instead of a small spoon drawn from the great basin of the European Development Fund (for ACP countries)'.[8]

Following this line of thinking, French Polynesia would like the EU to set up this 'small pot', separate from the EDF, and a separate EU administrative body to run it. This would make for efficient lobbying in Brussels, since nobody would then have to decide which share of the 'big pot' would go to the OCTs using the same criteria as for ACP countries. The political lobbying would then concentrate on the size of the 'small pot' given to OCTs. It is hoped that it would become easier to obtain a larger amount per capita for the OCTs (the benefit of being small being that you do not cost as much to aid; a mere drop in the big bucket of EU development aid):

The logic of cooperation (between the EU and the OCTs) relies on a series of standards similar to those applied to member countries of the group of ACP States.

The OCTs and the ACPs affairs are managed by the same services of the European Commission. The merging of their management within the administrative organization as well as the unified representation of their interests may have the perverse effect of marginalizing the OCTs' action. The diversity of their situations (OCTs and ACPs) makes the administrative unity of their management problematic.

> (Conseil économique et social de la Polynésie française 2008)

You can aid us more because we don't cost as much to aid as other (ACP) developing countries.

Indeed, being small and dependent should turn out to become an advantage in the bargaining process for aid: if they had a separate fund set up for them, the less populated OCTs could receive more aid per capita because there are fewer of them among which to spread the aid, and each of them has a small population.

It is verified statistically that for small islands (population less than 1 million), the amount of aid received per capita is inversely related to the island population. I have suggested that this fact is explained by a 'theory of aid as trade' (Poirine 1995; 1999): aid buys political goodwill and strategic benefits, an invisible service export to the donor nation. The amount of this strategic export does not depend on the island's population. As a result, it is cheaper to buy this indivisible (and invisible) export from islands with a small population, since the smaller the population, the greater the visible effect of aid on the standard of living of this population (for the same aid effort), and the greater the degree of commitment to expect from the receiving population to the donor nation (or group of nations).

So the smallness of the OCTs should warrant more aid – both because it is cheap to aid societies that are small on absolute accounts and because it is unfair to place the same demands on small societies as on large ones.

You owe us more aid because we have hosted the French atomic experiments, contributing to the security of Europe.

French Polynesia also believes that it has contributed to the security of France and the EU by serving as the testing ground for French atomic experiments from 1964 to 1995. In its view, this entitles the territory to compensation from France and the EU (in other words: compensation for past invisible geostrategic services exported to Europe):

> the Economic and Social Council wishes to recall that French Polynesia had been the site for the nuclear testing of France, a member of the EU, thus enabling her to develop the nuclear weapon and, offering herself and all of the countries of the European Union a guaranty of security.
>
> (Conseil économique et social de la Polynésie française 2008: 2)

One might remain sceptical about the force of this argument to obtain more aid from the EU. But it represents a very explicit attempt to exploit a colonial past as a tool to acquire benefits in the future (see Hannibal, Holst, *et al.*, this volume).

To sum up: French Polynesia employs its marginality in relation to the EU to place itself on both the inside (we are Europeans and should therefore have aid) and the outside (we are non-EU members and should not be bound by EU regulations); French Polynesia employs its size to argue for more aid; and Polynesia employs wrongs committed in the colonial past to be cashed in on in the postcolonial present and future.

France would like the EU to assume more responsibility for the OTs

France would like the EU to provide more aid to the French overseas territories, even though they are not part of the EU's territory. As far as the manipulation of hybridity goes, France agrees with Polynesia: they belong to the 'European family' and should therefore be privileged when considering aid, and not amalgamated with the ACP countries associated with Europe.

> Marie-Luce Penchard, French Minister of the overseas affairs, requests a 'differential treatment' as the OCTs are not ACPs; and a 'preferred treatment' because the OCTs are part of the European family. Like the ACP countries, the OCTs benefit from the European Development Fund, but so as to differentiate them, they want another "tool" of funding for 2013, a simpler one, as the current procedures are overly cumbersome. Minister of the Overseas, Marie-Luce Penchard, also deems it necessary to 'reduce' and 'simplify' them.
>
> (*Les Nouvelles de Tahiti*, 26 March 2010)

Rather than following the Polynesian arguments about size, however, not to speak of the colonial past, France argues that Polynesia helps Europe reach otherwise unattainable parts of the globe.

> The French overseas territories are 'outposts' of Europe in the Pacific zone, they can promote European values in that region. And the French Pacific overseas territories are a geostrategic asset to Europe (they command vast oceanic zones, for example, the size of Europe for French Polynesia). 'In order to win over Brussels authorities', France and its Overseas Departments and Territories emphasize that they are assets for the EU: biodiversity, maritime space, and a presence in every ocean.
>
> (*Les Nouvelles de Tahiti*, 26 March 2010)

This argument resonates squarely with the important element in French identity, which Holm identifies (this volume): for France to be France, it must have a strong global voice. However, this is not necessarily an argument which resonates with the conceptions that other member states have of what Europe should be.

The other EU members do not feel that they should have to share the cost

The other EU member states do not consider the economic and geostrategic benefits of France's Pacific territories to be coming to the EU, but rather to the French state. Consequently, they are reluctant to share the costs without being able to share in the benefits.

The member states have no diplomatic or strategic interests in the Pacific Ocean since Britain left its last colonies (except minuscule Pitcairn Island).

Australia and New Zealand (non-EU members) are at present the only regional powers in the South Pacific and see the French presence as a positive element for the stability of the region. Recently, most of the French naval forces have been transferred from French Polynesia to New Caledonia, which is much closer to Australia.

France, Australia, and New Zealand signed the FRANZ agreement in 1992 to cooperate in matters of humanitarian aid and maritime surveillance. An Australia–France Defence cooperation agreement entered in force in July 2009, whereby both countries agreed on joint military exercises, the use of the Noumea Naval Base by Australian forces, and joint efforts to assist the regional stability and security.

As regards the oceanic zone, tuna fishing appears to be the most lucrative activity at the moment, but very few European vessels sail the South Pacific. Most of them are Japanese, Korean, Chinese, or American.

Moreover, the EU does not need an additional launching pad close to the equator for the Ariane space project in addition to the existing Kourou space facility in French Guyana (South America). The South Pacific islands therefore have no geostrategic interest in that regard.[9]

Most of the member states tend to think that the aid given to the French overseas departments and territories is already too costly compared to the benefits for the non-French member states, some of which are poorer than the richer territories, such as French Polynesia.

According to one Commission official:

> a majority [of the member states] said, "there is no reason why we should go on financing the co-operation under the EDF, when the majority of the OCTs have a [GDP] level which is superior to the EU average GDP. There is no reason why we should go on financing the cooperation under the EDF".
> (Interview with Commission official, 4 November 2009)

To sum up: the French OCTs feel that they do not receive enough aid from the EU compared to what the French DOMs receive (which are ORs and therefore EU territory) and that they should receive more than the ACP countries aided by the EDF. To that aim, they rhetorically employ their marginality, size, and colonial history (first part of this section). France would like the EU to assume more responsibility in sharing the cost of aid to its overseas territories but is unwilling to share its sovereignty over them (second part of this section). Other EU members consider they should not bear the burden of aid to French territories since only France benefits from the geostrategic or economic advantages and the new member states do not see why they should have to contribute to the development of OCTs with a higher GDP per capita than their own (third part of this section).

The euro debate

One of the most striking ways in which the triangular sovereignty games play out relates to the euro debate. The assembly of French Polynesia voted to replace the Pacific Franc with the euro on 6 January 2006, at a time when the president (elected by the assembly) was the separatist leader Oscar Temaru. The resolution read:

> The Assembly of French Polynesia makes a request to the government of the Republic to adopt the set of legislative and regulatory measures necessary to introduce the European currency in French Polynesia and to obtain to that effect the agreement of the European authorities.
>
> (L'Assemblée 2006)

France has agreed to take the necessary steps to introduce the euro with the European Commission – provided, however, that the two other entities which use the CFP (New Caledonia, Wallis and Futuna) – also agree to request it. For the moment, however, only French Polynesia has officially made this request.

The Polynesian separatists want to do away with the Pacific Franc because of its neo-colonial connotations (Franc CFP means *Franc des Colonies Françaises du Pacifique*). 'The Pacific Franc is not a real currency; it is an administrative currency, a substitute money, an anomaly. You cannot change euros for pacific francs in any French or European bank. The euro is not a colonial currency', says Louis Savoie, a former foreign affairs advisor to former President Oscar Temaru (and leader of the Polynesian delegation to the OCTA conference in 2007).

The separatists also see the euro as a means to deal directly with Europe and to become less dependent on France alone: 'Introducing the euro in French Polynesia would be a way to go beyond the bilateral relation with France' (Louis Savoie, personal communication).

However, while the separatists see the euro not only as a currency without colonial connotations but as the currency for a future independent Polynesia, they may very well be on the wrong track: the agreement signed with France would have to be renegotiated in the event of independence, and it is doubtful that the EU would grant the privilege to become a member of the euro zone to a small independent Pacific island state with a relatively large budget and foreign trade deficits. This would represent an unprecedented move for the EU, in any case, since all euro zone members are currently European states, geographically speaking (Andorra and Monaco use the euro even though they are not EU members).

Paradoxically, it is only because it is *not* independent and belongs to an EU member state that French Polynesia could adopt the euro as its currency. In the case of independence, it would have to print its own currency, possibly pegged to the euro.

The Polynesian separatists are also probably incorrect in thinking that a strong currency like the euro would help their economy in the case of independence. Most small Pacific states, such as Fiji, could only develop tourism and exports with the help of significant currency devaluation.

The Polynesian autonomists are ambivalent towards introducing the euro: they think that the euro would be beneficial to the local economy (less uncertainty, no risk of devaluation, more convenient for tourism and exports), but they fear a devaluation (i.e. converting the Pacific Franc to euros at a lower rate than at present).[10] They also fear that French Polynesia would lose part of its fiscal autonomy by joining the euro zone. They are interested in the benefits of the euro without the constraining European rules and regulations (the Maastricht criteria would not apply to French Polynesia, since it is not a member state, but the European tax on income from savings might apply).

This is why the resolution cited above also includes the following reservations:

> The assembly points out, however, that the introduction of the euro:
>
> - Should definitely not entail a change in the actual exchange rate of the Pacific Franc in euros.
> - Should definitely not modify the competences that the statute of 1984 granted to French Polynesia.
> - Implies that the French State should help French Polynesia to support the cost of the currency change.
>
> (L'Assemblée 2006)

The European Commission would probably agree to introduce the euro in French Polynesia provided the French state first makes a formal request to that effect. Two French OTs are already using the euro: Saint Pierre et Miquelon and Mayotte (the latter recently became an overseas department), but both were using the French franc before the euro, so substituting the euro for the French franc was a natural move.

As mentioned, the French Pacific Franc is also the currency for New Caledonia and Wallis and Futuna – and France insists that the three take the same course. The euro is, however, employed in a curiously different way in the domestic games around sovereignty in these entities. The separatists in New Caledonia do not (as detailed by Brown, this volume) want the euro because its banknotes do not carry distinctive signs of the Kanak identity, whereas the Pacific Franc does (this was also an argument used against the euro in France: no national identity signs appear on any euro notes).

At present, the euro question has been at a standstill since 2006, since there is no agreement is the New Caledonian Assembly on this question, and the French state does not seem ready to introduce the euro in only one of the three territories. It seems as though it would be possible to adopt the euro in French Polynesia alone and let the Pacific Franc still be used in New Caledonia and Wallis and Futuna, but the French government does not seem ready to do so.

France has successfully turned the CFP/euro question into a stalemate by interlocking two separate sovereignty games – the Polynesian and New Caledonian. The EU – probably wisely – stays clear of attacking the Gordian Knot constructed by France. Meanwhile, the Pacific Franc continues to hold an ambiguous status as both a colonial symbol and sign of autonomy from European legislation.

Conclusion

This chapter shows how triangular sovereignty games are played between the EU, France, and the political parties of French Polynesia. It has shown that the EU is often constituted by French Polynesian politicians as a way out of French domination. However, Europe has multiple meanings. For France, the EU offers a helping hand with economic aid to this distant French territory.

The French government is lobbying the EU to help the French OTCs obtain increased aid through a dedicated fund separate from the EDF.

The French OTCs argue their geostrategic value as 'outposts' of the EU in the Pacific and want to be recognized as quasi-states when dealing with the EU. At the same time, however, they would like to be considered as deserving special treatment as members of the 'European family'. Being very small, they argue that the cost of this dedicated fund would be a mere drop in the bucket of development aid and structural development funds.

But many other member states do not see why they should contribute to pay for the costs of the remnants of the French Empire, since they feel as though the latter are no longer 'underdeveloped', judging by their GDP per capita, which is higher than the per capita GDP of many member states.

Furthermore, there is at present no perceived geostrategic interest in the French territories of the South Pacific for the (non-French) EU member states. Yet this may change in the future. Who would have thought in 1949 that the Tuamotu Archipelago would become of great strategic interest to France in 1964? Or that French Guyana would become the cornerstone of the European satellite launching program? The oceanic zone of French Polynesia covers an area the size of Europe. Should the deep sea mining of polymetallic nodules become feasible, for example, it could one day become of great economic interest to Europe.

The French Polynesian separatists view Europe as a tool for decolonization. They welcome a multilateral relationship instead of the bilateral one they used to have with France only. At a time when their leader is the president of French Polynesia and wants to push diplomatic efforts to support listing the territory on the list of the UN decolonization committee, he hopes to find support from some EU member states.

The autonomists want to remain in the French Republic, but they feel as though the EU might do more for them: they compare the aid received from the EU (per capita) to what is received by the French DOMs, which have OR status and receive much more. At the same time, they want to maintain their autonomy from France and the EU and are not ready to accept all of the European rules (e.g. fiscal regulation, free entry of labour and goods from the EU). They want to maintain their autonomous status and do not want to become a French DOM (where the citizens pay income tax to the French state, in addition to local taxes) just for the sake of receiving more EU aid.

Both the autonomists and the separatists would like to introduce the euro to replace the Pacific Franc as their currency, and France would agree to begin the required procedure with the European Commission. For the moment, however, the New Caledonian Congress has not found a majority to request the euro, and the French government therefore waits for a unanimous request from the three territories. If New Caledonia or French Polynesia became independent, it is very unlikely that they could negotiate with the EU to use the euro as the currency of their new state.

Notes

1 The next paragraphs are based on Toullelan (1991) and de Deckker (1997).
2 'Unfortunately, the letter soliciting the French protectorate was signed by the Queen on her own will' ('Malheureusement, la lettre par laquelle le protectorat français fut sollicité, a été signée de la Reine de son plein gré'). Letter of Lord Aberdeen, Secretary of the Foreign Office, to Consul Pritchard, 25 September 1843, cited in de Deckker (1997: 270), author's translation.
3 Around the same time, France and England had agreed to guarantee the independence of the kingdom of Hawai'i after a British officer had decided, on his own, to take possession of the kingdom for the British Crown.
4 A judicial inquiry is under way about the conditions surrounding the choice of this company by the local communication monopoly, *L'office des Postes et Telecommunications*, who hired former executives from Alcatel to design the specifications for the project.
5 Foreigners must obtain authorization from the local government to acquire real estate in French Polynesia. A European citizen from Luxembourg was recently denied the authorization to purchase a house on the island of Moorea. He appealed to the administrative court (*tribunal administratif*) to have this decision judged unlawful. He won this case on the basis of the discriminatory treatment of a European citizen, since no such authorization is required of French citizens. Consequently, all European citizens are now free to acquire property in French Polynesia.
6 For an account of the OCTs as a category between the ORs and the ACP, see Hannibal, Holst, *et al.*, this volume.
7 Comment at a conference in Copenhagen, 31 May–1 June 2010.
8 This statement, made by Alexandre Léontieff, was mentioned to me by Louis Savoie (personal communication), his minister of economic affairs at the time.
9 It should be noted that the Hao Atoll (Tuamotu Archipelago), a former French military base built for French atomic testing in Mururoa, has long been an emergency runway for the US space shuttle.
10 Devaluation would appear logical, since the average price level is about 50 per cent higher than in metropolitan France, according to a recent study. Entering the euro with a lower exchange rate would reduce this difference and stimulate exports. Entering the euro with an overvalued exchange rate, on the other end, would perpetuate the high cost handicap of tourism and the local industry.

References

L'Assemblée de la Polynésie française (2006) 'Resolution en faveur de l'euro', *Journal officiel de la Polynésie française*, 6 January 2006.

European Commission (2009) *Communication from the Commission to the European Parliament, The Council, The European Economic and Social Committee and the Committee of the Regions: Elements for a new partnership between the EU and the overseas countries and territories (OCTs)*, COM (2009) 623, Brussels, 6 November 2009.

Conseil économique et social de la Polynésie française (2008) 'Avis sur la rénovation de la relation d'association entre les PTOM et l'UE', Rapport N° 49/2008, 14 October 2008.

de Deckker, P. (1997) *Jacques-Antoine Moerenhout, ethnologue et consul*, Papeete: Au Vent des îles.

Haut commissariat de la république française en Polynésie française (2009) *Communiqué de presse*, 3 November 2009.

Herrera, J. and Merceron, S. (2010) 'Les approches de la pauvreté en Polynésie française: résultats et apports de l'enquête sur les conditions de vie en 2009', *Document de travail AFD*, N° 103, November 2010.

Institut d'émission d'outre-mer (IEOM) (2011) 'La balance des paiements en Polynésie française'.

Institut de statistique de la Polynésie française (2011) *La Polynésie en bref Edition 2010*. Online. Available at: www.ispf.pf (accessed 23 March 2012).

Les Nouvelles de Tahiti (2010), 25 and 26 March.

Poirine, B. (1995) *Les petites economies insulaires: Théories et strategies de développement*. Paris: L'Harmattan.

Poirine, B. (1999) 'A theory of aid as trade with special reference to small islands', *Economic Development and Cultural Change*, 47(4): 833–52.

Sarkozy N. (2011) New Year's speech to the overseas departments and territories, Guadeloupe Island, 9 January 2011.

Toullelan, P.Y. (1991) *Tahiti et ses archipels*, Paris: Karthala éditions.

12 Negotiating postcolonial identities in the shadow of the EU

New Caledonia

Peter Brown

New Caledonia is an archipelago in the southwest Pacific, 20,000 km from Europe. Its nearest neighbours are Vanuatu (500 km), Australia (1,500 km), and New Zealand (2,000 km). This Overseas Country and Territory (OCT) of the European Union (EU) is a special case within the French Republic, being neither a *Département* (overseas region) nor a *Territoire*: it is a *sui generis* entity, a *collectivité* known simply as 'New Caledonia'. In the past generation, it has experienced serious social unrest, tantamount to 'civil war', followed by a process of 'reconciliation' leading to a highly innovative plan for constitutional change. From being relatively isolated in its Pacific context, indeed the subject of concern to a number of its neighbours 30 years ago, it is now actively engaged in efforts at regional 'integration' and sometimes seen as a force of stability in the so-called 'Melanesian arc of instability'.

Yet the country's official social project of a 'common destiny' for its diverse peoples is taking place within the context of significant socio-economic disparities, continuing divisions over the question of 'independence', and a finely balanced demography, where no 'ethnic group' has a numerical majority. This means that census gathering in New Caledonia has been a highly charged political activity in recent years: President Chirac issued a directive for the 2004 census that the ethnic category be removed, and various local boycotts also affected the census. Nevertheless, it is safe to say that the population of about 250,000 is demographically diverse: 44 per cent Melanesian (Kanak), 34 per cent of European descent, 15 per cent Polynesian (mostly Wallisian), and 5 per cent Asian (Vietnamese, Indonesian).[1] Another important factor in New Caledonia's potential development is that the island is rich in natural resources, having one of the largest nickel deposits in the world;[2] the EU Green Paper estimated its GDP to be €22,734, which is close to the EU average.[3]

This chapter analyses New Caledonia's geo-strategic position, the composition of its population, and its natural riches as important resources for intersecting and interlocking sovereignty games. The section following this introduction has three objectives. First, it briefly presents the history of colonization and de-colonization in New Caledonia; second, it analyses this history as a postcolonial negotiation of identities; and third, it situates these negotiations in the wider Pacific and international contexts. The subsequent section analyses the roles the EU takes upon itself and those for which the Union is enlisted in the sovereignty games involving New Caledonia. A concluding section offers some perspectives for the future involvement of the EU.

The complementarity and divergence of interests between the EU, France, and New Caledonia are multi-faceted, engaging conceptions of regional integration, reconfigurations of colonial histories, questions of aid and development, military presence and the projection of soft power, and constitutional matters. Past histories, present negotiations, and posturing for the future are entangled in this three-cornered game, where the challenge can sometimes appear to be how to square the circle.

History, identity – New Caledonia in the Pacific context

After 3,000 years of indigenous settlement originating from southwest China, the island was 'discovered' by James Cook in 1774. France annexed New Caledonia in 1853 and established a penal colony (1864–97). Encroachments were made on indigenous lands, and ensuing Kanak uprisings were vigorously suppressed (notably in 1878 and 1917). The Native Law (*Indigénat*, 1887–1946) displaced sections of the indigenous population onto reserves, restricted movement, imposed a head tax, and introduced forced labour. In 1940, the island rallied to the cause of de Gaulle and served as a major American base in the Pacific War.

In 1946, New Caledonia officially ceased being a colony, instead becoming a French Overseas Territory. Kanak were, henceforth, French citizens, but they found themselves to be in a minority in their 'own' country.[4] Following decolonization in the English-speaking Pacific (1960s and 1970s), culminating in the independence in 1975 of the largest Melanesian island, Papua New Guinea, a pro-independence movement gained momentum in New Caledonia. This radicalized the politics in the Territory between pro- and anti-independence forces and further divided it along racial lines, particularly in the 1980s when conflict spilled over into quasi civil war, still generally known, euphemistically, as *les événements* (the events), 1984–8.

The Matignon Accords brokered between the French State, the pro-independence *Front de Libération National Kanak et Socialiste* (FLNKS), and the 'loyalist' *Rassemblement pour la Calédonie dans la République* (RPCR) restored peace in 1988.[5] The Accords provided for greater recognition of Kanak culture and social and economic development needs. They also foreshadowed a referendum on independence for 1998, but out of general concern that this would again polarize pro- and anti-independence supporters, this was deferred for up to a further 20 years with the signing of the Noumea Accord (1998).

The Matignon Accords had made no reference to the original colonization of the island and hence no reference to the legitimacy of sovereignty. The preamble to the Noumea Accord, on the other hand, acknowledged France's 'unilateral acts', and the 'enduring trauma' caused by the 'shock of colonization' to the indigenous population. It recognized the need to restore to the Kanak people its 'confiscated identity', which it said implied 'a recognition of its sovereignty, a pre-requisite to the establishment of a new sovereignty, to be shared in a common destiny' (Noumea Accord 1998: para. 3). The Noumea Accord thus made a decisive discursive break with the past in announcing a project of 'decolonization'. Conversely, the pro-independence parties accepted the present legitimacy of France as the sovereign authority over the island. That is, paradoxically, in the very same gesture, France acknowledged its former illegitimate presence, and the pro-independence movement accepted the legitimacy of the same colonizer's current presence – as a pre-condition to a process of 'decolonization'.

To this end, the Noumea Accord created a New Caledonian government and a Kanak Senate to advise on customary matters and provided for a gradual and 'irreversible' transfer of powers from Paris to Noumea – except five sovereign (*régalien*) powers (foreign policy, defence, law and order, justice, currency). These remaining powers would be decided in a referendum to be held during the period 2014–18. In the meantime, the Noumea Accord called upon the diverse populations of the island to overcome the racial antagonisms of the past and create a 'common destiny'. Yet this latter term can be seen as ambiguous in the context: it can be read both as referring to the need for the peoples of New Caledonia to develop a new mode of social interaction – a 'new social contract', as the official *Legifrance* site puts it[6] – and to the relation between these peoples and the French Republic.

Negotiations of identity and postcolonialism

In her study of the 'Caldoche' settlers of European extraction (*Expériences Coloniales* 1995), Isabelle Merle draws a picture of an ambiguous – not to say contradictory – relationship between them, many being descendants of convicts, and the French state. In political terms, however, and whatever the built-up resentments that New Caledonian settlers might historically feel towards the metropolitan French, they have a clear desire to remain French and accept subordination in exchange for fixed and limited responsibility. They certainly differ from the Kanak in that they have hitherto never questioned France's ultimate authority over New Caledonia in a traditional conception of sovereignty. Yet they are also increasingly negotiating between dependence and self-affirmation ('autonomy').

On the Kanak side, there is no illusion about what 'independence' might actually mean, at least not among a number of significant leaders; indeed, on occasion, they have suggested that they have already achieved 'sovereignty' through the transfer of powers underway. Whilst they are prepared to push a legalistic position on certain matters (e.g. voter eligibility as defined in the Noumea Accord), they are also conscious of living in a world of 'interdependencies', as Jean-Marie Tjibaou put it a generation ago (Tjibaou 1996[1976]: 179). The search for legitimacy, including recourse to outside bodies, both regional and global, can be viewed as a source of sovereignty gamesmanship. Political debate within New Caledonia itself, as well as negotiations between the New Caledonian parties and metropolitan France, is replete with discourse that can stress divergence or convergence, as the need arises.

In his article on the instruments of European law and Melanesian integration, Jacques Ziller, Professor of Law at the European Institute in Florence, refers to the notion of 'shared sovereignty' that he claims was first used in May 1950 in the Schuman Declaration. In what could be seen as a (surely) unintended example of European ethnocentrism, he presents the signatories of the Matignon–Oudinot Accords of 1988 and the Noumea Accord of 1998 as 'the direct descendants of Jean Monnet and Robert Schuman, saying in their way, "let us concentrate on what unites us, not on what divides us, let us create institutions to work together"' (Ziller 2009: 248, author's translation). This functionalist approach may well be, as Ziller says, the one regularly used by the European Court of Justice. It could also be claimed, however, that signatories to the Matignon and Noumea Accords were working off other genealogies, more specifically those of the Pacific, in reaching a consensus, even if this was in turn locked in through a more formalistic, organic, and institutional approach, codified in the French Constitution.

In this perspective, the Noumea Accord, in which the colonizing nation acknowledges the 'shadows of colonization', including the illegitimacy of its own original presence, and announces a process of 'decolonization', could be seen as at once confirming and challenging the notion of 'hybridity' as used, for example, by Homi Bhabha, for whom it is a sign of the postmodern and postcolonial condition, undoing essentialism and binary oppositions, and enabling, Bhabha claims, to 'entertain difference without an assumed or imposed hierarchy' (Bhabha 1994: 4). Similarly, Edward Saïd affirms that 'all cultures are involved in one another, none is single and pure, all are hybrid, heterogeneous, extraordinarily differentiated, and unmonolithic' (Saïd 1994: xxv). Accordingly, the Noumea Accord could be said to set up a paradigm of constant negotiation and reinterpretation about the project of 'decolonization', all the more in that the UN itself allows for a nuanced sense of the process and end result, including the (re-)integration of a territory previously to-be-decolonized.[7]

If authority is undermined or subverted, however, it is not necessarily only that of the colonizer. Whilst it is clear that this is not about 'incompatible systems' (Sharrad 2007: 107), one may wonder whether it is simply a question of 'hybridity'. Bhabha's argument turns on the idea that because colonial culture can never faithfully reproduce itself in its own image, each act of mimesis necessarily involves a slippage or gap whereby the colonial subject produces a hybridized version of the 'original'. But what is missing from this view is reflection on how what one could call 'reverse mimetic behaviour' operates. This is relevant in New Caledonia, where almost everyone, every group, is someone's/some other's 'Other'. Indeed, one may ask: what is the 'dominant discourse' here, when all parties talk of 'decolonization', as they did of 'emancipation' at the time of the signing of the Noumea Accord?[8] What are the implications if, now, as then, different meanings are attached to the same terms: 'independence', as presented by the Kanak leadership to convince its supporters that they were successful in their negotiations; greater 'autonomy' with more financial support from France, as presented by the anti-independence leadership to convince its sceptical supporters; proof of its role as 'arbiter', as presented by the French State to convince both the other groups and the international community of its 'neutrality'.[9]

The call made in the Noumea Accord for the creation of a 'common destiny' could also be seen in the light of Paul Gilroy's notion of 'community' that 'can be defined, on one level, through desire to transcend both the structures of the nation state and the constraints of ethnicity and national particularity' (Gilroy 1993: 19). This is coherent with when Philippe Gomes told the UN in New York in 2009 that the Noumea Accord:

> calls us to transcend the colonial. It requires us to write an original page of world history where the indigenous people and people from elsewhere conjoin their desires to build together, where Caledonians of all ethnic backgrounds transcend their parallel histories to write a common history.
>
> (Gomes 2009)

Yet this is the same Philippe Gomes whose government fell just before the EU–OCTA meeting in Noumea in March 2011. Gomes was therefore a kind of phantom chairman at the meeting due to internal division amongst the anti-independence ranks and collusion by parts of the pro-independence movement. Gomes was then disavowed by the French government, itself playing as 'both arbiter and authority', to quote an expression from the 1988 Matignon Accords. Gomes refused to accept the new dispensation in New Caledonia, however, invoking 'democracy' and 'freedom of expression' in seeking to force fresh elections over the question of the New Caledonian flag as an identity marker, whilst partisans on both sides of politics started lining up in the streets. The New Caledonian Congress may have passed a law in late 2010 making the official motto of the country, *Terre de Parole. Terre de Partage* ('Land of the Word, Land of Sharing').[10] The Noumea Accord is nonetheless still often referred to locally, *sotto voce*, as *Le Désaccord de Nouméa* ('the Noumea Discord').

Pacific regional context and wider international context

The Noumea Accord refers to the need for 'greater integration' of New Caledonia within its regional context, and the various parties in New Caledonia have been engaging strategically with international fora, including Pacific Regional bodies. Notably, there is the Pacific Islands Forum (PIF), originally established in 1971 as a political counterpart to the Secretariat of the Pacific Community. The latter is a multi-state development, aid, and cultural organization with 22 island members with headquarters based in Noumea and whose charter, at France's request, excludes the consideration of political issues. Without being formal members of the PIF, both France and New Caledonia are briefed about meetings. New Caledonia, which already has associate membership, unsuccessfully lodged a formal application for full membership at the annual PIF meeting held in Vanuatu in August 2010. It renewed this request, again unsuccessfully, at the meeting held in Auckland, New Zealand in September 2011, which was also attended by French Foreign Minister Alain Juppé and European Commission President José-Manuel Barroso.

It should be remembered that this body had, out of sympathy for the Kanak pro-independence movement, played a leading role in the 1980s in seeing the French territory inscribed on the Decolonization Committee's list and a General Assembly Resolution on the Question of New Caledonia. This helps indicate how much more complex and shifting things have become that it is now also, if not especially, the non-independence forces that seek confirmation of their legitimacy through membership of the Forum, coherent with the Noumea Accord's call for greater regional integration.[11] In 2009–10, New Caledonia's then President Philippe Gomes travelled to New York to make a presentation on behalf of New Caledonia – indeed, Gomes indicated his government's intention to make this an annual event – with a view to having the UN recognize that New Caledonia was fully engaged in a process of 'decolonization' on the way to its 'emancipation'[12] towards the long-term aim of having the country removed from the Decolonization Committee's list.

There is also the Melanesian Spearhead Group (MSG) composed of the independent countries of Papua New Guinea, the Solomon Islands, Fiji, Vanuatu – and the FLNKS of New Caledonia, support for whose pro-independence cause was the *raison d'être* for creating the MSG in 1986, as tensions in New Caledonia were escalating and the independence question came to a head. The FLNKS still sees itself as the sole legitimate representative of New Caledonia in this body, which it considers to be a check on French actions.

But there is now a twist in the postcolonial games. In the 1990s, Caldoche identity discourse followed Kanak identity claims in a kind of mimesis,[13] even implicitly reaching back to other traditions of resistance under colonial rule such as *la Négritude*, on which was based the expression *la Caldochitude*. Thirty years later, Philippe Gomes, the anti-independence 'Caldoche' president of the New Caledonian government, turned the tables by using the 'decolonization' category in an attempt to have New Caledonia, still a French sovereign territory, accepted as a member of the MSG. If this were successful, it would give the non-independence government legitimacy in the eyes of the very organization that was set up to support Kanak independence of New Caledonia-Kanaky. A step further along this path was taken in late February 2012, when the New Caledonian *Congrès*, led by President Roch Wamytan, former leader of the FLNKS, signed an agreement in Vanuatu (the pre-independence Franco-British condominium, the New Hebrides) with the MSG. According to this agreement, New Caledonia will henceforth provide financial support for the MSG which, in return, will promote French as one of its official working languages.

The European Union

Relations with the EU are – in their own peculiar way – another significant dimension of New Caledonia's broadening array of diplomatic overtures and the jockeying for position by various New Caledonian players with respect to international bodies.[14] In terms of relations with the EU, the Noumea Accord not only confirmed the logic of the special dispensations regarding non-reciprocal rights that

France had negotiated with the EU for its overseas territories; it also extended these rights by adding specific provisions for New Caledonia.

As with other OCTs, New Caledonia can export goods to the EU at preferential rates whilst maintaining protectionist policies for the local economy, for example, through tariff and customs duties (Faberon and Ziller 2007: 271). Currency arrangements are similar to those of the other French Pacific territories, in accordance with the special exemption that France negotiated in the Maastricht Treaty when it adopted the euro.[15] As French citizens, New Caledonians are entitled to EU passports and have the right to travel, work, and settle in EU countries. French nationals residing in French Pacific OCTs are also entitled to vote for special overseas seats in European elections (Faberon and Ziller 2007: 252–4).

Three special European Parliament seats represent the French overseas *collectivités*. Moreover, since the 2009 European elections, the EU has accommodated the French Pacific OCTs specifically by allocating a non-proportional distribution of seats to the EU Parliament. Previously, Réunion Island, the most populous French overseas possession, had received all three seats. Now, one seat goes to the Indian Ocean (*Réunion*), one to the Caribbean (French *Départements*), and one to the Pacific. In 2009, this seat was won by New Caledonian Kanak anti-independence politician Maurice Ponga, a former member of the New Caledonian government.

On a number of accounts, however, New Caledonian identity politics and the related sovereignty games with France make the EU appear rather peculiar. The remainder of this section provides four cogent examples: the role which the EU has been given in relation to New Caledonian citizenship and voting rights; the debate on the euro; the framing of the European Development Fund (EDF); and the French policy for (Europe in) the Pacific.

Citizenship and voting rights

The Noumea Accord was also sensitive to local calls to control immigration, employment, and voter eligibility. It proposed a New Caledonian 'citizenship', something distinct from the 'nationality' that could be introduced at the end of 20 years if the referendum so determined it.

Restricting voter eligibility was one of the key demands of the independence movement in negotiations leading to the signing of the Noumea Accord. Under the terms of this Accord and the subsequent Organic Law (1999), three electorates were established for the residents of New Caledonia: one for municipal, legislative, and presidential elections for which universal suffrage applies; one for provincial/Congress elections requiring ten years residence in New Caledonia by the end of 1998; one for the exit referendum to the Noumea Accord, for which 20 years residence is required by 31 December 2013.[16]

The pro-independence FLNKS movement was not very happy with the first category that, in conformity with European law, allows European (and therefore French) citizens with six months residence in New Caledonia to vote in municipal elections, because the new arrivals from Europe could have a possible impact on local politics. The second provision in particular gave rise to much public discussion and political negotiation between a sliding and restricted requirement of ten years residence. In the end, President Chirac ensured that the electorate would be restricted to those with ten years residence up to the Noumea Accord (i.e. who have been residents in New Caledonia since 1988), with a number of complex cases to be determined on a case-by-case basis.

European institutions subsequently endorsed these provisions, both within the EU Commission and the European Court of Human Rights to which anti-independence complaints had been referred. The Court argued that the Noumea Accord exceptions should prevail, thereby confirming the exclusion of EU voters from New Caledonia's provincial and congressional elections, including French nationals who are not 'citizens' of New Caledonia.[17]

Conversely, despite the great interest shown in the question of voter eligibility within New Caledonia, New Caledonian citizens have shown little enthusiasm for European Parliamentary elections. The local turnout for the 2004 EU Parliamentary elections was 25.42 per cent.[18] In 2009, it was even lower, with just 21.82 per cent of the electorate voting,[19] and this despite New Caledonia now having its own elected member of the European Parliament.[20] Moreover, the general lack of appreciation of any benefits to be gained from the EU has been widespread in the general community, both in the pro- and anti-independence camps. In this context, it is interesting to note that for the May 2005 French referendum on the proposed EU Constitution, one leading Kanak party (Palika) called for a boycott. This party saw the referendum as being about 'European' affairs, 'a product of history in a context of globalization and the rise of new powers'. With the electoral question in New Caledonia still unresolved, Palika wanted EU–New Caledonia relations to instead be pursued on the basis of 'cooperation', the objective being the further integration of New Caledonia within its own region (Palika 2005).[21]

In short, in the field of voting rights, the EU's legal system has been enrolled in 'domestic' New Caledonian games to little effect, whilst the invitations to New Caledonians to engage in European Parliamentary politics has had limited effect. In New Caledonia, energies have simply been directed elsewhere, principally to internal matters and to working out relations with France.

The euro

The euro is another European issue of concern to New Caledonia. In 2007, President Sarkozy indicated that he would support the introduction of the euro in the Pacific territories on the condition that all three French Pacific OCTs agreed to do so. Whilst both autonomy and independence forces in French Polynesia are in favour of having the euro (see Poirine, this volume), as Wallis and Futuna also would be, New Caledonia is divided. In short, anti-independence supporters would like to see the euro introduced as soon as possible, but the pro-independence forces are opposed for political, economic, and symbolic reasons.

Politically, this proposal would seem to anticipate the consideration of the currency as one of the five sovereign powers to be determined in the post-2014 exit referendum. This proposal would therefore not appear to fully respect the Noumea Accord schedule. Economically, it would lock in the artificially high cost of living in New Caledonia and pre-empt any possibility of devaluing of the currency (see Poirine, this volume).[22] Symbolically, in a country seeking new forms of identity markers,[23] including a replacement of the CFP Franc, as part of a process of decolonization,[24] adoption of a European currency might seem a step backwards. The political importance of these identity markers should not be underestimated: debate over the flag produced such emotion that it was the nominal reason for the fall of the New Caledonian government and the protracted political crisis of early 2011.

The European Development Fund

The OCTs receive approximately 1.25 per cent (286 million euros) of the total EDF 10th budget 2008–13 (22,682 billion euros). Within the Pacific, the 10th EDF amounts to 400 million euros, of which the OCTs receive nearly 59 million; 56.5 million of this goes to the French OCTs.

New Caledonia receives approximately 20 million euros from the 10th EDF, that is, about 3.5 million annually (20 per cent of which is supplied by French contributions to the EDF) (European Commission, Noumea Bureau (undated)). This compares with over 1 billion euros transferred annually to New Caledonia from France,[25] a figure that does not account for some of the spending on military personnel.[26] This means that French transfers exceed 300 times the EU contribution.

The primary interest for New Caledonia/France in terms of the EU's EDF scheme might therefore not appear to be economic. However, given that the Outermost Region (OR) budget is 100 times larger than that for the OCTs and that the EU structural funds are of an altogether different magnitude, one can see the interest in pursuing the matter for its potential economic benefits, as the Common Position adopted by OCTA in Noumea in 2011 shows.[27] This is of particular concern to New Caledonia, which not only has a university but also an important research centre, the *Institut de Recherche pour le Développement* (IRD). The IRD has taken an active role in promoting 'Europe' in New Caledonia, having hosted a 'Europe awareness' week in 2009 and 2010, the latter (November 2010) including a biodiversity conference and European cinema festival.

However, difficulties, including in perception, remain. Whilst the EU does promote its research, education and training programmes (respectively worth 53.2 billion euros and 7 billion euros for 2007–13) (European Commission, Noumea Bureau (undated)) as being accessible to the Pacific OCTs, bureaucratic obstacles are seen in New Caledonia at best as an impediment to access to such funds, and new arrangements would be welcomed. As the OCTA Joint Position Paper (2011: 10) recommended:

> The new partnership framework should be at least as beneficial as it is under the current OAD [Overseas Association Decision] and should further improve the quality and standard of living in the OCTs whilst striving to reduce the

difference between the OCTs and the ORs. Funding over the period after 2013 should match the ambition of the renewed OAD.

If New Caledonians of all persuasions, including politicians, are not always well informed or enthusiastic about the advantages of being associated with the EU, there is a converging interest amongst local decision-makers[28] to limit responsibility and maximize returns in relations with the EU. What is interesting, however, is the difference in the object of development to be supported by the EDF in relation to the varying perspectives and separate histories of the players concerned. The 2007 publication by the New Caledonian Government, *Ensemble depuis 1957* ('Together since 1957. New Caledonia and Europe: a half-century of cooperation') is a case in point.

In this publication, all of the parties use the discourse of 'development', albeit to a different end. The then president of the New Caledonian government, Marie-Noëlle Thémereau, assimilates the whole of New Caledonia to the needs of indigenous development for the purpose of securing EU funds, including to the wealthy 'European' parts of the south; the president of the pro-independence Kanak Northern Province, Paul Néaoutyine, sees EU aid as a strategy for redistributing wealth and infrastructure within New Caledonia, as consistent with the discourse of the Noumea Accord on '*le rééquilibrage*' (rebalancing). Jean-Pierre Piérard, the then head of the EU Delegation to the Pacific, also refers to development, but qualifies it with the word 'sustainable', an expression absent from the other two presentations. Whereas Marie-Noëlle Thémereau stresses the need for development in New Caledonia, making no reference to sustainability, Paul Néaoutyine speaks in terms of internal Kanak needs, that is, Kanak sustainability. For his part, the EU Delegation Head has a wider brief extending to all of the Pacific OCTs, not just New Caledonia; indeed, he sees the latter as the means to another end, namely, as a way of 'strengthening our partnership with the Pacific islands' (i.e. the sovereign states associated with the EU through the ACP status), particularly given the already 'developed' nature of the OCTs.[29]

Subsequently, President Gomes encouraged the moves by the Kanak anti-independence politician Maurice Ponga to lobby the EU Commission for support for the island that they both call a 'little slice of Europe . . . a member of the great European family' (Gomes 2011).[30] Indeed, it is this very 'fact' of being 'part of the European family . . . promoting the values, the convictions and the projects of Europe' that justifies the view that 'a differentiated and privileged treatment must be afforded to us . . . The support of the Commission is indispensable' (Gomes 2011).

European 'soft power' and French foreign policy in the Pacific

The EU's Green Paper (European Commission 2008) on future relations with the OCTs proposes a new approach linking the long-term viability of the islands and global European influence. According to the Paper, these relations should:

no longer rest on a classic approach of development cooperation but rather a reciprocal partnership with the aim of supporting the sustainable development of the OCTs, and promoting the values and norms of the EU in the rest of the world.

The Green Paper admittedly goes on to place emphasis on economic matters: the strengthening of competitiveness, adaptability, and cooperation with other partners. Whilst these priorities are not necessarily those of New Caledonia, the recognition given to the importance of taking account of the diversity of the OCTs and their different strengths, vulnerabilities, and specific characteristics certainly does correspond to New Caledonia's interest. Further, New Caledonia has no difficulty fulfilling the Green Paper's wish to improve the OCTs' responsibility to promote the regional operations of the EU and other partners and their 'potential . . . as strategically important outposts, spread all over the world, as proponents of EU's values' (European Commission 2008: 2).

The New Caledonian President Gomes echoed this language when he chaired the OCTA–EU meeting in Paris in March 2010, indeed even took it a step further when he declared that the OCTA nations not only have the potential to be the EU's 'outposts', but also its 'bridgeheads in our geographic zones . . . and to reaffirm our role in the promotion of European values' (Gomes 2010a). In March 2011, at a conference organized by the New Caledonian government on future constitutional arrangements and relations with France, which immediately followed the OCTA–EU meeting that President Gomes chaired in Noumea, the island's EU parliamentarian, Maurice Ponga, said that his country 'could spread European values to the neighbouring countries and enable the EU to exert its influence faced with the great powers in the region such as China and Japan' (Ponga 2011: 389–90).

However, this apparent convergence of foreign policy perspectives must also factor in the particular interests of France, the only European country to have islands in the Pacific (with the exception of the tiny British Pitcairn Island, with a population of 50). As the Noumea Accord specifies (section 3.3), foreign relations are one of the residual '*compétences régaliennes*' (sovereign powers) of France – subject to the provisions of section 3.2.1 concerning the 'shared relations' in the area of international and regional affairs, where France will include New Caledonia in discussions; for its part, the island is entitled to have its own representation on international bodies and conclude agreements with Pacific countries.

France clearly supports the attempts being made by the New Caledonian government within the region and in the wider international sphere: to have the island – French sovereign territory, after all – removed from the UN Decolonization Committee's list; to join the PIF and the MSG. Yet Paris has also been taking its own regional initiatives. It has organized three *France–Océanie* summits (Tahiti 2003, Paris 2006, Noumea 2009) to show its willingness to assume a leadership role with regard to its Pacific island neighbours and has been developing closer ties with the region's larger players, Australia and New Zealand. These moves reflect France's domestic and foreign policy agenda regarding the Pacific, where it has been an interested power for over two centuries, rather than being part of a concerted EU policy effort.

On a different note, France has also been developing closer defence relations with Australia and New Zealand, through the FRANZ agreement, concerning disaster relief provisions, and through the 'Southern Cross' military manoeuvres, which also involve other regional countries. In August 2011, it extended these activities by engaging in military exercises with the United States (US), on Tonga, an island which has experienced civil unrest in recent years. New Caledonia plays a key role in these developments, particularly since the 2008 decision to transfer the French military command for the Pacific to the archipelago from Polynesia, where it had previously been based.

Europe thus has a *de facto* military presence in the Southern Ocean, paid for by the French taxpayer, and with the strong support of the two major powers in the region and US encouragement.[31] Indeed, Australia and New Zealand, which barely 20 years ago were clamouring for France's departure from the Pacific, now look to the continued presence of France and to maintenance of the status quo in New Caledonia, seen as the only 'stable democracy' in the so-called Melanesian 'arc of instability'.[32] Arguably, the EU has a cheap form of soft power projection across the vast space of the Pacific, allowing it, moreover, to present itself as (merely) an aid donor, without any clear global foreign policy, let alone any defence force, through its development programs and promotion of human rights, democracy, and trade liberalization in its democratic OCTs. At the same time, Europe's gain underscores the continued legitimacy of France's presence in the Pacific.

The EU's OCT arrangements may thus be interpreted as Europe's attempt at extending its 'late sovereignty' mode of interaction beyond the European continent, thereby gaining greater impact than its 'soft power' usually allows in foreign affairs. This projection of soft power through its Pacific OCTs and its own engagement as donor and dialogue partner with Pacific island states and regional bodies comes at a relatively low cost (aid programs to non-OCT Pacific countries amount to just 114 million euros over the period 2008–13), yet the EU can still lay claim to being the second greatest aid donor in the Pacific over the past 20 years, after Australia; it could even be said to be the principal aid donor if the French support to its own OCTs was taken into account. But the very significance of the French support for New Caledonia (and its other Pacific OCTs) shows how it has a different conception of 'development aid' and hence of postcolonial politics to that of the EU, particularly as the latter attempts to reconfigure the region in its own image in the post-sovereignty game.

As stated above, the referendum on self-determination upon the expiration of the Noumea Accord in 2018 is to concern the transfer of the five remaining sovereign powers. Currency, one of these powers, has given rise to debate in New Caledonia and elsewhere in the French Pacific, including the FLNKS's political critique of this issue being raised ahead of any referendum to decide the matter. Remarkably, however, no such significant debate or critique has taken place, either in New Caledonia or in the region, concerning the new French defence arrangements in its Pacific territories and its developing partnerships with other sovereign Pacific powers eager for French support and its ongoing presence – and little reference is made to the subject in EU papers on the Pacific OCTs.[33] The latter lacuna is the more remarkable in that the French plans for the 'integration' of New Caledonia within the region do not coincide with the EU's understanding of the 'integration' of the OCTs (compare the discussion of how the French take the lead in the EU's regional cooperation in the Indian Ocean by Muller, this volume).[34]

Over time, it is likely that the EU will come to feature more prominently in such positioning and repositioning than it has in the past, particularly as it develops Economic Partnership Agreements with Pacific island nations and multi-lateral relations through organizations such as the PIF. Conversely, it is not clear that, under current conditions, New Caledonia would easily heed the EU's call for greater participation in regional economic activity through bodies such as the Pacific Islands Countries Trade Agreement or through the Pacific Agreement on Closer Economic Relations, conscious as New Caledonian players are of the difficulties regarding the liberalization of trade in a protectionist environment with a high per capita GDP and a strong, even overvalued currency, notwithstanding the euro's recent difficulties.

Conclusion

The very diversification of relations to the outside world can (as discussed in the Introduction to this volume) be seen as postcolonial, including the preparedness of France to relinquish or redistribute some of its 'sovereign' power in order, paradoxically, to secure its wider interests in the same region. Thus, as per Walker (2008),[35] it could be seen to be an example of the overlapping and functionally differentiated claim to authority under 'late sovereignty'.

The EU is assuming greater institutional importance for New Caledonia. Whilst the Noumea Accord (3.2.1) affirms that '[i]nternational relations are the competence of the State', it adds that France 'will take into account New Caledonia's own interests in the international negotiations led by France and will associate it in these discussions'. More specifically, it states that New Caledonia 'will be associated with the re-negotiation of the EU–OCT Decision of Association'.[36]

Whilst it remains fair to say that the front running on this issue continues to be done by French officials, New Caledonian activity has recently increased in this regard. Maurice Ponga, elected to the European Parliament in 2009, has taken a keen interest in the issue, and the recently deposed New Caledonian President Philippe Gomes saw the importance of capitalizing on this opportunity for lobbying in Brussels.[37] In March 2010, New Caledonia assumed the presidency of OCTA and took the lead[38] in drawing up a 'common position' on the future of OCTA–EU relations, at which meeting President Gomes asserted that 'more than being simple spectators of discussions that concern us directly in the first place, this is about being the actors of such discussions, of being the real driving force for proposals' (Gomes 2010a). Ponga's own Obama-inspired electoral slogan for the European elections had been '*Quand l'Europe veut, l'Europe peut*' ('When Europe wants, Europe can').

During its presidency of OCTA, the New Caledonian government made a full-time appointment of a civil servant, Chloé Calvignac, to work on the OCTA dossier at its impressive new headquarters in Paris, the *Maison de la Nouvelle-Calédonie*. Since the March 2011 OCTA–EU meeting in Noumea, Madame Calvignac, who had previously worked in Brussels for EURODOM – the association working for the interests of the French ORs vis-à-vis the EU – has become the Executive President of OCTA. New Caledonia is thus clearly trying to position itself to play a key role in OCT–EU negotiations. This is also related to the timetable for internal developments in New Caledonia and its negotiations with France on its constitutional future. The OCTA–EU meeting in Noumea in March 2011, which presented a Joint Position Paper on a new Treaty of Association (OCTA 2011), was immediately followed by a New Caledonia government-sponsored conference devoted to the constitutional situation of different entities, particularly in the Pacific, with a view to seeing the range of flexible options available.[39] That very week, however, the Philippe Gomes government collapsed, ushering in a period of instability. The French government went so far as to ban 'civic marches' – indeed, public gatherings of more than ten people – that had been planned in Noumea for Saturday 2 April, fearing confrontations between opposed groups, reminiscent of the troubled years of the 1980s.

The triangular relations between New Caledonia, France, and the EU are destined to assume greater prominence in the years ahead as the next EDF post-2013 overlaps with the crucial political and social decisions that will need to be made in the 2014–18 period concerning the island's future.

Notes

1 The Institut de la Statistique et des Etudes Economiques puts the 2009 population at 245,580 (www.isee.nc/chiffresc/chiffresc.html, accessed 2 April 2012).
2 As New Caledonian President Philippe Gomes told the United Nations (UN) in October 2010, New Caledonia will be the world's second largest producer of nickel by 2012 (Gomes 2010c).
3 European Commission (2008: 7). The figure was an estimate for 2006. According to President Gomes (2010c), New Caledonia's per capita GDP will reach 35,000 euros per annum by 2013.
4 See www.isee.nc/tec/popsociete/popugeneral.html; also Christnacht (1987: 25).
5 It must be said that there was abiding resistance to this in some quarters; the murder in May 1989 of independence leader Jean-Marie Tjibaou is one glaring example of this.
6 www.legifrance.gouv.fr/affichTexte.do?cidTexte=JORFTEXT000000555817&dateT exte
7 UN Resolution 1541, December 1960 (XV), Annex. http://daccess-dds-ny.un.org/doc/ RESOLUTION/GEN/NR0/153/15/IMG/NR015315.pdf?OpenElement
8 Brown (1998: 134). The leader of the FLNKS at the time of the Noumea Accord was Roch Wamytan, also the then President of the New Caledonian Congrès (Parliament). In a meeting that I attended on 21 March 2012 (Australian National University, Canberra), Mr Wamytan said on several occasions that New Caledonia remained on a path to 'émancipation'. He studiously avoided using the word 'independence'. He was accompanied on this visit to Australia by other members of the New Caledonian

Congrès, some of whom are opposed to 'independence'; one even said that everyone had to be very mindful of which words could not be uttered, what questions could not be asked.

 9 As President Mitterrand said in his Open Letter to All the French People in 1988 concerning the Matignon Accords, 'the guarantor of peace in New Caledonia can only be the French Republic; there is no other arbiter'.

10 New Caledonian President Gomes, himself a settler of the North African *pied noir* origin, told the UN in October 2010 that this was introduced 'in order to translate the importance of rootedness (*enracinement*) in the land, as a reminder that *la parole* is foundational in Kanak society and in the political accords as bearers of peace'.

11 President Gomes went as far as to present a collective 'Pacific-island' identity for New Caledonia when he stated to the UN Regional Seminar in Noumea in May 2010: 'We share ancestral lines with the Pacific islands, and our future is inconceivable without a deepening of our relations with them' (Gomes 2010b).

12 Terms that he used in his presentation to the UN in New York on 6 October 2009 (Gomes 2009).

13 See, for example, Collective (1993, 1996).

14 Philippe Gomes told the UN that international and regional relations were a 'major element' of New Caledonia's 'emancipation', being one of the areas of 'shared sovereignty' (Gomes 2010b).

15 'France will retain the right to issue currency in its overseas territories . . . and will be the only authority to determine parity of the CFP franc' (Special Protocol no 13, Maastricht Treaty). As of 1 January 1999, the CFP was linked to the euro at a specified rate. This was further confirmed by the Protocol on France in the Treaty of Amsterdam.

16 It could be argued that there is a fourth electorate, for European Parliamentary elections, for non-French EU nationals living in New Caledonia who are not otherwise eligible to vote in the other consultations above. But the Noumea Accord makes no explicit reference to this fourth category.

17 The European Court of Human Rights found that after 'a turbulent political and institutional history, the ten-year residence requirement . . . has been instrumental in alleviating the bloody conflict' (Py vs France, 11 January 2005, point 62; see also the same court's ruling of 9 June 2009). This received further support through a resolution passed by the UN General Assembly, which refers to 'the concerns expressed by representatives of the indigenous people regarding incessant migratory flows'. Resolution A/Res/64/102 (19/1/2010), paragraph 4.

18 www.interieur.gouv.fr/sections/a_votre_service/resultats-elections/eur2004/008/988/08988.html

19 www.interieur.gouv.fr/sections/a_votre_service/resultats-elections/ER2009/08/COM/988/988.html. It must be said that this does not vary greatly from the overall French *outre-mer* turnout of 22.96 per cent. www.interieur.gouv.fr/sections/a_votre_service/resultats-elections/ER2009/08/08.html

20 Law no 2007–224 passed by French Parliament, 21 February 2007.

21 More recently, one of Palika's militants, also a member of the New Caledonian government, told me that Europe is 'too far away' and therefore not a major preoccupation (personal communication, March 2011).

22 Paradoxically, it might seem as though the Kanak proposal to devalue New Caledonia's currency echoes the EU call for the OCTs to strengthen the competitiveness of their economies and their capacity to adapt and even promote their cooperation with other regional partners.

23 The Noumea Accord (1.5) referred to the importance of this 'in order to express Kanak identity and the future shared by all'.

24 Even the pro-euro President of New Caledonia, Philippe Gomes, passed laws in the New Caledonian Congress in late 2010 concerning the effigy on local bank notes, as he proudly told the UN in New York in October 2010 (Gomes 2010c).

25 The statistical bureau of New Caledonia (ISEE) puts the provisional 2009 figure at 136,990 million CFP, i.e. 1.15 billion euros. www.isee.nc/chiffresc/chiffresc.html#fin ances%20publiques (accessed 2 April 2012).

26 See Fisher (2011). President Gomes told a UN Regional Seminar in May 2010 that French spending amounted to 6,500 euros per capita per annum, in terms of provision for local budgets only, together with tax relief for 'economic projects', thereby also seemingly excluding certain French transfers (Gomes 2010b).

27 'The real accessibility of the OCTs [to these funds] is, however, limited, by dint of their complexity and their rules that do not take sufficiently into account the special features of the OCTs' (Celulle de coopération régionale et des relations extérieures 2010: 7). Maurice Ponga (2011: 390) has evoked the possibility of New Caledonia becoming a OR.

28 Interestingly, the same Kanak pro-independence militant referred to above, who claimed that Europe was 'too far away', also added, parenthetically, that it was nonetheless 'important, of course'.

29 Subsequent to the EU Green Paper (European Commission 2008) and the Copenhagen Summit (2009), the New Caledonian government has tried to make a greater play of its commitment to ecological considerations and sustainable development, stating that some 40 per cent of Europe's flora and fauna species are endemic to the island. But this approach must fit together with New Caledonia's serious commitment (by both independence and anti-independence leaders) to major mining developments that are likely to have a massive impact on the island's eco-systems.

30 For his part, EU Deputy Maurice Ponga told the conference on New Caledonia's future, held in Noumea in March 2011, immediately after the EU–OCTA meeting, that the EU has a 'privileged relationship' with New Caledonia due to the island being 'a member of the European family' (Ponga 2011).

31 The French navy helps with fisheries surveillance, which is of assistance to Australia and New Zealand, and arguably also to the EU via small islands, as well as with emergency intervention and humanitarian aid, as in East Timor in 1999, Papa New Guinea drought and famine relief in 1997–8, and as it proposed to do in 2003 with regard to the civil war in the Solomon Islands.

32 The Annual Report of the Delegation of the European Union for the Pacific (2010) states 'poverty reduction' as the main objective of the EU. Yet it also refers to 'human rights, democracy and the rule of law' as 'the core values of the EU'. The two are linked in the document in so far as overseas development policy will only be achieved if a democratic state is in place. There is no reference to this issue in the OCT document, undoubtedly on the assumption that all of the Pacific OCTs are already parliamentary democracies.

33 In a personal communication on 6 September 2011, before attending the 40th anniversary Pacific Islands Forum meeting in Auckland, EU Commission President Barroso told me that Europe had no intention or capacity to put 'soldiers on the ground in the Pacific'. However, the lecture he gave that day at the Australian National University in Canberra, entitled, 'Shared futures: Europe and Australia in the 21st century', made the point that 'the rise of this region does not mean the demise of Europe. The European Union is and will remain a global player' (Barroso 2011a). Moreover, the Council of the European Union's position paper on 'East Asia Policy Guidelines' (2007: 4) states: 'Given the great importance of transatlantic relations, the EU has a strong interest in partnership and cooperation with the US on the Foreign and Security policy challenges arising from East Asia.' And in late 2011, the US announced a major shift in its military policy towards a greater Pacific focus.

34 Manuel Barroso, in his plenary address to the Pacific Islands Forum on 7 September 2011, referred to the need for greater regional and institutional cooperation, having 'mandated the European Commissioner for Development to formulate a proposal for a bold renewal of the European Union development partnership with the Pacific: we

need to do more and to do it better . . . we cannot afford fragmentation in our efforts of development assistance' (Barroso 2011b).
35 Referred to in Gad and Adler-Nissen's Introduction, in this volume.
36 See also Articles 30 and 89 of the 1999 Organic Law for New Caledonia, and Faberon and Ziller (2007: 271).
37 As Philippe Gomes told the OCTA partners: 'We must . . . intensify our dialogue with the European institutions . . . in particular the European Parliament with which, as the PM of Greenland has stressed, and as Maurice Ponga has encouraged us to do, we must share our vision and our perspectives that we must use to legitimize our activities' (Gomes 2010a).
38 This is confirmed in interviews with officials from other OCTA members, Brussels, 24 March 2010.
39 Philippe Gomes had referred to such deliberations in his presentation to the UN in New York (Gomes 2010c). Further, the Pacific Ocean already shows that there are a number of flexible arrangements possible under the umbrella of decolonization and independence that comply with UN resolutions, such as the free Association model (Cook Islands–New Zealand) and the compact model (Palau–USA), the latter, unlike the former, even allowing for a separate UN seat.

References

Barroso, J.M. (2011a) 'Shared futures: Europe and Australia in the 21st century', lecture delivered at the Australian National University, Canberra, 6 September.
Barroso, J.M. (2011b) 'The EU and the Pacific: a renewed partnership for a new era', plenary speech, The Pacific Islands Forum, 7 September
Bhabha, H. (1994) *The Location of Culture*, London and New York: Routledge.
Brown, P. (1998) 'Strangers in paradise, stranger than paradise', *International Journal of Francophone Studies*, 1(3): 125–39.
Cellule de coopération régionale et des relations extérieures, New Caledonian Government (2010) 'Mémo sur les relations UE–PTOM', Noumea, 22 October.
Christnacht, A. (1987) *La Nouvelle-Calédonie*, Paris: La Documentation française, No. 4839.
Collective (1993) *Etre Caldoche Aujourd'hui*, Noumea: Ile de Lumière.
Collective (1996) *Notre Pays Demain*, Noumea: Ile de Lumière.
Council of the European Union (2007) *East Asia Policy Guidelines*, 16468/07.
Delegation of the European Union for the Pacific (2010) *Annual Report 2009*, Fiji.
European Commission (2008) *Green Paper. Future relations between the EU and the Overseas Countries and Territories* COM (2008) 383. Brussels, 25 June 2008.
European Commission, Noumea Bureau (undated) *Programmes européens accessibles aux Pays et Territoires d'Outremer du Pacifique*.
Faberon, J.-Y. and Ziller, J. (2007) *Droit des collectivités d'Outre-mer*, Paris: Librairie Générale de Droit et de Jurisprudence.
Fisher, D. (2011) 'France in the South Pacific: power and politics', MPhil thesis, Australian National University, Canberra.
Gilroy, P. (1993) *The Black Atlantic: Modernity and the Double Consciousness*, Cambridge MA: Harvard University Press.
Gomes, P. (2009) Speech to United Nations, New York, 6 October.
Gomes, P. (2010a) Speech to OCTA countries, Paris, 26 March.
Gomes, P. (2010b) Presentation to Regional Seminar of the United Nations, Noumea, 18–20 May. Online. Available at: www.un.org/en/decolonization/regsem2010.shtml (accessed 28 March 2012).

Gomes, P. (2010c) Speech to United Nations, New York, 6 October. Online. Available at: www.franceonu.org/spip.php?article4190 (accessed 28 March 2012).

Gomes, P. (2011) Radio interview, Radio Nouvelle-Calédonie, 1 February.

Matignon Accords (1988) Online. Available at: www.nouvellecaledonie.gouv.fr/site/content/search?SearchText=matignon&x=6&y=6 (accessed 28 March 2012).

Merle, I. (1995) *Expériences coloniales. La Nouvelle-Calédonie (1853–1920)*, Paris: Belin.

New Caledonian Government (2007) Ensemble depuis 1957. La Nouvelle-Calédonie et L'Europe: Un Demi-Siècle de Coopération.

Noumea Accord (1998) Online. Available at: www.legifrance.gouv.fr/affichTexte.do?cidTexte=JORFTEXT000000555817&dateTexte (accessed 28 March 2012).

OCTA (2011) *Joint Position Paper*. Online. Available at: www.octassociation.org/visual%20identity%20and%20publications/reports/joint%20position%20280211.pdf (accessed 28 March 2012).

Palika (2005) Press Release. Online. Available at: http://fr.groups.yahoo.com/group/kanaky/message/9921 (accessed 25 April 2005).

Ponga, M. (2011) 'L'Union européenne et l'Océanie', in J.-Y. Faberon, V. Fayaud and J.-M. Regnault (eds) *Destins et collectivités politiques d'Océanie*, Aix-Marseille: Presses Universitaires d'Aix-Marseille.

Saïd, E. (1994) *Culture and Imperialism*, London: Vintage.

Sharrad, P. (2007) 'Strategic hybridity: some Pacific takes on postcolonial theory', in J. Kuorti and J. Nyman (eds) *Reconstructing Hybridity: Post-Colonial Studies in Transition*, Amsterdam: Rodopi.

Tjibaou, J.-M. (1996[1976]) *La Présence Kanak*, A. Bensa and E. Wittersheim (eds) Paris: Odile Jacob.

Walker, N. (2008) 'The variety of sovereignty', in R. Adler-Nissen and T. Gammeltoft-Hansen (eds) *Sovereignty Games: Instrumentalizing State Sovereignty in Europe and Beyond*, New York: Palgrave Macmillan.

Ziller, J. (2009) 'Les ressources du droit de l'Union européenne pour l'intégration mélanésienne', in P. de Deckker and J.-Y. Faberon (eds) *La Nouvelle-Calédonie pour l'intégration mélanésienne. La Nouvelle Revue du Pacifique*, 4(1) Paris: L'Harmattan.

13 Between Europe and Africa
Mayotte

Karis Muller

Mayotte is a French group of islands lying off the Mozambique coast in the Indian Ocean. The two inhabited islands measure $374\,km^2$. The mainly Bantu population of roughly 200,000 has increased five-fold in 35 years; 56 per cent are under the age of 20. Population density has reached over 510 people per km^2. Geographically, Mayotte belongs to a four-island group, the Comoros; politically, it is an anomaly in as much as its population voted several times to remain French or to become more so, unlike the other islands, which chose independence in 1974. In 2011, Paris acceded to the Mahorans' long-standing desire to become an Overseas Region and Department (DROM). France's four other DROMs, one of which, Réunion, is also in the Indian Ocean, joined the European Community (EC) in 1957 and today belong to the EU's Outermost Regions (OR) (see Hannibal, Holst, *et al.*, this volume). New DROM Mayotte is expected to transfer from the Overseas Country or Territory (OCT) to the OR category in 2014 (Rakotondrahaso 2009). The Mahorans reject independence, as the departure of France would invite annexation by the nearest island, Anjouan (Nzwani), or the Comoros as a whole, which they regard as a disastrous colonial occupation worse than the protective, wealthy French administration. For this reason, they have long sought the fullest degree of integration possible into France (Martin 2010; Caminade 2003/10).

Mayotte's progressive integration into France and the EU is in conflict with its Afro-Islamic customs. Younger, urbanized Mahorans generally see themselves as modern French citizens rather than as akin to the conservative, Muslim Comorians. In contrast, most of the older Mahorans retain their animist-Muslim beliefs and customs and resist the social changes that being a DROM and 'European' necessitates. The substitution since 2003 of the French civil code for local customary law exacerbates existing generational and cultural tensions, encouraging the emigration of educated youth. Will social changes further drive a wedge between island populations that circulated freely until the mid-1990s? Will the EU Charter of Rights and Council of Europe (CoE) Conventions, which enforce European values, apply from 2014? Or do they do so already?

Some French analysts suggest negative consequences should Mayotte be transformed into a DROM and consequently an OR of the EU (Salesse 1995; Gaymard 1987). The disparity between this artificial enclave, the second in the Indian Ocean to add to Réunion, would, they warned, further increase once the island becomes eligible for European Structural Funds, encouraging more economic refugees from the Comoros, who would compete for resources on an already densely populated island. The situation would be particularly volatile, since Mayotte has poor and unstable states to its east and west. The seizure of arriving boats and the deportation of their passengers, as well as of many of those settled in the slums around the capital Mamudzu, does not stem the rate of arrivals, instead providing a regular spectacle for the locals. These deduce, first, that independence has been a catastrophe for their neighbours, and second, that overcrowding in schools and hospitals is due more to the presence of foreigners than to either French neglect or their own high birth rate.

Mayotte is possibly the most complex of all the case studies chosen for this volume. There are five main players on the field: France, Mayotte, the Comoros, the EU, and the United Nations (UN), and the African Union and Arab League are also occasional players. Omitting multiple combinations and the Indian Ocean players that make an occasional appearance, we have ten possible team combinations, although a few are inoperative (e.g. Mayotte lacks the formal statehood to make it a 'real' player in the UN). The following four sections deal, first, with games pitting the geopolitical priorities of France (and, implicitly, the EU) against those of Moroni (the capital of the Comoros) and its allies, especially the UN; second, the processes that depoliticize the 'otherness' of Mayotte, harnessing euro-identity formation to this end; third, the ways in which the marine traffic in (from France's point of view) 'illegal' Africans, mainly from the nearest Comoros island, Anjouan, serves Comorian and French interests in different ways; finally, widening the focus to the Indian Ocean, how far does France's request to transfer Mayotte from OCT to OR status implicate the EU in sovereignty games there? How does France attempt to neutralize opposition in the Indian Ocean? The conclusion briefly ties the different threads together, suggesting that the French move to implicate the EU, which Mayotte regards as its best guarantee against Moroni's (very theoretical) temptation to 'invade', may instead exacerbate tensions.

Competing sovereignty claims

As the Comoros contest the political status of Mayotte (in the local dialect, Maore), the EU risks being drawn into France's late-imperial game. France has EU support, as both prepare the island for its change from OCT to OR in 2014, and neither responds to appeals from Moroni. France's game fields as team players a supportive government, a mostly acquiescent national parliament, and a divided public. The EU member states are indifferent or prefer not to play. The EU as goalkeeper is cautious because its member states cannot agree on the rules, although the Commission implicitly regards France's geopolitical priorities as its own. The other team, the Comoros, the UN, the Arab League, and the African Union, discuss their entirely opposed set of rules vociferously; their enthusiasm is volatile and not inclined to action. Finally, the *Francophonie* and Franco-African Summits sit and watch the game. The playing field is in fact a mine field.

French governments, politicians, and diplomats consider the right to self-determination absolute provided a consultation has taken place and the population desires it (Martin 2010). Article 53 of the French Constitution states that no part of the Republic may secede unless its population consents. Hence, Paris cannot hand over Mayotte to another state against the wishes of its inhabitants. Scholars have highlighted the UN commitment to the self-determination principle (Weller 2009; Pomerance 1982). Why then does the UN reject French Mayotte? And why did European member states repeatedly do likewise or abstain when the issue was put to the vote? The reason is *uti possidetis juris*, 'as you possess by law'; that is, former colonies must respect colonial boundaries, thereby removing the right of minorities to secede. In Mayotte's case, the point of international contention was and is whether self-determination applied globally in 1974 to all four islands of the then Overseas Territory Comoros, or singly to each island. A first, global referendum revealed that Mayotte alone rejected independence; a second referendum was counted separately. French loyalists argue that since most Mahorans dreaded likely domination by one or all of the remaining islands in the archipelago, it was right to 'save' their island (Martin 2010; Mouhoutar 2011). Others consider that the results of Mayotte's self-determination consultations are themselves predetermined, since there is no tradition for open debate, and agree with the UN that *uti possidetis* applies (Caminade 2003/10: 49–72; Salesse 1995; Saïd 2010).

In fact, the UN has evolved over the years. The UN founding Charter and other early UN texts neither condemned colonialism nor mentioned the sanctity of colonial borders. The paramount concern then was that subject peoples should have the right to self-determination. Empires or scattered states were legitimate as long as local populations approved. Decolonization could mean autonomy within a greater whole, including the existing ruling power (Pomerance 1982; Miles 2005; Hannibal, Holst, *et al.*, this volume). Today, French officials still define decolonization not as the process by which a colony becomes independent but as a democratic majority choice. That is why the Mahorans claim that they are 'French to be free'. After all, with the brief exception of New Caledonia, no French dependency has ever appeared on the UN list of non-self-governing territories requiring remedial action.

The sovereignty dispute over Mayotte erupted in the mid-1970s after the second vote on independence. By then, the communist and non-aligned blocs held the majority in the UN, and *uti possidetis* was the new norm (UN Resolution 1514 (XV) 1960). Hence, a referendum (or plebiscite, see below) in Mayotte alone (and not in all of the Comoros) was illegal, so irrelevant, insist Comorians, international organizations and French pro-Comoros sympathizers (Caminade 2003/10; Saïd 2010; Theilleux 2011). Besides, which 'people' has the right to vote for self-determination – the Mahorans, never a people, or all Comorians, who share a language, a culture, and a religion (Salim 2011)? The French term *le peuple* denotes the state or collective sovereign, as opposed to *la population*, a demographic term. This distinction is carefully preserved in the Constitution (Article 3 Title 1 and Articles 53, 72–3). Some French and Comorian experts therefore argue that the principle of the supremacy of the will of the people is infringed when an overseas population alone votes. So-called referendums in Mayotte are simply non-binding plebiscites; all of France should have been consulted, as in Algeria in 1961. Departmentalization and OR status are also illegal (Thréard 2009).

France's Constitutional Court has warned of the governments' confusing, legally doubtful use of consultations overseas (Consitutional Council 2000). The sovereignty issue has been instrumentalized as all select the evidence and the arguments they require to convince world opinion of the legality of their position. For the Mahorans, sovereignty cannot signify independence, but instead only the freedom to choose one master or the other, and few choose Moroni (Kashkazi 2006). Over the years, writers on both sides have suggested shared sovereignty or a federal solution as a way out of the impasse. Recently, a Réunion academic and former Comoros President Sambi have independently suggested similar projects (Kashkazi 2006; Oraison 2009). Such projects would demand considerable creativity in practice; neither putative scenario considers, for example, how the island could possibly be part of both the Comoros and the EU.

Who are the Mahorans?

Identity games are many and contradictory in Mayotte, owing both to a historically weak local identity typical of all the Comoros islands and to the political choices the Mahorans have made (Salesse 1995; Walker 2007). French state representatives urge assimilation to French norms but encourage local colour, or 'folklore'. However, reconciling the blend of Islam and African animism with both French norms and those of the Council of Europe and the EU is problematic. Until recently, most chose the personal, Muslim legal code as opposed to the secular civil code, a choice the French Constitution explicitly allows (article 75), as a French Parliamentary Report reminded the government (Quentin *et al.* 2009). The French State is nonetheless bringing the practices of the often reluctant islanders into line with laws prevailing in the metropole (Salesse 1995; Michalon 2009). A French edict has declared, for example, that family conflicts may henceforth be settled only by the civil courts, not by Muslim judges (Quentin 2010a). Family, property, and taxation laws are to be made consistent with EU and CoE norms.

Nowhere in the *Outre-mer* is French spoken less than in Mayotte. In the early 1990s, the figure was around 20 per cent (Salesse 1995). Language policies, however, contribute to the Europeanization of Mayotte. Sovereignty games in this area fall into two broad categories, depending upon whether the weak and somewhat artificial local identity asserts itself against the metropole/Europe or the Comoros. The first, more prevalent game is played by educated, francophone Mahorans. These situate the defence of their mother tongue within the long-standing struggle between French and the (mainland) regional languages. Article 75-1 in the Constitution states that 'regional languages are part of France's cultural heritage'. In 2000, the French Parliament legalized the protection of France's languages overseas, as regional languages subaltern to French (Legifrance 2000, Title IV). Since 2009, Mamudzu's General Council has a Direction of Regional

Languages of Mayotte. Its members refer to the European Charter of Regional and Minority Languages, 1992, in defence of Shimaore (the name given to the local version of the Swahili-derived language used throughout the Comoros archipelago) despite the obstacles to its implementation in the metropole (Jean-jean 2002). The moral authority of the CoE Charter will raise the status of and preserve Shimaore (dominant) and Shibushi (declining, minority status), which are being creolized and may disappear. Metro officials see the rules of the game otherwise, imposing French aggressively, and valuing local tongues less than is the case in other dependencies, owing probably to their very prevalence. President Sarkozy's declaration in Mamudzu in January 2010, that all non-francophone children be immersed in a French-speaking school environment from age three in the classroom (Sarkozy 2010), impressed neither participants at a workshop that May (see below) nor many francophone, educated Mahorans. When a metro education official implied that Shimaore was a quaint, exotic relic, suggesting that speakers of 'bad French' compromised their job prospects, linguists and local politicians alike argued the merits of early education in the vernacular. Locals protested that all of France's 'regional' languages were of equal status (Perrot 2010; Aly 2011). This debate is reminiscent of metro regionalist movements of the 1970s and 1980s; locals have internalized French micro-nationalism. Or, they are behaving tactically, knowing that no other argument will be acceptable. Mayotte remains the overseas area which most discourages the use of the mother tongue in early education, precisely because French is neither dominant, nor always 'properly' spoken.

Linguists, officials, and the elite, both in Mayotte and in the Comoros, play the second language game. This has each team playing by rules that mirror the other's. Both start from the ideological position that language and political borders are 'naturally' identical. Ergo, Mayotte, which is part of France, has its own language reflecting its unique choices. Pan-Comorians, in contrast, insist that all four islands speak the same language with minor variations, proving that the Comoros archipelago is 'really' a single political entity. In sum, the Mahoran language game assumes an imagined scattered French Republic spread over several oceans, while the second game assumes its playing field to be the south-west Indian Ocean, a geographical reality impervious to externally imposed political abstractions.

Accounts of a May 2010 conference on language policy and practice held in Mamudzu show the two rival games in action. A conservative account in *Mayotte Hebdo* cites mainly metro officials and a French linguist, Foued Laroussi, who define local languages as distinct markers of Mayotte's specificity as regional languages of France, French being the official language (Laroussi 2009). In contrast, a Comorian account of the same conference highlights fellow national and linguist Mohamed Ahmed-Chamanga. He warns that, in all four islands, French is driving out the national language, Shikomori, and acknowledges that each island has its variant and has invented a standard written form that is being applied in schools. Interestingly, former Mayotte Senator Ramadani, defending the languages and identity of his island in the Senate, asked for a standardized writing system for Shimaore and Shibushi, which he wanted introduced as optional classes in schools. If that were to happen, Shikomori would have two, similar written systems, one used in the independent Republic and based on the variant used in Grand Comoros, and the other used in Mayotte, based on the near identical variants used in near neighbours Anjouan and Mayotte (MOM 2010b; Anon 2011a). Most linguists agree with Chamanga that there is but one common tongue, Shikomori, with its local variants, avoiding political conclusions. Deciding at what point a dialect becomes a language is obviously a pointless exercise; educational and mobility factors determine the range of inter-comprehension. Such battles around language only draw shifting civilizational boundaries around islands. In Mayotte, the game is to deny the evidence of linguistic kinship. In the Comoros, the game is to create some language uniformity in a failed island state (Walker 2007: 2–3). As the Mahorans struggle to identify as Muslim-French-European Africans, rather than simply richer Comorians, the language game is central to the political and ideological battle.

Identity games also function in Mayotte's secondary school history syllabus, where metro teachers introduce children to salient events of French history, neglecting local pre-occupation history. Manufacturing consent for the existing power relations and devaluing alternative histories is obviously no more unique to France than is imposing a national language (Fairclough 1989). In May 2010, secondary level children acquired an extra identity layer in view of the expected statutory change to OR: European rituals are now an annual event. The lavish public programme to celebrate Europe Day is organized by the Prefecture and the Europe cell of the General Council and involves schools and the military, blue and yellow balloons, posters of Schuman in the streets, the Ode to Europe in Shimaore, and sundry quizzes and prizes (Orcier 2010; Perrot 2010).

Is top-down indoctrination effective? Some aspire to be non-Comorian, that is, metro French albeit with 'regional' particularities, adopting mainly European lifestyles and internalizing secular values (Hassani 2009). France's game of turning 200,000 Muslim Africans into Franco-European citizens meets little overt resistance, because of greatest importance for the Mahorans is being First, not Third, World. School curricula reinforce this by detaching Mayotte from its natural neighbourhood as for example they introduce pupils to the Free French rhetoric of the Second World War rather than the fact that the Comoros were actually part of Vichy (Mgueni 2011a, 2011b). Will Mayotte emerge as a successful exemplar of a post-national European identity based on a non-spatial logic? Should and will this African island invent itself as home to a people firstly European and only secondly African? European identity may be an abstract, non-territorial phenomenon, a top-down normative project (Balibar 2004; Habermas 1992; Nicolaïdis and Howse 2008), but how credible is it to invent a piece of Europe off the Mozambique coast? Morocco was, after all, deemed 'non-European' when it applied for EU membership.

As Afro-Muslim customs and local languages are progressively devalued, resistance is growing. Shortly before the official protest of Senator Ramadani, local writer and pro-French loyalist Salim Mouhoutar argued strongly in the columns of the conservative *Mayotte Hebdo* that France was breaking its 1841 promise to protect local identity, culture, beliefs, and languages. Departmentalization risked destroying his society. Why was local and regional history not taught? Shimaore and Shibushi were invaluable at the regional level. The media must be obliged to show that they were disseminating local languages adequately (Mouhoutar 2011).

Immigration also raises especially difficult questions concerning political and identity frontiers. How does and how will the intrusion of a privileged enclave affect the regional stability and population movements within Mayotte and beyond?

Immigration as a security issue

Illegal immigration from Africa to Europe has become a security issue (Dover 2008; Youngs 2008). The EU encourages the states at its southern periphery to inhibit migration control from Africa by making aid conditional on border security. France is at the forefront of such action (Othily and Buffet 2006). Although Article 1 of the Constitution states that the Republic is indivisible, parts of the Republic operate de facto on federal, perhaps colonial, principles, since even those French–European citizens born in the overseas departments do not have exactly the same rights as those born in the metropole. This is especially so on the European plane, as both France's OCTs and ORs lie outside the Schengen zone. To settle within the metropole, which alone is in Schengen, a Mahoran must have long-standing family connections there. This situation does not contravene Article Eight of the European Convention of Human Rights, as living in Schengen is legally indistinct from living in non-Schengen. Mahoran students, for example, must prove their status if asked. They are shocked to discover that they are checked upon arrival and often thereafter, and if lacking papers are liable to deportation (MOM 2010a). Since perhaps half of Mahorans lack identity papers, instructions now allow Mahorans in the metropole time to acquire them (AFP 2008). These difficulties encourage some to conclude that they will never be accepted as other than Africans (Bamana 2010).

While efforts are being made to counter the conditional acceptance of Mahorans in Marseille, Lyon, or Paris, Mayotte itself is a second Lampedusa, overwhelmed by African illegal immigration from the Comoros, East and even Central Africa (Torre 2008). Comorans are not illegal in the view of the UN and Moroni. All use Anjouan traffickers, and some intend later to enter the EU with false 'French' papers. With one Comoran so far having been identified as a terrorist, French Member of Parliament (MP) Quentin declared Mayotte an entry point of Muslim extremism into geographical Europe (Quentin 2006). It is true that Moroni fails to check the identity of Africans taking *kwassa-kwassa* (local fishing boats) from Anjouan, presumably because most are in their view only in transit on Comorian soil.

Cooperation with Moroni is limited and sporadic controls in Mayotte are ubiquitous, due to the difficulty (to *wazungu*, i.e. whites) of distinguishing Mahorans from other ethnic Africans. The unintended consequence is that any African may be deported unless they have French papers on hand at all times. The *wazungu* are never importuned, so the Mahorans feel unsafe, even strangers in their own island. Yet the Constitution's Article 66 states that 'No-one shall be arbitrarily detained' (ML 2010; Majarou 2010). The full integration of Mayotte into France and the EU is premature until a French-style digitized civil register of the Mahorans is complete, with all of the necessary family names and affiliations. This problem dates from the 1995 visa introduction and has nothing to do with the EU.

One two-pronged game, as mentioned, is the difficult reconciliation of a non-racial greater France with the EU's restrictive regulations in and beyond the Schengen area. Regularization of migration traffic in the face of absent papers and the prevalence of Islamic naming practices require increased funds and personnel as a standard French family nomenclature and identity card system are created (Quentin 2010a). Immigration to and from Mayotte is complicated further by a second sovereignty game, the 1995 visa system applied to visitors to Mayotte from the neighbouring islands, denounced by all except the French and the EU. In response to recent suggestions by a few left-wing metro MPs that the visa system should be abolished, at least until all had a modern, digitized identity card, the General Council, concerned that their little enclave would be further obliged to share its scant resources with strangers, parried the suggestion with implausible republican arguments: visa abolition would negate their (unending?) right to self-determination and undermine the integrity of the Republic. The Comoros was to blame for the flight of their nationals, not the visa (Bamana 2010).

In 2010, the French consul in Anjouan, Eric Weiss, introduced cheap, simplified three-month visas to Mayotte and tried to arrange a half-price ferry fare, greatly undercutting the at least 100 euro cost of a seat on a *kwassa-kwassa*. He also accepted doubtful family addresses, knowing the police would later check on over-stayers (Perrot and Macone 2010). One year later, however, Weiss increased the visa fee from 9 to 60 euros once more, saying that that was the fee applicable in all the *Outre-mer* (Chaban 2011). Weiss's short-lived easing of entry requirements did not impress Comorians, who lack dual citizenship, or do not 'understand' France's position. These people complain that their right to obtain French, hence Schengen, visas is illegally restricted only to those uncritical of French Mayotte. Since the two French visa delivery points manage travel throughout Schengen, political criteria are, they allege, applied that other Schengen states would not countenance (Canavate 2011).

In Mayotte, securing the contested border requires four radars at the cardinal points, numerous police and border guards, and new speedboats and planes. Nevertheless, the *kwassa* continue to arrive. By mid-2011, 27,000 expulsions had already taken place that year. One move Comorians sporadically consider and use is to refuse to allow deportees to disembark on the grounds that internal deportation contravenes international law. If prolonged, such action would quickly bankrupt the ferry business, which depends upon regular state-funded deportations. Better still from their point of view, the ensuing humanitarian crisis might attract international attention (Hassani 2009; GRDC 2010). For three weeks in 2008, the government of Anjouan did refuse to accept deportees, citing slack recordkeeping and the desperate condition of the arrivals, some of whom were not from Anjouan. Deportations resumed when the Prefect agreed to ensure that all were adequately dressed, had their possessions with them, and were returned to their island of origin. This face-saving arrangement, hardly consistent with Moroni's own stance, may have included financial inducements (RC 2008).

As departmentalization approached, Moroni decided to express its disapproval by announcing that only deportees with papers would be accepted in the future (Perrot 2011). This sovereignty game was calculated once more to cause havoc, as deportees discarded their papers. In reprisal, the French Embassy ceased issuing official and diplomatic visas and ultimately all visas (Mgueni 2011a, 2011b). Moroni then decided to emulate Anjouan's brief experiment, refusing not only those without papers, but all deportees, since forced population movements were illegal (Anon 2011a; Bounou 2011). Both sides were engaged in a diplomatic game, the better to extract concessions. The usual arrests and expulsions resumed during the absence of the Comorian foreign minister, who was furious upon learning of the capitulation.

While diplomats on both sides score points, the press plays its own games. Moroni's press claims that people only want to visit family and return home. The conservative Mayotte press echoes popular prejudice that all illegals are sick or starvelings willing to work 'black' for subsistence wages. The same press hardly notices how some Mahoran employers denounce their 'black' labourers just before payment is due, ensuring their immediate deportation. The employer is not charged with any crime. Deflecting hostility towards non-visa holding Comorians distances some Mahorans from taking responsibility for their fertility, while dependence on French subsidies reduces anger towards the *wazungu*. Parents see schools working two shifts a day and overwhelmed medical services (especially maternity facilities) and attribute these and other ills to the Comoran foreigners (Kashkazi 2008; Hopquin and Canavate 2005).

This being France, demonstrations are also part of the immigration game; two demonstrations were held in early 2011 in Mamudzu. The first was organized by non-governmental organizations (NGOs) and Comoran activists and publicized human rights abuses, attracting mostly *wazungu*. No Mahoran public figure took part. Police blocked the access roads, obliging marchers to walk 2 km to the assembly point, then lined the route, watching as onlookers abused the marchers (Chanfi 2011; Trannois 2011a, 2011b). Two weeks later, a large counter demonstration thronged the main streets of Mamudzu, organized and joined only by Mahorans, the men in front. They declared the earlier demonstration a sell out to the Comoros and demanded tougher border controls. The Prefect received a delegation from the second march only (Perrot 2011).

Will Mayotte's integration into the EU make it more attractive to economic refugees, aggravating social tensions, as some French analysts have warned (Salesse 1995; Gaymard 1987)? Will the methods used to deal with the constant arrival of *kwassa* be challenged once Mayotte is an OR, whether by the CoE Convention on Human Rights or by the EU Charter of Fundamental Freedoms? Educated Mahorans concerned about human rights violations are loath to make their concerns public at home, believing that the European institutions will intervene and effect the changes that they themselves feel powerless to demand. Mayotte-born legal academic Faneva Tsiadino Rakotondrahaso conjectures that from 2014, the European Court of Human Rights may well signal contraventions (Rakotondrahaso 2009). Mayotte Senator Ramadani believes that the EU will insist on minimum standards despite derogations granted (Girardin and Gaymard 2010). Such faith in Europe (whether the EU or CoE) is perhaps optimistic. France may exempt its overseas from the CoE's Conventions (Declaration 3 May 1974). Metro MP Didier Quentin warned the Parliament that EU and CoE legislation, if applied, would render immigration control impossible. Ensuring that no nationals were deported would cause lengthy delay. On another occasion, Quentin assured Parliament that Mayotte's new status as an OR would not interfere with detentions and deportations, as the Article 73 of the Constitution allowed derogations to national legislature overseas (Quentin *et al.* 2009; Quentin 2010a, 2010b). He possibly overlooked the fact that although Articles 73, 74 and 74–1 allow the overseas (DROM and COM) to adapt statutes and regulations in the light of their specific circumstances, Article 73 excludes derogations that undermine civil liberties anywhere on French territory, with the exception of Réunion.

During its EU Presidency in 2008, France had approved common rules for the treatment of illegal immigrants in the member states (European Pact for Immigration and Asylum). After a video made at Mayotte's Pamanzi detention centre showing the disregard for human rights that was posted on the *Libération* newspaper website (Rousselot 2008; Carayol 2008), the Commission and MEPs investigated conditions in detention centres, including Mayotte's, pointing out that whether Mayotte was in the EU or not, human rights applied there (AFP 2008). Commission Vice-President Jacques Barrot said that the EU 2008 Return Directive did not (yet) apply in the OCT Mayotte, although the CoE Convention on Human Rights did. He did not mention possible derogations. In response to mild criticisms of Pamanzi levied at a subsequent European Parliament hearing on the matter, Réunion MEP Margie Sudre assured her fellows that the high proportion of illegals in Mayotte was unmatched anywhere on European territory, that renovations to the existing detention centre and the construction of a second detention centre were in train, and that Mayotte, due to be integrated into the EU, needed not stigmatization but solidarity (European Parliament 2009).

Whatever the status of CoE Conventions post-2014, Mayotte will remain outside the Schengen zone and the EU's common immigration control mechanism, *Frontières extérieures* (FRONTEX) (Council ruling Articles 1–4, no. 2007/2004). MP Abdoulatifou Aly believed that Mayotte would accede to FRONTEX (Aly 2009), asking the European Affairs Minister whether the government intended to 'be inspired' by the actions of the FRONTEX agency to better control illegal immigration. The Minister replied that Mayotte would not be covered by FRONTEX despite its future OR status, as the non-European territories of the Netherlands and France were excluded. That said, the French authorities would indeed be 'inspired' by FRONTEX (Aly 2010b). In the meantime, a local magistrate signalled his disapproval of the fact that thousands of children were roaming the streets after their parents had been deported by transferring the guardianship of a Comorian girl to the (then) Prefect (Anon 2011a).

Europe in the Indian Ocean

Mayotte is in the euro zone yet remains a 'least developed OCT'. Mamudzu politicians had hoped that OR status would follow immediately after departmentalization, not delayed until 2014, which signals the next round of EU funding programmes. The island will then have access to POSEIDOM, the European Regional Development Fund and European Structural Funds (Rakotondrahaso 2009).

French officials consider the Indian Ocean as 'our region', and its chequebook diplomacy aims at overcoming opposition to this perception. The Commission has a Delegation in Mauritius, while the French delegation is the only EU member state embassy in Moroni. The role of the EU is central to France's 'game' in consolidating the acceptance of French Mayotte in the Indian Ocean. (For the Pacific parallel, see Brown, this volume.)

Mayotte, Paris, and, despite its discretion, the Commission too assume that whatever the theoretical impediment (possible lack of unanimity in the European Council), OR status is as good as certain. Both OR and OCT officials at the Commission in Brussels confirm as much in discussions with visiting Mayotte MPs and officials (interview, 25 June 2010).

Legally, the passage from DROM to OR is not automatic; MP Quentin warned that EU member states might insist upon protracted negotiations or even veto the application at the Council level. It might be safer, he suggested, to combine Mayotte's request with the probable application of the Netherlands islands of Bonaire, Saba, and St Eustatius (Bockel 2009; Quentin 2010b). More modestly, Marie-Luce Penchard, French Minister for the Overseas, declared that cooperation with the Comoros would remove objections (Cointat 2010).

While the General Council has been preparing for OR integration for several years, the French government formally first put Mayotte's change of status to the Commission in April 2011. French received wisdom, echoed by Mahorans, is that Europe will gain from its territorial projection off the African coast, while with France and the EU on its side, Mayotte will be protected from Comorian claims (Rakotondrahaso 2009).

This combination of objectives demonstrates the dissonance between Mayotte's legal status and its geographical location; Europe and the Indian Ocean are awkwardly collapsed. Acceptance in the Indian Ocean is part of France's global imperial ambitions. The quid pro quo is that the recipient should 'respect the wishes of the Mahorans' (Préfecture de Mayotte n.d.). Whether or not the Comoros should receive French and EU largesse in part in proportion to its understanding of French global priorities, as a francophone nation and former colony it deserves aid despite spats over Mayotte. Paris remains Moroni's leading state donor via the French Development Agency and the Mayotte and Réunion Cooperation Fund, contributing in addition 20–24 per cent of the EDF (France Diplomatie 2006–10; Europa 2007).

France is also a major donor to the Indian Ocean Commission (IOC) (Gaymard 1987), because it 'serves to reinforce acceptance of France in the region' (Aly 2010a). The Commission, though, facilitates cooperation between Madagascar, the Comoros Mauritius, Seychelles, and Réunion is a member – but not Mayotte, to the General Council's chagrin (Préfecture de Mayotte 2009). Paris organizes annual Conferences on Regional Cooperation in the Indian Ocean to raise the profile of 'France of the Indian Ocean' and publicize Europe's role in the region. Mahoran counsellors add their own sub-imperial ambition to ensure the integration and *rayonnement* of Mayotte in the Indian Ocean and become, with Réunion, Europe's relay in the region (Abdourraquib 2009; see also Holm, this volume).

Appropriately, regional sport competitions are a terrain for the playing of sovereignty games. Excluded from regional sports competitions after a 1995 Organisation of African Unity Resolution, Mayotte has gradually reintegrated into them thanks to French lobbying and inducements. Mahoran athletes compete in both the Indian Ocean Island Games (under a neutral flag) and the European Island Games (under the *Tricolore*).

Conclusion

Why has Paris finally agreed to fully integrate Mayotte after six decades of lobbying by local leaders? Some cite geostrategic advantages (Collective 2011; Massey and Baker 2009), others Mayotte's extensive marine resources (Bensoussan 2009). Since departmentalization is not a prerequisite in either case, a more pertinent driving force might be presidential vanity and global ambitions, in particular the revived determination to rehabilitate the overseas.

Officials have warned the Mahorans not to expect large, immediate economic benefits given the financial crisis in the euro zone. Will the crisis dampen the EU's acceptance of the geopolitical advantages France cites to encourage 'solidarity' for its overseas (European Commission 2008)? Regionally, that solidarity attracts attention to an awkward past. In vain Saïd Dhoifir Bounou, President of the Comoros Assembly, asked Hans Gert Pöttering, President of the European Parliament, not to accept Mayotte as an OR (Anon 2010); Interim President Sambi appealed to the EU at the Third Africa–EU Summit in Tripoli in November 2010 (Anon 2011b), and later, again in Moroni, asked the EU not to incorporate part of a sovereign state, to no avail (Mgueni 2011b).

Will the European Council set conditions before the 27 member states agree to expand EU territory into Southern Africa? Further, angrily fought sovereignty games over Mayotte are likely to add to those already ritually re-enacted over language, culture, immigration, human rights, and sport.

References

Abdourraquib, T. (2009) 'Mayotte: Quelle relation d'entente et de concorde au sein de l'Océan indien?' Online. Available at: www.etatsgenerauxdeloutremer.fr (accessed 9 December 2010).

AFP (2008) 'Bruxelles appelle la France à respecter les droits de l'homme dans le centre de rétention', 23 December.

Aly, A. (2009) 'Mayotte demain: département français et région européenne', 2 November. Online. Available at: www.aly-mayotte.fr (accessed 8 January 2010).

Aly, A. (2010a) Question no. 8044, Assemblée Nationale, *Journal officiel*, 20 July, Reply, p. 8088.

Aly, A. (2010b) 27 April, Question no. 77478, Assemblée Nationale, *Journal Officiel*, p. 4598, and 23 November 2010, Reply, p. 12679.

Aly, A. (2011) 'Question no. 111000 au Ministère de l'Education', 14 June. Online. Available at: www.nosdeputes.fr (accessed 8 April 2012).

Anon (2010) 'Comores: Dhoiffir Bounou seul candidate credible', 11 September. Online. Available at: http://wongo.skyrock.com (accessed 31 August 2012).

Anon (2011a) 'A Mayotte, les mineurs isolés, victime par ricochet de la lutte contre les clandestins', *Le Nouvel Observateur*, 30 March.

Anon (2011b) 'Troisième Sommet Afrique Union européenne: Le President des Comores accuse la France', 30 November. Online. Available at: http://wongo.skyrock.com (accessed 31 August 2012).

Assemblée Nationale (1958, revised) Constitution de la République française. Online. Available at: www.assemblee-nationale.fr (accessed 14 February 2011).

Balibar, E. (2004) *We, the people of Europe? Reflections on transnational citizenship*, Princeton NJ: Princeton University Press.

Bamana, Z. (2010) 'Accession de Mayotte au statut de RUP', *Mayotte Hebdo*, 24 September. Online. Available at: www.mayottehebdo.com (accessed 3 November 2010).

Bensoussan, O. (2009) 'La mer, menace ou espoir de développement pour Mayotte?', *Cahiers de l'Outre-mer*, 248: 489–512.

Bockel, F. (2009) 'La perspective d'une accession de Mayotte au statut de Région ultrapériperique', *Revue juridique de l'Océan indien*, Special issue on Mayotte, pp. 91–7.

Bounou, S. (2011) Interview with Adou El-Aniou, *Albalad-Comores*, No. 473, 25 March 2011.

Caminade, P. (2003/10) *Comores-Mayotte: une histoire néocoloniale*, Paris: Agone.

Canavate, L. (2011) 'Cracher dans la soupe', *Courrier international*, 11 March. Online. Available at: www.courrierinternational.com (accessed 10 April 2011).

Carayol, R. (2008) 'Mayotte: le centre de rétention, une zone de non-droit', *Libération*, 18 December.

Chaban, B. (2011) 'Anjouan/Mayotte: le visa de Mayotte passe de 9 à 60 euros', *Albalad-Comores*, 28 June. Online. Available at: www.albaladcomores.com (accessed 17 July 2011).

Chanfi, I.M. (n.d.) 'Comores: Manifestation Mayotte le 23 février 2011 – Appel à signature et à soutien'. Online. Available at: http://blogidriss.blogspot.com (accessed 25 February 2011).

Cointat, C. (2010) Projet de loi relative au Département de Mayotte, Rapport No. 17, 6 October.

Collective (2011) 'Livre bleu Sud Océan indien', French Ministry for the Overseas, December.

Constitutional Council (2000) *Decision no. 2000–428 DC*, 4 May. Online. Available at: www.conseil-constitutionnel.fr (accessed 8 April 2012).

Dover, R. (2008) 'Towards a common EU immigration policy: a securitization too far', *Journal of European Integration*, 30(1): 113–30.

Europa (2007) Union des Comores-Communauté européenne. Online. Available at: http://ec.europa.eu/development/ (accessed 4 September 2012).

European Commission (2008) *Green Paper. Future relations between the EU and the Overseas Countries and Territories.* COM (2008) 383. Brussels, 25 June 2008.

European Parliament (2009) 'Situation préoccupante dans les centres de rétention pour immigrés, notamment dans les iles de Mayotte et Lampedusa', 3 February. Online. Available at: www.europarl.europa.eu (accessed 13 November 2010).

Fairclough, N. (1989) *Language and Power*, London: Longman.

France Diplomatie (2006–10) Document Cadre de Partenariat France-Union des Comores. Online. Available at: www.diplomatir.gouv.fr (accessed 4 September 2012).

Gaymard, H. (1987) 'Une politique de la France dans l'Océan indien', *Revue de la défense nationale*, 2: 69–84.

Girardin, A. and Gaymard, H. (2010) 'L'avenir des relations entre l'Union européenne et les pays et territoires d'outre-mer' (E3902) in Assemblée Nationale, 10 February.

GRDC (2010) 'Adresse au futur Président de l'Etat de l'Union des Comores, SOS Democratie Comores'. Online. Available at: www.sosdemocratiecomores.skyrock.com (accessed 13 January 2011).

Habermas, J. (1992) 'Citizenship and national identity: some reflections on the future of Europe', *Praxis International*, 12(1): 1–19.

Hassani, M. (2009) 'Quand il y a acceptation des autorités d'Anjouan, cela va très vite', *La Chronique de Madjuwani, Al-Watwan*, 19 January.

Hopquin, B. and Canavate, L. (2005) 'A Mayotte, sur fond d'immigration clandestine massive, le débat sur le droit du sol enflamme les esprits', *Le Monde*, 9 October.

Jeanjean, H. (2002) 'Jack Lang and minority languages: a radical change in French linguistic policies or more of the same?', in A. Liddicoat and K. Muller (eds) *Perspectives on Europe, Language Issues and Language Planning in Europe, Language*, Melbourne: The National Languages and Literacy Institute of Australia.

Kashkazi (2006) 'Maore française? Maore comorienne? Et après?', No. 57. Online. Available at: http://migrantsoutremer.org (accessed 13 November 2010).

Kashkazi (2008), ' "Etrangers" à Maore; le fantasme', No. 73, June/July (accessed 13 November 2010).

Laroussi, F. (ed.) (2009) *Langues, identité et insularités: regards sur Mayotte*, UPRES, CRNS.

Legifrance (2000) Loi d'orientation pour l'outre-mer, no. 2000-1207 du 13 décembre 2000, Article 34, Du développement de la culture et identités d'outre-mer.

Majarou, M. (2010) 'Un Mahorais expulsé de Mayotte à cause de son apparence', 3 April. Online. Available at: http://wongo.skyrock.com (accessed 11 November 2010).

Martin, J. (2010) *Histoire de Mayotte*, Paris: Les Indes savantes.

Massey, S. and Baker, B. (2009) *Comoros: Eternal Involvement in a Small Island State*, Chatham House: London.

Mgueni, A. (2011a) 'Comores: les autorités comoriennes interdites de visa d'entrée en France', *Malango*, 25 March. Online. Available at: www.malango-actualite.fr (accessed 3 August 2011).

Mgueni, A. (2011b) 'Les Comores ont symboliquement denoncé la France', *Malango*, 28 March. Online. Available at: www.malango-actualite.fr (accessed 3 August 2011).

Michalon, T. (2009) *L'Outre-mer français: Evolution institutionelle et affirmations identitaires*, Paris: L'Harmattan.

Miles, W. (2005) 'Democracy without sovereignty: France's post-colonial paradox', *Journal of International affairs*, XI(2): 223–34.

ML (2010) 'Désormais à Mayotte, les Blancs doivent exiger qu'on exige leurs papiers'. Online. Available at: http://wongo.skyrock.com (accessed 8 April 2012).

MOM (2010a) 'OQTF prises en France à destination de Mayotte'. Online. Available at: www.migrantsoutremer.org (accessed 29 July 2011).

MOM (2010b) 'Articles publiés par *Mayotte Hebdo* à l'occasion d'un colloque intitulé Plurilinguisme, politique linguistique et éducation, quels éclairages pour Mayotte?' Online. Available at: www.migrantsoutremer.org (accessed 5 August 2010.)

Mouhoutar, S. (2011) 'Tribune libre', *Mayotte Hebdo*, 4 May.

Nicolaïdes, K. and Howse, R. (2008) 'Democracy without sovereignty: the global vocation of political ethics', in T. Blonde and Y. Sharry (eds) The shifting allocation of authority in international law: considering sovereignty, supremacy and subsidiarity, Oxford: Hart.

Oraison, A. (2009) 'Le différend franco-comorien', *Diplomatie*, No. 40. Online. Available at: www.diplomatie-presse.com (accessed 8 March 2011).

Orcier, P. (2010) 'Mayotte et sa première fête de l'Europe', *Nouvelle Europe*, 2 June. Online. Available at: www.nouvelle-europe.eu (accessed 29 November 2010).

Othily, G. and Buffet, F.N. (2006) 'Immigration clandestine: une realité inacceptable, une réponse ferme, juste et humaine', Senate Report No. 300, 6 April.

Perrot, J. (2010) '60e anniversaire: Mayotte fête l'Europe', *Mayotte Hebdo*, 7 May.

Perrot, J. (2011) 'Regain de tension entre la France et les Comores', *Mayotte Hebdo*, 25 March.

Perrot, J. and Macone, F. (2010) 'Entretien avec le vice-consul de France à Anjouan', *Mayotte Hebdo*, 22 March.

Pomerance, M. (1982) *Self-determination in Law and Practice: The New Doctrine in the United Nations*, The Hague: Martinus Nijhof.

Préfecture de Mayotte (n.d.) 'Cadre stratégique du Fonds de co-opération régionale de Mayotte 2006–10'. Online. Available at: www.mayotte.pref.gouv.fr (accessed 7 November 2010).

Préfecture de Mayotte (2009) 'Comité de suivi du CIOM de Mayotte', 18 December.

Quentin, D. (2006) Assemblée National, *Rapport* No. 2932, 8 March.

Quentin, D. (2010a) *Rapport sur l'Outre-mer,* 14 October, No. 2863, National Assembly.

Quentin, D. (2010b) 'Les négotiations concernant les départements et régions d'outre-mer et le statut de Mayotte vis-à-vis de l'Union européenne', 17 November, *Rapport* No. 2946, National Assembly.

Quentin, D., Gosselin, P. and Dosière, R. (2009) *Rapport d'information*, 18 February, No. 1485, National Assembly.

Rakotondrahaso, F.T. (2009) 'Mayotte, le statut de pays et territoire d'outre-mer de l'Union européenne: un pis-aller?' *Revue juridique de l'Océan indien*, Special issue on Mayotte, pp. 73–89.

RC (2008) 'Le gouvernement anjouanais refuse les Comoriens des autres iles refoulés de Mayotte', *Malango*, 23 October. Online. Available at: www.malango-actualite.fr (accessed 4 March 2009).

Rousselot, R. (2008) 'Honte', *Libération,* 18 December.

Saïd, I. (2010) 'Le contentieux de l'Ile comorienne de Mayotte: La France à l'épreuve du mépris du droit international'. Online. Available at: http://legavox.fr/blog/issa-said (accessed 10 September 2010).

Salesse, Y. (1995) *Mayotte, L'Illusion de la France: Propositions pour une décolonisation*, Paris: L'Harmattan.

Salim, A.B.S. (2011) 'Comores: respecter le choix du peuple Mahorais: quel chox, quel peuple?', *Albalad-Comores*, No.452, p. 11.

Sarkozy, N. (2010) Speech, 18 January, Mamudzu.

Theilleux, F. (2011) 'Mayotte/histoire: Une mémoire torturée', *Albalad-Mayotte*, 14 March (accessed 11 July 2011).

Thréard, Y. (2009) 'Le scandaleux vrai-faux référendum', *Le Figaro*, 31 May.

Torre, H. (2008) 'Un éclairage budgétaire sur le défi e l'mmigration clandestine', Senate, 10 July, *Rapport d'information* No. 461.

Trannois, E. (2011a) 'Mayotte-une manifestation pour un 'rappel à la loi' ', *Malango*, 25 February. Online. Available at: www.malango-actualite.fr (accessed 3 March 2011).

Trannois, E. (2011b) 'Manifestation en memoire des victimes de la traversée Anjouan – Mayotte', *Malango*, 19 February. Online. Available at: www.malango-actualite.fr (accessed 4 June 2011).

Walker, I. (2007) 'What came first: The nation or the state? Political process in the Comoro Islands', *Africa*, 77(4): 582–605.

Weller, M. (2009) 'Settling self-determination conflicts: recent developments', *European Journal of International Law*, 20(1): 111–65.

Youngs, R. (2008) 'Fusing security and development: Just another platitude?', *Journal of European Integration*, 30(3): 419–37.

14 Postcolonial sovereignty games with Europe in the margins

The Netherlands, the Antilles, and Europe

Gert Oostindie

The Kingdom of the Netherlands is trans-Atlantic, uniting a mid-sized European country with six tiny Caribbean islands, the remnants of a once-impressive colonial empire. In order to understand how this Kingdom relates to the European Union (EU), we should first explore how and why its constituent parts still cling together. The first section of this chapter therefore outlines the decolonization of the Dutch colonial empire, focusing on its remarkable outcome, the persistence of non-sovereign polities in the Antilles. The next part discusses the *Statuut*, the constitution of the Kingdom. Moving to contemporary politics, the third section analyses the highly contested rhetoric, process, and outcome of the recent restructuring of the trans-Atlantic Kingdom and the role allotted to the EU in the debates. The conclusion questions whether the Green Paper might change the parameters of the debate anytime soon and offers some reflections about the status quo.

Inspired by the conceptual framework presented in the introduction to the volume, this chapter probes into the 'sovereignty games' played out in the triangle formed by the Netherlands, the six Dutch Antillean islands, and the EU. Bearing in mind the treatment of the concepts of, and interfaces between, small-scale and non-sovereignty in Baldacchino's contribution to this volume, it may, however, be appropriate to indicate that precisely because small-scale and non-sovereignty imply a delicate relation between the subordinate and dominant polities, the playful concept of 'sovereignty games' should not conceal that much of this is dead serious, at least from the perspective of the smaller polities (see Baldacchino and Milne 2009).

Decolonization and postcolonial (re-)arrangements

Under the aegis of its East and West Indian Companies, the Netherlands forged an empire connecting the metropolis to Asia, Africa, and the Americas. After the Napoleonic Wars, the UK took over parts of the empire. From the mid-nineteenth century until the Second World War, the Netherlands (East) Indies was crucial to the Netherlands, certainly from an economic and geopolitical perspective, but to some degree also in the domains of culture and sciences. At the margins of the empire were the Dutch West Indies, the former plantation colony Suriname on the Northern coast of South America, and six tiny islands in the Caribbean Sea.[1]

While parliamentarians occasionally suggested that the unprofitable Caribbean colonies should be passed on to the highest bidder – as indeed Denmark had sold its Caribbean islands to the United States (US) in 1917 – there was no interest whatsoever in parting with the East Indies. Colonial reform was discussed with reluctance, partly out of sheer self-interest, partly because of a lack of confidence in the native elites. A mixture of feelings of racial and/or cultural superiority and an urge to compensate for colonial exploitation resulted in the formulation of an 'ethical policy' around 1900. Of course, this hybrid paralleled the British concept and policy of a 'white man's burden' and the French *mission civilisatrice*.

As late as the 1930s, the prospect of the independence of the vast colony in Asia was widely rejected. The East Indies were considered 'the cork that keeps the Dutch economy floating' and the Dutch ticket to geopolitical prominence. As one parliamentarian had it, without this colony, the Netherlands would demote to the 'rank of a country like Denmark'. But there was also a genuine – certainly in retrospective highly naive – belief that 'the natives' delighted in the supposedly beneficial Dutch colonial rule.

The Second World War changed all that. Germany occupied the Netherlands from 1940 to 1945, while Japan took over the Netherlands Indies in 1942. The West Indies retained their Dutch colonial status, but their defence was taken over by the Allied forces, in particular the Americans. After liberation in May 1945, the Dutch anticipated a return to pre-War normality in the colonies, but the declaration of an independent Republic of Indonesia on 17 August 1945, two days after the Japanese capitulation, proved to be a decisive step in the other direction. It took four years of protracted negotiations, bloody military combat, and increasing international pressure on the Netherlands before the Dutch reluctantly accepted the transfer of sovereignty to Indonesia in late 1949.

In the shadow of these seminal events, negotiations about the decolonization of the West Indies were initiated. During the war, the Dutch government, exiled in London, had cautiously promised colonial reform after the defeat of the Axis powers. This promise was not an unconditional transfer of sovereignty, but rather a reform in which the constituent parts of the Kingdom would cling together on a voluntary basis, autonomous in internal affairs and assisting one another where appropriate. A Kingdom government under the Dutch monarch would be the highest authority in all Kingdom matters.

Obviously, this was all too little and too late for the Indonesian nationalists, but raised hopes in Suriname and the Antilles for colonial reform. Between 1945 and 1954, a long-winded negotiation process resulted in the *Statuut* or Charter for the Kingdom of the Netherlands, confirming that the West Indies would remain within the Kingdom while attaining autonomy in domestic affairs. More radical alternatives (a transfer of sovereignty or full integration into the Dutch state) were not seriously considered.

Able Dutch Caribbean politicians made sure that Dutch promises intended to lure Indonesia to remain within the Kingdom now materialized for their nascent micro-states. Matters of scale were turned on their head. The 'equality' within the Kingdom offered by the Netherlands (10 million inhabitants by 1940) to Indonesia (90 million) was now extended to two colonies totalling less than 300,000 citizens. In the latter stages of the process, prominent Dutch politicians became wary of the concessions made. Yet after the international fiasco with Indonesia, the reluctance to be branded a reactionary colonial power again by the United Nations (UN) prevailed.

The Netherlands emerged highly frustrated from the war and the loss of Indonesia, initially with widespread pessimism regarding the future. Yet within a decade, the Dutch reinvented themselves as an enthusiastic actor in the European unification process. The Netherlands undoubtedly benefitted enormously from its strategic location in Europe and the growth of the European open market. Euroscepticism would only come to the fore at the turn of the century, despite the evident economic gains to the Netherlands, past but also present, of European unification.

Until the late 1960s, the Netherlands and two new Caribbean states appeared content with the new arrangement and there were no serious tensions. This changed by 1970, primarily because Dutch politicians started to worry about the downsides (latent or manifest) of this postcolonial arrangement. In short, there were three clusters of problems, the common denominator being that the Kingdom and its *Statuut* mainly favoured the Caribbean polities – all this, of course, from a Dutch point of view. First, there was a feeling that the Dutch had a responsibility to bear to correct for poor governance in the West Indies, whereas the autonomy of these entities makes pre-emptive Dutch intervention difficult. As had transpired in May 1969 in Curaçao, a local conflict could turn into a revolt in which Dutch marines were invited in to restore order – impossible to explain to an international audience that this was *not* a neo-colonial action. Next, there was concern about the increasing amount of development aid producing uncertain results. Finally, there was growing apprehension about the unrestricted right of abode of West Indians in the Netherlands.

Within a year after the May 1969 revolt, the Dutch parliament adopted a position in favour of an early – immediate, if possible – transfer of sovereignty to both Suriname and the six islands (dominated by Curaçao) forming the Netherlands Antilles. Suriname, with a serious nationalist movement but nonetheless deeply divided over this issue, indeed became an independent republic in 1975, stimulated by a golden handshake worth (corrected for inflation) over 10,000 euro per capita in today's currency. In contrast, the Netherlands Antilles refused the 'gift' of sovereignty and has consistently continued to do so to this day. The major Antillean arguments in favour of a continuation of non-sovereignty are that the Kingdom (for all practical purposes, the Netherlands) guarantees democracy, human rights and liberties, and territorial integrity (not a completely abstract concern with respect to the lengthy history of Venezuelan claims); provides development funds and makes the islands a more trustworthy focus of foreign investments; and that Dutch citizenship entails the right of abode in the Netherlands and the EU in general. Obviously, the same kinds of arguments are keeping the citizens of other non-sovereign territories from rallying to demand full independence.

Since 1990, successive Dutch governments have accepted the inability to impose independence on the islands against their will. The Hague's priority has turned to improving the quality of governance on the islands by strengthening the role of the Kingdom, if need be at the cost of local autonomy. The results were mixed. The other Dutch priority was to keep the six islands together, which failed miserably.

Thus, the Netherlands has maintained a reluctant postcolonial presence in the Caribbean, not so much driven by a desire to cling to empire but rather due to the inability to leave the scene. This impossibility stems not only from the consistent Antillean refusal to accept independence as much as from the fact that the constitution of the Kingdom of the Netherlands, the *Statuut*, makes no provision for unilateral dissolution of, or secession from, the Kingdom.

Up to this very day, The Hague has struggled to propose a serious national Dutch interest in the prolongation of the trans-Atlantic Kingdom. The three arguments in favour of a Dutch retreat remain relevant. The surge of international crime in the Caribbean has only served to step up the concern with the quality and integrity of Antillean governance and the functioning of local politics. There are additional worries now about territorial integrity with respect to the position of Hugo Chávez' Venezuela vis-à-vis the Dutch presence in the Caribbean – Aruba, Bonaire, and Curaçao lie only a few dozen miles from the Venezuelan coast. Recently the Dutch saw no alternative but to invest an astonishing 1.7 billion euros in the restructuring of Antillean public debt. Finally, the Antillean community in the Netherlands has increased tenfold from a mere 13,000 in 1970 to over 130,000 today, and this group suffers from integration problems.

Small wonder, in a hardening political climate, enthusiasm for the Antilles and for a continuation of the trans-Atlantic is once again waning. Despite the attempts to formulate a more positive engagement, the bottom line of Dutch Kingdom policies is to minimize what the British refer to as the 'contingent liabilities' of this type of postcolonial constitutional legacy. The option of a unilateral transfer of sovereignty is sometimes advocated, in spite of the legal impediments. Suffice it to say that the international context would not be supportive of any unilateral Dutch policy aimed at enforcing independence. The UN has long accepted the permanent association of former colonies or their incorporation into a postcolonial constitutional arrangement if the former colony's right to self-determination has been exercised in choosing this option. Moreover, close allies of the Netherlands, in particular the US, France and the UK, would not welcome a Dutch retreat from the Caribbean (Hillebrink 2008).

The *Statuut* or Charter for the Kingdom of the Netherlands

The Charter was proclaimed in 1954 and has since remained the constitutive document regarding relations between the Netherlands and its former colonies in the Caribbean (Oostindie and Klinkers 2003: 84–8). Its major formal features may be briefly summarized. The participants state that they are partners in the Kingdom on a voluntary basis, exercising their right to self-determination by participating in the Kingdom of the Netherlands. The Kingdom of the Netherlands is defined as an entity consisting of autonomous countries, pledging to promote common interests on the basis of equality and to accord each other assistance and cooperation where appropriate.

The countries constituting the Kingdom – in 1954, the Netherlands, Suriname, and the Netherlands Antilles – are autonomous in internal affairs. A number of specific issues are defined as 'affairs of the Kingdom', the most important being nationality matters, foreign affairs, defence, and the guarantee of good govern-ance. The constitutional monarch presides over all of the countries in the King-dom; a governor in the Caribbean countries represents the monarch, and hence the Kingdom, while at the same time heading the local government, formed by a democratically elected parliament.

Kingdom affairs are decided upon by the government of the Kingdom, consist-ing of the Dutch cabinet and supplemented by ministers plenipotentiary of the par-ticipating Caribbean countries. There is no Kingdom parliament, but analogous to the arrangement of the Kingdom cabinet, other Dutch institutions, such as the Council of State, function as Kingdom institutions by adding a representative of each Caribbean country.

In its preamble, the Charter literally claims to be 'no eternal edict', yet its con-tents remained unaltered for over half a century. This reflects the rigidity of the *Statuut*, which stipulates that no changes can be made without the consent of all of the involved partners; this applies to changes of content as well as to secession or any other change in the Kingdom's membership. By mutual consent, membership of the Charter *has* changed several times. Suriname opted out and became inde-pendent in 1975; Aruba seceded from the Netherlands Antilles in 1986 to become a country in its own right within the Kingdom; and on 10 October 2010 (10/10/10), the 'Antilles-of-five' were dismantled, with Curaçao and St Maarten attaining country status within the Kingdom and the three smallest islands (Bonaire, St Eustatius, and Saba, together 'BES') becoming 'public bodies', a special type of municipalities of the Netherlands.

Several observations are pertinent at this stage. First of all, some of the lofty pretentions of the *Statuut* pale in view of reality. In view of the wide divergences in scale (the Netherlands has 16.5 million inhabitants, the six islands together 300,000) and resources, the equality as defined in the Charter applies to individual civil rights rather than to the real equivalence of the countries involved. Likewise, the ideal of 'mutual' assistance is fictitious, as material and immaterial support has been a one-way street for the past 60 years.

Next, the Kingdom government lacks democratic legitimacy, as there is no Kingdom parliament. However, none of the partners has attached high priority to repairing this 'democratic deficiency'. More generally, while the Kingdom has a semi-federal character, the Netherlands-dominated Kingdom government has the final say in all conflicts. In this sense, as pro-independence Antilleans emphasize, the Kingdom may be said to have remained a neo-colonial structure.

The Charter allows for intensive cooperation in all fields, including matters pertaining to good governance, but Dutch efforts to intensify such cooperation have often been interpreted, and thus rejected and/or resented, as a means to sub-vert Caribbean autonomy. On the other hand, the very concept of autonomous countries so central to the *Statuut* is disputable. Over the past decades, (the Kingdom of) the Netherlands has ceded much of its sovereignty and hence autonomy to the EU, but the rhetoric of Caribbean autonomy still dominates much of the debate on governance within the trans-Atlantic Kingdom.

Not only has the meaning of sovereignty changed fundamentally since the proclamation of the Charter, but so has the virtual distance separating the European from the Caribbean part of the Kingdom. The Charter is based on geographically separate populations, yet the Antillean population has become truly transnational in recent decades, with 45 per cent of the total Curaçaoan community living in the Netherlands. As a result, problems on the islands and resulting migration pressures affect the Netherlands more directly than ever before.

The EU in the debates on dismantling the Netherlands Antilles

There is no reason to assume that the Dutch constitutional presence in the Caribbean will end anytime soon, and this is only confirmed by the re-organization of the trans-Atlantic Kingdom implemented on the symbolic – and from a bureaucratic perspective not particularly practical – date of 10/10/10. This restructuring was implemented in response to a number of challenges and responded to several, partially conflicting ambitions. The outcome therefore remains contested.[2]

The first priority of the islands was to sever the constitutional bonds linking them together while at the same time maintaining their constitutional links with the Netherlands – in other words, attaining a direct bilateral relation with The Hague within the Kingdom of the Netherlands without having to bother too much about the other five Dutch Antilles.[3] They were also in dire need of the restructuring of the massive national debt. The Hague wanted to pursue its policy of extending Kingdom powers to improve the quality and integrity of the governance on the islands. A majority in the Dutch parliament also strived for simultaneous legislation in order to restrict free migration between the various parts of the Kingdom. This package deal was consistently rejected by all of the Antillean politicians, and The Hague eventually dropped the migration issue as part of the package to be negotiated.

Otherwise, the outcome represented a compromise for all those involved, with the exception of Aruba. The island gave its constitutionally indispensable consent but ensured that its own 'full' autonomy, as defined in the Charter, remained unaffected. Curaçao and St Maarten both attained country status within the Kingdom but had to abide with direct metropolitan involvement with financial affairs, the administration of justice, and police matters. This involvement implies a curtailment of the extent of autonomy enjoyed by the former country of the Netherlands Antilles and even today by Aruba. The 10/10/10 agreement allows for a future downgrading of Dutch involvement, but it is uncertain whether this will materialize.

The BES islands have been incorporated into the metropolitan state, neither as municipalities nor as part of a (new or existing) province, but rather as *sui generis* 'public bodies', allowing for some discrepancies with the Netherlands with regard to legislation, administrative rules, and practice. Thus, whereas formally only the tripartite Kingdom of the Netherlands was located on both sides of the Atlantic, now the Netherlands itself extends into the Caribbean.

There have been gains and losses for all parties. The Netherlands eventually had to consent to breaking up the Antilles and paid 1.7 billion euros in debt servicing, but did acquire a stronger hold on Dutch Caribbean governance. Curaçao and St Maarten attained country status and a fresh financial start but had to accept restricted autonomy. The BES islands will enjoy more Dutch support but at the expense of a considerable stepping up of metropolitan control. Aruba was left alone but faces the possibility that The Hague will attempt to extend some of its new powers to the island at the first opportunity. Only in the field of migration did the islands not compromise whatsoever.

The process that ended on 10 October 2010 started ten years earlier, with a plebiscite in St Maarten disclosing a clear majority for secession from the Antilles. Throughout this decade, there were heated debates about the meaning of self-determination and about the contemporary relevance of the concept of autonomy as laid down in the *Statuut* half a century before. Surely this was a lengthy process of postcolonial sovereignty games, and 'Europe' was indeed included in some stages in the contestations. However, remarkably, the debate about the European dimension of the trans-Atlantic Kingdom was postponed before it could acquire serious political significance.

Upon closer inspection, this is not a remarkable outcome. The Caribbean countries within the Kingdom have been officially associated with the EU since the early 1960s, attaining their current Overseas Countries and Territories (OCT) status in 1970. Over the decades, there has been little public debate on the islands regarding their relations with the EU, presumably because these are deemed a rather technical matter of limited significance. The focus of all policy and popular debates on external relations has always been the relationship with the Netherlands. The Hague, in turn, has briefly and cautiously suggested the possibility of upgrading Antillean–EU relations to a status similar to the French departments in the Caribbean but dropped this idea in the face of Antillean opposition.

Antillean politicians are obviously aware of the advantages the EU may bring. The first, of course, is that the EU means additional financial support. This argument has hardly figured in the debates about the restructuring of the trans-Atlantic Kingdom, and certainly not as an Antillean argument in favour of moving from OCT to OR status. Dutch financial aid is of far greater importance, and the islands therefore prioritize the securing of continued Dutch support. This makes sense. Brussels feels no particular responsibility for the Antilles, the less so as the successive extensions of EU membership have brought several continental countries into the EU with lower per capita income than the Antilles. The Hague might have nurtured hopes of transferring some of its financial burden regarding the Antilles to the EU, as France has done successfully. It stands to reason, however, to assume that the new EU, with its centre of gravity moving towards Central and Eastern Europe, will be more inclined to actually cut financial aid to the former colonial territories, including the French overseas provinces, than to expand the number of such extra-European territories qualifying for additional EU support. Thus, in this field, attempts to play sovereignty games, whether by the metropolis or the former colonies, would soon meet insurmountable limits.

The EU could mean support for upgrading the quality of local governance. This type of argument is not prominent, either. Again, relations in this field are predominantly bilateral and unidirectional, from the Netherlands to each of the six islands. The parameters here are set by the Kingdom and Dutch legislation, bureaucratic rules and procedures, including the Dutch language. EU intervention is of secondary importance here at best, and there is little indication that any of the partners feels this should change. Once more, this leaves little room or need for postcolonial sovereignty games.

The EU might mean new economic opportunities. This argument is part of a globalization discourse which has created sharp divisions, not so much between the Netherlands and the islands, but rather in all camps. Not surprisingly, due to the small scale and economic vulnerability of the islands, protectionist leanings have been dominant. Certainly, the debates of the past decade did not include voices or moves aimed at substituting EU structures for the bilateral, postcolonial arrangements with The Hague – historically, the opposite has prevailed, thus Antillean calls for the Netherlands to ward off EU pressure to liberalize their island economies.

A less rosy image of the EU seems to be dominant on the islands, being that 'Europe' means excessive regulations, potentially increased intervention, and less autonomy. This argument, indeed, has been used and possibly decisively so, at least in the short run. The 2002 Dutch initiative to explore the possibility of a transition to OR status was defended by the Dutch government as well as the Council of State, not only as a potential avenue to ensure more European support, but also as a logical implication of the fact the Antilles will remain part of the Kingdom. The Council of State argued that as the Kingdom will remain trans-Atlantic, one should consider not only the Netherlands, but all parts of the Kingdom to be European territory. Hence, like the Azores, the Canary Islands, or the French *départements d'outre-mer*, the Antilles should become an OR (CDA, VVD and D66 2003: 14; Raad van State 2003).

This reasoning has provoked strong (though not unanimous) rejection on the islands. Opponents argued that a transition to OR status would not simply open the door to the Brussels bureaucracy, but would also sustain the covert Dutch attempt to further reign in Antillean autonomy – the previous strongly autonomist Aruban government in particular hoped for OCT+ status, meaning the same arrangement but with additional material advantages.

This argument has therefore certainly provoked postcolonial sovereignty games, not so much by using the EU as a strategic partner against Dutch 'recolonization' but rather by lumping the Netherlands and EU together as twin powers eager to crush Antillean autonomy. The mid-2000s saw passing parliamentary debate in the Netherlands on the pros and cons of the OCT and OR options, but this debate has ended inconclusively. While the Dutch government was cautiously positive about a transition towards OR, state-commissioned external reports were more critical, warning against the excessive bureaucratic burden of the *acquis com-*

munautaire and the economic disadvantages of taking the islands out of the dollar economy prevalent in the Americas (Van Beuge 2004).

Neither the former Netherlands Antillean government nor the aspiring new countries Curaçao or St Maarten came to any definitive conclusions on the subject. In 2005, a joint Dutch–Antillean decision was made to postpone discussions about possible changes in the relation to the EU altogether. Five years after 10 October 2010, the evaluation of the new arrangements within the Kingdom will include the reassessment of the relationship with the EU. Even for the newly incorporated BES islands, the decision regarding a possible transition from OCT to OR status has been postponed. Brussels, in turn, seems to have demonstrated no particular interest in revising present relations with the Dutch Antilles apart from its overall intention to reform the OCT arrangement as indicated in the 2008 Green Paper.

The case of Aruba illustrates most clearly how arguments within the Dutch Caribbean about the EU are grounded in attitudes towards the Netherlands and about autonomy within the Kingdom. As explained above, the dominant Aruban interest in the dismantling of the Netherlands Antilles was simply to ascertain that there would not be any consequences for its own status. Any possible change in the relation to the EU was evaluated from this perspective. From 2001 until 2009, Aruba was governed by the uncompromising pro-autonomy party People's Electoral Movement (MEP). The MEP had no interest whatsoever in revising the Aruban relationship to Brussels. Its sworn political adversary the Aruban People's Party (AVP), in opposition after many years of rule, was known for its more accommodating stance to The Hague and its close relation to the ruling Dutch Christian-Democrats.[4] Thus, when the oppositional AVP produced a report arguing in favour of OR status for Aruba, using many of the same arguments as forwarded by the Council of State, the Aruban government immediately rejected this suggestion as part of a sell-out to the Netherlands. Conversely, when the AVP returned to political power in 2009, the new Aruban government was quick to publish a strong pro-Europe and hence pro-OR White Paper (Government of Aruba 2010). Sovereignty games indeed, mainly used in domestic politics.

Arguably the most significant political use made of the link to the EU pertains to the debate about free migration and the right of abode. Ever since the late 1960s and particularly in the last decade, Dutch government has explored ways of restricting Antillean migration to the Netherlands. Such moves were vehemently opposed by Antillean politics and by the Antillean community on both sides of the Atlantic – in fact, this is probably the only issue on which politicians and citizens on all islands agree. Arguably, the *Statuut*, with its definition of a single shared citizenship for all members of the polity of the Kingdom, provides solid ground for the position that there cannot be a generic restriction on Antillean immigration. Yet successive Dutch governments have argued that the *Statuut* does allow for specific legislation, such as obligatory citizenship training, the banning of criminals, and imposing state supervision on underage immigrants.

No progress was made with this type of legislation due to serious objections, not only from Antillean and some Dutch politicians as well as Antillean organizations in the Netherlands but also from the Dutch Council of State on strictly constitutional grounds. In this context, the European connection has aptly been utilized by all opponents to restrictive legislation. The argument that all Antilleans are not simply citizens of the Kingdom but equally of the EU has become standard in the Antillean repertoire. It implies that its European citizenship provides legal guarantees as well as practical opportunities which further weaken the case for curtailing Antillean migration – and the warning that there is always the ultimate remedy of pleading the case for unrestricted migration with European courts. It therefore stands to reason that in a Dutch Caribbean context, the strategic use of the Brussels connection has nowhere been played out as competently as in the issue of migration policies. If these postcolonial sovereignty games have ever been triangular, it is in this field.

There is some irony in this observation. One of the central questions addressed in this book is how postcolonial entities at the margins of Europe use the EU in their efforts to put their colonial status behind them. From the reasoning above, it should be clear that the EU connection has not been a major issue within Kingdom relations over the past decades at all. Much of the political effort of Aruba, Curaçao, and St Maarten has rather been to cling as much as possible to a constitutional arrangement made in 1954 guaranteeing a high degree of local autonomy, and at the same time to hold tight to The Hague rather than to Brussels. Much of the debate and most of the postcolonial sovereignty games thus aimed at safeguarding the interests of the former colonies have been acted out on an intra-Kingdom level, with only limited use of the broader European playing field. 'Brussels' has mainly been used in the Antilles as an additional argument in the debate about autonomy (with a tendency to presume that 'more Brussels' would imply 'more The Hague' and therefore less autonomy) and in the debate about migration (the otherwise scarcely valued European connection nurtured here as an additional argument in favour of unrestricted migration and rights of abode).

The Green Paper

This conclusion probably sets the Dutch case apart from the others discussed in this book. The question remains, nevertheless, how the Green Paper published by the European Commission in 2008 will affect all of the parties involved. The core of the Green Paper, of course, is to move away from the extant development aid character – privileging the OCT over the African, Caribbean and Pacific (ACP) countries – towards a relationship aiming at improving the competitive powers of the OCTs in the global economy (Hannibal, Holst, *et al.*, this volume). This new policy should be codified in the sequel to the present OCT arrangement dating from 2001 and expiring in 2013 (European Commission 2008).

Not surprisingly, a comparison of the governmental reactions of the three countries to the Green Paper discloses consensus on all major issues (Aruba 2008; Netherlands 2008; The Dutch Antilles 2008). All three governments politely agree with the Commission's intention to break away from the classic development aid model but proceed by emphasizing the structural problems of small-scale to all of the six islands – and hence the need to continue helping them to increase their competitiveness with various types of policies. In the words of the Antillean cabinet, '[t]he larger OCTs, including the Netherlands Antilles, need help in building up infrastructure and institutional capacity' (2008: 3). Similarly, Aruba is of the opinion that the 'Community should support the OCT in achieving their objectives in the face of their challenges', adding that this 'could mean technical, financial, and trade [related], or any other kind of assistance' (2008: 1).

The fact that the islands have relatively high per capita incomes is not withheld, but this does not lead any of the three governments to state that EU support may be reduced. Neither the Antilles nor Aruba exhibit much enthusiasm for the suggestion to construct an index to measure the relative vulnerability of the OCTs, while The Hague expresses only lukewarm support.

From the above, it will have become clear that over the years the major economic support for the islands has rather come from the Netherlands itself; indeed, there has been a permanent policy debate and hence the deployment of postcolonial sovereignty games within the Kingdom. The playing field is clearly different here, but both the islands and the metropolis concur in proposing that the EU should continue to contribute its share in the future. There is also broad consensus on priorities, in particular strengthening local governance; capacity building; developing intraregional and intercontinental transport in support of the tourism industry; and at the same time, potentially conflicting, stimulating sustainable development and the advance of alternative sources of energy and preserving biodiversity. All three governments emphasize that the Antilles and Aruba may serve as a bridge between Europe and the Americas in much the same way as the islands continuously attempt to persuade the Netherlands that the extension of the Kingdom into the Caribbean is also a Dutch strategic interest.

There is also consensus that not only the European connection, but equally firmer regional integration is important to minimizing contingent liabilities as discussed above. Thus, the Antillean government writes:

> Given the common and border crossing interests in e.g. transnational migration, education and scientific research, agriculture and fisheries, environmental protection, tourism and combating money laundering and drugs, closer cooperation is probably possible between relevant organizations and departments within the region.
>
> (The Dutch Antilles 2008: 5)

But this clearly does not lead to a preference for regional integration over the European link: 'In conclusion it is highly questionable whether participation in regional economic integration in the Caribbean will lead to prosperity in the Netherlands Antilles' (2008: 5).

Hence, the Antillean reaction stresses the 'Europeanness' of the OCTs and suggests that they might be 'encouraged to meet European norms and standards in terms of administrative and legislative facilities' – all this, in an implicit reference to the treasured autonomy, as 'a voluntary adoption of these standards' (2008: 3). Likewise, Aruba stresses the significance of 'historical ties, shared values and solidarity' (2008: 1) as an argument for European support. The Hague also discusses partnership between the OCTs and the EU in terms of 'greater reciprocity' and adaption of 'European standards over time and on a voluntary basis' (2008: 2).

Likewise, the three governments have mainly positive things to say in response to the question on the present structures within the EU to discuss possible conflicting views between the Commission, an OCT, and a member state. All governments qualify the current consultation structures as 'sufficient' (The Netherlands 2008: 2; Aruba 2008: 5; The Dutch Antilles 2008: 6) and do not refer to past, present, or future conflicts either within the Kingdom or between the Netherlands, the islands, and/or the EU. In sum, if sovereignty games are played here, they take the form of a strategic consensus to ensure continued European support in addition to the more vital constitutional postcolonial link. The central aim of the Caribbean players has been to each have their own direct connection to The Hague – connections which are inevitably asymmetric in a way that makes formal Dutch sovereignty a shield (against interference from the outside world) and possibly a platform (for Caribbean agency), but these are played out without opening up to more interference from The Hague than absolutely necessary. If the EU can be employed to secure that aim, fine. If not, then there is no need to engage the EU.

Of course we should also question what the OCTs mean for the EU. The OCTs are generally small-scale and vulnerable – that is why these 'confetti of empire' have generally refused sovereignty in the first place (Aldrich and Connell 1998). From this follows a host of contingent liabilities for the individual European metropolitan states, but these obviously accrue indirectly to the EU at large. There is also another side to this equation. Spread around the globe, Europe's OCTs (and ORs) also enhance Europe's geopolitical position in world politics and economic fields such as mineral exploration in the world's oceans.

The Antillean reaction to the Green Paper does hint at this:

> The European Commission Green Paper seems to find that the OCT relationship mostly imposes responsibilities and obligations on Europe. That raises the question of what is Europe's own interest in the relationship with the OCTs. Are the OCTs for instance of strategic importance for the European Union?
>
> (The Dutch Antilles 2008: 1)

The question is submitted but not taken up in the rest of the reaction, and even weakened as the following sentence implicitly returns to the issue of contingent liabilities ('Or should the OCTs take more responsibility in areas of importance to the European Union, such as the protection of biodiversity?' (2008: 1)). And yet the question of real European interest beyond responsibilities stemming from the colonial era remains.

Conclusion

In conclusion, then, the Green Paper and ensuing European decision might affect how the EU deals with the OCTs, in particular in diminishing preferential aid arrangements. The four semi-autonomous countries making up the Kingdom of the Netherlands concur in striving for maximization of European support for the Caribbean OCTs. The divergence remains where it always been: within the Kingdom, with the Caribbean partners striving for maximum autonomy and support and the Dutch conversely striving to strengthen the Kingdom government in its role as guarantee for good governance and trying to minimize the various contingent liabilities. 'Europe' was mainly an indirect argument in the postcolonial identity games of the past decade. First, and as shared by all Dutch Caribbean players, in the argumentation in favour of unrestricted migration by reference to a shared European citizenship. Second, by opponents to a stepping up of Dutch involvement in local governance, by suggesting that any argumentation in favour of a transition from OCT to OR status was nothing but another pretext for 'recolonization'.

The recent history of the trans-Atlantic Kingdom of the Netherlands might be read as a story of reluctant embraces for old time's sake, of lack of trust, ignorance, and hypocrisy; but we might also understand these in a more positive light as a case of postcolonial solidarity, no matter how ambivalent. And of course, much of the argumentation of the former colonial powers in the EU to convince the more recent member states from Central and Eastern Europe to consent to a continuation of European support for the 'confetti of empire' reflects much the same attitude.

Notes

1 The section is mainly based on Oostindie and Klinkers (2003) and Oostindie (2009).
2 The analysis of the period since 2000 is based on Oostindie and Klinkers (2012). For the European dimension, see Besselink (2004), Van Beuge (2004), Oostindie and Klinkers (2012: 91–4), and Raad van State (2003).
3 Only St Eustatius opted in vain for continuation of the Antilles-of-five.
4 A.G. 'Mito' Croes, the driving force behind the AVP's European policy, defended a PhD thesis on this very subject at Tilburg University (Croes 2006). His thesis advisor was Professor Ernst Hirsch Ballin, an expert in Kingdom relations both as a politician and constitutional scholar – he was a minister in the Dutch cabinet for the Christian-Democrat CDA from 1989 through 1994 and again from 2006 through 2010. In between, he served in the Council of State (2000–6), as one of the authors of the report arguing in favour of a transition to OR status (Raad van State 2003).

References

Aldrich, R. and Connell, J. (1998) *The Last Colonies*, Cambridge: Cambridge University Press.

Aruba (2008) 'Aruba's Response to Green Paper Questionnaire', *Response to COM (2008) 383*.

Baldacchino, G. and Milne, D. (eds) (2009) *The Case for Non-Sovereignty: Lessons from Sub-National Island Jurisdictions*, London: Routledge.

Besselink, L.F.M. (2004) 'De Europese Unie en de Koninkrijksrelaties', in L.J.J. Rogier and H.G. Hoogers (eds) *50 jaar Statuut voor het Koninkrijk der Nederlanden. Bijdragen voor het congres 50 jaar Statuut voor het Koninkrijk der Nederlanden*, Rotterdam: Erasmus University Rotterdam.

CDA, VVD and D66 (2003) 'Meedoen, meer werk en minder regels'. Hoofdlijnenakkoord voor het kabinet CDA, VVD, D66, 16 May (available in TK, 2002–3, 28 637, No. 19).

Croes, A.G. (2006) *De herdefiniëring van het Koninkrijk*, Nijmegen: Wolf Legal Publishers.

The Dutch Antilles (2008) 'The Dutch Antilles' Response to Green Paper Questionnaire', *Response to COM (2008) 383*.

European Commission (2008) *Green Paper. Future relations between the EU and the Overseas Countries and Territories* COM (2008) 383. Brussels, 25 June 2008.

Government of Aruba (2010) 'Visie Arubaanse regering op de relaties met de Europese Unie'. *Response to COM (2008) 383*.

Hillebrink, S. (2008) *The Right to Self-Determination and Post-Colonial Governance: The Case of the Netherlands Antilles and Aruba*, The Hague: Asser Press.

Netherlands (2008) 'Netherland's Response to Green Paper Questionnaire', *Response to COM (2008) 383*.

Oostindie, G.J. (2009) 'Dependence and autonomy in sub-national island jurisdictions: the case of the Netherlands Antilles and Aruba', in G. Baldacchino and D. Milne (eds) *The Case for Non-Sovereignty: Lessons from Sub-National Island Jurisdisctions*, London: Routledge.

Oostindie, G.J. and Klinkers, I.A.J. (2003) *Decolonising the Caribbean: Dutch Policies in a Comparative Perspective*, Amsterdam: Amsterdam University Press.

Oostindie, G.J. and Klinkers, I.A.J. (2012) *Gedeeld Koninkrijk. De ontmanteling van de Nederlandse Antillen en de herstructurering van het trans-Atlantische Koninkrijk*, Amsterdam: Amsterdam University Press.

Raad van State van het Koninkrijk (2003) *Verdieping of geleidelijk uiteengaan? De relaties binnen het Koninkrijk en met de Europese Unie*, 's-Gravenhage: Raad van State.

Van Beuge, Ch.R. (2004) *Banden met Brussel. De betrekkingen van de Nederlandse Antillen en Aruba met de Europese Unie*, Rapport van de Commissie ter bestudering van mogelijke toekomstige relaties van de Nederlandse Antillen en Aruba met de Europese Unie.

15 Greenland projecting sovereignty – Denmark protecting sovereignty away

Ulrik Pram Gad[1]

In 1985, Greenland became the first territory to ever leave the European Community (EC) when it opted for a status as an Overseas Country or Territory (OCT). The way Greenland had to follow Denmark into the EC in 1973 – whereby Greenlanders saw control over its fisheries transferred from Copenhagen to even further removed Brussels – was crucial to the Greenlandic demands for home rule, which succeeded in 1979 and made the 1985 withdrawal possible. On 9 June 2009, a majority of the people of Greenland voted in favour of enhanced home rule – 'self-government' – still under formal Danish sovereignty. Denmark and Greenland alike are preparing for a future envisioned as one of climate change, intensive raw material extraction, new transportation corridors and new claims to sovereignty over the Arctic. Greenland uses this envisioned future as a lever to enhance its subjectivity, not least when dealing with the European Union (EU).

The Greenland–EU relationship can only be understood as a negotiation of the postcolonial development from a past Danish colonialism to a future independent Greenlandic state: this development involves, first, a tension between being able to pay for one's own welfare system and the preference for deciding for one self. It is felt that the annual cheque from Copenhagen comes with strings attached. In relation to the EU, the challenge is how to maintain the cash flow from Brussels while returning as few fishing quotas as possible and keeping sovereignty from going south. Second, the development involves tension between two distinct approaches to gaining recognition and subjectivity on the world scene. On the one hand, protecting certain practices deemed central to indigenous Inuit culture – specifically, the killing and consumption of certain wild animals – even if achieved by utilizing Danish sovereignty as a lever. On the other hand, posing as a polity in charge of its own business – formal Danish sovereignty or not.

This chapter analyses how the Greenlandic self-image as being on the way to sovereignty – and the tensions involved – structures the triangular relation between the EU, Greenland, and Denmark. Primarily, the chapter focuses on the Greenlandic perspective – but as this is shaped by the mutual relations to Copenhagen and Brussels, the perspectives of Denmark and the EU necessarily come into view.

The next section, first, explains how Greenlandic identity involves the transition towards a sovereign nation-state modelled on the Danish. Second, the section identifies a number of tensions that follow from combining – on the road to sovereignty – a process towards economic self-sufficiency with the protection of symbolic elements of Inuit culture.

The section that follows recapitulates how Greenland's relations to the EU have developed and interfered with the Greenlandic ambitions to move towards independence – and analyses how the Government of Greenland rhetorically presents the relations to the EU of this Greenland working to leave non-sovereignty behind. Particularly, it notes how Denmark is 'photoshopped out' of the stories.

The subsequent section zooms in on the practical games necessary to beef up the bureaucratic muscle of a fragile microstate. Even if the Greenlandic approach has – pragmatically – been to utilize the Danish membership as a platform for its relations to the EU, the tension between development towards self-sustainability and self-government – as well as the tension between indigenous identity and statehood – must be handled. This handling has involved producing independent Greenlandic visibility by downplaying the role of Denmark while relying on an intricate relation in the practical handling of the EU. The chapter concludes that Greenland has used the Danish EU membership wisely as a platform for building its own subjectivity. However, it also concludes that Denmark has had little choice when facilitating the staging of Greenlandic subjectivity.

A postcolonial inconvenience to national identities

Greenland's recent history as a Danish colony began when Norwegian missionary Hans Egede landed in 1721. From the point of departure – the meeting between Inuit and Europeans – identification was straightforward: The Danes were the ones who made the decisions (*naalagat*), were responsible for trade, did the teaching, and lived in wooden or stone houses – whereas the Greenlanders were decided over, went hunting, and lived in tents or turf huts. For a long time, Denmark limited access for Europeans to protect Inuit culture – and thereby protect the supply of tradables provided by the traditional hunters spread along the coast. German romantic nationalism – in a specifically Danish version filtered by the Lutheran theologian N.F.S. Grundtvig – came to apply to Greenland as well: the true potential of the nation – of any nation – demanded the enlightenment of the common man in his own language. As bilingual interlocutors were necessary for transmitting enlightenment from Denmark, an independent Greenlandic elite formed – an elite that aspired to equality with the Danes. But as formal equality was established with the incorporation of Greenland in Denmark in 1953, the everyday experience remained one of a clear ethnic hierarchy. The result was Greenlandic nationalism – a nationalism both formulated against Denmark and formed with a picture of the ideal nation-state which mirrors the 'perfect' coincidence of state, nation, culture, and religion which (after a series of lost wars) is Denmark's self-image.

So when Greenland identifies itself today – that is, when Greenlanders talk about what Greenland is and ought to be – diverse elements are articulated. On the one hand, Greenlandic identity relates to cultural roots. The Greenlandic language is pivotal. So is a close relation to nature and a traditional material culture developed for survival in the High North – therefore a series of practices involving the killing and consumption of wild animals must be protected, practised along the coast (compare Neumann 2002: 110–15), and promoted abroad.

On the other hand, political debates make clear that modern phenomena such as democracy and welfare are equally indispensable elements in what Greenland is and ought to be. And so is the nation-state: no one imagines a Greenland which is not a democratic welfare state. In Greenlandic identity discourse, the national principle is what ties aboriginality and modernity together: Greenland *ought to be* an independent state to allow Greenlandic culture to flourish within a welfare society. Some deem it impossible – some deem it a perspective far removed to the horizon – yet others would declare independence soon. So in terms of Greenlandic discourse, the present situation is not as it ought to be: Greenland is not an independent nation-state. Greenland's present identity is transitional – Greenland sees itself on the way from colonial dependency to future independence. In that sense, becoming independent is part of Greenlandic identity (Gad 2005, 2009a). And in that sense, most Greenlandic domestic politics are almost by definition postcolonial sovereignty games: linguistic games allowed by the concept of sovereignty, played on the way to the realization of independence. These domestic games structure the relations between three political priorities: legal self-government, economic self-sufficiency, and aboriginal cultural identity. Greenland must be allowed to govern itself, and Greenland needs to be able to sustain itself – all the while Greenland must preserve the symbolic elements of Inuit culture anchoring its identity.

To Greenland, then, the relation to Denmark is not as it ought to be. But the relation to Greenland is also peculiar from the Danish perspective. Denmark and the Danes are accustomed to seeing themselves as a cultural nation which built a state for itself (Gad 2010). In Denmark-the-nation-state, there is (ideally) no room for cultural plurality. To have this conception of the nation-state co-exist with an intimate relation to a former colony necessitates linguistic and legal games. Particularly, Danish discourse requires the concept of 'Community of the Realm' *(Rigsfæl-lesskabet)* to make sense of the relation (see Gad 2008, 2009b): The 'realm' works as an extension of 'our state' – necessitated by how the state is intimately tied to 'our nation'. And as Denmark sees itself as on the side of the weak and working for equality (Gad 2008, 2009b, 2010), this 'realm' cannot be conceived of as a hierarchical relation. Being colonizers does not fit Denmark's self-image, so the realm is something which the Danes have 'in common' *(fælles)* with the Greenlanders.[2] The main element in the 'Community of the Realm' – apart from legal submission – is an annual block grant from Denmark to Greenland. This element adds to the Danish self-image of being a force for good in the world: Denmark prides itself on being in the very top when it comes to giving development aid. In the same way, the annual grants to Greenland serve as proof of maternal benevolence – only in this relation, the colonial past makes conditionality impossible: Denmark paternalistically demands good governance in sub-Saharan Africa – but interference in Greenlandic affairs is a much more sensitive issue (Gad 2008, 2009b).

So Greenlandic and Danish self-images overlap sufficiently to allow the continuation of the relation. The basic way of legitimizing constitutional and economic dependency on both sides of the Atlantic Ocean is an agreement that Greenland requires assistance in developing towards self-sustenance and self-government (Gad 2008, 2009b). The flip side of this is that the continuation of this narrative of the *raison d'être* of the Community is endangered whenever it is implied that Greenland will never be capable of independence – or when it is implied that Denmark has other motives than assisting Greenland towards this goal. To keep up appearances, both sides engage in games – games that are ultimately made possible but also made necessary by the either/or concept of sovereignty.

Meanwhile, a new sovereignty game is taking shape: the Arctic is envisioned as opening up to new players by a changing climate melting the ice. On one dimension, this is a traditional horizontal sovereignty game between the five Arctic states (Russia, Canada, the US, Norway, and Denmark), each seeking to secure the largest share of the Arctic Ocean by submitting geological evidence of continental continuity in accordance with the UN Convention on the Law of the Seas (Strandsbjerg 2011) – and with huge corporations ready to step in to extract resources (Refsnes 2011). On another level, the either/or concept of sovereignty implied in the claims of the 'Arctic 5' is challenged both by indigenous peoples submitting claims for sovereignty which structure space differently (Shadian 2010; Gerhardt 2011) and by environmentalists as well as non-Arctic states proposing further international regulation to protect nature or allocate resources differently. In this game, Denmark's strategy has been to promote the Arctic Council as the relevant body of governance, thereby escaping the 'realist' version of sovereignty-as-either/or (determined by the raw *power* to protect sovereignty). The Arctic Council uniquely bolsters the traditional 'legal positivist' version of sovereignty-as-either/or (determined by the *right* of the member states to have sovereignty) with the extra legitimacy obtained from granting a special status as 'permanent participants' to a number of indigenous peoples. Meanwhile, Greenland utilizes this new game to separate itself further from its former colonizer – as will be clear from the next sections analysing how the EU is engaged.

Greenlandic visions of sovereign equality

Greenland was until recently the only part of the EC which has ceded membership status. The urge to leave the EC was so strong that it was decisive in the struggle for home rule (see Lauritzen 1997: 15–21). In 1973, Denmark became a member of the EC. Greenland was, since the 1953 constitution, considered a part of Denmark – so despite a 70 per cent majority in Greenland against accession in the 1972 referendum, Greenland joined Denmark in the EC (N. Petersen 2006). The referendum campaign in Greenland focused on fisheries: now Copenhagen decides who may catch our fish – in the future, the decisions will be taken even further away; in Brussels (Skydsbjerg 1999: 25). To allow for more – not less – subjectivity, new legal arrangements were called for.

Greenlandic home rule was established in 1979 – and in 1982, a 53 per cent majority in a consultative referendum asked for Greenland to leave the EC. The negotiations on the unprecedented situation took a couple of years and involved

European, Danish, and Greenlandic officials (see Motzfeldt 2003, 2006; Vester-birk 2006). The result was 'The Greenland Treaty', which moved Greenland from being part of the Danish membership to the provisions included in the treaty for the OCTs of the member states. Concerning fishery products – Greenland's sole export – the tax-free access to the EU market provided by the OCT arrangement became conditional on '[satisfactory] possibilities for access to Greenland fishing zones granted to the Community'.[3] The package deal negotiated did indeed include such a 'satisfactory' fishery agreement. This meant that the EC could keep its fishing rights in the Greenlandic Exclusive Economic Zone, but Greenland kept the payments from the EC it had received thus far from the social and structural funds; the figure on the check actually even increased (Skydsbjerg 1999: 26).[4]

In sum, Greenland left the EC and took the money with it – both the lump sum development money converted into fisheries payments and the tax-free access to the EU market. As the Greenlanders had already 'taken home' from Copenhagen the fisheries policy as a home rule issue – and as Copenhagen had left its fisheries policy to Brussels – Nuuk has had de facto sovereignty over fisheries since 1985; a sovereignty used to trade fish for cash. But the cash stream soon appeared uncertain, and sovereignty did not in itself secure cultural identity.

First, concerning the money, the problem sprang from the fact that some of the fish sold were 'paper fish' which the Commission had, in the first instance, invented so that they could be redistributed in the continuous haggling over quotas.[5] The Greenlandic cod fisheries collapsed in 1990, as the sea temperature had fallen slightly (Government of Greenland 2005) – the EU continued to buy the right to catch cod, should they return. In parallel, the EC paid for a stock of red-fish which remained a biological hypothesis (Kommissionen 2003). During the 1990s, the Commission – pressured by the European Court of Auditors and the European Parliament, which had gained influence on the fisheries policy – found that the money spent on Greenlandic paper fish could be spent better on material fish along the coastlines of African states. A substitute for the EU budget line for 'fisheries agreements' appeared increasingly urgent. Access to the EU's external development fund was not a viable option: the average level of income and welfare in Greenland was well over that of the African, Caribbean and Pacific (ACP) countries. Access to the EU's internal regional fund would not do the trick, either: after the inclusion of the new Eastern European member states in the 2004 enlargement, Greenland was more affluent than the average EU member state.

In 2006, a solution was found: a joint declaration concerning an EU/Greenland partnership was issued as an umbrella covering the fisheries agreement and a new special partnership agreement foreseeing increased cooperation in a number of areas presumably of interest to the EU, such as minerals, transportation, and climate research. Crucially, the partnership agreement legitimized a budget line allowing the funding of Greenlandic sustainable development. In the first programming period (2007–12), funding is directed to the Greenlandic budget for education and the development of human resources. Greenlandic society *is* far from sustainable in this area, as many of the jobs requiring formal education are manned by short- or long-term immigrants (mainly Danes, but also other nationalities). Again, Greenland and Denmark secured the payment from Brussels despite the change in Greenland's legal position.[6]

Second, and less immediately reparable, formal sovereignty did not immediately secure cultural identity: one of the weightiest arguments for seceding from the EC was that Greenland would be better at managing its fisheries for its own benefit than Denmark and the EC. A couple of decades later, there is not entire agreement that this turned out to be the case. Crucial in this regard is, of course, what is meant by 'better management'. Lars Mathæussen, president of a local union of fishermen, explains why he now favours re-accession to the EU: 'We need to accept that fisheries management hasn't improved, and deep sea fishing is controlled by a handful of people' (Mølgaard 2010). This quote highlights a central struggle taking place domestically in Greenland – which produces a separate category of problems in relation to the EU. On the one hand, the Greenlandic identity discourse implies development towards self-sufficiency under the conditions of a globalizing world economy. This has implied the centralization of deep sea fishing on very few boats, controlled by very few people. On the other hand, Greenlandic identity discourse involves care for a traditional culture – which is implied to involve a distribution of the population in small settlements along the coastline, depending for their livelihood on small-scale fisheries and hunting.

Western animal rights groups have attacked a series of indigenous hunting practices (e.g. whaling, sealing, trapping). These practices do not have the same bearing on the Greenlandic budget as deep sea fisheries, but they carry weight as they pertain to icons of Inuit culture. In a series of these cases, Greenland has worked to influence the EU – either to change EU regulations threatening Greenlandic interests or to gain European support in preventing international regulation or challenging national regulation in the US and other countries. In these cases, Greenland has variously attempted to limit and influence but also to employ Danish and EU sovereignty further abroad.

As the present Greenlandic prime minister explains, Greenland has consciously chosen to 'use the Danish platform' when dealing with the EU.[7] The choice of metaphor is interesting: a platform is something you stand on to reach things you would otherwise not be able to reach. In terms of the metaphor, the Greenlanders are the active part doing their own thing, while the Danish platform is passive. When the Government of Greenland presents its visions of the relations in public, it goes even further and ends up retouching Denmark out of the picture.

First, when speaking of the relation to EU in the Greenlandic parliament, Denmark already disappears from the *present* picture: the present status – supplementing the OCT status with the partnership and fisheries agreements – allows direct dialogue with the EU without Danish interference. The Government contrasts this situation to a *future* return to membership – which would mean a return to depending on Danish goodwill.[8]

Second, the Government of Greenland takes the Commission Green Paper on the revision of the OCT decision (cf. Hannibal, Holst *et al.*, this volume) as an occasion to present its general view of the relation to the EU[9] – and the substance of the vision is unique when compared to the other OCTs: Greenland avails itself of the discourse about a future Arctic bonanza to describe itself as in command of unique resources. Thus constructed, the subjectivity allows Greenland to choose to offer the resources either to the EU or someone else, depending on how forthcoming the partners turn out to be in relation to Greenland's need for both cash flow and recognition of the symbolically important cultural practices involving the hunting of wild animals. Notably, Denmark is not mentioned when this future is described. In that way, Greenland presents itself as an independent subject capable of engaging in a traditional zero-sum sovereignty game with the EU.[10]

This tendency to retouch Denmark out of the picture is not only present in rhetoric. It also structures the practical handling of the relation, which is the focus in the next section.

Handling the relation in diplomatic practice[11]

The Prime Minister of Greenland describes Denmark as a 'platform' for Greenland's relation to the EU – and when the government of Greenland envisions the future relation to the EU, it is one of sovereign equality. However, the practical games played in Brussels seem to imply a distribution of agency which is more complex than the platform metaphor would allow. A number of games particularly serve the purpose of upholding the image of an (active) Greenlandic subject performing on a (passive) Danish platform – or even an image which does not include Denmark at all. This section analyses these games, first, to see how Greenlandic equality and independent visibility are produced. Second, the section zooms in on the distribution of roles between the Greenlandic and Danish bureaucrats involved in the substance of Greenlandic EU affairs.

Producing independent visibility in Brussels

The 1978 Home Rule Act stipulated that '[t]he home rule authorities may demand that in countries in which Greenland has special commercial interest Danish diplomatic missions employ officers specifically to attend to such interests' (section 16(1)). Since 1992, a Greenlandic representative has worked in the Danish diplomatic mission in Brussels and held diplomatic status. Even if the arrangement departed in the renewal of the fisheries agreement, what was described in the legal text as 'commercial' interests was immediately re-interpreted to be the 'full spectre' national interests of Greenland in relation to the EU (Vesterbirk 2006). Today, four persons work full-time in Brussels for Greenland, two of whom have (Danish) diplomatic passports.

One of the ways the first Greenlandic representative interpreted the national interest of Greenland was to insist on an independent visual presence (see Vesterbirk 2006: 131). This priority took a number of forms. One result was that when the Danish representation moved to new offices, a visitor to the representatives of Greenland or the Faroes no longer had to enter through a door flanked by a Danish coat of arms and a Danish flag – rather, they would enter through a separate door guided by the Greenlandic and the Faroese insignia.[12]

More recent renovations to the interior of the building have finally put an end to the flip side of independent visibility: the demand for a separate entrance door outside the control of the Danish authorities meant that a security door had to be installed between the Greenlandic and Faroese representations and the Danish representation. Unfortunately, no bathrooms or even running water were on the 'North Atlantic' side of the door. Employees could enter using a magnetic card – but visitors without security clearing, such as a Greenlandic minister, had to be escorted to a Danish bathroom.[13] This year – after the introduction of self-government, coincidentally – independent bathrooms were installed.[14]

There are two reasons for mentioning what might seem a trivial detail. First, of course, the anecdote symbolizes in an irresistible manner that independence has a price. Second, it is the first in a series of examples of how Denmark is still around, even when Greenland is on its own in Brussels. Notably, however, the presence and absence of Denmark is carefully measured and explained – by Greenlanders and Danes alike – in different ways on different occasions. The elephant may be in the room. It may be right next door. Or it may turn into a mouse. But most of the time it is there.

Let us continue our narrative of a Greenlandic politician visiting Brussels: a regular point on the programme is a visit to the Danish ambassador to receive a briefing on how Denmark handles current EU affairs of interest to Greenland.[15] Here, the distinction between the Greenlandic and Danish sides is upheld, but two hierarchies are constructed simultaneously: first, the colonial hierarchy is re-installed as the Greenlandic minister has to go from 'his own' premises to those of the metropole. But second, a different hierarchy is constructed as the ambassador briefs the minister: that between a civil servant and a political executive.

Back on the Greenlandic side of the door, Denmark's presence will continue to be felt even if only Greenlanders are present. When talking to the Greenlandic representatives, repeated references are made to 'our member state' or to 'in there', both often accompanied by a nod in the direction of the Danish representation behind the wall.[16]

On one of the main points on the programme of a Greenlandic minister's visit to Brussels, however, Denmark tends to turn invisible: when a Greenlandic minister goes to talk to a Commissioner, Denmark does not interfere. There might be a junior Danish diplomat present in the room – they might be visible to the accompanying Greenlandic officials and perhaps to the Commission officials. But the Greenlandic minister would not necessarily notice.[17] Such a set-up not only requires Danish acceptance but also acceptance from the third party: in this case, the EU facilitates the independent Greenlandic appearance.

In one specific venue in Brussels, Greenlandization is already implemented 100 per cent: Denmark never follows Greenland to meetings in the OCT Association (OCTA)[18] – when its political leadership meets in annual ministerial meetings in one of the OCTs or when the executive committee meets more frequently in Brussels. Danish representatives are still present in tripartite meetings (Commission, metropole member states, OCTs) – but mainly to show symbolic support to

Greenland. As two Danish officials explain (the one repeating the other almost verbatim), Greenland usually behaves reasonably, so there is really no need to control them in detail.[19] Most of the OCTA business relates to projects and pro-grammes under the European Development Fund (EDF). Greenland, however, does not have access to the EDF – except as part of certain special, cross-cut-ting projects dedicated to the OCTs. Given that the economic interest of Green-land in this main focus of OCTA is rather marginal,[20] why has Greenland become involved, and even done so in leading roles?

When speaking with Greenlandic officials, they explicitly mention two very different reasons. The first is about boosting the importance of Greenlandic con-cerns by being part of something larger. Whereas the fisheries agreements are solidly rooted in EU's interest in gaining access to Greenlandic fish stocks, the partnership agreement is much more fragilely anchored on the EU side: the devel-opment of Greenland appears a bit lonesome as a purpose when listed in the EU budget – but when by inscribing itself as 'one of the OCTs' (even if a special one), a number of potential allies are constructed. Greenland might be special but it is not alone. And in parallel; even if Greenland counts itself as comparably well-known in Brussels, OCTA is judged to be a valuable platform for gaining attention as worthy partners in issues like climate change because it makes visible how the Greenlandic concerns are part of a larger pattern which echoes in the OCTs of other member states.[21] As summed up by the then Greenlandic Minister for For-eign Affairs in a parliamentary debate in 2007: 'OCTA has shown itself to have a much greater clout than the individual OCT countries can have'.[22] By contributing more work to OCTA than appears to be in Greenland's immediate self-interest, Greenland expects to gain general goodwill with member states other than its own – which can be spent later in specific cases when needed.[23]

The second reason for engaging in OCTA initially appears to be much more mundane: it prepares Greenlandic officials for greater tasks. The work in OCTA's executive committee is explicitly described as a place where young Greenlandic diplomats learn the trade of international relations in practice. The forum is not terribly important for Greenland, but spending time and effort there is regarded as useful because it provides experience which will be useful in other fora.[24]

The way Greenlandic officials describe their experiences with the work in OCTA suggests, however, that this rather mundane reason has extra dimensions to it: OCTA seems to be the ideal place to practise sovereign equality. The first extra dimension to this argument is that the organization might have the same function for the Greenlandic ministers: contrary to the OCT fora, which are tri-partite (Commission, metropole member states, OCTs), the Greenlandic ministers are on their own among equals in the OCTA ministerial meetings. In that sense, these meetings – with no authorities posing as superiors – are the perfect place to practise for sovereign equality. And more than that, it provides a forum in which Greenland is not only equal but in many ways slightly superior – a point repeat-edly mentioned by Greenlandic officials: Greenland may contribute to OCTA because it has more bureaucratic muscle (in Brussels and in general) than most OCTs[25] and – related – because Greenland has one of the most 'advanced' home rule arrangements;[26] which of course relates to the fact that, as one leading Greenlandic official puts it, 'not all the OCTs have the same aspirations' for independent agency and, perhaps, for future formal sovereignty.[27]

Finally, the concern for visibility has also involved taking a number of individual EU counterparts to Greenland to let them see for themselves. A saying in the select circle of Greenlandic foreign policy bureaucrats is that 'the most profitable tourism in Greenland is ministerial tourism'. The point is that it is much easier to have it your way in negotiations, if the politician presiding over the counterpart has experienced first-hand the hardship of survival in the High North – and marvelled over the beauty of the Ilulissat Icefiorth.[28] Whether organizing such trips really pays off is, of course, difficult to decide. But it appears as though Danish ministers are also susceptible to the charms of inviting counterparts to Greenland: where else may you, due to logistical necessity, have the undivided attention of a member of the European Commission for days? However, the protocols of the Dano-Greenlandic relation generally demands that the Greenlandic third party is invited along. Under the 2000 visit of the then President of the European Commission Romano Prodi, everything seems to have formed a synthesis: personalities which hit it off, upcoming negotiations on Greenlandic agreements with the EU, a Danish prime minister preparing enlargements under an upcoming Danish presidency, a Commission president and his wife in a holiday mood. The logistics even failed at the perfect time: for hours, the party (including the VIPs) were isolated, way out of the reach of mobile phones, at the solitary ruins of the old Norse church at Hvalsey – and the Air Greenland helicopter first returned to pick them back up after a considerable delay. Considerable, that is, to the civil servants – the VIPs seemed to enjoy the break without making much of the fact that they were out of reach of the world and vice versa. The fact that the hosts of the final informal dinner at the sheep owners' annual gathering had become a bit tipsy when the honorary guests arrived only made everyone involved more positively spirited.[29]

Increased independent visibility appears to have paid off. Greenlandic officials stress that it is now easier to get to business in Brussels when needed than a decade ago[30] – simply because there is a higher degree of awareness that Greenland exists. In recent years, the active promotion of Greenlandic visibility has been aided by the rising position on the agenda of global warming and related visions of both increased access to natural resources in the Arctic and the potentially ensuing conflicts and environmental problems (Strandsbjerg *et al.* 2011). The EU is currently formulating an Arctic Policy, and the Greenlandic officials in Brussels feel almost overwhelmed by invitations to present their positions as everyone seems to want to arrange their own 'Arctic seminar'.[31]

From continuity to change

Most of those interviewed on the topic agree that persons matter when a fragile, small-scale diplomatic corps is working.[32] Since the branching off of Greenlandic EU relations from Danish EU relations in the mid-80s, they have basically been handled by the same trio: Greenland's representative in Brussels, Greenland's chief fisheries negotiator – both were Danes with personal ties to Greenland, who began their carriers in the Danish colonial administration but were 'taken home' by the home rule government after it was established in 1979 – and the Danish Ministry of Foreign Affairs' (MFA) old hand on Greenland's EU relations.

A basic benefit of continuity was, of course, first-hand experience with previous rounds of negotiations with the EU and the opportunity to consistently build up 'textual levers' for future benefits by contributing to the self-description of the other: as part of the reason for annually subsidizing the development of Greenland with 25 million euros, the EC states that 'the European Community has a continuing geostrategic interest in treating Greenland, being part of a member state, as a privileged neighbour and in contributing to Greenland's wellbeing and economic development'. Tracing this sentence backwards, it must have passed through computers in Copenhagen and Nuuk.[33]

Furthermore, the continuity of the Greenland/EU portfolio in the Danish MFA secured that at least one person in Denmark had qualified attention to EU issues that might be relevant for Greenland in a way that does not conform to regular Danish priorities.[34] This concern was why the Government of Greenland requested the continuity.[35] The flip side of the continuity, however, was Greenlanders ultimately worrying that the Danish MFA might find that loyalty shifted from Copenhagen to Nuuk, endangering the point of the whole set-up.[36]

In more subtle ways, the continuity of portfolios – and the continuity of personal experience and contacts across the fine line between Danish and Greenlandic bureaucracy – provided advantages to the home rule government in negotiations. When comparing his conditions to those of his Icelandic colleagues, one Greenlandic official notes that inside knowledge of the EU's internal coordination procedures has made a significant difference – not only in terms of the elegance with which the negotiations could be conducted but also in terms of the results. The inside knowledge came both from personal experience from earlier assignments within what was then the Danish Ministry for Greenland – but also from relating to sympathetic Danish colleagues sitting on the European side of the table representing Denmark as a member state in the internal EU coordination.[37]

Moreover, continuity allowed the trio to develop a distinct distribution of roles. Particularly interesting is the postcolonial blame games (see Kristensen 2004) occasionally played by one Greenlandic official. They involved kicking doors open to get access and slamming them behind him when leaving meetings in anger.[38] It also involved 'publically' criticizing the Danish official present at a meeting with European counterparts for acting in a 'colonialist' manner.[39]

Overall, it is difficult not to find the outcome of the games to be successful, when considering the core priorities of Greenland: to keep both the cash flow from Brussels and self-government in fisheries intact. When asked to explain this success, however, interviewees place the decisive agency differently: while some insist that the result came about because the assets which Greenland commands (fish) were simply necessary for the EU to acquire,[40] others ascribe the success to the elaborate and broad-spectrum preparatory efforts coordinated between Greenland and Denmark, including the combination of ministerial tourism, writing the self-interest of the EU, and documenting Greenland's needs and potentials in detail.[41] And yet others insist that what made the EU agree was a high-level conversation in which the Commission President asked the Danish Prime Minister whether 'the member state *really* meant' the demands put forward by the Greenlanders.[42] More interesting than the question of which story might be the best approximation to reality is to note how the three narratives match three different political stances to the present and future of the Community of the Realm (see above): an unnecessary straitjacket for Greenland; a handy working relationship; or the framework for maternalistic Danish benevolence.

In the cases in which Inuit hunting and fishing traditions have been under attack, Danish support – especially in the Council of Ministers – has undoubtedly been central to any success with influencing the EU. But Danish support has neither been unlimited nor automatic, as the Danish position is to be formulated as a compromise between North Atlantic priorities versus Danish public opinion and consistency with the position Denmark advocates in comparable cases outside the Community of the Realm.[43] A recent case provides a vivid example of the importance attached to the issue and the trappings of handling it: in 2009, the EU prepared a ban on the import of sealskin. In a letter to addressed to the presidents of the European Commission and the European Parliament, the speaker of the Greenlandic parliament warned that Europe was repeating the colonial policies pursued in South America 400 years ago and thereby committing 'cultural genocide' (Motzfeldt, in KNR 2009; see also ICC 2009). Behind the fears for the collapsing market was the threat against cultural practices described as essential to Inuit identity (Gad 2005: Ch. 2; Fægteborg 1990) posed by Western standards of 'humane' treatment of animals.[44] Concerted and persistent Danish–Greenlandic action secured that the recent ban on import of sealskin exempts skins harvested by traditional hunters. However, this exemption did not alleviate the fears of the Government of Greenland that sealskin would for all practical purposes be impossible to sell in Europe (Government of Greenland 2009). At one point, the Greenlandic government considered asking Denmark to act on its behalf in the World Trade Organization to challenge the ban on the import of sealskin which the EU (including Denmark) had introduced.[45]

The members of the trio handling Greenland's EU relations all retired between 2007 and 2011. The generational change has entailed the 'Greenlandization' of the handling of Greenland's EU relations, which is described as 'only natural'.[46] The relations are now handled by Greenlanders, products of Danish and international higher education with the home rule administration as their central job experience. Apart from the Greenlandization, however, the generational change also seems to involve a Danish detachment: the Greenland/EU file in the MFA has been merged with the general Greenland file and allocated to a Greenlander temporally employed and a career diplomat without previous Arctic experience now appointed as 'Arctic Ambassador' – while the Greenland file at the Danish permanent representation in Brussels is now a side task for younger diplomats circling in and out of town every few years.[47] It already seems as though the bulk of the workload and the initiative in handling the more day-to-day business of Greenland vis-à-vis the

EU has gradually shifted from the Danish to the Greenlandic side.[48] Asked about the possible consequences of the generational change for the – more heavy-duty – negotiations of Greenland's partnership and fisheries agreements with the EU, a central Greenlandic official finds that losing the memory of alternatives left behind 'may, after all, be both bad *and* good'.[49]

Conclusion

Greenland has kept the size of its payments from Brussels constant across a series of potential hurdles: across the introduction of home rule in the face of a Danish bureaucracy accustomed to taking care of Greenlandic affairs; across withdrawal from membership and 'taking home' sovereignty over fisheries from Brussels to the home rule government established partly for this purpose; and across the introduction of parliamentary scrutiny of the EU budget. In terms of output, this can hardly count as anything but sovereignty games well played.

However, the combination of the use of 'the Danish platform' with a national identity narrative projecting a sovereign Greenlandic nation-state has necessitated that games are played with present Danish sovereignty in both the practical handling and the discursive presentation of the relations to the EU. Particularly, in a number of ways, Denmark is gradually retouched out of the picture.

This arrangement has also been convenient for Denmark: by 'allowing' Greenland to act independently, Denmark can escape the embarrassment of having the 'colonialist' label applied internationally. More importantly, however, Denmark seems to have realized that in relation to Greenland, playing traditional colonialist games is the only sure way to cut a postcolony loose. Especially when the postcolony may avail itself of a discourse on booming resources in the Arctic to beef up its visions of itself as a future independent player.

This far down the road, the combination of independent Greenlandic visibility and the Danish platform has worked: Greenland is envisioning its own sovereignty into being; it is telling a narrative of independent agency which is successfully inviting others to partake in the realization of the narrative. All the while Denmark is protecting its sovereignty over Greenland in the sense that it downplays formal Danish authority in relation to Greenland and facilitates Greenlandic agency in relation to the EU. But continuing these narratives without ending in full formal Greenlandic sovereignty will demand considerable creativity in both Greenland and Denmark, bearing in mind how the concept of a homogenous nation-state structures identity on both sides of the Atlantic.

Notes

1 Special thanks to the politicians, civil servants, and diplomats who gave their time for interviews – and to Rebecca Adler-Nissen, Uffe Jacobsen, and Iver Neumann for valuable comments on an earlier version of this article.
2 The Greenlandic term for 'Community of the Realm', *naalagaaffeqatigiinneq*, literally translates into a relation which is even more explicitly equal than the Danish version: *naalagaq*, meaning the one who decides – in this case what is done is qatigiinneq,

something done together with someone (else) (Lennert 2006: 1, n. 2; Gad 2008: 122). Critics insist that, in legal terms, the 'community' part of the label is void, as the label covers unilateral delegations from the Danish Parliament (Høydal 2000), even if some legal scholars doubt that the delegations may be withdrawn (Harhoff 2003).

3 This treaty and other documents which comprise the legal relation between Greenland and the EU are available via http://eu.nanoq.gl/Emner/EuGl.aspx, accessed 19 January 2012.

4 The economic transfer which resulted from the negotiations was so large that it surprised some of those who had wanted to stay in the EU (Lauritzen 1997: 289f), but others argued that the fish sold should have been processed by the developing Greenlandic fisheries industry (Skydsbjerg 1999: 26).

5 Former Greenlandic official, interviewed in Copenhagen, 17 December 2010. The EC not only needs these fishing rights for their own fishing vessels: parts of the rights are traded on to Norway, Iceland, and Russia in exchange for EU fishing rights in the Exclusive Economic Zones of these countries.

6 Danish transfers cover 56 per cent (400 million euros) of the annual home rule budget of roughly 700 million euros. From 2001 to 2006, the EU fisheries agreement secured a further 6 per cent (42.8 million euros). For the period 2007–13, this amount has been split in two: 17.8 million euros for fisheries rights and 25 million euros for sustainable development. See Government of Greenland (2006: 8).

7 Prime Minister Kuupik Kleist, telephone interview, 28 March 2011.

8 For a detailed analysis, see Gad (forthcoming).

9 The Greenlandic response to the Commission was not co-ordinated with the Danish MFA (Danish official, interviewed in Copenhagen, 14 September 2009).

10 For a detailed analysis, see Gad *et al.* (2011) and Hannibal and Holst (2010). The vision is picked up by a German EU analyst advocating for EU support to Greenlandic independence (Schymik 2009).

11 This section builds on 19 interviews – plus a number of informal conversations – with diplomats, bureaucrats, and politicians from Greenland, Denmark, and the EU currently or previously handling the relations between the EU and Greenland. The interviews were conducted in Brussels, Copenhagen, and Nuuk in 2009–11, most face-to-face, a few via telephone. The reading of the interviews – as well as how they were conducted – was influenced by the 'field work' conducted by the author while employed in the home rule bureaucracy in 1998–2001 and 2004. All of the quotes have been anonymized to secure the anonymity of the interviewees who stipulated this as a condition for their participation. A number of the interviews were conducted by Ida Hannibal and Kristine Holst – I am grateful for being allowed to use their material and for being inspired by their analysis reported in (2010). Two of the interviews were conducted together with Rebecca Adler-Nissen.

12 According to Greenlandic officials in Brussels, the arrangement is especially noticed and commented on by visitors from other self-governing micropolities (Greenlandic official, interviewed in Brussels, 24 March 2011).

13 A parallel issue may have more serious repercussions: as the computers of the Greenlandic officials are not hooked up with the – security-cleared – network of the Danish Ministry of Foreign Affairs (MFA), certain security-cleared information may not be sent to them. This might have been of limited consequence were it not for the fact that the outside status means that Greenland misses not only security-cleared mails but also other mails circulated which are only circulated to insiders.

14 Greenlandic official, interviewed in Brussels, 24 March 2011.

15 Greenlandic official, interviewed in Brussels, 24 March 2011.

16 Greenlandic official, interviewed in Brussels, 24 March 2011.

17 Greenlandic official, interviewed in Copenhagen, 24 February 2011. Neither would the Commissioner, for that matter, even if his staff would probably expect a Danish diplomat to be present – to secure that the Commission does not interfere in the

constitutional arrangements of a member state (Commission official, interviewed in Brussels, 24 March 2011).

18 This organization is introduced in Hannibal, Holst *et al.*'s contribution to this volume.

19 Four former and present Danish and Greenlandic officials, interviewed in Copenhagen and Brussels, 9 September 2009, 17 December 2010, 28 January 2011, and 24 March 2011.

20 Three Greenlandic officials, interviewed in Copenhagen, 17 December 2010, 12 January 2011, and 28 January 2011.

21 Two Greenlandic officials, interviewed in Copenhagen and Brussels, 28 January 2011 and 24 March 2011. One Commission official (interviewed in Brussels, 24 March 2011) mentions a related practical reason for prioritizing OCTA and the tripartite OCT Fora: it secures institutionalized face-time – and even leisure time, when fora are annually held in one of the OCTs – with high-level Commission officials, including the Commissioner. This concern might, however, not be as important for Greenland due to how it excels in 'ministerial tourism', as described below.

22 Josef Motzfeldt (Inuit Community Party), Minister for Finances and Foreign Affairs, 24 April 2007.

23 Former and present Greenlandic officials, interviewed in Copenhagen, 17 December 2010, and 28 January 2011. This idea of getting abstract credit to cash in on later for helping others out has been found to be generally perceived as a norm in the EU, particularly in the committees under the Council of Ministers (Adler-Nissen 2009).

24 Two Greenlandic officials, interviewed in Copenhagen, 12 January 2011 and 28 January 2011.

25 Three former and present Greenlandic officials, interviewed in Copenhagen, 17 December 2010, 12 January 2011, and 28 January 2011.

26 Two leading Greenlandic officials, interviewed in Copenhagen, 12 January 2011 and 28 March 2011.

27 Leading Greenlandic official, interviewed in Copenhagen, 28 March 2011.

28 The two aspects of the trips – tourism and knowledge-gathering – are stressed to varying degrees by the Greenlandic officials interviewed. But most imply – sometimes by intonation or facial gestures – that the touristic aspect is not always insignificant. The whole business of inviting the right people to secure smooth negotiations seems, however, to have become much more difficult, as the European Parliament is increasingly involved in approving the international agreements of the EU (former Greenlandic official, interviewed in Copenhagen, 28 March 2011).

29 Former Greenlandic official, interviewed in Copenhagen, 28 March 2011. Photos available at: www.greenland-guide.dk/leif2000/day2day.htm.

30 Two former and present Greenlandic officials, interviewed in Copenhagen and Brussels, 17 December 2010 and 24 March 2011.

31 Three former and present Greenlandic officials, interviewed in Copenhagen and Brussels, 17 December 2010, 28 January 2011 and 24 March 2011.

32 This was a basic tenet in almost all of the interviews on the Greenlandic case – but also in interviews on other OCTs (Hannibal and Holst 2010; see also H. Petersen 2006: 12–13).

33 An earlier example of Greenland writing itself into EU policy documents via Copenhagen is the invention of an 'Arctic Window' in the 'Northern Dimension' EU policy. The Northern Dimension was originally devised by Finland to focus on Russia as a counterweight to the focus on the Mediterranean neighbours of the EU. Following a Greenlandic initiative (Vesterbirk 2006: 157), however, an 'Arctic Window' stretched the area covered by the Dimension to the West. The formulations of the Arctic Window were later used as one hook among others for arguing the necessity of a benevolent agreement with Greenland to serve the EU's interests in the Arctic (Former Greenlandic official, telephone interview, 28 March 2011).

34 Even if this 'filter' has not been able to identify all potential problems, let alone defuse them (such as the case of the EU ban on the import of seal skins discussed below).
35 Greenlandic official, interviewed in Denmark, 12 January 2011.
36 Both former and present Greenlandic officials mentioned as a potential problem – for Greenland, but also for the interlocutor in question, and ultimately for the Community of the Realm – that the Danish MFA might judge him as being too loyal to Greenland (and therefore not sufficiently loyal to Denmark). Three former and present Greenlandic officials interviewed in Copenhagen, 17 December 2010, 12 January 2011, and 24 March 2011.
37 Former Greenlandic official, interviewed in Copenhagen, 17 December 2010.
38 Former Greenlandic official, interviewed in Copenhagen, 2 October 2009.
39 Whether or not these allegations from the Greenlandic representative were spontaneously prompted or strategically devised with or without the consent of the Danish representative (former and present Greenlandic and Danish officials, interviewed in Copenhagen and Brussels, 14 September 2009, 2 October 2009, and 24 March 2011).
40 Greenlandic official, interviewed in Copenhagen, 12 January 2011.
41 Former Greenlandic official, interviewed in Copenhagen, 2 October 2009.
42 Danish official, interviewed in Copenhagen, 14 September 2009.
43 Three Danish and Greenlandic officials, interviewed in Copenhagen and Brussels, 14 September 2009, 12 January 2011, and 24 March 2011.
44 Sealskin (and in parallel whaling, etc.) arguably, also has importance for the household budgets of a certain number of individual Greenlanders living off subsistence and/or subsidized hunting and fishing.
45 Kuupik Kleist (Inuit Community Party), Chairman of the *Naalakkersuisut* (prime minister), speaking in *Inatsisartut* (parliament), 16 June 2009.
46 Leading Greenlandic official, interviewed in Copenhagen, 28 March 2011. The term 'Greenlandization' is notoriously polyvalent. It involves at least the formal transfer of decisions and administration from Copenhagen to Nuuk – but may as a programmatic slogan also involve linguistic, ethnic, and mental changes (Tobiassen 1995; Gad 2008: 121–2).
47 Informal conversations with three Danish and Greenlandic officials, Copenhagen, 15 March 2011, Brussels 24 March 2011, Nuuk 17 April 2011, and Copenhagen 31 January 2012.
48 Five present and former Danish and Greenlandic officials, interviewed in Copenhagen and Brussels, 9 September 2009, 17 December 2010, 28 January 2011, and 24 March 2011. High tension cases involving 'wild animals' necessarily provoke work on both sides as well as in Nuuk and Copenhagen.
49 Three leading Greenlandic officials interviewed in Copenhagen, 12 January 2011, 24 March 2011, and 28 March 2011. Not all non-leading officials appear equally confident (former Greenlandic official, interviewed in Copenhagen, 17 December 2010).
50 Leading Greenlandic official, interviewed in Copenhagen, 28 March 2011.

References

Adler-Nissen, R. (2009) 'Late sovereign diplomacy', *Hague Journal of Diplomacy*, 4(2): 121–41.

Fægteborg, M. (1990) 'Den menneskelige dimension', *Tidsskriftet Grønland*, 8: 98–100.

Gad, U.P. (2005) *Dansksprogede grønlænderes plads i et Grønland under grønlandisering og modernisering*, Copenhagen: Eskimologis Skrifter, No. 19.

Gad, U.P. (2008) 'Når mor/barn-relationen bliver teenager: kompatible rigsfællesskabsbilleder som (dis)integrationsteori', *Politica*, 40(2): 111–33.

Gad, U.P. (2009a) 'Post-colonial identity in Greenland?', *Journal of Language and Politics*, 8(1): 136–58.

Gad, U.P. (2009b) 'Un avenir postcolonial groenlando-danois? Trois scénarios pour la dissolution de la Communauté du royaume: et trois autres pour son maintien et sa modification', *Nordiques*, 18: 69–87.

Gad, U.P. (2010) '(How) can they become like us? Danish identity politics and conflicts of "Muslim Relations"'. PhD dissertation, Department of Political Science, University of Copenhagen.

Gad, U.P. (forthcoming) 'Greenland: a post-Danish sovereign nation state in the making', in *Cooperation & Conflict*, special issue on 'Post-Imperial Sovereignty Games in Norden'.

Gad, U.P., Hannibal, I., Holst, K. and Adler-Nissen, R. (2011) 'EUs oversøiske lande og territorier: postkoloniale suverænitetsspil og Grønlands arktiske muligheder', *Tidsskriftet Politik*, special issue on the Arctic, 14(1): 15–24.

Gerhardt, H. (2011) 'The Inuit and sovereignty: the case of the Inuit Circumpolar Conference and Greenland', *Tidsskriftet Politik*, 14(1): 6–14.

Government of Greenland (2005) *Fakta om dyrene: Art: Torsk/banketorsk (den atlantiske torsk)*. Online. Available at: http://dk.nanoq.gl/Emner/Landsstyre/Departementer/Lands styreformandens%20Departement/Tusagassiivik/Projekter/Tulugaq/Fakta_om_dyrene/ Fisk_rejer_krabber/Torsk.aspx (accessed 16 April 2011).

Government of Greenland (2009) *Ban on sealskin products is catastrophic for Greenland*, press release, Minister for Fishing, Hunting and Agriculture. Online. Available at: http:// uk.nanoq.gl/Emner/News/News_from_Government/2009/05/sealskin.aspx (accessed 16 April 2011).

Hannibal, I. and Holst, K. (2010) 'Europas permanente paradoks? EUs oversøiske lande og territoriers suverænitetsspil i Brussels', unpublished MA thesis, Department of Political Science, University of Copenhagen.

Harhoff, F. (2003) *Rigsfællesskabet*, Aarhus: Klim.

Høydal, H. (2000) *Myten om rigsfællesskabet: vejen til en selvstændig færøsk stat*, Copenhagen: Lindhardt og Ringhof.

ICC (2009) *Response from the Inuit Circumpolar Council*. Online. Available at: www. inuit.org/index.php?id=293&contUid=0 (accessed 6 April 2011).

KNR (2009) *Jonathan Motzfeldt til EU: Skam dig, Europa*, 20 March. Online. Available at: http://knr.gl/index.php?id=297&tx_ttnews[tt_news]=43357&tx_ttnews[backPid]=8 44&cHash=3d539d2ee6&cHash=318c8bf3c5 (accessed 1 May 2010).

Kommissionen (2003) 'Forslag til Rådets forordning om indgåelse af protokollen om ændring af den fjerde protokol om betingelserne for det fiskeri, der er fastsat i fiskeriaftalen mellem Det Europæiske Økonomiske Fællesskab på den ene side og den danske regering og det grønlandske landsstyre på den anden side' (KOM/2003/0609 endelig udg.). Online. Available at: http://eur-lex.europa.eu/LexUriServ/LexUriServ. do?uri=CELEX:52003PC0609:DA:HTML (accessed 6 April 2011).

Kristensen, K.S. (2004) *Greenland, Denmark and the Debate on Missile Defense: A Window of Opportunity for Increased Autonomy* (DIIS Working Paper 2004/14), Copenhagen: Danish Institute for International Studies.

Lauritzen, P. (1997) *Philip Lauritzen i Grønland. 21 års journalistik*, Copenhagen: Tiderne Skifter.

Lennert, K.H. (2006) 'The Danish interests in the Community with Greenland', unpublished MA thesis, Department for History, International Studies and Society, Aalborg University.

Motzfeldt, J. (2003) 'Grønland og EU', in J. Blom-Hansen and J.G. Christensen (eds) *Danmark i EU i 30 år. Et Festskrift*, Copenhagen: Gyldendal.

Motzfeldt, J. (2006) 'Hjemmestyre og Udenrigspolitik', in H. Petersen (ed.) *Grønland i Verdenssamfundet: Udvikling og forandring af normer og praksis*, Nuuk: Atuagkat.

Mølgaard, N. (2010) 'Nuuk fishermen ready to rejoin Europe', *Sermitsiaq*, 4 February 2010. Online. Available at: http://sermitsiaq.gl/erhverv/article110073.ece?service=print &lang=EN (accessed 6 April 2011).

Petersen, H. (2006) 'Grønland på verdenskortet', in H. Petersen (ed.) *Grønland i Verdenssamfundet: Udvikling og forandring af normer og praksis*, Nuuk: Atuagkat.

Petersen, N. (2006) *Dansk udenrigspolitiks historie 6: Europæisk og globalt engagement 1973–2006*, 2nd edn, Copenhagen: Gyldendal.

Refsnes, A. (2011) 'Global miljøstyring av olje- og gassaktiviteter i Arktis: et institusjonalisert samarbeid eller en uforrmell dialog?', *Tidsskriftet Politik*, 14(1): 33–42.

Schymik, C. (2009) 'Grönland in selbstregierung. Die EU als chance für den weg in die staatliche unabhängigkeit'. *SWP-Aktuell* 49. Online. Available at: www.swpberlin.org/ common/get_document.php?asset_id=6244 (accessed 16 March 2011).

Shadian, J. (2010) 'From states to polities: Re-conceptualizing sovereignty through Inuit governance', *European Journal of International Relations*, 16(3): 485–510.

Skydsbjerg, H. (1999) *Grønland. 20 år med Hjemmestyre*, Nuuk: Atuagkat.

Strandsbjerg, J. (2011) 'Geopolitik, naturlige grænser og "kartopolitik" i Arktis', *Tidsskriftet Politik*, 14(1): 51–60.

Strandsbjerg, J., Schlæger, J. and Gad, U.P. (2011) 'Introduktion', *Tidsskriftet Politik*, 14(1): 3–4, special issue on 'The Arctic: sovereignties, governance and geopolitics'.

Tobiassen, S. (1995) 'Fra danisering til grønlandisering. Forventninger og realiteter om grønlandisering', unpublished MA thesis, Nuuk: Ilisimatusarfik, Institut for Administration.

Vesterbirk, L. (2006) 'Grønlands diplomati i Bruxelles', in H. Petersen (ed.) *Grønland i Verdenssamfundet. Udvikling og forandring af normer og praksis*, Nuuk: Atuagkat.

16 Conclusion

When European and Postcolonial Studies meet

Rebecca Adler-Nissen and Ulrik Pram Gad

From its very beginnings in the 1950s, European integration has been entangled in practices of colonization and decolonization. This entanglement continues. A number of the Overseas Countries and Territories (OCTs) of the member states – small at least in terms of population if not in terms of territory – have not been 'properly' decolonized as formally sovereign states. The EU therefore still finds itself implicated in peculiar versions of postcolonial sovereignty games revolving around these islands.

For a number of reasons, however, this story has not been told. This is unfortunate – not only because it deserves to be part of the broader accounts of European integration, but also because postcolonial theory and European integration studies can learn from each other. We hope that the insights presented in this volume may serve to bring the two fields closer together. Concluding this volume, we wish to highlight a number of theoretical and empirical insights: first, we revisit the concept of sovereignty in light of the contributions of the volume. Second, we take a second look at the EU as an imperial polity. Third and fourth, we summarize how imperial metropoles as well as discourses, resources, and regions make a difference to the OCTs. We then address the limits of our approach before discussing perspectives for future research.

Revisiting postcolonial sovereignty in the light of European integration

One of the first lessons to draw from this book is that sovereignty is not only a question of either/or. Sovereignty is more mendable than most International Relations (IR) scholars would want us to believe. If we draw on theoretical insights from both fields, we can see how other polities than formally fully sovereign states matter. We can also see how the system of sovereign states – despite its constraining effects – is unable to withhold alternative forms of polities and subjectivities.

More specifically, we need to acknowledge various hierarchical relations that most accounts of the so-called Westphalian international have relegated to the past. By only focusing on the roughly 200 states with equal formal status, as most IR scholars do, we paint a partial picture of international relations. Focusing only on the largest, materially most powerful states have led us to overlook the realized and potential influence which micropolities may have on the metropole states and on the international system.

Yet in both European and Postcolonial Studies, the sovereign state remains the dominant template. There seems to be no way of fully escaping sovereignty. However, there is a variety of possibilities of escaping the choice between either sovereignty or not. The late sovereign EU and postcolonial entities illustrate that by playing creatively, institutionally, discursively, and in everyday practice on the sovereign state system, one can obtain certain benefits. The relation between the EU and a number of the overseas territories are – with the respective metropole as link – illustrative of what Palan (this volume) calls symbiotic sovereignty; that is, complicated forms of division of labour allowing states, Unions and formally non-sovereign micropolities to do things that they would not otherwise be able to do.

Sovereignty and subjectivity, hence, is not the same thing in international politics. On the one hand, a polity may have (or be) a state – but have no sovereignty beyond the thinnest formal notion of the concept; no substantial measure of the subjectivity supposedly accompanying sovereignty (Grovogui, this volume). On the other hand, a polity may have considerable subjectivity – without neither statehood nor sovereignty (cf. in each their way the case studies by Gad, Oostindie, Vlcek, Muller, Baldacchino, this volume).

If we acknowledge the possibility of other forms of subjectivity than the state, even within what counts as the international, and at the same time insist that we have not moved beyond sovereignty – as some critical Postcolonial Studies and European scholars would want us to do – we can address some of the central questions in IR. In the following, we focus on two of these questions where we believe that Postcolonial Studies and EU studies can inspire each other – the future of the EU as a postcolonial empire and the future of postcolonial relations along the margins of Europe.

Revisiting the EU as empire

In the Introduction, we argued that the EU can be seen as an imperial construction: it radiates its way of ordering from a centre, the forms and ambitions of ordering varying, roughly descending with distance from the centre, and accepting more and more compromises and anomalies further away from the centre. We believe that the case studies support this argument. Seeking to establish itself as a global 'normative power', the EU builds on a long imperial history. The OCTs – and with them, their metropole member states – present themselves (some more eagerly than others) to the EU as 'strategic outposts'. The EU, however, does not quite appear to know what to do with this offer. First, it is unclear to member states with little or no imperial history why and how far islands will prove an asset in the role set aside for the EU. Second (and this is interesting, if we view the EU as an empire) the EU does not itself claim the kind of authority that comes with a state-like monopoly of violence. In other words, despite its military ambitions (see also Mérand 2006, 2008), the EU still promotes its power as a 'soft power', which places great limits on its 'strategic' capability. Third, because the EU organizes its centre in a late sovereign manner, it is more open to marginal subjectivities – like the formally non-sovereign micropolities analysed in this volume. Taken together, these particularities make the EU very different from the former empires of Europe. Nonetheless, the EU *does* seek to shape the world in its image – as such, the EU qualifies as an empire. Embodied by European Commission President José Manuel Barroso, the EU even embraced such a label when characterizing the EU as the 'first non-imperial empire' (Marks 2011: 2).

Because of its particularities – the uneven memory of empire in the centre; the self-image as a soft power; the late sovereign internal organization – the EU as an imperial project takes many forms. And so the image of Europe is different on each of the overseas islands. Geography and different regional contexts invariably colour the image and change the meaning of the European project(s).

In the British overseas territories covered by this volume, the main issue related to the EU is global finance. Here, the EU's imperial project assumes the form of imposing regulation and taxation on otherwise freely floating capital. Odd local effects and reactions come about. In the British Virgin Islands, the colonial and racist past of slavery is reactivated as self-defence against foreign interference (Maurer, this volume). In the Caymans Islands, the European imperial project presents itself in legal terms – and the sovereignty game is institutional. First, the European imposition of regulation was challenged at the European Court of Justice. Second, it turned out that the 'one size fits all' regulatory mechanism implemented did not make much of a difference to the particular financial products in which the Cayman Islands specialized. The primary effect of the regulation, hence, was to contribute to the image of the Cayman Islands as a well-regulated tax haven (Vlcek, this volume); an image which – as for all the British overseas tax havens – basically depends on their being protected by British sovereignty.

In the French OCTs covered in this book, the European imperial project reveals itself as the promoter of regional integration by cross-border cooperation. In this sense, the EU seeks to shape the world in its own image. The analyses of Mayotte and New Caledonia show, however, that this is not easy to do in the shadow of the French empire. In Mayotte, the most obvious candidates for cooperation (the neighbouring islands which comprise the Republic of the Comoros) reject cooperation with Mayotte as a French island because they insist that the island belongs to the Comoros. Consequently, the closest cooperator is – equally French – Réunion, far removed across the Indian Ocean (Muller, this volume). Similarly, in new Caledonia, ethnically defined pro- and anti-independence forces compete to represent New Caledonia in regional bodies – while neighbouring islands with formal sovereignty deny France and dependencies a seat at the table in regional coordination (Brown, this volume). More classic imperial authority – in this case, French sovereignty – comes in the way of European 'soft' imperialism.

If we take the Caribbean as an example, the EU seems to have no luck in facilitating regional integration: each island is oriented not towards its neighbour islands but to a European metropole (or Miami) (Sutton 1991; 2008). Even within each former European empire, 'regional disintegration' rather than integration appears to be the main trend – as exemplified by the devolution of the Netherlands Antilles, each island preferring to have an individual link to The Hague (Oostindie, this volume).

So not only does the EU do different things in relation to different OCTs. The EU is also used for different purposes in different OCTs: in Greenland, the EU is mainly a – willing – counterpart helping Greenland appear independent on its way to sovereignty (Gad, this volume). In French Polynesia, the EU appears in political debates in a way which is, on the one hand, parallel – the EU is presented as an alternative to the metropole in the sense that Polynesia may (potentially) relate to Brussels directly and unmediated by Paris. On the other hand, the relation to Brussels is not envisioned – as in Greenland – as one of sovereign equality, but one of an alternative submission: the European late sovereign imperial project appears to some as more attractive than the more traditional French colonial empire (Poirine, this volume). Conversely, in Mayotte, integrating in the EU as an 'outermost periphery' (with the *acquis* and all of the pooled sovereignty that comes with it) is seen as an extra way – on top of the integration in France – to make oneself secure from decolonization to Comoro sovereignty (Muller, this volume). In the British overseas, one seeks to secure oneself *against* EU authority, particularly in taxation and finance (Vlcek, Maurer, Palan, this volume).

The OCTs, in their corner of the triangular relation to their metropoles and to the EU, find themselves in very different positions on a number of dimensions. To understand Europe as a global power involves taking the variety of imperial legacies and current postcolonial situations into account. The EU is not one thing, but many different things, depending on the local context in which it seeks to play – or is used – as an imperial authority.

Consequently, we must temper the claims that it is possible to construct a grand theory of how the EU projects itself, that is as a 'normative power Europe' (see Manners 2002) or a 'tragic' power (Hyde-Price 2008). In short, if EU scholars want to study what Europe does in the former European empires, they need to take past and postcolonial present into account. Moreover, they need to study the *variety* of imperial legacies and how these legacies mediate material resources discursively as well as the different regional contexts into account. We now turn to these varieties.

How is the metropole imperial?

Another major finding in this book is that the imperial metropole makes a difference. As already hinted at in the discussion above, it matters whether you play games in the context of a French empire with a worldview focused on *gloire* and geo-politics (Holm, Muller, Brown, Poirine, this volume), or if you play games in the context of a pragmatic British empire with a worldview that has gradually shifted its focus from commerce to finance (Hedetoft, Palan, Vlcek, Maurer, this volume). Altogether different conditions meet the tiny islands left in a Dutch empire specifically designed for other purposes – Indonesia, that is (Oostindie, this volume).[1] If you are placed in a Danish empire whose metropole system-atically forgets that it ever has been an empire, former colonies are nothing but particularly privileged receivers of enhanced development aid (Gad, this volume). In terms of theory, these observations serve to stress (contra Sørensen 2002) that the sovereignty games played cannot be adequately characterized by looking at the unit. Sovereignty games are relational – postcolonial sovereignty games are played in relations between a (post-)colony and a metropole; the specific version of a postcolonial sovereignty game can only be understood by analysing the lega-cies and strategies of both parties.

But the imperial metropole does not just make a difference on its own. The influ-ence of the metropole is mediated by the available alternatives. In other words, resources make a difference. It makes a difference if you are a tiny population on a tiny island or if you are a tiny population on an enormous island. There are plenty of tiny islands and they are as such substitutable – even if prudence may make it an attractive SITE for extracting PROFIT from the outside (see Baldacchino, this volume). In contrast, enormous islands which may be imagined as enormous repositories of scarce resources have more to bargain with. Or at least that's how Greenland presents itself (Gad, this volume). But resources are not just material. To the British overseas territories which have established themselves as financial centres, the 'imperial whiteness' that comes with British sovereignty – the trust one can supposedly put in a judicial system whose proceedings are overseen by the Queen of England – is an invaluable resource to be marketed beyond the island (Maurer, this volume).

However, material resources depend on specific discourses: Greenland's sup-posed material resources have for millennia been buried under permafrost and kept from accessibility by the deceptive icebergs of the Arctic Ocean – and they still are. But with the discourse of global warming, the resources become avail-able as a lever – so far immaterial – for a Greenlandic nationalism on the path to sovereignty (Gad, this volume). Come independent sovereignty, and Greenland must prove that it does not need the Danish empire to guarantee stability. French Polynesia, on the other hand, commands an Exclusive Economic Zone the size of Europe – but no political discourse values it in a way comparable to Greenland's melting ice. Yet.

Nevertheless, for a number of the OCTs, the sovereignty of the metropole is *the* most important resource: not a resource to be marketed, but a resource for the island as a polity to extract resources from the metropole (Baldachino, Muller, Poirine, this volume) and/or for the individual citizen of the island to use for, among other things, travelling freely to the metropole (Muller, Oostindie, this volume). The population of the OCTs may travel freely to the metropole – while people from neighbouring sovereignties are barred from going (Muller, Maurer, this volume). In the meantime, the OCT becomes a meeting place for metropole people seeking profit by escaping the constraints of sovereignty in the metropole by disappearing in the ambiguity of sovereignty in the OCT (Vlcek, Palan, Maurer, this volume).

The metropole makes a difference. But the difference is relational, depending on which material and discursive resources are available to the OCT. In other words, it depends on alternatives. Regions therefore also matter.

Regions matter

On top of the metropole, resources, and discourses, regions matter. When in a geopolitical security mind-set, in the Caribbean (and perhaps also in the Arctic), the sovereignty of European metropoles is – post-Grenada, Monroe doctrine kept in mind – also perceived as a shield against US intervention. Off the African coast, it appears even more pertinent to keep the regional context at a distance (Muller, this volume). When in an economic mind-set, the regional context plays a role by being absent both in the Arctic and in the Pacific (and, outside the cases covered in this volume, in the South Atlantic): merely establishing contact and commerce is a separate and daunting task (Gad, Poirine, this volume). Even in the relatively densely populated Caribbean basin, the day-to-day traffic in persons and goods (legal and illegal) is directed to European or North American metropoles rather than to the neighbouring island (sharing, possibly, the 'comparative advantages' of the OCT of departure in question).

In some cases, the regional context is so important that we can hardly argue that we are analysing a triangular relation but rather a quadrilateral. Does it make sense to tell a story of any Caribbean island without including the US in the story? Whether as a source of capital (Vlcek, Palan, this volume); a source of demand for labour – whether forced (Maurer, this volume) or comparatively well paid (Vlcek, this volume); a source of tourists (Maurer, Baldacchino, this volume); a market for goods – whether legal or illegal; or a source of fear for invasion (see Baldacchino, this volume).[2]

The triangular relations presented in the analytical framework may have a fourth corner imposed on it from another angle: does it make sense to analyse the case of New Caledonia with one analytical corner allocated to the island – when it is obvious that the domestic politics produces so much more difference than identity that the imperial metropole may credibly present itself as the necessary (if not neutral) arbiter (Brown, this volume)? In terms of future applications of the framework (to which we will return below), the lesson must be, first, that the analytics be kept open as to the number of corners in the polygon, and second, that important insight about the individual case springs from the way in which it refuses to fit the framework (see Wæver 2009; 2011).

More important for the theoretical setup is that the UN is important in all case studies – not just as a fourth corner in the polygon but as a fundamental alternative. The UN embodies international society. It is also the organization that recognizes sovereignty claims. The UN has played very different roles in the cases analysed: the sovereignty of the French over both Mayotte and New Caledonia remains challenged by the UN – in different ways, though, as the Comoro claim to Mayotte is favoured over the French (Muller, this volume), while the alternative in New Caledonia is a separate sovereignty (Brown, this volume). Copenhagen cleverly pre-empted a parallel challenge by integrating Greenland in due time (Gad, this volume; forthcoming). In the British and Dutch Caribbean, the flagpole in front of the UN primarily plays a role as an unattractive alternative (Baldacchino, Oostindie, this volume).

Strategic agency and subjectivity in sovereignty games

Non-sovereign subjectivity may – even for the very tiny player – culminate in formal sovereignty. Yet independent subjectivity sometimes needs to submit itself to cooperating with others at a very basic level to be successful. One example is how the OCTs gain leverage by cooperating in OCTA (Hannibal, Holst *et al.*, this volume). Moreover, subjectivity inevitably depends on the recognition from *some* others. Any independent OCT agency depends on the acceptance and facilitation of the metropole – but it *also* depends on the acceptance and facilitation of the EU (Hannibal, Holst, *et al.*, Introduction, this volume).

Perhaps due to the fact that the EU's founding treaties were formulated in the context of early decolonization, the EU has imposed on itself an obligation to facilitate agency for remote, non-sovereign polities. This might, somewhat paradoxically, offer a separate reason for why the polities do not (all, so far) seek full sovereignty – even if the possibility exists, manifest in the alternative chosen by the neighbouring islands. Siba Grovogui's chapter on the – typical, if there is such a thing – postcolonial experience with sovereignty testifies to the grave consequences of the sovereignty claims made in the heyday of decolonization. The disappointments of realized postcolonial sovereignty possibly account for the propensity of micropolities for choosing(!) *non*-sovereignty. The volume testifies to a parallel preference for the late sovereign arrangements embodied in the logic of European integration (even if it has drawbacks) *and* in the balanced relation of both dependence and distance; of both non-sovereignty and dependence with the metropole so far preferred by these micropolities. 'Mature manhood', wrote Nietzsche, 'that means to have rediscovered the seriousness one had as a child at play' (1973: 94). Sovereignty claims are serious business – whether polities make them or not. If they do not claim sovereignty, they will have to live with the consequences – and after decolonization, they also have to live with the knowledge that they themselves have chosen submission. If – on the contrary – they do make a successful sovereignty claim it is also serious. Then they have to not only live with the consequences, they also have to take responsibility for managing the consequences themselves. Even worse if they make a sovereignty claim which is *not* successful. Sovereignty is always only a claim (Mac Amhlaigh, this volume) waiting to be explicitly or implicitly accepted – or challenged. Moreover, one infelicitous claim will make future claims difficult, so timing is crucial.

As mentioned, our case studies – illuminated by both postcolonial and European experience with sovereignty – suggest that it is hardly possible to escape the question of sovereignty altogether. There is no way of escaping the dilemmas of this predicament – the seriousness of the games. The arrangements inhabited by the formally non-sovereign micropolities may not look very heroic from the perspective of a staunch anticolonialist quest for a position and subjectivity independent from the powers and categories of Western modernity. In many cases, the arrangements do not live up to Kantian ethics: not every island can sustain itself as a tax haven. Rather, the arrangements which some of these micropolities have made are grossly parasitic not only on metropole resources and global economic structures in the abstract but also on other postcolonial micropolities: the sovereignty games which have benefitted Switzerland at the expense of the Congo by allowing Mobuto to reallocate the riches of the postcolony (see Grovogui, this volume) might very well also have benefitted, say, the Cayman Islands. Nevertheless, from the perspective of a number of the individual micropolities analysed in this volume, non-sovereignty makes a sensible choice when compared to available alternatives, even if by opting out of the destructive sovereignty games otherwise played in their geographical region they eventually come to assist in upholding them. If 'there is no escape from modernity, or indeed from colonial authority or European domination more generally', as Paolini (1999: 85) sums up what postcolonialism looks like after giving up essentialism, one can strategically embrace concepts such as sovereignty or empire (see Baldacchino, this volume) – to get the best out of the situation. And 'In learning to live with the hybridity and ambivalence of contemporary life' – instead of insisting on a clear cut, homogenous, sovereign nation-state – 'subjects can begin to carve out a space for future action and reflection' (Paolini 1999: 107).

Nevertheless, there are different ways of side-tracking the either/or concept of sovereignty. As one example, we have the EU which is *internally* structured in a late sovereign manner – pooling sovereignty functionally. Externally, the EU functions more like an empire: it employs the blurring of its borders under the flag of 'regional integration' as a means to let its ordering ambitions reach further. Peculiarly, the project of this particular empire is to (unilaterally, hierarchically) model the outside in its own (networked, interdependent) picture. To the outside, then, the late sovereign approach taken by the EU does facilitate a measure of ambiguity, and the EU therefore appears less prone to deny acknowledgement of subjectivities posing as if they make sovereignty claims. And then again, there are limits: the European Commission is always careful to avoid being accused of interfering in the constitutional affairs of the member states. Sovereignty is there – but it is convoluted in complexities and its iron fist is hidden in a velvet glove of postcolonial shame (see Hannibal, Holst, *et al.*, this volume).

Another way of going post- or late sovereign is found in the British Virgin Islands where sovereignty still exists (Maurer, this volume), but the voice claiming it – or just casually posing 'sovereign but not quite' – is just one among others. The sovereign voice comes across more as a convenient register in which to issue certain, more limited claims. Playing sovereign, in other words, is a way of saying and achieving something different than sovereignty. So the sovereign state system does provide for OCT agency – for an agency for polities which should not have any if we conceive of international society as either/or, whether in terms of a legal *right* to sovereignty or in terms of a realist *capability* of sovereignty. 'It is precisely because th[e] everyday space is ambivalent and identity is multiple that post-colonial subjects are able . . . to improvise, bargain with, and reshape their environment' (Paolini 1999: 119, paraphrasing Mbembe). Grovogui reminds us (this volume) that postcolonial sovereignty is not just about the transfer of the regalia of power – but postcolonial subjectivity may mean even less without being insignificant, when we are looking for a gradual reconfiguration rather than a wholesale rejection of the categories of Western modernity.

However, a separate issue which challenges this argument is the question of strategic agency in relation to sovereignty games: How strategic are the players? How constrained are they by structures beyond sovereignty? If we take the example of the British overseas, are the overseas financial centres the result of ingenious agency on the islands and/or dependent on the structures of capitalism? One issue is the balance between agency and structure – on this question, there are nuances in the contributions to this volume (Vlcek, Maurer, Palan, Baldacchino, this volume). Another issue is whether our theoretical framework focuses on the wrong structure: the structures of capital studied by International Political Economy (IPE) are possibly of greater consequence than the structures of international law and power conceptualized by international legal and political theory. While the case studies in this volume do not sum up to allow a conclusion to the relative merits of economic structures versus legal and political structures, they do demonstrate that sovereignty is an important resource in and of itself and that it is possible to employ it whether it is your own or not.

Perspectives for further research

Combining insights from postcolonial and European integration studies pays off. It leads to a more nuanced understanding of the status of sovereignty in a world of overlapping claims to authority. In the Introduction to this book, we presented a framework inspired by the European, the postcolonial, and the micropolity experiences with sovereignty as laid out in the three theoretical chapters. This framework has framed the empirical analyses in nine case chapters on the experiences with the present versions of four empires in four oceans and Brussels.

The framework consists of four elements, each representing a move away from the either/or concept of sovereignty – and away from how this either/or concept organizes the international as a system (only) of equal sovereign states: first, sovereignty gives rise to Wittgensteinian language games among polities. Second, each polity may – must! – simultaneously engage in different sovereignty games with different polities. Third, some of these games might resemble the archetypical, Westphalian 'high sovereignty' game between equal, non-intervening units – but most are 'hierarchicized' in complexly temporalized ways. Postcolonial games involve – in a variety of ways – imperial metropoles under dissolution and their postcolonies. Late sovereignty games involve the dissolution of what was previously 'properly' sovereign states into a pooling of sovereignty in functionally circumscribed spheres. Fourth and finally, these different games may – must! – intersect when polities engage with polities with different imperial legacies and ambitions, different geographical circumstances, and different resources.

In this volume, the framework has been applied to the intersection of, on the one hand, (a specific version of) postcolonial sovereignty games and, on the other hand, European, late sovereign games. However, each of the four elements of the framework can be applied analytically on its own or in combination. There are a range of past and current relations that could be explored through the lenses of sovereignty games. Here, we suggest a few examples.

The entire framework can be applied wherever two sovereignty games intersect – and as soon as there are three (sovereign or potentially sovereign) polities involved, two different games *do* in principle intersect, as no two games are exactly alike.

Staying within the closest neighbourhood of case studies involving micropolities, a number of comparative projects present themselves as obvious: first, the framework can be applied in a comparison of a series of obvious twin cases – one (micro-)polity opting for sovereignty, one opting for non-sovereignty.[3] Second, the framework is applicable wherever there is a potentially or almost or fragilely or recently sovereign polity. Again, a series of comparative projects are waiting.[4] Third, this volume has only just begun the *tour d'horizon* centred on the EU: we need to compare the EU's relations to the sovereign European microstates outside (or inside?) the EU with their respective 'metropoles' – and we should compare them with the EU's mini member states.[5] Not all of these cases are postcolonial per se, but they all involve the postcolonial problematique par excellence: how to acquire subjectivity from a disadvantaged position in a relationship.

The framework presented in this volume can also be used to explore intersecting sovereignty games between polities in decidedly central positions: What goes on in the corridors and banquet halls of an African capital when the Chinese arrive to present their alternative to the standard postcolonial sovereignty game? How does it play out when the Russians insist on playing 'high' sovereignty games with individual EU member states accustomed to pooling their late sovereignty – and accustomed to engaging the rest of the world by inviting it to become like itself? How does this late sovereign EU handle the Cypriot twin polities constituted in both their postcolonial relation to the UK and by the high sovereignty games played with and by their two local metropoles, Turkey and Greece? Which complexities arise when two late sovereign games – the EU version and the World Trade Organization version – intersect, as when a state, member of both, is pressured by a non-sovereign micropolity for whom it conducts foreign policy to act in the one to curb the policies of the other?

These and more questions are still waiting to be answered. We hope that this book will inspire further collaboration between postcolonial and European scholars and that the framework will be useful for further empirical investigations.

Notes

1 Granted; there is an issue of case selection of the volume, here – the British Empire in particular could have provided different cases. Anguilla might fit the 'Dutch' category; the Falklands the 'French'.

2 See also a recent call for papers for a special issue of *The Round Table, the Commonwealth Journal of International Affairs*, which takes a particular interest in the micropolities that have come out of the British Empire, www.tandf.co.uk/journals/cfp/ctrtcfp.pdf (accessed 20 March 2012).
3 (Western) Samoa vs US Samoa. Suriname and (British) Guyana vs. French Guyana. St Kitts-Nevis versus Anguilla – why did Nevis stay with St Kitts while Anguilla insisted on returning to the UK? And so on and so forth.
4 In Europe, for instance: the Nordic micropolities – Iceland, Greenland, the Faroes, Aaland (this comparative analysis is forthcoming as a special issue of Cooperation & Conflict on 'Postimperial Sovereignty Games in Norden'). The British micropolities – Jersey, Guernsey, Alderney, Isle of Man, Gibraltar (even if it is conceived of as 'Overseas' when observed from London). The post-Soviet breakaway entities – Abkhasia, Transdnistria, South Ossetia. The small, post-Yugoslav entities with different sovereignty status – Montenegro, Republika Srpska, Bosnia and Herzegovina, Vojvodina.
5 San Marino, Andorra, Liechtenstein, Monaco vs Luxembourg, Malta, Cyprus.

References

Gad, U.P. (forthcoming) 'Greenland: a post-Danish sovereign nation state in the making', forthcoming in *Cooperation & Conflict*, special issue on 'Post-Imperial Sovereignty Games in Norden'.

Hyde-Price, A. (2008) 'A "tragic actor"? A realist perspective on "ethical power Europe" ', *International Affairs*, 84(1): 29–44.

Manners, I. (2002) 'Normative power Europe: a contradiction in terms?', *Journal of Common Market Studies*, 40(2): 235–58.

Marks, G. (2011) 'Europe and its empires: from Rome to the European Union', *Journal of Common Market Studies*, 50(1): 1–20.

Mérand, F. (2006) 'Social representations in the European security and defence policy', *Cooperation and Conflict*, 41(2): 131–52.

Mérand, F. (2008) *European Defence Policy: Beyond the Nation State*, Oxford: Oxford University Press.

Nietzsche, F. (1973) *Beyond Good and Evil [Jenseits von Gut und Böse: Vorspil einer Philosophie der Zukunft]*, Harmondsworth, Middlesex, England: Penguin Books.

Paolini, A.J. (1999) *Navigating Modernity: Postcolonialism, Identity & International Relations*, Boulder, CO: Lynne Rienner.

Sørensen, G. (2002) 'The global polity and changes in statehood', in M. Ougaard and R. Higgott (eds) *Towards a Global Polity*, London: Routledge.

Wæver, O. (2009) 'Waltz's theory of theory', *International Relations*, 23(3): 201–22.

Wæver, O. (2011) 'Politics, security, theory', *Security Dialogue*, 42(4–5): 465–80.

Index